Contents

How to use this guide

This official VisitEngland guide is packed with information from where to stay, to how to get there and what to see on arrival. In fact, this guide captures everything you need to know when exploring England.

Choose from a wide range of quality-assessed accommodation to suit all budgets and tastes. This guide contains a comprehensive listing of all bed and breakfast properties participating in the VisitEngland Quality Assessment Scheme, as well as hotels, guesthouses, farmhouses, inns, hostels and campus accommodation.

Each property has been visited annually by professional assessors, who apply nationally agreed standards, so that you can book with confidence knowing your accommodation has been checked and rated for quality.

Check out the places to visit in each region, from towns and cities to spectacular coast and countryside, plus historic homes, castles and great family attractions! Maps show accommodation locations, selected destinations and some of the National Cycle Networks. For even more ideas go online at www.visitengland.com.

Regional tourism contacts and tourist information centres are listed – contact them for further information. You'll also find events, travel information, maps and useful indexes.

Accommodation entries explained

Each accommodation entry contains detailed information to help you decide if it is right for you. This has been provided by proprietors and our aim is to ensure that it is as objective and factual as possible.

(1) (2) (3) (4) (5) (6) (7)

ASHBOURNE, Derbyshire *Map ref 4B2* SatNav DE6 1QU B

enjoyEngland.com ★★★★ GUEST ACCOMMODATION

enjoyEngland.com Silver AWARD

B&B PER ROOM PER NIGHT
S: £61.00 - £83.00
D: £66.00 - £88.00

Peak District Spa

Buxton Road, Nr Alsop en le Dale, Ashbourne, Derbyshire DE6 1QU **T:** (01335) 310100
F: 01335 310100 **E:** PeakDistrictSpa@rivendalecaravanpark.co.uk
W: www.peakdistrictspa.co.uk **£ BOOK ONLINE**

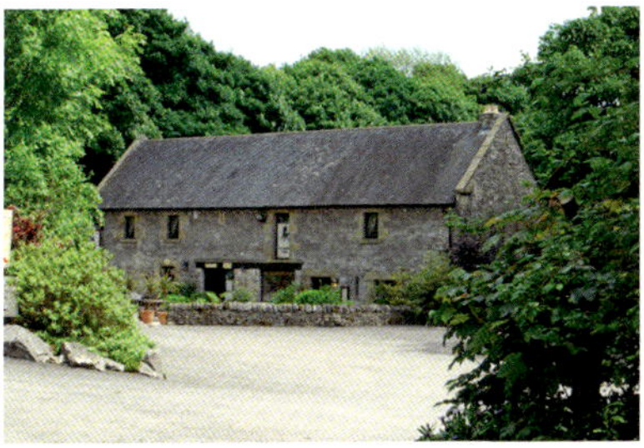

Occupying a secluded location on part of Rivendale's 37 acre site with its own parking, terrace and garden with superb views over Eaton Dale. Ideal for cycling, walking & outdoor pursuits (fly fishing lake on site). Convenient Chatsworth, Alton Towers, Carsington Water. All rooms with en suites, oak or travertine floors, under floor heating. Ground floor rooms accessible for wheelchairs,

Directions: Travelling north from Ashbourne towards Buxton on the A515, find Rivendale on the RHS.

Bedrooms: 2 double, 2 twin. Ground floor rooms with wheelchair access & shower room wet rooms en suite. 1st floor rooms with over bath showers en suite
Open: All year except closes 2nd Jan - 31st Jan

Site: P **Payment:** **Leisure:** **Property:** **Children:** **Catering:**
Room:

WALKERS WELCOME

(8) (9) (10) (11) (12)

1. Listing under town or village with map reference
2. Rating (and/or) Award where applicable
3. Prices per room per night for bed and breakfast (B&B)
4. Establishment name, address, telephone and email
5. Website information
6. Satellite navigation
7. Indicates whether a property is a Hotel (H) or Guest Accommodation (B)
8. Accessible rating where applicable
9. Walkers, cyclists, pets and families welcome where applicable
10. Travel directions
11. Indicates when the establishment is open
12. At-a-glance facility symbols

Key to symbols

Information about many of the accommodation services and facilities is given in the form of symbols.

Site Features

- Private parking
- Garden
- Euros accepted
- Visa/Mastercard/Switch accepted

Leisure Facilities

- Tennis court(s)
- Swimming pool – outdoor
- Swimming pool – indoor
- Sauna on site
- Health/beauty facilities on site
- Gym on site
- Games room
- Riding/pony-trekking nearby
- Golf available (on site or nearby)
- Fishing nearby
- Cycles for hire nearby

Property Facilities

- Real log/coal fires
- Passenger lift
- Night porter
- Lounge for residents' use
- Laundry facilities
- WiFi or internet access
- Dogs/pets accepted by arrangement
- Conference facilities
- Air conditioning

Children

- High chairs available
- Cots available
- Children welcome

Catering

- Special diets available
- Licenced (table or bar)
- Evening meals

Room Facilities

- DVD player
- Television
- Satellite/cable/freeview TV
- Telephone
- Tea/coffee making in bedrooms
- Hairdryer
- Bedrooms on ground floor
- Four-poster bed(s)
- Smoking rooms available

Campus/Hostels

- Cooking facilities available

Visitor Attraction Quality Scheme

Participating attractions are visited by a professional assessor. High standards in welcome, hospitality, services, presentation; standards of the toilets, shop and café (where provided) must be achieved to receive this VisitEngland award.

Visitor Attraction Quality Scheme Accolades

- For top-scoring attractions where visitors can expect a really memorable visit.
- For 'going the extra mile', ensuring that visitors are really well looked after.
- For small, well-run attractions that deserve a special mention.
- For particularly innovative and effective interpretation or tour, telling the story to capture visitors' imaginations.
- For attractions with cafes and restaurants that consistently exceed expectations.

Pets Come Too - accommodation displaying this symbol offer a special welcome to pets. Please check for any restrictions before booking.

Businesses displaying this logo have undergone a rigorous verification process to ensure that they are sustainable (green). See page 23 for further information.

VisitEngland's Breakfast Award recognises hotels and B&Bs that offer a high quality choice of breakfast, service and hospitality that exceeds what would be expected at their star rating. Look out for the following symbol in the entry

National Accessible Scheme

The National Accessible Scheme includes standards for hearing and visual impairment as well as mobility impairment – see pages 10-11 for further information.

Welcome Schemes

Walkers, cyclists, families and pet owners are warmly welcomed where you see these signs – see page 9 for further information.

Motorway Service Area Assessment Scheme

The star ratings cover a wide range of aspects of each operation including cleanliness, the quality and range of catering and also the quality of the physical aspects, as well as the service provided. – See page 326 for further information.

A special welcome

To help make booking your accommodation easier, VisitEngland has four special Welcome schemes which accommodation in England can be assessed against. Owners participating in these schemes go the extra mile to welcome walkers, cyclists, families or pet owners to their accommodation and provide additional facilities and services to make your stay even more comfortable.

Families Welcome

If you are searching for the perfect family holiday, look out for the Families Welcome sign. The sign indicates that the proprietor offers additional facilities and services catering for a range of ages and family units. For families with young children, the accommodation will have special facilities such as cots and highchairs, storage for push-chairs and somewhere to heat baby food or milk. Where meals are provided, children's choices will be clearly indicated, with healthy options also available. They'll have information on local walks, attractions, activities or events suitable for children, as well as local child-friendly pubs and restaurants. However, not all accommodation is able to cater for all ages or combinations of family units, so do remember to check for any restrictions before confirming your booking.

Welcome Pets!

Do you want to travel with your faithful companion? To do so with ease make sure you look out for accommodation displaying the Welcome Pets! sign. Participants in this scheme go out of their way to meet the needs of guests bringing dogs, cats and/or small birds. In addition to providing water and food bowls, torches or nightlights, spare leads and pet washing facilities, they'll buy in pet food on request and offer toys, treats and bedding. They'll also have information on pet-friendly attractions, pubs, restaurants and recreation. Of course, not everyone is able to offer suitable facilities for every pet, so do check if there are any restrictions on the type, size and number of animals before you confirm your booking.

Walkers Welcome

If walking is your passion, seek out accommodation participating in the Walkers Welcome scheme. Facilities include a place for drying clothes and boots, maps and books for reference and a first-aid kit. Packed breakfasts and lunches are available on request in hotels and guesthouses, and you have the option to pre-order basic groceries in self-catering accommodation. On top of this, proprietors provide a wide range of information including public transport, weather forecasts, details of the nearest bank, all night chemists and local restaurants and nearby attractions.

Cyclists Welcome

Are you an explorer on two wheels? If so, seek out accommodation displaying the Cyclists Welcome symbol. Facilities at these properties include a lockable undercover area, a place to dry outdoor clothing and footwear, an evening meal if there are no eating facilities available within one mile and a packed breakfast or lunch on request. Information is also available on cycle hire, cycle repair shops, maps and books for reference, weather forecasts, details of the nearest bank, all night chemists and much much more.

For further information go online at www.qualityintourism.com/types-of-schemes/welcome-schemes

National Accessible Scheme

Finding suitable accommodation is not always easy, especially if you have to seek out rooms with level entry or large print menus. Use the National Accessible Scheme to help you make your choice.

Proprietors of accommodation taking part in the National Accessible Scheme have gone out of their way to ensure a comfortable stay for guests with hearing, visual or mobility needs. These exceptional places are full of extra touches to make everyone's visit trouble-free, from handrails, ramps and step-free entrances (ideal for buggies too) to level-access showers and colour contrast in the bathrooms. Members of staff may have attended a disability awareness course and will know what assistance will really be appreciated.

Appropriate National Accessible Scheme symbols are included in the guide entries (shown opposite). If you have additional needs or specific requirements, we strongly recommend that you make sure these can be met by your chosen establishment before you confirm your reservation. The index at the back of the guide gives a list of accommodation that has received a National Accessible Scheme rating.

'Holiday in the British Isles' is an annual guidebook produced by Disability Rights UK. It lists NAS rated accommodation and offers extensive practical advice to help you plan your trip.

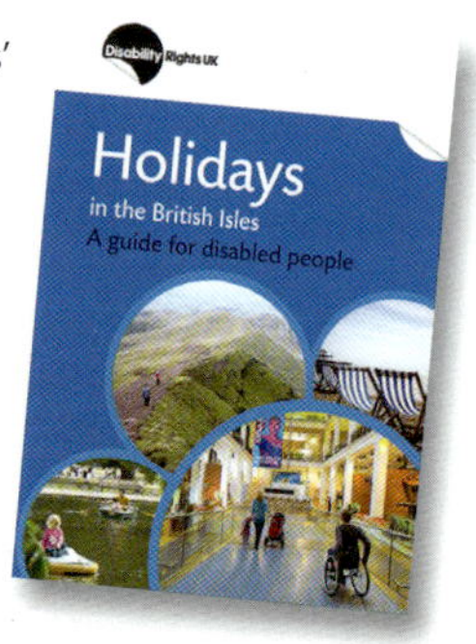

£12.99 (inc. P&P), www.disabilityrights.uk.org

The criteria VisitEngland has adopted does not necessarily conform to British Standards or to Building Regulations. They reflect what the organisation understands to be acceptable to meet the practical needs of guests with mobility or sensory impairments and encourage the industry to increase access to all.

For more information on the NAS and tips and ideas on holiday travel in England go to:
www.visitengland.com/accessforall

Additional help and guidance on accessible tourism can be obtained from the national charity Tourism for All:

Tourism for All

Tourism for All UK
7A Pixel Mill
44 Appleby Road
Kendal
Cumbria LA9 6ES

Information helpline 0845 124 9971
(lines open 9-5 Mon-Fri)
E info@tourismforall.org.uk
W www.tourismforall.org.uk
www.openbritain.net

England

Mobility Impairment Symbols

Older and less mobile guests
Typically suitable for a person with sufficient mobility to climb a flight of steps but who would benefit from fixtures and fittings to aid balance.

Part-time wheelchair users
Typically suitable for a person with restricted walking ability and for those who may need to use a wheelchair some of the time and can negotiate a maximum of three steps.

Independent wheelchair users
Typically suitable for a person who depends on the use of a wheelchair and transfers unaided to and from the wheelchair in a seated position. This person may be an independent traveller.

Assisted wheelchair users
Typically suitable for a person who depends on the use of a wheelchair and needs assistance when transferring to and from the wheelchair in a seated position.

Access Exceptional is awarded to establishments that meet the requirements of independent wheelchair users or assisted wheelchair users shown above and also fulfil more demanding requirements with reference to the British Standards BS8300.

Visual Impairment Symbols

Typically provides key additional services and facilities to meet the needs of visually impaired guests.

Typically provides a higher level of additional services and facilities to meet the needs of visually impaired guests.

Hearing Loss Symbols

Typically provides key additional services and facilities to meet the needs of guests with hearing loss.

Typically provides a higher level of additional services and facilities to meet the needs of guests with hearing loss.

Peace of Mind with Star Ratings

Many hotels and bed and breakfast properties in England are star rated by VisitEngland. We annually check that our standards are comparable with other British tourist boards to ensure that wherever you visit you receive the same facilities and services at any star rated accommodation.

All the accommodation in this guide is annually checked by VisitEngland assessors and an on site assessment is made every year. This means that when you see the Quality Rose marque promoting the star rating of the property, you can be confident that we've checked it out.

The national standards used to assess accommodation are based on VisitEngland research of consumer expectations. The independent assessors decide the type (classification) of accommodation, for example if it's a 'small hotel', 'country house hotel', 'bed and breakfast', 'guest accommodation' etc. and award star ratings based on the quality of the service and accommodation offered, as well as, where appropriate, a further special quality award.

Our assessors consider every aspect of your stay, such as the warmth of welcome, comfort of furnishings, including beds, food quality (breakfast and dinner for hotels, breakfast for guest accommodation), cleanliness and the level of care offered.

The Quality Rose marque helps you decide where to stay, giving you peace of mind that the accommodation has been thoroughly checked out before you check in.

Accommodation Types

Always look at or ask for the classification of accommodation, as each offers a very distinct experience.

The hotel designators you'll find in this guide are:

Hotel – minimum of 5 bedrooms, but more likely to have over 20.

Small Hotel – maximum of 20 bedrooms, usually more personally run.

Country House Hotel – set in ample grounds or gardens, in a rural or semi-rural location and an emphasis on peace and quiet.

Town House Hotel – maximum of 50 rooms in a city or town-centre location, high quality with distinctive and individual style, high ratio of staff to guests. Dinner may not be served but room service available. Might not have a dining room so breakfast may be served in bedroom.

Metro Hotel – can be any size and in a city or town centre location - offering full hotel services, but not dinner (although will be within easy walking distance of a range of places to eat).

Budget Hotel – part of a large, 'branded' hotel group offering clean and comfortable en suite facilities, many with 24-hour reservations. Budget hotels are not awarded individual star ratings.

Accredited Hotel – accredited hotels have been visited by VisitEngland assessors to check the standards of cleanliness and maintenance meet or exceed guests' expectations. This annual assessment does not include an overnight stay and no star ratings are awarded.

Looking for something a little different?

Within this guide you'll find some interesting alternatives to hotels. **Restaurants with Rooms** are just that – the restaurant is the main business and they will be licensed. **Hotel Boats** are generally narrow boats and are worked by a crew. They can be booked by individuals or groups and provide all the services of a hotel, including meals and refreshments.

Star ratings you can trust

Hotels are awarded a rating from 1 to 5 stars. All star ratings assure you of certain services which are:

- All rooms have an en suite or private bathroom
- Designated reception and staff available during day and evening (24 hrs in case of emergency)
- Licence to serve alcohol
- Access to hotel at all times for registered guests
- Dinner available at least five days a week (except Town House or Metro Hotels)
- All statutory obligations will be met, including Fire Safety

The bed and breakfast designators you'll find in this guide are:

Guest Accommodation – wide range of establishments from one-room bed and breakfast to larger properties, which may offer dinner and hold an alcohol licence.

Bed and Breakfast – accommodating generally for no more than six people, the owners of these establishments welcome you into their home as a special guest.

Guest House – generally comprising more than three rooms. Dinner may be available (if it is, it will need to be booked in advance). May possibly be licensed.

Farmhouse – bed and breakfast, and sometimes dinner, but always on a farm.

Inn – pubs with rooms, and many with restaurants as well.

Room Only – accommodation that either does not offer breakfast or, if it does, it will not be served (ie self-service or breakfast pack)

Hostel – safe, budget-priced, short-term accommodation for individuals and groups. The Hostel classification includes Group Hostel, Backpacker and Activity Accommodation (all of which are awarded star ratings).

Campus – accommodation provided by educational establishments, including university halls of residence and student village complexes. May be offered on a bed and breakfast or sometimes on a self-catering basis.

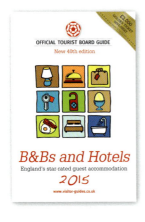

Star ratings you can trust

All bed and breakfast accommodation that is awarded a star rating (from 1 to 5 stars) will assure you of minimum standards, so you can be confident that you will find the basic services that you would expect, such as:

- A clear explanation of booking charges, services offered and cancellation terms.
- A full cooked breakfast or substantial continental breakfast.
- May offer ensuite facilities, but also shared bathroom facilities.
- For a stay of more than one night, rooms cleaned and beds made daily.
- Printed advice on how to summon emergency assistance at night.
- All statutory obligations will be met, including Fire Safety.

To achieve higher star ratings, an increasing level of facilities and services are offered. For example, at 3-star, bed and breakfast must offer a guest bathroom which cannot be shared with the owners and bedrooms must have a washbasin if not en suite. At 4-star, 50% of bedrooms will be en suite or with private bathroom. At 5-star, all rooms must be en suite or with a private bathroom.

Star ratings are based on a combination of the range of facilities, the level of service offered and quality - if an establishment offers facilities required to achieve a certain star rating but does not achieve the quality score required for that rating, a lower star rating is awarded. Accommodation with limited facilities but high quality standards may be capped at a lower star rating, but may achieve a Silver or Gold Award.

Gold and Silver Awards

How can you find those special places to stay – those that, regardless of the range of facilities and services, achieve top scores for quality (for hospitality and service, bedrooms and bathrooms, food and cleanliness)? Look for VisitEngland's Gold and Silver Awards. These awards are given to establishments offering the highest level of quality within their particular star rating.

High star ratings mean top quality in all areas and all the services expected of that classification. Lower star ratings with a Silver or Gold Award indicate more limited facilities or services but top quality. You may therefore find that a 2-star Gold Award hotel offering superior levels of quality may be more suited to your needs if, for example, enhanced services such as a concierge or 24-hour room service are not essential for your stay.

Sometimes a bed and breakfast establishment has exceptional bedrooms and bathrooms and offers guests a very special welcome, but cannot achieve a higher star rating because, for example, there are no en suite bedrooms. This is sometimes the case with period properties. Look out for accommodation with Gold or Silver Awards which recognise quality rather than specific facilities.

VisitEngland's unique Gold and Silver Awards are given in recognition of exceptional quality. A list of all Gold and Silver Award winning accommodation with a detailed entry in this guide is given on page 348.

The more stars, the higher the quality and the greater the range of facilities and level of service. The following refers to the Hotel scheme:

★★ Two-Star must provide

Dinner five nights a week (unless Metro hotel)

★★★ Three-Star must provide

All en suite bedrooms (i.e. no private bathrooms)
Telephones in all rooms
Room service during core hours
A permanently staffed reception

★★★★ Four-Star must provide

Enhanced guest services e.g. 24 hour room service, porterage, afternoon tea etc.
Superior bedrooms and bathrooms

★★★★★ Five-Star must provide

Some permanent suites
Enhanced services, such as concierge, valet parking etc.

Gold and Silver Awards

VisitEngland's unique Gold and Silver Awards are given in recognition of exceptional quality in hotel and bed and breakfast accommodation.

VisitEngland professional assessors make recommendations for Gold and Silver Awards during assessments. They look for aspects of exceptional quality in all areas, in particular, housekeeping, hospitality, bedrooms and bathrooms.

While star ratings are based on a combination of quality, the range of facilities and the level of service offered, Gold and Silver Awards are based solely on quality. Therefore a 2 star property with limited facilities but exceptional quality could still achieve the Gold Award status.

Hotels and Bed & Breakfast establishments with a Gold Award are featured below. Detailed entries for these properties are also included in the regional pages and can be found using the property index on page 360.

An index of Gold and Silver Award-winning properties with a detailed entry in this guide can be found at the back of this guide.

Gold Award Hotels with entries in the regional pages

Coworth Park
Ascot, Berkshire

Barnsley House
Barnsley, Gloucestershire

Lucknam Park Hotel and Spa
Bath (6 miles), Somerset

Stanley House Hotel & Spa
Blackburn, Lancashire

Collingwood Arms Hotel
Cornhill-on-Tweed, Northumberland

Northrepps Cottage Country Hotel
Cromer, Norfolk

Clare House
Grange-over-Sands, Cumbria

Rudding Park
Harrogate, North Yorkshire

Stone House Hotel
Hawes, North Yorkshire

Langley Castle Hotel
Hexham, Northumberland

Combe House Devon
Honiton, Devon

Chewton Glen
New Milton, New Forest, Hampshire

Scafell Hotel
Rosthwaite, Cumbria

Rye Lodge Hotel
Rye, Sussex

Hotel Riviera
Sidmouth, Devon

Calcot Manor Hotel
Tetbury, Gloucestershire

Hanbury Manor, A Marriott Hotel
Ware, Hertfordshire

Gilpin Hotel & Lake House
Windermere, Cumbria

Gold Award Guest Accommodation
with entries in the regional pages

Abbey Guest House
Abingdon-on-Thames, Oxfordshire

Bow House
Alnwick, Northumberland

The Barn at Penfolds
Arundel, Sussex

The Old Pump House
Aylsham, Norfolk

Marlborough House Guest House
Bath, Somerset

Woodside Luxury B&B, Spa and Glamping
Battle (4.7 miles), Sussex

Fenham Farm Coastal Bed & Breakfast
Berwick-upon-Tweed, Northumberland

Pendragon Country House
Camelford, Cornwall

Druid House
Christchurch, Dorset

Hubert House Guesthouse
Dover, Kent

The Astor Wing at Hever Castle
Edenbridge, Kent

Broom House at Egton Bridge
Egton Bridge, North Yorkshire

Cold Cotes Guest Accommodation, Gardens & Nursery
Harrogate, North Yorkshire

Underleigh House
Hope, Derbyshire

Hazelmere House
Lostwithiel, Cornwall

Highcliffe House
Lynton, Devon

Powe House
Portinscale, Cumbria

St Cuthbert's House
Seahouses, Northumberland

The Barn & Pinn Cottage Guest House
Sidmouth, Devon

No1
St. Ives, Cornwall

1 Woodchester Lodge
Stroud, Gloucestershire

The Old Coach House
Stroud, Gloucestershire

The Avalon
Tintagel, Cornwall

Bradle Farmhouse
Wareham, Dorset

Beryl
Wells, Somerset

Meadow View Guest House
Wighton, Norfolk

The Homestead Lodge
Windermere, Cumbria

The Manor House
York, North Yorkshire

VisitEngland Awards for Excellence

In 2014 the annual VisitEngland Awards celebrated 25 years of excellence. Years during which the breadth of tourism experience offered to visitors in England has grown to suit every purse and preference whilst matching, and often exceeding, the quality and choice available on the international stage.

With a history stretching back over 25 years, the VisitEngland Awards for Excellence are firmly established as representing the highest accolade in English tourism. The Awards recognise businesses that incorporate best practice and demonstrate excellence in customer service throughout their operation and celebrate the very best in quality and innovation. The Awards are open to all tourism businesses and tourism support organisations which meet the published criteria for the award category or categories they are entering.

Competition to win one of the 15 categories is hotly contested with the majority of finalists having won their destination heats and truly out to show that they are the best of the best! A panel of expert judges review the entries and this year a total of 76 finalists, 15 gold, 16 silver, 15 bronze and 30 highly commended winners were selected from a total of 368 entries from areas spanning the length and breadth of England.
You can find a complete list of winners online at:
www.visitenglandawards.org

Large Hotel of the Year 2014

GOLD WINNER

Burleigh Court, Leicestershire ★★★★

SILVER WINNER

hope street hotel, Merseyside ★★★★

HIGHLY COMMENDED

Ellenborough Park, Gloucestershire ★★★★★

Peckforton Castle Hotel, Cheshire ★★★★

Rockliffe Hall, County Durham ★★★★★

Small Hotel of the Year 2014

GOLD WINNER

The Old Rectory Hotel, Devon

SILVER WINNER

Swinton Park, North Yorkshire ★★★★

BRONZE WINNERS

Rothay Garden, Lake District ★★★★

HIGHLY COMMENDED

Brockencote Hall, Worcestershire ★★★★

Hell Bay Hotel, Isles of Scilly ★★★★

The hunt for the **Large Hotel of the Year** shone the spotlight onto stellar establishments. The range of accommodation offer available is highlighted by the three Highly Commended experiences to be had at the elegant Ellenborough Park near Cheltenham, Gloucestershire; the enchanting Peckforton Castle near Tarporley, Cheshire and exhilarating Rockliffe Hall, Hurworth-on-Tees in County Durham. The Silver Award went to Liverpool to the hope street hotel, an urban boutique experience of 89 individually designed hotel rooms, variously described by the media as " a symbol of Liverpool's renewed prosperity" to "Isambard Kingdom Brunel meets Carrie Bradshaw". Winner of the Gold Award is Burleigh Court, situated in Loughborough, and one of the Midlands largest four star accredited residential conference centres and hotels. It combines outstanding meeting facilities with first class accommodation and putting customers at the forefront of everything the team does. It has an enviable reputation as a leader in the hospitality industry, evidenced by the number of awards it has achieved.

The winner of the Gold Award for **Small Hotel of the Year**, The Old Rectory Hotel in Devon, is a stylish boutique country house close to the stunning Exmoor coast in North Devon that offers delicious food and sumptuous accommodation in a relaxed and friendly atmosphere. The Silver Award went to Swinton Park at Ripon in North Yorkshire, a luxury castle hotel in the Yorkshire Dales, with fine dining, cookery school, spa and extensive grounds.

For the **B&B of the Year Award** hidden gems of the English tourism world shone brightly. Highlighting wonderful locations, superb hospitality and exquisite establishments, the two Highly Commended, five star, finalists were Browns of Holbeck in Holbeck, Nottinghamshire and the Low Mill Guesthouse in Bainbridge, North Yorkshire. The Bronze Award winner, Kester House is a 16th century Grade II listed home in the bustling conservation village of Sedlescombe, East Sussex with rooms which capture different aspects of the rich historic character of this village in the heart of 1066 country. On the edge of the Cotswolds, at Silver Award winner Eckington Manor in rural Worcestershire, great food is at the centre of the offer. Time at Eckington Manor can be spent brushing up on your cookery skills, relaxing in luxurious bedrooms or simply soaking up the countryside air. This year's Gold Award winner is a beautiful 200 year-old former church, St. Cuthbert's House, at much-loved Seahouses in Northumberland. This lovely, historic building has been tastefully renovated with great attention to detail to preserve its charm and history yet provide guests with beautiful, luxury Bed and Breakfast accommodation incorporating high-quality facilities. The passion and pride shown by the proprietors, who demonstrate a huge commitment to the environment, to sustainability and to the community is infectious. Customer service is exceptional whilst providing a warm and homely feel. A solid gold experience.

Bed & Breakfast / Guest Accommodation of the Year 2014

GOLD WINNER

St Cuthbert's House, Northumberland ★★★★★

SILVER WINNER

Eckington Manor, Worcestershire ★★★★★

BRONZE WINNERS

Kester House Bed & Breakfast, East Sussex ★★★★

HIGHLY COMMENDED

Browns of Holbeck, Nottinghamshire ★★★★★

Low Mill Guesthouse, North Yorkshire ★★★★★

VisitEngland

Awards for Excellence 2014

GOLD WINNER

Award-winning B&B

St Cuthbert's House

When Jeff Sutheran, a senior officer in the uniformed services, and his wife Jill relocated to Northumberland 16 years ago they wanted to escape the day-to-day pressures of modern life and enjoy the beauty of the area's amazing coastline.

But finding a simpler way to live wasn't that easy once they had fallen in love with a Minister's house attached to St Cuthbert's Church in Seahouses.

"The house was perfect for us," says Jeff. "The problem was, it came with a dilapidated church as part of the sale. At first we were hesitant, because buying a historic, falling-down listed building didn't seem like a good way to simplify our life. But we went ahead with the purchase and figured we'd decide what to do about the church in due course."

Jeff and Jill did nothing with the church for six years while they renovated the house, so had plenty of time to think through the possibilities and issues. Slowly they began to see the potential for a high-quality bed and breakfast business in the old building.

The planning process was fraught with difficulty - it's a Grade 2 listed building - but once they moved into the build phase, the job went smoothly, taking ten months from starting the 'internal demolition' and rebuild, to receiving their first guests.

"We worked on the project full-time alongside local tradesmen," explains Jeff. "We began by stripping everything back to the stone shell - and then we built a new building inside it. We now have ultra-modern and very beautiful facilities combined with the beautiful, historic ambience of this ancient building. It's perfect for us, and for guests too, because the house attached is still our family home, and the old church, which is now St Cuthbert's House, is given over entirely to spectacular guest accommodation."

St Cuthbert's House, which has six ensuite double rooms, is now regarded as high-quality place to stay, and winning gold in the VisitEngland Awards for Excellence 2014 is a remarkable achievement for Jeff and Jill.

"We know that St Cuthbert's House is a stunning building, which creates a real 'wow' factor when guests arrive - and that helps to set the scene for a great stay," adds Jeff. "But we know that guests are no longer looking simply for a place to stay, with a comfortable bed. It's not just about the building, or the bedroom. They're looking for an 'experience' - one which they can go home to tell their friends and family about. We work hard to create that experience with them and for them. If there was one thing which we had to say was the key, we would say 'attention to detail' – if you're looking after the little things then the big things are also being taken care of in the process."

Achieving such high standards takes a lot of time and effort – in fact, it's a seven-day-a-week full-time job for the couple from March to October. They employ two part-time housekeeping staff, and friends help throughout the season.

Jeff and Jill are also committed to sustainability. They're passionate about local produce and local services, and helping to keep visitor-spend in the local economy. "We buy lots of supplies which we could get cheaper from other parts of the country but we choose to buy local in order to support our colleagues locally. This makes it possible for young people to make a decent living – rather than having to go away from the rural communities for work."

The couple have a passion for live music and they stage a number of house-concerts at St Cuthbert's House, attracting world-class musicians to play in

the guest lounge. It's part of the old church's former sanctuary, and so it's a really beautiful space to enjoy fabulous music. "We can get about 50 people in, who get to see and hear these amazing musicians at close quarters," says Jeff.

It has been a fantastic journey turning a dilapidated church into award-winning accommodation but it certainly hasn't resulted in a simpler way of life for Jeff and Jill. So have there been any regrets?

"None at all," admits Jeff. "Northumberland is undoubtedly one of England's 'hidden gems'. We're excited to be offering the very best accommodation and hospitality in the whole country, and helping to enhance and develop the visitor experience in a way which makes this area a better place to visit - and also a better place to live."

Contact St Cuthbert's House, Seahouses, Northumberland NE68 7UB. Tel: 01665 720456 www.stcuthbertshouse.com

Sustainable Tourism in England

More and more operators of accommodation, attractions and events in England are becoming aware of sustainable or "green" issues and are acting more responsibly in their businesses. But how can you be sure that businesses that 'say' they're green, really are?

Who certifies green businesses?

There are a number of green certification schemes that assess businesses for their green credentials. VisitEngland only promotes those that have been checked out to ensure they reach the high standards expected. The members of those schemes we have validated are truly sustainable (green) businesses and appear amongst the pages of this guide with our heart-flower logo
on their entry.

Businesses displaying this logo have undergone a rigorous verification process to ensure that they are sustainable (green) and that a qualified assessor has visited the premises.

The number of participating green certification scheme organisations applying to be recognised by us is growing all the time. At the moment we promote the largest green scheme in the world - Green Tourism Business Scheme (GTBS) - and the Peak District Environmental Quality Mark.

Peak District Environmental Quality Mark

This certification mark can only be achieved by businesses that actively support good environmental practices in the Peak District National Park. When you buy a product or service that has been awarded the Environmental Quality Mark, you can be confident that your purchase directly supports the high-quality management of the special environment of the Peak District National Park.

Green Tourism Business Scheme

GTBS recognises places to stay and attractions that are taking action to support the local area and the wider environment. With over 2000 members in the UK it's the largest sustainable (green) scheme to operate globally and assesses hundreds of fantastic places to stay and visit in Britain. From small bed and breakfasts to large visitor attractions and activity holiday providers.

Businesses that meet the standard for a GTBS award receive a Bronze, Silver, or Gold award based on their level of achievement. Businesses are assessed in areas that include Management and Marketing, Social Involvement and Communication, Energy, Water, Purchasing, Waste, Transport, Natural and Cultural Heritage and Innovation.

How are these businesses being green?

Any business that has been certified 'green' will have implemented initiatives that contribute to reducing their negative environmental and social impacts whilst trying to enhance the economic and community benefits to their local area.

Many of these things may be behind the scenes such as energy efficient boilers, insulated lofts or grey water recycling, but there are many fun activities that you can expect to find too. For example, your green business should be able to advise you about traditional activities nearby, the best places to sample local food and buy craft products, or even help you to enjoy a 'car-free' day out.

VisitEngland
Awards for Excellence 2014
GOLD WINNER

Award-winning Hotel

imago goes for gold

Tasked with generating profit for reinvestment into Loughborough University's academic and research provision, imago has created a set of outstanding venues that offer high-level conference and sporting facilities as well as sumptuous accommodation.

imago is a wholly owned subsidiary of the university and was launched in 2003 to offer first class accommodation, training, catering and event facilities.

imago's portfolio of venues includes:

- Burleigh Court; boasts 26 meeting rooms, 225 bedrooms and 150sqm of exhibition space
- Holywell Park; a conference centre for up to 300 delegates, set in landscaped grounds
- Loughborough University; with conference, training and exhibition facilities for up to 2,000 delegates with good quality accommodation
- The Link Hotel; an excellently located hotel for delegates to meet and network or rest before the next stage of a journey

One of its venues – the four-star international **Burleigh Court** – has set the standard really high by winning Gold in the Large Hotel of the Year category of the VisitEngland Awards for Excellence 2014.

The four star hotel has retained the prestigious Visit England Silver Award for the second year running, scoring an impressive 100% for hospitality. In addition to the Silver Award, Burleigh Court achieved the Breakfast Award and also renewed their mobility level three accreditation, which is part of its National Accessible Accreditation Scheme.

The venue offers business and leisure guests 26 meeting rooms, 150 square metres of exhibition space and 225 en-suite bedrooms with a range of facilities to suit all needs, including a well-equipped gym complete with swimming pool, sauna and a spa offering a range of relaxing treatments.

"imago unifies Loughborough University's first class conference and catering activities under a distinctive brand, collectively offering outstanding meeting venues and accommodation, delicious food and the UK's most extensive sport and leisure facilities," says Burleigh Court, Operations Manager, Guy Hodge.

The company targets mainly business guests as all venues offer conference facilities, but around 20% of its revenue comes from B&B business at The Link Hotel and Burleigh Court.

One of the most popular deals offered by imago is the 'Stay, Play & Explore' theme-park package, which includes accommodation at Burleigh Court and a family ticket to Drayton Manor Park.

So what sets imago apart from the crowd? "We have a lot of experience so we know what works and what doesn't," adds Guy. "We put a lot time and effort into providing great customer service, and often get fantastic reviews for going above and beyond the call of duty. This is backed up by the numerous awards we have won recently."

"The fact we have four venues across one location makes us very unique, and the fact Burleigh Court won Large Hotel of the Year in 2014 demonstrates our good practice and outstanding facilities."

But like all award-winning business, imago is constantly looking at ways to improve its offering. Burleigh Court has just undertaken a refurbishment of its restaurant, bar and lounge, and there are also plans in the pipeline for new postgraduate campus, Loughborough in London, to offer conference facilities in the Olympic Park.

"These are exciting times for the company, continues Guy. "We are very proud of our achievements but want to continue to offer the best in accommodation, conference and sporting facilities."

One final thing: where does the name imago orginate? "imago is the final and fully developed adult stage of an insect, typically winged – it's essentially the transformation of a living thing (metamorphosis). It's what this company is all about," says Guy.

imago is well located with fantastic transport links - 1 mile from junction 23 of the M1, 8 miles from Nottingham East Midlands International Airport, 3 miles from Loughborough mainline station.

Contact:
Tel: 01509 633030
Email: info@welcometoimago.com
Website: www.welcometoimago.com

Don't Miss...

Eden Project

St. Austell, Cornwall PL24 2SG
(01726) 811911
www.edenproject.com

Explore your relationship with nature at the world famous Eden Project, packed with projects and exhibits about climate and the environment, regeneration, conservation and sustainable living. Be inspired by cutting-edge buildings, stunning year round garden displays, world-class sculpture and art, as well as fabulous music and arts events. See all the sights and immerse yourself in nature with a walk among the the treetops on the Rainforest Canopy Walk or a ride on the land train.

Paignton Zoo

Paignton, Devon TQ4 7EU
(0844) 474 2222
www.paigntonzoo.org.uk

One of Britain's top wildilfe attractions, Paignton Zoo has all the usual suspects with an impressive collection of lions, tigers, gorillas, orangutans, rhinos and giraffes. It is also home to some of the planet's rarest creatures and plants too. For a day jam-packed with family fun and adventure there's Monkey Heights, the crocodile swamp, an amphibian ark and a miniature train, as well as the hands-on interactve Discovery Centre.

Roman Bath

Bath, Somerset BA1 1LZ
(01225) 477785
www.romanbaths.co.uk

Bathe in the naturally hot spa water at the magnificent baths built by the romans, indulge in a gourmet getaway, or enjoy a romantic weekend exploring the wealth of historic architecture. You can find all of this in the beautiful city of Bath and attractions such as Longleat Safari Park and Stonehenge are all within easy reach too.

Sherborne Castle & Gardens

Sherborne, Dorset DT9 5NR
(01935) 812072
www.sherbornecastle.com

Built by Sir Walter Raleigh in c1594, the castle reflects various styles from the Elizabethan hall to the Victorian solarium, with splendid collections of art, furniture and porcelain. The grounds around the 50-acre lake were landscaped by 'Capability' Brown and the 30 acres of tranquil lakeside gardens are the perfect place to escape.

Stonehenge

Amesbury, Wiltshire SP4 7DE
(0870) 333 1181
www.english-heritage.org.uk/stonehenge

The Neolithic site of Stonehenge in Wiltshire is one of the most famous megalithic monuments in the world, the purpose of which is still largely only guessed at. This imposing archaeological site is often ascribed mystical or spiritual associations and receives thousands of visitors from all over the world each year.

South West

Cornwall & Isles of Scilly, Devon, Dorset, Gloucestershire, Somerset, Wiltshire

A spectacular combination of ancient countryside and glorious coastline, Britain's South West is its most popular holiday area. It stretches from the soft stone and undulating hills of the Cotswolds in the north, through Wiltshire with its historic monuments, to the wild moors, turquoise waters, golden sands and pretty harbours of Dorset, Devon and Cornwall. The beauty of this region and all it has to offer never fails to delight.

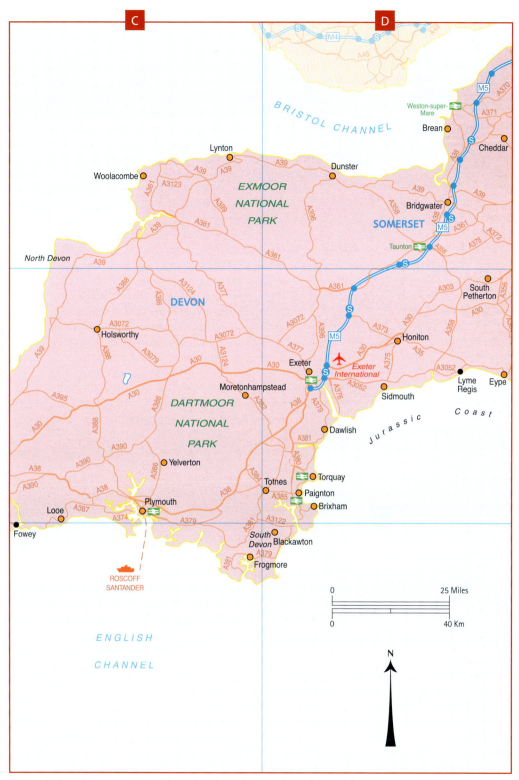

Explore – South West

Cornwall

Spectacular turquoise seas and white sands dotted with fishing harbours, beautiful gardens and the remnants of Cornwall's fascinating industrial heritage draw visitors from far and wide. The pounding waves to be found along the coastline attract surfers from all over to the world famous beaches around Newquay and make Cornwall a mecca for watersports enthusiasts of all kinds.

Hotspot: Boardmasters, Europe's largest surf and music festival, takes place at Fistral Beach and Watergate Bay near Newquay in early August.
www.boardmasters.co.uk

The majestic and largely untouched wilderness of Bodmin Moor is only one example of the rich natural environment that can be found here, with miles of walking paths criss-crossing the impressive landscape and offering panoramic views.

The captivating landscape of West Cornwall continues to intrigue and inspire a vibrant art scene centred around St Ives, and Cornwall has a diverse history with prehistoric, Celtic and medieval roots. There are a huge number of heritage attractions, such as Tintagel Castle which overlooks the dramatic windswept Atlantic coast and the Grade I listed Port Eliot House & Gardens, a hidden gem nestling beside a secret estuary near Saltash.

Devon

Take a hike or a mountain bike and discover the rugged beauty of Exmoor, explore the drama of the craggy coastline, or catch a wave on some of the region's best surf beaches. North Devon is also rich in heritage with many stately homes and historic attractions including Hartland Abbey and the picturesque Clovelly village.

Stunningly beautiful, Dartmoor is perhaps the most famous of Devon's National Parks and offers miles of purple, heather-clad moorland, rushing rivers and stone tors. Walk the length and breadth of the moor or cycle the Drake's Trail, where you'll come across wild ponies and plenty of moorland pubs, perfect for a well earned rest. Head east and discover the imposing Blackdown Hills Area of Outstanding Natural Beauty, stopping off in one of the area's picture-postcard villages for a delicious Devon Cream Tea.

Plymouth is famous for its seafaring heritage, with Plymouth Hoe as the backdrop for Sir Francis Drake's legendary game of bowls, as well as being one of the most beautiful natural harbours in the world. Climb Smeaton's Tower for the incredible views if you're feeling energetic, visit the world-famous Plymouth Gin Distillery at Sutton Harbour, or take the kids to the National Marine Aquarium for an afternoon of fishy fun.

Torquay, gateway to the English Riviera, boasts elegant Victorian villas, iconic palm trees, a sweeping sandy beach and a rich maritime history. Paignton offers great days out including its famous zoo, and the traditional fishing harbour of Brixham is awash with seafood restaurants, waterside pubs and cafés. This whole area is also home to a huge selection of beaches from small, romantic coves to larger, award-winning stretches. The Jurassic Coast is a UNESCO World Heritage Site which stretches for 95 miles along the Devon/Dorset coast, revealing 185 million years of geology and is a must for visitors to the South West.

Hotspot: The Dartmouth Steam Railway runs from Paignton along the spectacular Torbay coast and through the wooded slopes bordering the Dart estuary. With stunning scenery and seascapes right across Lyme Bay to Portland Bill on clear days. www.dartmouthrailriver.co.uk

Gloucestershire

Perfect for a relaxing break or as a base for touring the Cotswolds, Cheltenham is an elegant spa town where Regency town houses line the historic promenade and leafy squares. Relax in award-winning gardens or visit one of the impressive range of sporting and cultural events such as The Cheltenham Gold Cup or The Cheltenham Festival of music.

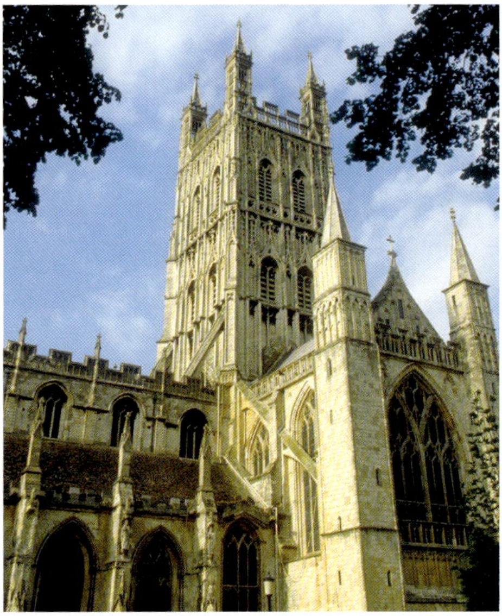

Dorset

Stretching from historic Lyme Regis in the west to Christchurch in the east, and including a number of designated heritage areas, the whole Dorset coastline is a treasure trove of geology. Interesting landforms are plentiful - Durdle Door, Lulworth Cove, the Isle of Portland with the famous Portland Bill lighthouse and the shingle bank of Chesil Beach to name but a few. Weymouth and Portland are two of the best sailing locations in Europe and offer water sports galore, as well as pretty harbours. For traditional English seaside resorts visit Victorian Swanage, or Bournemouth with its fine sandy beach, perfect for families.

Inland, enchanting market towns, quaint villages and rolling countryside play host to delightful shops, museums, family attractions, historic houses and beautiful gardens such as the Sub-Tropical Gardens at Abbotsbury. Explore Dorset's natural beauty on foot or by bicycle at Stoborough Heath and Hartland Moor nature reserves.

Hotspot: Step back in time at Lulworth Castle or the majestic ruins of Corfe Castle, perched above the Isle of Purbeck.

In the North of the Severn Vale, the ancient settlement of Tewkesbury, famous for its fine half-timbered buildings, network of alleyways and 12th Century Norman Abbey, is one of the best medieval townscapes in England. Enjoy a riverside stroll along the River Severn or a boat trip along the Avon. At the centre of the Severn Vale, Gloucester is a vibrant and multicultural city, combining historic architecture with numerous visitor attractions, shops and a collection of mouth watering tea shops, restaurants, bars and pubs. The city, with its impressive cathedral, is linked to Sharpness Docks via the historic 16 mile ship canal and the ancient woodlands of Forest of Dean are only a stone's throw away.

Hotspot: Stow-on-the-Wold is one of the best known Cotswold market towns. The large market square, with its ancient cross and stocks, is bordered with an elegant array of Cotswold stone town houses, antique shops, art galleries and gift shops.

Hotspot: Featuring over 300 flights, world records, special shape balloons from all over the world, nightglows, spectacular fireworks and air displays, the annual Bristol Balloon Fiesta at the beautiful Ashton Court Estate, to the West of Bristol City Centre is an experience not to be missed. www.bristolballoonfiesta.co.uk

Somerset & Bristol

The maritime city of Bristol is packed with historic attractions, exciting events and fabulous festivals. Cabot Circus offers first class shopping, while stylish restaurants and cafés on the Harbourside serve up locally produced food to tempt and delight. Out and about, Isambard Kingdom Brunel's Clifton Suspension Bridge and the Bristol Zoo Gardens are firm favourites.

Topped by the tower of the ruined 15th Century church, Glastonbury Tor is the stuff of myth and legend, rising high above the Somerset Levels near the delightful town of Glastonbury. Believed to be the site of a Saxon fortress, it has breathtaking views reaching to Wells, the Mendips and the Bristol Channel in the North, Shepton Mallet and Wiltshire in the East, South to the Polden Hills and to the Quantocks and Exmoor in the West.

Wiltshire

Surrounded by stunning scenery and home to a magnificent Cathedral, a wealth of heritage and cultural, dining and shopping venues, the medieval city of Salisbury is the jewel in the crown of South West England's rural heartland.

Further afield you can find an abundance of quintessential English market towns including Chippenham, Devizes, and the county town of Trowbridge. Marlborough, famed for its charming high street and independent shops, is stylish and sophisticated with a cosmopolitan café culture, while Wilton, the ancient capital of Wessex, is home to Wilton House and a beautiful Italianate Church.

Indulge – South West

Deli on the Quay serves fabulous fudge brownies, ideal with a coffee while the kids indulge in an ice cream. Dolphin Quays, The Quay, Poole.
www.delionthequay.com

Enjoy delicious seafood at the fun and quirky **Rum & Crab Shack**, Wharf Road, St Ives, Cornwall
www.rumandcrabshack.com

Relax with a sumptuous afternoon tea at **The Salty Monk**, Church Street, Sidford in Devon.
T: 01395 513174

Indulge your sweet tooth with handmade luxury chocolates from **Cockington Chocolate Company** at Cockington Court in Devon.
www.cockingtonchocolate.co.uk

Visit **Temple Quay Food Market** in Bristol for Jamaican patties, Thai curry, handmade falafel, home-made cakes, artisan breads and cheeses, hearty pies and much more!

Sample the delights and discover the history and heritage of Wadworth brewing at **Wadworth Visitor Centre**, Devizes, Wiltshire.
T: (01380) 732277
www.wadworthvisitorcentre.co.uk

Attractions with this sign participate in the Visitor Attraction Quality Assurance Scheme.

Cornwall

Blue Reef Aquarium
Newquay, Cornwall TR7 1DU
(01637) 878134
www.bluereefaquarium.co.uk
A dazzling undersea safari through the oceans of the world.

Cornwall Film Festival
November, Cornwall
www.cornwallfilmfestival.com
A month long festival of fabulous films.

Cornwall's Crealy Great Adventure Park
Wadebridge, Cornwall PL27 7RA
(01841) 540276
www.crealy.co.uk/cornwall
Enter the magical land of Cornwall's Crealy and hold on tight for a thrilling ride.

Crantock Bale Push
September, Crantock, nr Newquay
www.balepush.co.uk
Over 100 teams pushing giant hay bales around the village.

Lost Gardens of Heligan
St. Austell, Cornwall PL26 6EN
(01726) 845100
www.heligan.com
An exploration through Victorian Productive Gardens & Pleasure Grounds, a sub-tropical Jungle, pioneering Wildlife Project and more.

Minack Theatre
Porthcurno, Cornwall TR19 6JU
(01736) 810181
www.minack.com
Cornwall's world famous Minack open-air theatre is carved into the granite cliff and set in glorious gardens with spectacular views.

National Maritime Museum Cornwall
Falmouth, Cornwall TR11 3QY
(01326) 313388
www.nmmc.co.uk
This multi award-winning museum delivers something for everyone.

National Seal Sanctuary
Helston, Cornwall TR12 6UG
(01326) 221361
www.sealsanctuary.co.uk
The National Seal Sanctuary rescues, rehabilitates and releases over 40 seal pups a year, providing a home for those that can't be released back to the wild.

Newquay Fish Festival
September, Newquay, Cornwall
www.newquayfishfestival.co.uk
Three days celebrating Newquay harbour and delightful fresh local produce.

Newquay Zoo
Newquay, Cornwall TR7 2LZ
(01637) 873342
www.newquayzoo.org.uk
Multi-award winning Newquay Zoo set in sub-tropical lakeside gardens and home to over 130 species of animals.

St Michaels Mount
Marazion, Cornwall TR17 0EF
(01736) 710265
www.stmichaelsmount.co.uk
Explore the amazing island world of St Michael's Mount and discover legend, myth and over a thousand years of incredible history.

Tate St Ives
St. Ives, Cornwall TR26 1TG
(01736) 796226
www.tate.org.uk
Tate St Ives offers an introduction to international Modern and contemporary art, including works from the Tate Collection.

Devon

Bournemouth Air Festival
August, Bournemouth, Devon
www.bournemouthair.co.uk
Free four-day seafront air show.

The Agatha Christie Festival
September, Torquay, Devon
www.agathachristiefestival.co.uk
Celebrate the world's most famous crime writer, Dame Agatha Christie. A literary festival with a murder mystery twist!

Brixham Pirate Festival
May, Brixham, Devon
www.brixhampiratefestival.co.uk
Brixham turns pirate with live music, games, re-enactments, skirmishes on the Golden Hind.

Clovelly Village
(01237) 431781
www.clovelly.co.uk
Most visitors consider Clovelly to be unique. Whatever your view, it is a world of difference not to be missed.

Dartmouth Castle
Dartmouth, Devon TQ6 0JN
(01803) 833588
www.english-heritage.org.uk/dartmouthcastle
For over six hundred years Dartmouth Castle has guarded the narrow entrance to the Dart Estuary and the busy, vibrant port of Dartmouth.

Escot Gardens, Maze & Forest Adventure
Ottery St. Mary, Devon EX11 1LU
(01404) 822188
www.escot-devon.co.uk
Historical gardens and fantasy woodland surrounding the ancestral home of the Kennaway family.

Fishstock
September, Brixham, Devon
www.fishstockbrixham.co.uk
A one-day festival of seafood and entertainment held in Brixham.

Hartland Abbey & Gardens
(01237) 441496/234
www.hartlandabbey.com
Hartland Abbey is a family home full of history in a beautiful valley leading to a wild Atlantic cove.

Ilfracombe Aquarium
Ilfracombe, Devon EX34 9EQ
(01271) 864533
www.ilfracombeaquarium.co.uk
A fascinating journey of discovery into the aquatic life of North Devon.

Plymouth City Museum and Art Gallery
Devon PL4 8AJ
(01752) 304774
www.plymouth.gov.uk/museumpcmag.htm
The museum presents a diverse range of contemporary exhibitions, from photography to textiles, modern art to natural history.

Quay House Visitor Centre
Exeter, Devon EX2 4AN
(01392) 271611
www.exeter.gov.uk/quayhouse
Discover the history of Exeter in 15 minutes at the Quay House Visitor Centre on Exeter's Historic Quayside.

Dorset

Athelhampton House and Gardens
Athelhampton, Dorchester, Dorset DT2 7LG
(01305) 848363
www.athelhampton.co.uk
One of the finest 15th century Houses in England nestled in the heart of the picturesque Piddle Valley in the famous Hardy county of rural Dorset.

Christchurch Food and Wine Festival
May, Christchurch, Dorset BH23 1AS
www.christchurchfoodfest.co.uk
Celebrity chefs, over 100 trade stands, culinary treats, cookery theatres and some eminent food critics.

Corfe Castle Model Village and Gardens
Corfe Castle, Dorset BH20 5EZ
(01929) 481234
www.corfecastlemodelvillage.co.uk
Detailed 1/20th scale model of Corfe Castle and village before its destruction by Cromwell.

Dorset Knob Throwing Festival
May, Cattistock, nr Dorchester, Dorset
www.dorsetknobthrowing.com
World famous quirky festival.

Forde Abbey & Gardens
Chard, Dorset TA20 4LU
(01460) 221290
www.fordeabbey.co.uk
Founded 850 years ago, Forde Abbey was converted into a private house in c.1649 and welcomes visitors all year round.

Larmer Tree Festival
July, Cranborne Chase, North Dorset
www.larmertreefestival.co.uk
Boutique festival featuring over 70 diverse artists across six stages, a comedy club, 150 free workshops, street theatre, carnival procession, all in front of an intimate crowd of 4,000.

Lulworth Castle & Park
Wareham, Dorset BH20 5QS
0845 450 1054
www.lulworth.com
Walk in the footsteps of Kings & Queens as you enjoy wide open spaces, historic buildings & stunning landscapes. Enjoy the tranquillity of the nearby 18th century Chapel, wander through the park & woodland & bring a picnic.

Lyme Regis Fossil Festival
May, Lyme Regis, Dorset
www.fossilfestival.co.uk
A natural science and arts cultural extravaganza on the UNESCO World Heritage Jurassic Coast.

Portland Castle
Portland, Dorset DT5 1AZ
(01305) 820539
www.english-heritage.org.uk/portland
A well preserved coastal fort built by Henry VIII to defend Weymouth harbour against possible French and Spanish attack.

Sherborne Abbey Music Festival
May, Sherborne, Dorset
www.sherborneabbey.org
Five days of music performed by both nationally acclaimed artists and gifted young musicians.

Sturminster Newton Cheese Festival
September, Sturminster, Dorset
www.cheesefestival.co.uk
A celebration of the region's dairy heritage with quality local food and crafts.

Swanage Regatta
July - August, Swanage, Dorset
www.swanagecarnival.com
The South's premier carnival.

Bristol

At-Bristol
Bristol BS1 5DB
(0845) 345 1235
www.at-bristol.org.uk
21st century science and technology centre, with hands-on activities, interactive exhibits.

Avon Valley Railway
Bristol BS30 6HD
(0117) 932 5538
www.avonvalleyrailway.org
Railway that's much more than your average steam train ride, offering a whole new experience for some or a nostalgic memory for others.

City Sightseeing The Bristol Tour
Central Bristol BS1 4AH
(03333) 210101
www.citysightseeingbristol.co.uk
Open-top bus tours, with guides and headphones, around the city of Bristol, a service that runs daily throughout the summer months.

Bristol Zoo Gardens
Bristol BS8 3HA
(0117) 974 7300
www.bristolzoo.org.uk
A visit to this city zoo is your passport for a day trip into an amazing world of animals, exhibits and other attractions.

Brunel's SS Great Britain
Bristol BS1 6TY
(0117) 926 0680
www.ssgreatbritain.org
Award-winning attraction showing the world's first great ocean liner and National Brunel Archive.

Gloucestershire

Chavenage
Chavenage, Tetbury, Gloucestershire GL8 8XP
(01666) 502329
www.chavenage.com
Elizabethan Manor Chavenage House, a TV/ Film location is still a family home, offers unique experiences, with history, ghosts and more.

Corinium Museum
Cirencester, Gloucestershire GL7 2BX
(01285) 655611
www.coriniummuseum.org
Discover the treasures of the Cotswolds as you explore its history at this award winning museum.

Forest Food Showcase
October, Forest of Dean, Gloucestershire
www.forestshowcase.org
A celebration of the foods and fruits of the forest. Held annually at Speech House on the first Sunday in October. With many food stalls and demonstrations it's a great opportunity to try what the area has to offer.

Gloucester Cathedral
Gloucestershire GL1 2LR
(01452) 528095
www.gloucestercathedral.org.uk
A place of worship and an architectural gem with crypt, cloisters and Chapter House set in its precincts.

Gloucester Waterways Museum
Gloucester GL1 2EH
(01452) 318200
www.nwm.org.uk
Three floors of a Victorian warehouse house, interactive displays and galleries, which chart the story of Britain's waterways.

Hidcote Manor Garden
Chipping Campden, Gloucestershire GL55 6LR
(01386) 438333
www.nationaltrust.org.uk/hidcote
Famous for its rare trees and shrubs, outstanding herbaceous borders and unusual plants from all over the world.

Painswick Rococo Garden
Painswick, Gloucestershire GL6 6TH
(01452) 813204
www.rococogarden.org.uk
A unique Garden restoration, situated in a hidden valley.

Sudeley Castle Gardens and Exhibition
Winchcombe, Gloucestershire GL54 5JD
(01242) 602308
www.sudeleycastle.co.uk
Award-winning gardens surrounding Castle and medieval ruins.

Westonbirt, The National Arboretum
Tetbury, Gloucestershire GL8 8QS
(01666) 880220
www.forestry.gov.uk/westonbirt
600 acres with one of the finest collections of trees in the world.

Somerset

Glastonbury Abbey
Somerset BA6 9EL
(01458) 832267
www.glastonburyabbey.com
Glastonbury Abbey – Somewhere for all seasons ! From snowdrops and daffodils in the Spring, to family trails and quizzes during the school holidays and Autumn colour on hundreds of trees.

Glastonbury Festival
June, Pilton, Somerset
www.glastonburyfestivals.co.uk
Best known for its contemporary music, but also features dance, comedy, theatre, circus, cabaret and other arts.

Haynes International Motor Museum
Yeovil, Somerset BA22 7LH
(01963) 440804
www.haynesmotormuseum.co.uk
An excellent day out for everyone. With more than 400 vehicles displayed in stunning style, dating from 1886 to the present day, it is the largest international motor museum in Britain.

The Jane Austen Centre
Bath, Somerset BA1 2NT
(01225) 443000
www.janeausten.co.uk
Celebrating Bath's most famous resident.

Number One Royal Crescent
Bath, Somerset BA1 2LR
(01225) 428126
www.bath-preservation-trust.org.uk
The magnificently restored and authentically furnished town house creates a wonderful picture of fashionable life in 18th century Bath.

West Somerset Railway
Minehead, Somerset TA24 5BG
(01643) 704996
www.west-somerset-railway.co.uk
Longest independent steam railway in Britain at 20 miles in length.

Wiltshire

Castle Combe Museum
Castle Combe, Wiltshire SN14 7HU
(01249) 782250
www.castle-combe.com
Displays of life in Castle Combe over the years.

Longleat
Warminster, Wiltshire BA12 7NW
(01985) 844400
www.longleat.co.uk
Widely regarded as one of the best loved tourist destinations in the UK, Longleat has a wealth of exciting attractions and events to tantalise your palate.

Old Sarum
Salisbury, Wiltshire SP1 3SD
(01722) 335398
www.english-heritage.org.uk/oldsarum
Discover the story of the original Salisbury and take the family for a day out to Old Sarum, two miles north of where the city stands now. The mighty Iron Age hill fort was where the first cathedral once stood and the Romans, Normans and Saxons have all left their mark.

Salisbury Cathedral
Salisbury, Wiltshire SP1 2EJ
(01722) 555120
www.salisburycathedral.org.uk
Britain's finest 13th century cathedral with the tallest spire in Britain. Discover nearly 800 years of history, the world's best preserved Magna Carta (AD 1215) and Europe's oldest working clock (AD 1386).

Stourhead House and Garden
Warminster, Wiltshire BA12 6QD
(01747) 841152
www.nationaltrust.org.uk/stourhead
A breathtaking 18th century landscape garden with lakeside walks, grottoes and classical temples.

Wilton House
Wilton House, Wilton, Wiltshire SP2 0BJ
(01722) 746714
www.wiltonhouse.com
Wilton House has one of the finest art collections in Europe and is set in magnificent landscaped parkland featuring the Palladian Bridge.

Tourist Information Centres

When you arrive at your destination, visit the Tourist Information Centre for quality assured help with accommodation and information about local attractions and events, or email your request before you go.

Axminster	The Old Courthouse	01297 34386	touristinfo@axminsteronline.com
Barnstaple	Museum of North Devon	01271 375000 01271 346747	info@staynorthdevon.co.uk
Bath	Abbey Chambers	0906 711 2000	tourism@bathtourism.co.uk
Bideford	Burton Art Gallery	01237 477676	bidefordtic@torridge.gov.uk
Blandford Forum	Riverside House	01258 454770	blandfordtic@btconnect.com
Bodmin	Shire Hall	01208 76616	bodmintic@visit.org.uk
Bourton-on-the-Water	Victoria Street	01451 820211	bourtonvic@btconnect.com
Braunton	The Bakehouse Centre	01271 816688	brauntonmuseum@yahoo.co.uk
Bridport	Bridport Town Hall	01308 424901	bridport.tic@westdorset-weymouth.gov.uk
Bristol : Harbourside	E Shed	0906 711 2191	ticharbourside@destinationbristol.co.uk
Brixham	18-20 The Quay	01803 211 211	holiday@englishriviera.co.uk
Bude	Bude Visitor Centre	01288 354240	budetic@visitbude.info
Budleigh Salterton	Fore Street	01395 445275	info@visitbudleigh.com
Cartgate	South Somerset TIC	01935 829333	cartgate.tic@southsomerset.gov.uk
Chard	The Guildhall	01460 260051	chard.tic@chard.gov.uk
Cheltenham	Municipal Offices	01242 522878	info@cheltenham.gov.uk
Chippenham	High Street	01249 665970	info@chippenham.gov.uk
Chipping Campden	The Old Police Station	01386 841206	info@campdenonline.org
Christchurch	49 High Street	01202 471780	enquiries@christchurchtourism.info
Cirencester	Corinium Museum	01285 654180	cirencestervic@cotswold.gov.uk
Combe Martin	Seacot	01271 883319	mail@visitcombemartin.co.uk
Dartmouth	The Engine House	01803 834224	holidays@discoverdartmouth.com
Dawlish	The Lawn	01626 215665	dawtic@teignbridge.gov.uk
Dorchester	11 Antelope Walk	01305 267992	dorchester.tic@westdorset-weymouth.gov.uk
Exeter	Exeter Visitor Information Centre	01392 665700	tic@exeter.gov.uk
Exmouth	Travelworld	01395 222299	tic@travelworldexmouth.co.uk
Falriver	11 Market Strand	0905 325 4534	vic@falriver.co.uk
Fowey	5 South Street	01726 833616	info@fowey.co.uk
Frome	The Library	01373 465757	touristinfo@frome-tc.gov.uk

Glastonbury	The Tribunal	01458 832954	info@glastonburytic.co.uk
Gloucester	28 Southgate Street	01452 396572	tourism@gloucester.gov.uk
Honiton	Lace Walk Car Park	01404 43716	honitontic@btconnect.com
Ilfracombe	The Landmark	01271 863001	marie@visitilfracombe.co.uk
Ivybridge	The Watermark	01752 897035 01752 89222	info@ivybridgewatermark.co.uk
Launceston	The White Hart Arcade	01566 772321	info@launcestontic.co.uk
Looe	The Guildhall	01503 262072	looetic@btconnect.com
Lyme Regis	Guildhall Cottage	01297 442138	lymeregis.tic@westdorset-weymouth.gov.uk
Lynton and Lynmouth	Town Hall	01598 752225	info@lyntourism.co.uk
Malmesbury	Town Hall	01666 823748	tic@malmesbury.gov.uk
Minehead	19 The Avenue	01643 702624	minehead.visitor@hotmail.com
Modbury	5 Modbury Court,	01548 830159	modburytic@lineone.net
Moreton-in-Marsh	High Street	01608 650881	moreton@cotswold.gov.uk
Newquay	Municipal Offices	01637 854020	newquay.tic@cornwall.gov.uk
Newton Abbot	6 Bridge House	01626 215667	natic@teignbridge.gov.uk
Ottery St Mary	10a Broad Street	01404 813964	info@otterytourism.org.uk
Padstow	Red Brick Building	01841 533449	padstowtic@btconnect.com
Penzance	Station Approach	01736 335530	beth.rose@nationaltrust.org.uk
Plymouth: Mayflower	Plymouth Mayflower Centre	01752 306330	barbicantic@plymouth.gov.uk
Poole		0845 2345560	info@pooletourism.com
Salcombe	Market Street	01548 843927	info@salcombeinformation.co.uk
Salisbury	Fish Row	01722 342860	visitorinfo@salisburycitycouncil.gov.uk
Shepton Mallet	70 High Street	01749 345258	enquiries@visitsheptonmallet.co.uk
Sherborne	3 Tilton Court	01935 815341	sherborne.tic@westdorset-weymouth.gov.uk
Scilly, Isles Of	Hugh Street, Hugh Town	01720 424031	tic@scilly.gov.uk
Seaton	The Underfleet	01297 21660	visit@seaton.gov.uk
Shaftesbury	8a Bell Street	01747 853514	tourism@shaftesburydorset.com
Sidmouth	Ham Lane	01395 516441	ticinfo@sidmouth.gov.uk
Somerset Visitor Centre	Sedgemoor Services	01934 750833	somersetvisitorcentre@somerset.gov.uk
South Molton	1 East Street	01769 574122	visitsouthmolton@btconnect.com
St Austell	Southbourne Road	01726 879 500	staustelltic@gmail.com
St Ives	The Guildhall	01736 796297	ivtic@stivestic.co.uk
Street	Clarks Village	01458 447384	info@streettic.co.uk
Stroud	Subscription Rooms	01453 760960	tic@stroud.gov.uk
Swanage	The White House	01929 422885	mail@swanage.gov.uk
Swindon	Central Library	01793 466454	infocentre@swindon.gov.uk
Taunton	The Library	01823 336344	tauntontic@tauntondeane.gov.uk
Tavistock	The Den	01626 215666	teigntic@teignbridge.gov.uk
Tetbury	33 Church Street	01666 503552	tourism@tetbury.org
Tewkesbury	100 Church Street	01684 855040	tewkesburytic@tewkesbury.gov.uk
Tiverton	Museum of Mid Devon Life	01884 256295	tivertontic@tivertonmuseum.org.uk
Torquay	The Tourist Centre	01803 211 211	holiday@englishriviera.co.uk
Torrington	Castle Hill	01805 626140	info@great-torrington.com
Totnes	The Town Mill	01803 863168	enquire@totnesinformation.co.uk
Truro	Municipal Building	01872 274555	tic@truro.gov.uk
Wareham	Discover Purbeck	01929 552740	tic@purbeck-dc.gov.uk
Warminster	Central Car Park	01985 218548	visitwarminster@btconnect.com
Wellington	30 Fore Street	01823 663379	wellingtontic@tauntondeane.gov.uk
Wells	Wells Museum	01749 671770	visitwellsinfo@gmail.com
Weston-Super-Mare	The Winter Gardens	01934 417117	westontic@parkwood-leisure.co.uk
Weymouth	The Pavilion	01305 785747	tic@weymouth.gov.uk
Wimborne Minster	29 High Street	01202 886116	wimbornetic@eastdorset.gov.uk
Winchcombe	Town Hall	01242 602925	winchcombetic@tewkesbury.gov.uk
Woolacombe	The Esplanade	01271 870553	info@woolacombetourism.co.uk
Yeovil	Petters House	01935 462781	yeoviltic@southsomerset.gov.uk

Regional Contacts and Information

For more information on accommodation, attractions, activities, events and holidays in South West England, contact one of the following regional or local tourism organisations. Their websites have a wealth of information and many produce free publications to help you get the most out of your visit.

www.visitsouthwest.co.uk
www.visitdevon.co.uk
www.visitcornwall.co.uk
www.visit-dorset.com
www.visitsomerset.co.uk
www.visitbristol.co.uk
www.visitbath.co.uk
www.southwestcoastpath.org.uk

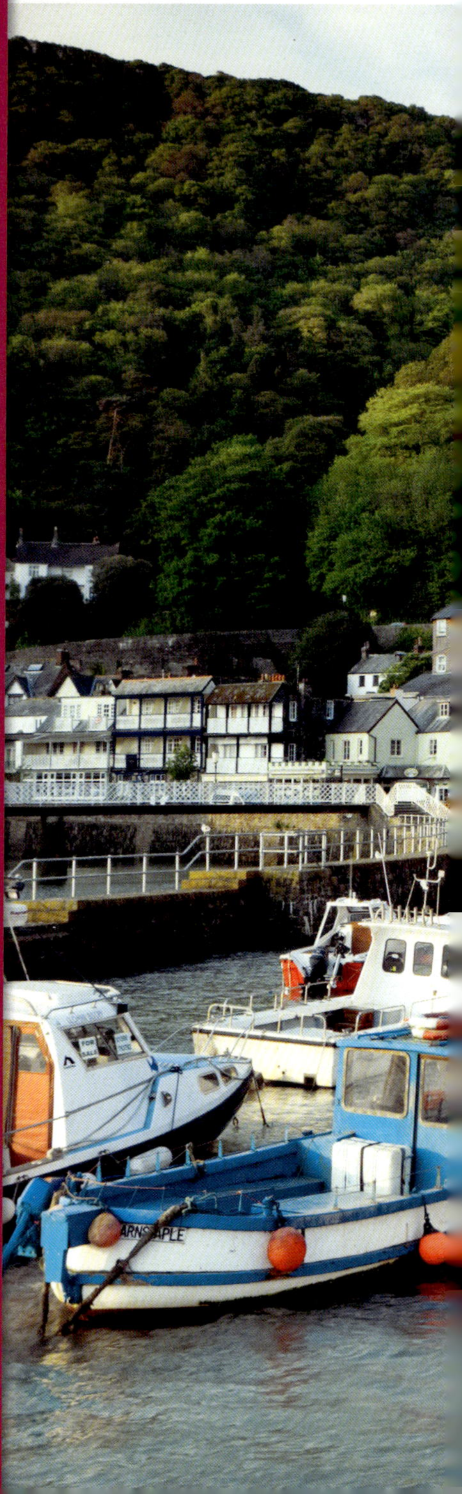

Stay – South West

Entries appear alphabetically by town name in each county. A key to symbols appears on page 7

CAMELFORD, Cornwall Map ref 1B2 SatNav PL32 9XR B

Pendragon Country House

Old Vicarage Hill, Davidstow, Camelford, Cornwall PL32 9XR **T:** (01840) 261131
E: enquiries@pendragoncountryhouse.com
W: www.pendragoncountryhouse.com **£ BOOK ONLINE**

B&B PER ROOM PER NIGHT
S: £60.00 - £65.00
D: £95.00 - £140.00
EVENING MEAL PER PERSON
£25.00 - £50.00

Beautifully presented, family-run luxury country guest house set in mature grounds offering bed & breakfast at its best. 7 en suite rooms offer a wide range of accommodation, from a spacious single to a grand superior king with a four-poster bed. **Directions:** From the East, entering Davidstow continue past church. Signposted Pendragon Country House will be on the right hand side 1/4 mile from A39. **Bedrooms:** All en suite, TV/DVD, tea tray and luxury furnishings **Open:** All Year except 24th-27th Dec

Site: P **Payment:** € **Leisure:** **Property:** **Children:** **Catering:** **Room:**

CHARLESTOWN, Cornwall Map ref 1B3 SatNav PL25 3NJ H

Pier House Hotel

Harbour Front, Charlestown Road, St Austell PL25 3NJ **T:** (01726) 67955 **F:** 01726 69246
E: pierhouse@btconnect.com
W: www.pierhousehotel.com

B&B PER ROOM PER NIGHT
S: £70.00
D: £114.00 - £148.00

Small, family-run hotel situated in a lovely 18th century harbour. We have a superb a la carte restaurant serving many exciting dishes and a selection of fish and seafood. **Directions:** Please see our website for full directions. **Bedrooms:** 7 single, 17 dble, 3 twin, 3 family **Open:** All year except Christmas day

Site: **Payment:** **Leisure:** **Property:** **Children:** **Catering:** **Room:**

CONSTANTINE BAY, Cornwall Map ref 1B2 SatNav PL28 8JH H

Treglos Hotel

Constantine Bay, Padstow PL28 8JH **T:** (01841) 520727 **F:** 01841 521163
E: stay@treglosshotel.com
W: www.treglosshotel.com **£ BOOK ONLINE**

B&B PER ROOM PER NIGHT
S: £73.50 - £115.00
D: £141.00 - £230.00
HB PER PERSON PER NIGHT
£98.00 - £139.50

SPECIAL PROMOTIONS
Prices vary throughout the seasons - please contact or visit website for further details.

This luxurious hotel on the North Cornish coast has 42 rooms and suites, many with dramatic views over Constantine Bay. Facilities include indoor pool, whirlpool, treatment rooms and award-winning restaurant. Treglos has its own golf course and self-catering apartments. Beaches and coastal paths are within a short stroll. Please contact for evening meal prices.

Directions: Please contact us for directions.

Bedrooms: 3 single, 23 double/twin, 10 family, 6 suite
Open: February - November

Site: P **Payment:** **Leisure:** **Property:** **Children:** **Catering:** **Room:**

FALMOUTH, Cornwall Map ref 1B3 SatNav TR11 5LG H

Budock Vean Hotel

Helford Passage, Mawnan Smith, Falmouth, Cornwall TR11 5LG **T:** (01326) 250288
F: 01326 250892 **E:** relax@budockvean.co.uk
W: www.budockvean.co.uk **£ BOOK ONLINE**

enjoyEngland.com ★★★★ COUNTRY HOUSE HOTEL · enjoyEngland.com Silver AWARD

B&B PER ROOM PER NIGHT
S: £73.00 - £141.00
D: £146.00 - £282.00
EVENING MEAL PER PERSON
£41.00

Budock Vean is a family-owned hotel nestled in 65 acres of organic subtropical gardens and parkland with private foreshore on the tranquil Helford river. Outstanding leisure facilities include golf, indoor swimming, sauna, outdoor hot tub, health spa, and award-winning restaurant.

Directions: Please contact us for directions.

Bedrooms: 7 single, 24 double, 23 twin, 2 family, 1 suite
Open: 24th January 2015 to 2nd January 2016

Site: **Payment:** **Leisure:** **Property:** **Children:** **Catering:** **Room:**

LANDS END, Cornwall Map ref 1A3 SatNav TR19 7RD B

Bosavern House

Bosavern, St. Just, Lands End TR19 7RD **T:** (01736) 788301 **E:** info@bosavern.com
W: www.bosavern.com

enjoyEngland.com ★★★★ GUEST HOUSE · enjoyEngland.com Silver AWARD

B&B PER ROOM PER NIGHT
S: £40.00 - £50.00
D: £80.00 - £98.00

C17th country house in attractive grounds. Centrally heated, comfortable accommodation. Most rooms have sea or moorland views. Home cooking using local produce. Ideally situated for exploring West Cornwall. Ample parking. **Directions:** Take A3071 from Penzance towards St Just, turn left onto B3306 signed Lands End. Bosavern House is 0.5 mile on left. **Bedrooms:** 1 single, 3 double, 2 twin, 2 family **Open:** All year except Christmas

Site: P **Payment:** € **Leisure:** **Property:** **Children:** **Catering:** **Room:**

LOOE, Cornwall Map ref 1C2 SatNav PL13 2DG H

enjoyEngland.com ★★★ HOTEL

B&B PER ROOM PER NIGHT
S: £50.00 - £72.00
D: £100.00 - £154.00

HB PER PERSON PER NIGHT
£52.00 - £92.00

SPECIAL PROMOTIONS
Special-event packages. Extensive range of conference and business facilities. Weddings and special occasions. Christmas and New Year celebrations.

Hannafore Point Hotel and Spa

Marine Drive, West Looe, Looe PL13 2DG **T:** (01503) 263273
E: stay@hannaforepointhotel.com
W: www.hannaforepointhotel.com

A warm welcome awaits you. Set in picturesque Cornish village with spectacular, panoramic sea views. Indulge in superb home-cooked food. Dining options include quality local produce and fresh fish. The terrace is a popular rendezvous for cream teas or cocktails. Spa pool, gym, sauna, steam and beauty therapies.

Directions: A38 from Plymouth, then A387 to Looe. Cross over stone bridge, turn 1st left (sign 'Hannafore') and uphill until overlooking bay.

Bedrooms: 4 single, 33 dble
Open: All year

Site: **Payment:** **Leisure:** **Property:** **Children:**
Catering: **Room:**

LOSTWITHIEL, Cornwall Map ref 1B2 SatNav PL22 0RA B

enjoyEngland.com ★★★★ BED & BREAKFAST
enjoyEngland.com Gold AWARD

B&B PER ROOM PER NIGHT
S: £50.00 - £55.00
D: £85.00 - £90.00

Hazelmere House

58 Grenville Road, Lostwithiel, Cornwall PL22 0RA **T:** (01208) 873315
E: hazelmerehouse@aol.com
W: www.hazelmerehouse.co.uk

Situated in the beautiful Fowey Valley with rural views overlooking the historic town of Lostwithiel, Hazelmere House offers exceptional bed and breakfast. Centrally situated, close to the Eden Project, Heligan Gardens and many National Trust properties, join us for a comfortable and informal base to explore all the joys of Southern Cornwall. **Directions:** On A390, North of Lostwithiel. **Bedrooms:** All rooms en suite, 1 kingsize, 1 super kingsize, 1 single **Open:** All year

Site: P **Payment:** € **Leisure:** **Property:** **Children:**
Catering: **Room:**

MEVAGISSEY, Cornwall Map ref 1B3 SatNav PL26 6ND B

enjoyEngland.com ★★★★ FARMHOUSE

B&B PER ROOM PER NIGHT
S: £35.00 - £40.00
D: £55.00 - £60.00

EVENING MEAL PER PERSON
£20.00 - £25.00

Tregilgas Farm

Gorran, St Austell PL26 6ND **T:** (01726) 842342 / 07789 113620 **E:** dclemes88@aol.com
W: www.tregilgasfarmbedandbreakfast.co.uk

Lovely 5-bedroomed detached farmhouse on working farm. Tastefully decorated. Very central for touring Cornwall. Lovely food for breakfast. Friendly welcome awaits you. **Directions:** Follow signs to Heligan Gardens. Go past gardens, take 4th turning on right, go to crossroads, go straight across. Tregilgas is 1st farm on right. **Bedrooms:** 2 double, 1 twin **Open:** March - September

Site: P **Payment:** € **Leisure:** **Property:** **Children:** 3 **Catering:** **Room:**

NEWQUAY, Cornwall Map ref 1B2 SatNav TR7 2NQ B

enjoyEngland.com ★★★ GUEST HOUSE

B&B PER ROOM PER NIGHT
S: £25.00 - £34.00
D: £46.00 - £58.00

Harrington Guest House

25 Tolcarne Road, Newquay TR7 2NQ **T:** (01637) 873581
E: harringtonguesthouse@yahoo.com
W: www.harringtonguesthouse.com **£ BOOK ONLINE**

The Harrington is a Bed & Breakfast with a central location situated within a short walk of all that Newquay resort has to offer. 5 mins walk from train station and local buses. Excellent value rooms with free Wi-Fi and free parking. **Bedrooms:** En suite, flatscreen TV, tea and coffee facilities **Open:** All year except Christmas

Site: P **Payment:** **Leisure:** **Property:** **Children:** 3 **Catering:** **Room:**

PADSTOW, Cornwall Map ref 1B2 SatNav PL28 8SB B

enjoyEngland.com ★★★ GUEST ACCOMMODATION

B&B PER ROOM PER NIGHT
S: £50.00 - £70.00
D: £55.00 - £120.00
EVENING MEAL PER PERSON
£6.00 - £30.00

The Harlyn Inn

Harlyn Bay, Padstow PL28 8SB **T:** (01841) 520207 **E:** mail@harlyn-inn.com
W: www.harlyn-inn.com **£ BOOK ONLINE**

The Harlyn Inn is situated adjoining the beautiful sandy beach of Harlyn Bay. Just a couple of miles outside Padstow it is the ideal place for an enjoyable Cornish holiday. The Inn has two bars and two restaurants, catering for the whole family. All of our accommodation is finished to a high standard and ranges from bed and breakfast rooms to fully equipped three-bedroom self-catering cottages. Our adjoining beach shop provides all your beach essentials, snacks and clothing as well as surf hire and surf school facilities.

Directions: Please contact us for directions.

Bedrooms: 11 single, 8 double, 4 twin, 3 family
Open: All year

Site: P **Payment:** **Leisure:** **Property:** **Children:** **Catering:**
Room:

PENZANCE, Cornwall Map ref 1A3 SatNav TR18 3AE H

enjoyEngland.com ★★★★ TOWN HOUSE HOTEL

B&B PER ROOM PER NIGHT
S: £85.00 - £95.00
D: £145.00 - £210.00
EVENING MEAL PER PERSON
£25.50

Hotel Penzance

Britons Hill, Penzance TR18 3AE **T:** (01736) 363117 **F:** 01736 361127
E: reception@hotelpenzance.com
W: www.hotelpenzance.com **£ BOOK ONLINE**

Enjoy high levels of comfort and friendly service at this award winning hotel. The Bay restaurant presents fine food served all day with evening a la carte and tasting menus. Traditional or contemporary-style rooms with sea views across Penzance Harbour. **Directions:** Enter Penzance on A30. At roundabout keep left towards Town Centre. Third turn right onto Britons Hill. Hotel 70m on right. **Bedrooms:** 4 single, 12 doubles, 9 twin. All Superior and most Classic rooms have sea views **Open:** All year

WALKERS WELCOME **Site:** **Payment:** **Leisure:** **Property:** **Children:**
Catering: **Room:**

PENZANCE, Cornwall Map ref 1A3 SatNav TR18 4HG H

Queens Hotel

The Promenade, Penzance, Cornwall TR18 4HG **T:** (01736) 362371 **F:** 01736 350033
E: enquiries@queens-hotel.com
W: www.queens-hotel.com **£ BOOK ONLINE**

enjoyEngland.com ★★★ HOTEL

SPECIAL PROMOTIONS
We have regular promotions, please check our offers webpage at http://www.queens-hotel.com/category/offers/

The Queens Hotel is the gateway to West Cornwall offering comfort and style, as well as great service and food. Enjoy a striking destination inspired by an extraordinary landscape, and a resilient culture rich in heritage. As a true family hotel, guests are welcome to bring their pets.

Directions: The Queens Hotel is located in the middle the promenade of Penzance, on one of the longest promenades in the UK. Just head to the seafront and you'll find us.

Bedrooms: All rooms en suite, with TV, Wi-Fi, tea and coffee and room service
Open: All year

Site: P **Payment:** **Leisure:** **Property:** **Children:** **Catering:**
Room:

ST. AGNES, Cornwall Map ref 1B3 SatNav TR5 0XX B

Little Trevellas Farm

Trevellas, St Agnes TR5 0XX **T:** (01872) 552945 **F:** 01872 552945
E: velvet-crystal@xlninternet.co.uk
W: www.stagnesbandb.co.uk **£ BOOK ONLINE**

enjoyEngland.com ★★★ FARMHOUSE

B&B PER ROOM PER NIGHT
S: £27.50 - £30.00
D: £50.00 - £60.00

A 250-year-old house on a working farm on the B3285 provides a peaceful, comfortable base for a holiday that will appeal to lovers of both coast and countryside. Wi-Fi now available. In the case of one night stays, a £5 surcharge will be added to room rates. **Directions:** Please contact us for directions. **Bedrooms:** 1 single, 1 double, 1 twin **Open:** All year

Site: P **Property:** **Catering:** **Room:**

ST. AGNES, Cornwall Map ref 1B3 SatNav TR5 0PA B

Penkerris

Penwinnick Road, St. Agnes TR5 0PA **T:** (01872) 552262 **E:** penkerris@gmail.com
W: www.penkerris.co.uk

enjoyEngland.com ★★ GUEST HOUSE

B&B PER ROOM PER NIGHT
S: £25.00 - £50.00
D: £50.00 - £60.00

Edwardian house with parking, lawned garden for relaxation and games, cosy lounge and delightful dining room serving real food. Close to dramatic cliff walks and iconic surfing beaches (nearest 1km). Beach hut available. Ideal location, central for all of Cornwall. **Directions:** From A30, big roundabout at Chiverton, 3 miles to village on B3277. Penkerris is just inside St Agnes and 30mph sign and before the Museum. **Bedrooms:** 2 Double, 2 twin, 2 family, 2 singles **Open:** All year

Site: P **Payment:** € **Leisure:** **Property:** **Children:** **Catering:** **Room:**

ST. IVES, Cornwall Map ref 1B3 SatNav TR26 1QP B

No1

1 Fern Glen, St Ives, Cornwall TR26 1QP **T:** (01736) 799047 **E:** info@no1stives.co.uk
W: www.no1stives.co.uk

SPECIAL PROMOTIONS
Please contact us for prices.

No1 is a bouchic style bed and breakfast in St Ives, Cornwall. Sleeping up to 8 in 4 bedrooms, 2 with distant sea views towards Godrevy lighthouse and beyond. Just a short walk from shops, galleries, bars, restaurants and our superb Porthmeor, Porthminster, Porthgwidden and Harbour beaches... This is No1.

Directions: Turn right at Porthminster Hotel. Turn left between the Natwest and the library. Over mini island, 200 metres on the right is abode.

Bedrooms: 1 superking, 1 kingsize, 1 double, 1 twin
Open: All year except Christmas

Site: P **Payment:** **Leisure:** **Property:** **Children:** 14 **Catering:** **Room:**

ST. MINVER, Cornwall Map ref 1B2 SatNav PL27 6RG B

Tredower Barton

St Minver, Wadebridge, Cornwall PL27 6RG **T:** (01208) 813501
E: dally.123@btinternet.com

B&B PER ROOM PER NIGHT
D: £60.00 - £80.00

Tredower Barton is a farm bed and breakfast set in beautiful countryside near the North Cornish coast. New for 2014, a lovely garden/sun room with beautiful panoramic views available for guests' use. Delicious breakfast and relaxing stay guaranteed. Near to local attractions, Padstow and Port Isaac. Wi-Fi available.
Directions: 3 miles from Wadebridge on road B3314 to Port Issac.
Bedrooms: 1 twin, 1 family (can be used as family or double)
Open: Easter to October

Site: P **Leisure:** **Property:** **Children:** **Room:**

TINTAGEL, Cornwall Map ref 1B2 SatNav PL34 0DD B

The Avalon

Atlantic Road, Tintagel, Cornwall PL34 0DD **T:** (01840) 770116
E: avalontintagel@googlemail.com
W: www.tintagelbedbreakfast.co.uk **£ BOOK ONLINE**

B&B PER ROOM PER NIGHT
S: £40.00 - £63.00
D: £76.00 - £100.00

Award winning, refurbished and beautifully redesigned B&B perfectly located within Tintagel Village. Luxury Superior and stunning Tintagel Island and sea-view rooms available. Extensive, award winning breakfast menu using all local produce. **Directions:** Off the A39 follow signs for Tintagel. Drive through the centre of the Village. Turn left down our drive immediately after the Olive Garden restaurant. **Bedrooms:** 5 double, 2 Superior twin/super-king. All en suite **Open:** March to November

Site: P **Payment:** **Leisure:** **Property:** **Children:** 3 **Catering:**
Room:

TRURO, Cornwall Map ref 1B3 SatNav TR1 2HX B

Townhouse Rooms

City Centre, 20 Falmouth Road, Truro TR1 2HX **T:** (01872) 277374 **F:** (01872) 241666
E: info@trurotownhouse.com
W: www.trurotownhouse.com **£ BOOK ONLINE**

★★★★ ROOM ONLY — Silver Award

B&B PER ROOM PER NIGHT
D: £59.00 - £79.00

The Townhouse is different, relaxed, friendly, flexible, our guests say so! Lovely rooms, fully equipped. Rates include Buffet continental breakfast & vat. Walking distance to all amenities.
Directions: Please see website for detailed directions.
Bedrooms: 10 en suite double rooms. Single or double guests
Open: All year except Christmas and New Year

Site: P **Payment:** **Property:** **Catering:** **Room:**

WADEBRIDGE, Cornwall Map ref 1B2 SatNav PL27 6LA H

St Enodoc Hotel Rock

Rock, Wadebridge PL27 6LA **T:** (01208) 863394 **F:** 01208 863970
E: info@enodoc-hotel.co.uk
W: www.enodoc-hotel.co.uk

★★★★ HOTEL — Silver Award

B&B PER ROOM PER NIGHT
S: £150.00 - £220.00
D: £180.00 - £285.00

SPECIAL PROMOTIONS
3 nights for the price of 2 available, please call us for details.

Distinctive style and a relaxed atmosphere. Ideally located for relaxing breaks, golf or visiting Cornwall's stunning gardens. The two restaurants are run by Nathan Outlaw and his team. 2 Michelin Star Restaurant Nathan Outlaw and the more casual dining room Outlaws a la Carte Restaurant.

Directions: M4 West to Exeter, M5 Southbound, A30 to Bodmin, A389 to Wadebridge and B3314 to Rock.

Bedrooms: 8 double, 8 twin, 3 family, 1 suite
Open: February to December

Site: **Payment:** **Leisure:** **Property:** **Children:** **Catering:**
Room:

BRYHER, Isles of Scilly Map ref 1A3 SatNav TR23 0PR H

Hell Bay Hotel

Bryher, Isles of Scilly TR23 0PR **T:** (01720) 422947 **F:** 01720 423004
E: contactus@hellbay.co.uk
W: www.hellbay.co.uk **£ BOOK ONLINE**

★★★★ HOTEL — Silver Award

B&B PER ROOM PER NIGHT
S: £115.00 - £365.00
D: £170.00 - £570.00

EVENING MEAL PER PERSON
£36.50 - £42.50

SPECIAL PROMOTIONS
Please see our website for all special rates and breaks.

Bryher's only hotel and England's last boasts a spectacular, natural location that blends with the contemporary style of the hotel to produce a unique venue. All accommodation is beautifully appointed, and most bedrooms have direct sea views. The award-winning food and informal service combine to complete the experience.

Directions: Flights from Exeter, Newquay or Land's End or ferry from Penzance all to the neighbouring island of St Mary's. A local boat transfer will take you to Bryher, a 15 minute journey.

Bedrooms: 4 family, 21 suite
Open: March to October

Site: **Payment:** **Leisure:** **Property:** **Children:** **Catering:** **Room:**

ST. MARY'S, Isles of Scilly Map ref 1A3 SatNav TR21 0NW B

Isles of Scilly Country Guest House

Sage House, High Lanes, St. Mary's TR21 0NW **T:** (01720) 422440
E: scillyguesthouse@hotmail.co.uk
W: www.scillyguesthouse.co.uk **£ BOOK ONLINE**

★★★ GUEST HOUSE

B&B PER ROOM PER NIGHT
S: £38.00 - £53.00
D: £78.00 - £112.00

Relax and get away from it all. A quiet and peaceful location with an off-island feel, yet still on St. Mary's with shops and services. We welcome all; families, couples, individuals, even pets. Wake up to the sound of nothing but birdsong. **Directions:** Isles of Scilly on Saint Marys near Telegraph Hill towards Pelistry Beach. **Bedrooms:** All en suite and have tea/coffee making facilities **Open:** March - October

WELCOME WALKERS — WELCOME PETS!

Site: **Payment:** **Leisure:** **Property:** **Children:** **Catering:** **Room:**

BLACKAWTON, Devon Map ref 1D3 SatNav TQ9 7BG B

The George Inn

Main Street, Blackawton, Devon TQ9 7BG **T:** (01803) 712342
E: tgiblackawton@yahoo.co.uk
W: www.blackawton.com

★★★ INN

B&B PER ROOM PER NIGHT
S: £63.00 - £76.00
D: £78.00 - £90.00

EVENING MEAL PER PERSON
£7.00 - £13.00

Traditional village inn at the heart of Blackawton village, offering well kept cask ales, good food, excellent service, real value and choice and comfortable en suite accommodation. **Directions:** Between Totnes and Kingsbridge take A3122 towards Dartmouth, turn right to Blackawton at Forces Cross, right into the village centre. **Bedrooms:** 3 double, 1 twin, 1 family **Open:** All year

Site: P **Payment:** **Property:** **Children:** **Catering:** **Room:**

For **key to symbols** see page 7

BRIXHAM, Devon Map ref 1D2 SatNav TQ5 9AJ

enjoyEngland.com ★★★ HOTEL

B&B PER ROOM PER NIGHT
S: £55.00 - £78.00
D: £96.00 - £168.00

HB PER PERSON PER NIGHT
£58.00 - £94.00

SPECIAL PROMOTIONS
Special-event packages. Extensive range of conference and business facilities. Weddings and special occasions. Christmas and New Year celebrations.

Berry Head Hotel

Berry Head Road, Brixham TQ5 9AJ **T:** (01803) 853225 **F:** 01803 882084
E: stay@berryheadhotel.com
W: www.berryheadhotel.com

Steeped in history, nestling on the water's edge in acres of outstanding natural beauty. Traditional hospitality, excellent, friendly and personal service with attention to detail. Comfortable accommodation, thoughtfully equipped. Imaginative menus, varied dining options, featuring quality local produce and fresh fish. Lounge, bars and terrace, popular with locals and residents.

Directions: Enter Brixham, continue to harbour and around, up King Street for 1 mile to Berry Head.

Bedrooms: 3 single, 12 dble, 10 twin, 7 family
Open: All year

Site: **Payment:** € **Leisure:** **Property:** **Children:** **Catering:**
Room:

DAWLISH, Devon Map ref 1D2 SatNav EX7 0NA

enjoyEngland.com ★★★ HOTEL

B&B PER ROOM PER NIGHT
S: £69.00 - £150.00
D: £69.00 - £150.00

EVENING MEAL PER PERSON
£8.50 £35.00

SPECIAL PROMOTIONS
Children under 10 free when sharing with 2 adults. Special cabaret weekend breaks throughout the year.

Langstone Cliff Hotel

Mount Pleasant Road, Dawlish Warren, Dawlish, Devon EX7 0NA **T:** (01626) 868000
F: (01626) 868006 **E:** info@langstone-hotel.co.uk
W: www.langstone-hotel.co.uk **£ BOOK ONLINE**

Set in 19 acres of Devon woodland overlooking the sea close to Exeter and Torquay. Extensive leisure facilities include 2 swimming pools, snooker, tennis, table tennis, fitness room and hairdressing Salon. Regular entertainment, children welcome, dinner dance and cabaret weekends, Dance Holidays, extensive Christmas and New Year Programme.

Directions: From M5 jct 31 follow A379 for Dawlish. Turn left at harbour after Starcross. Follow road approx 1.5 miles, hotel is on left.

Bedrooms: 1 single, 19 dble, 8 twin, 30 family, 6 suite
Open: All year

Site: P **Payment:** **Leisure:** **Property:** **Children:**
Catering: **Room:**

EXETER, Devon Map ref 1D2 *SatNav EX4 4HD* B

enjoyEngland.com ★★★★ GUEST HOUSE

B&B PER ROOM PER NIGHT
S: £48.00 - £55.00
D: £78.00

Raffles Hotel

11 Blackall Road EX4 4HD **T:** (01392) 270200 **E:** raffleshtl@btinternet.com
W: www.raffles-exeter.co.uk

Raffles is a large Victorian townhouse 5 minutes walk from city centre and close to the university. Car park available. Wildlife garden for guests use. Spacious accommodation. Vegetarian, organic breakfast on request. 24 hours notice for Haddock or Kippers. First choice for The Lonely Planet Exeter. Enjoy your stay. Trip Advisor certificate of excellence. Family Room £86-96. **Bedrooms:** All single, twin, double or family rooms have en suite, Wi-Fi, Television and tea/coffee making facilities **Open:** All Year

Site: P **Payment:** £€ **Property:** **Children:** **Room:** TV

EXETER, Devon Map ref 1D2 *SatNav EX2 9UP* B

enjoyEngland.com ★★★★ FARMHOUSE

B&B PER ROOM PER NIGHT
S: £35.00 - £40.00
D: £65.00 - £75.00

South View Farm B & B

South View Farm, Shillingford St George, Exeter, Devon EX2 9UP **T:** (01392) 832278
F: 01392 832278 **E:** info@southviewbandb.co.uk
W: www.southviewbandb.co.uk

4 star Silver Quality farmhouse accommodation near Exeter, A30, A38. Peaceful rural setting, en suite rooms, tea/coffee facilities. Delicious breakfast, superb views. Coarse fishing on site, ample parking. Payment by card, cash or cheque. **Directions:** From M5 take A38 then next exit Kennford. Follow sign to Clapham, then Shillingford St George. After 1 mile, South View Farm on left before the village. **Bedrooms:** En suite, TV, tea/coffee facilities and free Wi-Fi
Open: All Year

Site: P **Payment:** £€ **Leisure:** **Property:** **Children:** **Catering:** **Room:** TV

FROGMORE, Devon Map ref 1C3 *SatNav TQ7 2NR* B

enjoyEngland.com ★★★★ INN

B&B PER ROOM PER NIGHT
S: £60.00 - £70.00
D: £85.00
EVENING MEAL PER PERSON
£10.00 - £20.00

Globe Inn

Frogmore, Nr Kingsbridge TQ7 2NR **T:** (01548) 531351 **E:** info@theglobeinn.co.uk
W: www.theglobeinn.co.uk

The inn is situated in the pretty village of Frogmore, between Kingsbridge and Dartmouth, in glorious unspoilt South Hams countryside. The pub has undergone tasteful renovation and now boasts 8 well appointed en suite bedrooms. Downstairs the pub has a cosy bar restaurant frequented be friendly locals. **Directions:** Via Kingsbridge take the A379 to Dartmouth and Torcross. After 2 miles, look out for the Inn on the left as you enter Frogmore. **Bedrooms:** 5 double, 2 twin, 1 family. All rooms en suite **Open:** All year

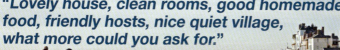

Site: P **Payment:** £€ **Leisure:** **Property:** **Children:** **Catering:** **Room:** TV

HOLSWORTHY, Devon *Map ref 1C2* — *SatNav EX22 6SJ* B

B&B PER ROOM PER NIGHT
S: £60.00 - £65.00
D: £70.00 - £90.00

EVENING MEAL PER PERSON
£20.00 - £25.00

SPECIAL PROMOTIONS
Please see our website for regular seasonal offers and discounts for longer stays.

Leworthy Farmhouse B&B

Lower Leworthy, Holsworthy, Devon EX22 6SJ **T:** (01409) 254484
E: leworthyfarmhouse@btconnect.com
W: www.leworthyfarmhouse.co.uk **£ BOOK ONLINE**

If it's the 'good life' you're seeking, look no further than Leworthy Farmhouse, tucked away in the peace and tranquility of a small hamlet, close to the North Devon/Cornwall border. This stunning Georgian farmhouse provides a relaxed base to explore the 'Ruby Country', the seaside town of Bude or spend a peaceful afternoon watching the rare breed livestock or coarse fishing in the lake.

Directions: From Holsworthy take the North Tamerton Road, after 3 miles turn left signed Leworthy/Southdown. Follow tarmac lane to island, stay left, B&B straight ahead. Enter via wooden gates to reception.

Bedrooms: Fresh towels, Freeview flatscreen TV/DVD player, Free Wi-Fi available. Hairdryer, radio/alarm, complimentary toiletries and tea/coffee making with fresh milk
Open: Closed from Christmas till February half term

Site: P **Payment:** **Leisure:** **Property:** **Catering:** **Room:** TV DVD

HONITON, Devon *Map ref 1D2* — *SatNav EX14 3AD* H

B&B PER ROOM PER NIGHT
S: £190.00
D: £220.00 - £460.00

HB PER PERSON PER NIGHT
£164.00 - £284.00

Combe House Devon

Gittisham, Honiton, Nr Exeter, Devon EX14 3AD **T:** (01404) 540 400
E: stay@combehousedevon.com
W: www.combehousedevon.com **£ BOOK ONLINE**

In top Best Foodie Hotels in South West England, 2014. Romantic, independently owned 450yr old Elizabethan Manor in 3,500 acres of some of England's finest countryside, with the South Devon coast nearby, Lyme Regis to Sidmouth. **Directions:** 15 minutes from M5/J29/Exeter Airport and A30/London-Honiton is 5 mins away. 'Halfway to Cornwall'. **Bedrooms:** 4 double, 9 twin king-size double, 2 suites and 2 thatched cottages. **Open:** All year

Site: **Payment:** **Leisure:** **Property:** **Children:** **Catering:** **Room:** TV

LYNTON, Devon *Map ref 1C1* — *SatNav EX35 6AR* B

B&B PER ROOM PER NIGHT
S: £75.00 - £112.00
D: £100.00 - £150.00

Highcliffe House

Sinai Hill, Lynton, Devon EX35 6AR **T:** (01598) 752235 **E:** info@highcliffehouse.co.uk
W: www.highcliffehouse.co.uk

Exclusively for adults, Highcliffe House is situated on the Exmoor coast with stunning sea views across the Bristol Channel to Wales. Six beautifully appointed bedrooms and an award winning breakfast makes this a special place to stay. **Bedrooms:** All rooms en suite, tea & coffee, flat screen TV's **Open:** Mid March to the end of October

Site: P **Payment:** € **Leisure:** **Property:** **Catering:** **Room:** TV DVD

MORETONHAMPSTEAD, Devon Map ref 1C2 SatNav TQ13 8QF B

Great Sloncombe Farm

Great Sloncombe Farm, Moretonhampstead, Dartmoor, Devon TQ13 8QF
T: (01647) 440595 **F:** 01647 440595 **E:** hmerchant@sloncombe.freeserve.co.uk
W: www.greatsloncombefarm.co.uk

enjoyEngland.com ★★★★ FARMHOUSE

B&B PER ROOM PER NIGHT
S: £45.00 - £50.00
D: £75.00 - £85.00

13th century farmhouse in a magical Dartmoor valley. Meadows, woodland, wild flowers and animals. Farmhouse breakfast with freshly baked bread. Everything provided for an enjoyable break. **Directions:** From Moretonhampstead take A382 towards Chagford. Take left turn (farm signed) up lane, through hamlet, farm is on right. **Bedrooms:** 2 double, 1 twin **Open:** All year

Site: **Payment:** **Leisure:** **Property:** **Children:** **Catering:** **Room:**

PAIGNTON, Devon Map ref 1D2 SatNav TQ3 2BQ B

Blue Waters Lodge

4 Leighon Road, Paignton TQ3 2BQ **T:** (01803) 557749 **F:** 01803 551842
E: info@bluewaterslodge.co.uk
W: www.bluewaterslodge.co.uk

enjoyEngland.com ★★★★ GUEST ACCOMMODATION

B&B PER ROOM PER NIGHT
D: £55.00 - £65.00

Blue Waters Lodge offers a warm friendly greeting and is conveniently situated within easy strolling distance of the seafront, shops and entertainments, yet still in a quiet location for a peaceful holiday. **Directions:** Please see website for details. **Bedrooms:** Freeview flatscreen TV, clock radio alarm, complimentary beverages and snacks, hairdryer and complimentary toiletries. **Open:** All year

Site: P **Payment:** **Property:** **Children:** **Catering:** **Room:**

PAIGNTON, Devon Map ref 1D2 SatNav TQ4 6EN H

Cleve Court Hotel

3 Cleveland Road, Paignton TQ4 6EN **T:** (01803) 551444 **F:** 01803 664617
E: info@clevecourthotel.co.uk
W: www.clevecourthotel.co.uk **£ BOOK ONLINE**

enjoyEngland.com ★★ SMALL HOTEL

B&B PER ROOM PER NIGHT
S: £36.00 - £44.00
D: £72.00 - £88.00
EVENING MEAL PER PERSON
£16.00

Situated between Paignton beach, Goodrington sands and Quaywest Water Park. Paignton harbour is just a 2 minutes stroll away, handy for fishing trips or sightseeing around the bay or cruise along the river Dart to Totnes. **Directions:** M5 onto 380 to Paignton Ringroad. Turn left second island, follow signs to seafront. Turn right at front to mini roundabout at end - turn left onto Roundham Road. Hotel half way up on the right. **Bedrooms:** En suite, TV, tea/coffee. **Open:** All Year

Site: P **Payment:** **Leisure:** **Property:** **Children:** **Catering:** **Room:** TV DVD

For **key to symbols** see page 7

PAIGNTON, Devon *Map ref 1D2* *SatNav TQ3 2NJ* H

B&B PER ROOM PER NIGHT
S: £20.00 - £35.00
D: £40.00 - £70.00

HB PER PERSON PER NIGHT
£35.00 - £50.00

SPECIAL PROMOTIONS
2-4 year olds half-price when sharing with adults. Winter 2 night breaks, B&B and 3 course evening meal from £30pppn.

Redcliffe Lodge Hotel

1 Marine Drive, Paignton TQ3 2NJ **T:** (01803) 551394 **F:** 01803 551394
E: davies.valleyview@tiscali.co.uk
W: www.redcliffelodge.co.uk **£ BOOK ONLINE**

Redcliffe Lodge occupies one of Paignton's finest seafront positions, in its own grounds with a large, free car park. All rooms are en suite and comfortably furnished with modern facilities. Licensed bar. Panoramic views from both our sun lounge and dining room, where you will enjoy our high standard of cuisine.

Directions: Follow A3022 to Paignton seafront. The hotel is situated at the end of Marine Drive, on the right adjacent to Paignton Green.

Bedrooms: 2 single, 10 dble, 3 twin, 2 family
Open: All year

Site: P **Payment:** **Leisure:** **Property:** **Children:** **Catering:** **Room:**

PAIGNTON, Devon *Map ref 1D2* *SatNav TQ4 6BU* B

B&B PER ROOM PER NIGHT
S: £35.00 - £40.00
D: £50.00 - £60.00

Rowcroft Lodge

14 Youngs Park Road, Goodrington Sands, Paignton, Devon TQ4 6BU **T:** (01803) 559420
F: 01803 500115 **E:** ellys14@btconnect.com
W: www.rowcroft-hotel.com **£ BOOK ONLINE**

A double fronted Victorian licensed guest house overlooking a beautiful park, lakes and sea. A short level walk to 2 sandy beaches, new children's play area, crazy golf, aquatic park and Leisure Centre. All rooms en suite with television. **Directions:** Along Paignton seafront to mini-roundabout at south end. Left past harbour to top of Roundham Road. Bear right into Alta Vista Road. Youngs Park Road 1st left. **Bedrooms:** En suite rooms, either overlooking garden or park **Open:** All year

Site: P **Payment:** **Leisure:** **Property:** **Children:** **Catering:** **Room:**

PLYMOUTH, Devon *Map ref 1C2* *SatNav PL1 2RQ* B

B&B PER ROOM PER NIGHT
S: £32.00 - £48.00
D: £54.00 - £62.00

Athenaeum Lodge

4 Athenaeum Street, The Hoe, Plymouth PL1 2RQ **T:** (01752) 665005
E: athenaeumlodge@gmail.com
W: www.athenaeumlodge.com **£ BOOK ONLINE**

Elegant, Grade II Listed guesthouse, ideally situated on The Hoe. Centrally located for the Barbican, Theatre Royal, Plymouth Pavilions, Ferry Port and the National Marine Aquarium. City centre and university are a few minutes walk. Wi-Fi. **Directions:** Please see website for comprehensive directions. **Bedrooms:** 3 double, 2 twin, 3 family **Open:** All year except Christmas and New Year

Site: P **Payment:** **Leisure:** **Property:** **Children:** **Catering:** **Room:**

PLYMOUTH, Devon Map ref 1C2 SatNav PL1 3BS

Caraneal

12-14 Pier Street, West Hoe, Plymouth PL1 3BS **T:** (01752) 663589 **F:** (01752) 663589
E: caranealhotel@hotmail.com
W: www.caranealplymouth.co.uk **£ BOOK ONLINE**

B&B PER ROOM PER NIGHT
S: £35.00 - £40.00
D: £55.00 - £60.00

Caraneal is a cosy family-run establishment near the famous Hoe and seafront and within easy walking distance of the city centre and the historic Barbican. Free Wi-Fi Available. **Directions:** From A38 follow signs for City Centre, then the Hoe and Seafront. On seafront pass Plymouth Dome and turn right at the next mini-roundabout. **Bedrooms:** 5 double, 2 twin **Open:** All year except Christmas and New Year

Site: P **Payment:** **Leisure:** **Property:** **Children:** **Catering:** **Room:**

PLYMOUTH, Devon Map ref 1C2 SatNav PL9 0AW

Gabber Farm

Gabber Lane, Down Thomas, Plymouth PL9 0AW **T:** (01752) 862269
E: gabberfarm@tiscali.co.uk
W: www.gabberfarm.co.uk

B&B PER ROOM PER NIGHT
S: £27.00 - £35.00
D: £27.00 - £30.00

A courteous welcome at this farm, near coast and Mount Batten Centre. Lovely walks. Special weekly rates, especially for Senior Citizens and children. Directions provided. Double and family rooms are en suite, single and twin non en suite. **Directions:** Directions of how to find the farm can be obtained by contacting Margaret directly or by email. **Bedrooms:** 1 single, 1 double, 1 twin, 2 family **Open:** All year

Site: P **Payment:** **Leisure:** **Property:** **Children:** **Catering:** **Room:**

PLYMOUTH, Devon Map ref 1C2 SatNav PL12HU

The George Guest House

161 Citadel Road, The Hoe, Plymouth PL1 2HU **T:** (01752) 661517
E: info@georgeguesthouse.com
W: www.georgeguesthouse.com **£ BOOK ONLINE**

Welcome to The George Guest House; we are a friendly family run guest house with a warm and welcoming atmosphere, located on Plymouth Hoe. We are within a short walking distance of all the local areas of interest and the cities amenities. Please contact for 2015 Rates. **Directions:** Please see website. **Bedrooms:** We have a range of rooms to suit everyone's needs, en suite rooms are also available **Open:** All year

Site: P **Payment:** **Catering:** **Room:**

SIDMOUTH, Devon Map ref 1D2 SatNav EX10 0ND B

The Barn & Pinn Cottage Guest House

Bowd, Sidmouth, Devon EX10 0ND **T:** (01395) 513613
E: barnpinncottage@btinternet.com
W: www.thebarnandpinncottage.co.uk

enjoyEngland.com ★★★★ GUEST HOUSE — enjoyEngland.com Gold AWARD

B&B PER ROOM PER NIGHT
S: £42.00 - £48.50
D: £78.00 - £118.00

EVENING MEAL PER PERSON
£19.00 - £22.50

SPECIAL PROMOTIONS
3+ nights 1 for free, 2+ Nights & 7+ Nights Special Rates please see our website for details. Open over Christmas & New Year. Special occasions & functions by arrangement. Please enquire for details.

This beautiful 15th Century thatched cottage nestles within two acres of award winning gardens 5 minutes drive from Sidmouth. All en suite rooms have full central heating, Digital TV, and tea/coffee making facilities. Dinner available Thur-Sun. Good home cooking, varied menu, well stocked bar. Comfortable guest lounge, large private car park.

Directions: Located on A3052 12 miles from Exeter, 15 miles from Lyme Regis. Between Newton Poppleford and Sidford. 5 mins from beach at Sidmouth using B3176.

Bedrooms: 1 single, 3 double, 1 kingsize, 2 luxury four posters with private garden, 2 twin, 1 holiday let as B&B or self catering. Family rooms possible
Open: All year

Site: P **Payment:** **Leisure:** **Property:** **Children:** **Catering:**
Room:

SIDMOUTH, Devon Map ref 1D2 SatNav EX10 8AY H

Hotel Riviera

The Esplanade, Sidmouth, Devon EX10 8AY **T:** (01395) 515201 **F:** 01395 577775
E: enquiries@hotelriviera.co.uk
W: www.hotelriviera.co.uk **£ BOOK ONLINE**

enjoyEngland.com ★★★★ HOTEL — enjoyEngland.com Gold AWARD

B&B PER ROOM PER NIGHT
S: £109.00 - £188.00
D: £218.00 - £356.00

HB PER PERSON PER NIGHT
£104.00 - £232.00

SPECIAL PROMOTIONS
Seasonal breaks available throughout the year. Christmas and New Year programme also available.

The Hotel Riviera is splendidly positioned at the centre of Sidmouth's esplanade, overlooking Lyme Bay. With its mild climate and the beach just on the doorstep, the setting echoes the South of France and is the choice of the discerning visitor in search of relaxation and quieter pleasures. Glorious sea views can be enjoyed from the recently re-designed en suite bedrooms, all of which are fully appointed and have many thoughtful extras. In the elegant bay-view dining room guests are offered a fine choice of dishes from extensive menus, prepared by English trained chefs with local seafood being a particular speciality. The hotel has a long tradition of hospitality and is perfect for unforgettable holidays, long weekends, unwinding breaks and all the spirit of the glorious Festive Season… you will be treated to the kind of friendly personal attention that can only be found in a private hotel of this quality.

Directions: Sidmouth is 165 miles from London and 13 miles from M5 exit 30 then follow A3052.

Bedrooms: 7 single, 10 doubles, 7 twin, 2 suite
Open: All year

Site: P **Payment:** **Leisure:** **Property:** **Children:** **Catering:**
Room:

SIDMOUTH, Devon Map ref 1D2 SatNav EX10 8AZ

enjoyEngland.com ★★★ HOTEL

B&B PER ROOM PER NIGHT
S: £45.00 - £82.50
D: £90.00 - £165.00

EVENING MEAL PER PERSON
£24.00

Royal York & Faulkner Hotel

The Esplanade, Sidmouth EX10 8AZ **T:** (01395) 513043 **F:** (01395) 577472
E: stay@royalyorkhotel.co.uk
W: www.royalyorkhotel.co.uk **£ BOOK ONLINE**

Magnificent Regency hotel on centre of Esplanade & adjacent picturesque town. Personally run by the Hook family with a long standing reputation for hospitality and service. Beautifully appointed throughout, with all amenities and superb spa. **Directions:** Exit M5 at junction 30. Follow A3052 signposted Sidmouth. All approach routes lead to Esplanade. **Bedrooms:** 22 single, 10 double, 30 twin, 8 family, 2 suites **Open:** Closed January

Site: P **Payment:** **Leisure:** **Property:** **Children:** **Catering:** **Room:**

TORQUAY, Devon Map ref 1D2 SatNav TQ1 3SN

enjoyEngland.com ★★★★ GUEST HOUSE — enjoyEngland.com Silver AWARD

B&B PER ROOM PER NIGHT
S: £36.00 - £40.00
D: £68.00 - £80.00

SPECIAL PROMOTIONS
Over 60's Discount for 4 nights or more, weekly discounts.

Babbacombe Guest House

53 Babbacombe Road, Babbacombe, Torquay TQ1 3SN **T:** (01803) 328071
E: info@babbacombeguesthouse.com
W: www.babbacombeguesthouse.com **£ BOOK ONLINE**

Ideally located in Babbacombe this Visit Britain 4* Silver Award and Breakfast Award Guest House offers free off road parking on-site and is a level 3 minute walk to the spectacular views of the Babbacombe Downs across Lyme Bay, Babbacombe Theatre and a number of pubs, restaurants, cafes and attractions. Continental buffet and cooked breakfast to order using locally sourced produce.

Directions: From the M5 South take the A380 to Torquay which leads to A3022 Riviera Way. Following the commercial park, turn left towards Hele onto the B3199. Continue towards St. Marychurch and turn onto A379.

Bedrooms: Pure white cotton linen, The White Company toiletries, branded hospitality tray, Wi-Fi, hairdryer, LCD TV, dressing robe and slippers, iPod dock radio
Open: All year

Site: P **Payment:** **Leisure:** **Property:** **Catering:** **Room:**

TORQUAY, Devon Map ref 1D2 SatNav TQ2 6RQ

enjoyEngland.com ★★★ HOTEL

B&B PER ROOM PER NIGHT
S: £35.00 - £110.00
D: £60.00 - £230.00

HB PER PERSON PER NIGHT
£40.00 - £140.00

Best Western Livermead Cliff Hotel

Sea Front, Torquay TQ2 6RQ **T:** (01803) 299666 **F:** (01803) 294496
E: info@livermeadcliff.co.uk
W: www.livermeadcliff.co.uk **£ BOOK ONLINE**

Privately owned, 3 star Best Western hotel on the water's edge with direct access to the beach. Panoramic views, sea view lounge and en suite rooms, licensed bar and stunning new Riviera Terrace. Free parking. Free Wi-Fi. Ideally located for touring the SW of England. **Directions:** Please contact us for directions. **Bedrooms:** 13 single, 29 double, 14 twin, 8 family, 1 suite **Open:** All year

WELCOME FAMILIES — WELCOME PETS!

Site: **Payment:** **Leisure:** **Property:** **Children:** **Catering:** **Room:**

For **key to symbols** see page 7

TORQUAY, Devon Map ref 1D2 SatNav TQ1 3LP B

B&B PER ROOM PER NIGHT
S: £40.00 - £53.00
D: £80.00 - £106.00

EVENING MEAL PER PERSON
£17.00 - £24.00

Coombe Court

67 Babbacombe Downs Road, Torquay TQ1 3LP **T:** (01803) 327097
E: enquiries@coombecourthotel.co.uk
W: www.coombecourthotel.co.uk

Coombe Court is a family-run establishment, situated in a level location just 50 yards from Babbacombe Downs, Babbacombe Theatre and the famous Cliff Railway. Within easy walking distance to St Marychurch and Wellswood. All bedrooms have en suite facilities, digital Freeview TV, complimentary tea and coffee tray and free Wi-Fi. There is private off road parking, licensed bar, guests TV lounge and guest lounge with views over the garden and out to the sea, nearby woodland and Babbacombe Bay. Traditional cooking and optional evening meal available. We look forward to offering you a warm and friendly welcome at Coombe Court Guest House.

Directions: Please contact us for directions.

Bedrooms: 1 single, 10 double, 3 twin, 1 family. Sea view rooms available
Open: All year except Christmas and New Year

Site: P **Payment:** **Leisure:** **Property:** **Children:** 10 **Catering:**
Room:

TORQUAY, Devon Map ref 1D2 SatNav TQ2 6RH H

B&B PER ROOM PER NIGHT
S: £39.00 - £121.00
D: £69.00 - £250.00

EVENING MEAL PER PERSON
£23.50 - £29.50

Corbyn Head Hotel

Sea Front, Torquay, Devon TQ2 6RH **T:** (01803) 213611 **F:** 01803 296152
E: info@corbynhead.com
W: www.corbynhead.com **£ BOOK ONLINE**

The Corbyn Head Hotel is one of Torquay's leading hotels with its seafront location. Most bedrooms enjoy stunning sea views, many have private balconies. Outdoor Swimming Pool. AA Rosetted Restaurant. Free Wi-Fi. Free on-site parking. **Directions:** Torquay Seafront, turn right and follow signs for Cockington Village. Hotel on right. **Bedrooms:** 3 single, 29 double, 10 twin, 3 family
Open: All year

Site: P **Payment:** **Leisure:** **Property:** **Children:**
Catering: **Room:**

TORQUAY, Devon Map ref 1D2 SatNav TQ1 3LN B

The Downs, Babbacombe

Seafront, 41-43 Babbacombe Downs Road, Babbacombe, Torquay TQ1 3LN
T: (01803) 328543 **F:** (01803) 670557 **E:** enquiries@downshotel.co.uk
W: www.downshotel.co.uk **£ BOOK ONLINE**

B&B PER ROOM PER NIGHT
S: £60.00 - £75.00
D: £75.00 - £90.00

EVENING MEAL PER PERSON
£17.95

SPECIAL PROMOTIONS
Stay 3 or more nights & get 1 extra night free - available Jan, Feb & November. Stay 7 nights & get 5% off - accom only. Upgrade to ½ Board for 6 consecutive nights and get dinner free for 1 night.

The Downs, Babbacombe in Torquay is family-run with 12 en suite rooms, 8 with balconies and uninterrupted sea views over Lyme Bay. We have a Lounge Bar and Restaurant serving optional evening meals and are fully licensed. We have an elegant feel whilst maintaining a comfortable, relaxed atmosphere. Dogs and Children welcome.

WINNERS OF SOUTH DEVON TOURISM & HOSPITALITY AWARDS 2013 - B&B, GUEST HOUSE & INN

Directions: M5 South to Torquay A380, at Torquay Harbour take left at r/a to Babbacombe. On entering Babbacombe take right turn into Princes Street, left onto Babbacombe Downs Rd, we are on the left.

Bedrooms: All bedrooms are fully en suite with simple yet stylish oak furniture and pocket sprung beds, luxurious toiletries and towels, in keeping with a 4*hotel.
Open: All year, Christmas breaks available

Site: P **Payment:** **Leisure:** **Property:** **Children:** **Catering:** **Room:**

TORQUAY, Devon Map ref 1D2 SatNav TQ2 6QJ H

Livermead House Hotel

Torbay Road, Seafront, Torquay TQ2 6QJ **T:** (01803) 294361 **F:** 01803 200758
E: info@livermead.com
W: www.livermead.com **£ BOOK ONLINE**

B&B PER ROOM PER NIGHT
S: £35.00 - £110.00
D: £60.00 - £230.00

HB PER PERSON PER NIGHT
£40.00 - £140.00

The Livermead House Hotel in Torquay, situated on the edge of the Cockington Valley was built in 1820 and is positioned on Torquay's sea front. The hotel offers breathtaking sea views, beautifully manicured lawns and exceptionally high standards of service and cuisine from award winning Chef, Tony Hetherington.
Directions: Full directions and map available on our website.
Bedrooms: 7 single, 34 double, 25 twin, 1 family, all en suite
Open: All year

Site: **Payment:** **Leisure:** **Property:** **Children:** **Catering:** **Room:**

TORQUAY, Devon Map ref 1D2 SatNav TQ1 2LL H

enjoyEngland.com ★★★★ HOTEL

B&B PER ROOM PER NIGHT
S: £75.00 - £105.00
D: £99.00 - £180.00

EVENING MEAL PER PERSON
£15.00 - £40.00

SPECIAL PROMOTIONS
Year round offers available, see website for details, or ring our friendly reception team.

The Osborne Hotel

Hesketh Crescent, Meadfoot Beach, Torquay TQ1 2LL **T:** (01803) 213311 **F:** 01803 296788
E: enq@osborne-torquay.co.uk
W: www.osborne-torquay.co.uk **£ BOOK ONLINE**

The Osborne Hotel, known by the discerning as 'The Country House Hotel by the Sea', is the centrepiece of an elegant Regency crescent. Most Rooms provide panoramic views of the broad sweep of Torbay. There are 2 hotel restaurants, the gourmet Langtry's offering regional specialities, and the more informal Brasserie.

Directions: From Torquay harbour, turn left at clocktower signposted Meadfoot Beach, turn right at traffic lights. Follow road straight ahead to the bottom of the hill.

Bedrooms: 1 single, 16 dble, 5 twin, 2 family, 8 suite
Open: All year

Site: **Payment:** **Leisure:** **Property:** **Children:**
Catering: **Room:**

TORQUAY, Devon Map ref 1D2 SatNav TQ2 5PD B

enjoyEngland.com ★★★ GUEST HOUSE

B&B PER ROOM PER NIGHT
S: £35.00 - £70.00
D: £45.00 - £70.00

Whitburn Guest House

Saint Lukes Road North, Torquay, Devon TQ2 5PD **T:** (01803) 296719
E: lazenby1210@btinternet.com
W: www.whitburnguesthouse.co.uk **£ BOOK ONLINE**

Anne and Joe warmly welcome you to our clean comfortable guest house, 5 mins walk or local bus to harbour, beach, seafront, town centre shops, clubs, restaurants. Lovely residential area and parking. Full cooked breakfast included in price. **Directions:** At Seafront go up Shedden Hill, take 2nd right into St Lukes Road, then 1st left into St Lukes Road North. Whitburn Guest House 150 metres on left. **Bedrooms:** En suite or private rooms, Freeview TV, tea, coffee **Open:** All year

Site: **Payment:** **Leisure:** **Property:** **Children:** **Room:**

TOTNES, Devon Map ref 1D2 SatNav TQ9 7LB B

enjoyEngland.com ★★★★★ GUEST ACCOMMODATION

B&B PER ROOM PER NIGHT
D: £65.00 - £70.00

Lower Horner

Halwell, Totnes, Devon TQ9 7LB **T:** (01548) 821448 **E:** lower-horner@hotmail.co.uk
W: www.lower-horner-totnes.co.uk

Walk through French doors into two individual beautifully furnished suites, sleeping 2 and 4. Both separate from the main house, located in a converted barn within the grounds where stunning far reaching views over rolling countryside await. **Directions:** From Totnes take A381 towards Kingsbridge. At Harbertonford take 2nd right. Travel 1.5 miles then turn right to Horner. Next right, we are 1st on right **Bedrooms:** En suite, flatscreen TV, tea and coffee and fridge **Open:** All year except Christmas and New Year

Site: **Property:** **Children:** **Room:**

WOOLACOMBE, Devon Map ref 1C1 SatNav EX34 8NR H

enjoyEngland.com ★★★ HOTEL

B&B PER ROOM PER NIGHT
S: £42.00 - £75.00
D: £96.00 - £149.00

EVENING MEAL PER PERSON
£23.50 - £28.50

Trimstone Manor Country House Hotel

Trimstone, Nr Woolacombe, Ilfracombe, North Devon EX34 8NR **T:** (01271) 862841
F: 01271 863808 **E:** info@trimstone.co.uk
W: www.trimstone.co.uk **£ BOOK ONLINE**

Trimstone Hotel is a beautiful Manor House in North Devon in 44 acres of gardens and countryside, within minutes of beaches such as Woolacombe, Saunton, Croyde. The Hotel boasts facilities including en suite bedrooms, Bar, Restaurant and indoor heated swimming pool. **Directions:** From Barnstaple drive north on A361 through Braunton. 3 miles after Knowle, beyond layby, turn left into Trimstone Lane. Hotel is 300 yards on left. **Bedrooms:** 2 single, 12 double **Open:** All year

Site: **Payment:** **Leisure:** **Property:** **Children:** **Catering:**
Room:

YELVERTON, Devon Map ref 1C2 SatNav PL20 6PS B

enjoyEngland.com ★★★★ FARMHOUSE

B&B PER ROOM PER NIGHT
S: £35.00 - £50.00
D: £65.00 - £75.00

Callisham Farm

Meavy, Yelverton, Devon PL20 6PS **T:** (01822) 853901 **F:** 01822 853901
E: esme@callisham.co.uk
W: www.callisham.co.uk

Traditional family run farm in the Dartmoor National Park, peaceful, natural location where clean, comfortable, cosy accommodation is offered. Scrumptious breakfast. 10 miles from Plymouth, easy access from A386. Direct access to the open moorland. Royal Oak Inn accessible by ancient footpath taking you across Lovaton brook by means of clapper bridge. Just lovely! **Directions:** Please see website for full directions. **Open:** All year

Site: P **Payment:** € **Leisure:** **Property:** **Children:** **Catering:**
Room:

YELVERTON, Devon Map ref 1C2 SatNav PL20 7RA B

enjoyEngland.com ★★★★ GUEST ACCOMMODATION

B&B PER ROOM PER NIGHT
S: £65.00 - £85.00
D: £75.00 - £95.00

Overcombe House

Old Station Road, Horrabridge, Yelverton PL20 7RA **T:** (01822) 853501
E: enquiries@overcombehotel.co.uk
W: www.overcombehotel.co.uk **£ BOOK ONLINE**

Offering a warm, friendly welcome in relaxed, comfortable surroundings with a substantial breakfast using local and homemade produce. The dining room and some bedrooms enjoy stunning views of Dartmoor. Conveniently located for exploring the varied attractions of Devon and Cornwall, in particular Dartmoor National Park and the adjacent Tamar Valley.

Directions: Located on edge of Horrabridge village just off A386 1 mile from Yelverton heading towards Tavistock.

Bedrooms: 4 Double [6ft] /Twin, 3 Double, 1 Twin
Open: All year

WALKERS WELCOME · CYCLISTS WELCOME

Site: P **Payment:** **Leisure:** **Property:** **Catering:** **Room:**

For **key to symbols** see page 7

BLANDFORD FORUM, Dorset Map ref 2B3 SatNav DT11 0LS B

Lower Bryanston Farm B&B

Lower Bryanston Farm, Blandford Forum, Dorset DT11 0LS
T: (01258) 452009 / 07794 200582 **F:** 01258 452009 **E:** andrea@bryanstonfarm.co.uk
W: www.brylow.co.uk

enjoyEngland.com ★★★★ FARMHOUSE

B&B PER ROOM PER NIGHT
S: £60.00 - £80.00
D: £75.00 - £100.00

Attractive, homely farmhouse B&B with spacious, peaceful rooms, beautiful rural views and off-road parking. Superb location to explore Dorset. Within walking distance of the Georgian town of Blandford. Farmhouse Breakfast a speciality. **Bedrooms:** En suite, Wi-Fi, flat screen TV's and hospitality trays. **Open:** All year, except Christmas and New Year.

Site: P **Property:** **Children:** **Catering:** **Room:**

BOURNEMOUTH, Dorset Map ref 2B3 SatNav BH1 3PF B

Balincourt

58 Christchurch Road, Bournemouth BH1 3PF **T:** (01202) 552962 **F:** 01202 552962
E: reservations@balincourt.co.uk
W: www.balincourt.co.uk £ BOOK ONLINE

enjoyEngland.com ★★★★★ GUEST ACCOMMODATION

B&B PER ROOM PER NIGHT
S: £65.00 - £120.00
D: £85.00 - £130.00
EVENING MEAL PER PERSON
£23.00

Elegant family-run Victorian guest accommodation. Prime location for attractions, seafront and town centre. Tastefully decorated en suite rooms. Warm and friendly service. Children minimum age 14 years. Evening meals by prior arrangement. **Directions:** Please contact for directions. **Bedrooms:** Special occasion flowers, chocolates, champagne available on request **Open:** All Year

Site: P **Payment:** **Leisure:** **Property:** **Catering:** **Room:**

BRIDPORT, Dorset Map ref 2A3 SatNav DT6 3LB H

Bridge House Hotel

115 East Street, Bridport, Dorset DT6 3LB **T:** (01308) 423371 **F:** 01308 459573
E: info@bridgehousebridport.co.uk
W: www.bridgehousebridport.co.uk £ BOOK ONLINE

enjoyEngland.com ★★★ HOTEL

B&B PER ROOM PER NIGHT
S: £82.00 - £122.00
D: £130.00 - £170.00

SPECIAL PROMOTIONS
Please check our website or call for our current offers.

18th Century Georgian character town house, next to the river and its gardens. Offers quiet elegance, traditional ambience and friendly service. Elegant lounge, ten en suite bedrooms and a fully licensed wine bar, offering the ideal venue for functions, from parties to funerals, buffets to full bespoke menus, using fresh local quality produce. Free parking, near the town centre.

Directions: Located at the eastern end of Bridport's main street; 400m from the town centre and 200m before the roundabout on the right-hand side.

Bedrooms: 3 single, 3 double, 1 twin, 3 family
Open: All year

Site: P **Payment:** € **Leisure:** **Property:** **Children:**
Catering: **Room:**

BRIDPORT, Dorset Map ref 2A3 SatNav DT6 4RJ B

Chesil Beach Lodge

Coast Road, Burton Bradstock, Bridport, Dorset DT6 4RJ **T:** (01308) 897428
E: enquiries@chesilbeachlodge.co.uk
W: www.chesilbeachlodge.co.uk

B&B PER ROOM PER NIGHT
D: £85.00 - £120.00

SPECIAL PROMOTIONS
Please contact for any special offers.

Chesil Beach Lodge is the perfect getaway, located on the beautiful World Heritage Jurassic Coast with unbelievable panoramic sea and coastal views from all the accommodation. Chesil Beach Lodge was voted one of the '50 best European Beach Breaks' by The Independent and has received a TripAdvisor Certificate of Excellence for each of the last 4 years!

Ideal for walkers and dog owners, Chesil Beach Lodge is located on the cliff-top, just a few minutes walk across National Trust Land to the South West Coast Path and Chesil Beach at Burton Bradstock. All rooms have panoramic coastal views from Portland Bill right round to Start Point on a clear day – 99 miles of Coastline! Enjoy a home-cooked breakfast in the comfort of your own room while you enjoy the magnificent views and Free-Range eggs from our own Chickens.

Directions: Located on the Coast Road (B3157) ½ a mile out of Burton Bradstock towards Weymouth. Chesil Beach Lodge is located at the top of the hill on the right hand side.

Bedrooms: 1 Suite, 2 Bedrooms. All with sea views and sleep 2 Adults and 2 Children
Open: All Year

Site: P **Payment:** **Property:** **Children:** **Catering:** **Room:**

BRIDPORT, Dorset Map ref 2A3 SatNav DT6 4PE B

Dippers

42 Uploders, Bridport DT6 4PE **T:** (01308) 485504 / 07855 344121
E: liz@dipperswestdorset.co.uk
W: www.dipperswestdorset.co.uk **£ BOOK ONLINE**

B&B PER ROOM PER NIGHT
S: £30.00 - £35.00
D: £60.00 - £70.00

EVENING MEAL PER PERSON
£12.50 - £15.00

Dippers sits on the banks of the River Asker in the beautiful West Dorset village of Uploders. 2 miles from Bridport: a wonderful location for exploring Jurassic Coast and Hardy Country.
Directions: Uploders is ½ mile north of the A35, 2 miles east of Bridport. Turn right at Crown Inn and Dippers is 200m on the left.
Bedrooms: 1 single, 1 double, 1 twin **Open:** All year

Site: P **Property:** **Children:** **Catering:** **Room:**

BRIDPORT, Dorset Map ref 2A3 SatNav DT6 3LY B

The Tiger Inn

14-16 Barrack Street, Bridport DT6 3LY **T:** (01308) 427543
E: jacquie@tigerinnbridport.co.uk
W: www.tigerinnbridport.co.uk

B&B PER ROOM PER NIGHT
D: £70.00 - £140.00

Award winning 'CAMRA - West Dorset town Pub of the Year 2012'. Free house. Excellent town centre location. Boutique style bedrooms, all en suite, flatscreen TV and free Wi-Fi. **Directions:** Please contact us for directions. **Bedrooms:** 4 Double, 2 family
Open: All year

Site: **Payment:** **Leisure:** **Property:** **Children:** **Catering:** **Room:**

For **key to symbols** see page 7

CHRISTCHURCH, Dorset Map ref 2B3 SatNav BH23 1JE B

enjoyEngland.com ★★★★★ GUEST ACCOMMODATION
enjoyEngland.com Gold AWARD

B&B PER ROOM PER NIGHT
S: £50.00 - £90.00
D: £80.00 - £135.00

SPECIAL PROMOTIONS
Weekend 3 day breaks £119-£130 pp 3 night stay. Weekday breaks available upon request. November - March inc. Prices based on 2 people sharing

Druid House

26 Sopers Lane, Christchurch BH23 1JE **T:** (01202) 485615 **F:** (01202) 473484
E: reservations@druid-house.co.uk
W: www.druid-house.co.uk

Overlooking park, this delightful family-run establishment is just a stroll from the High Street, Priory and Quay. Bedrooms, some with balconies, are modern and very comfortably DVD/CD and Wi-Fi access. Beautiful rear garden, patio and relaxing lounge and bar areas.

Directions: A35 exit Christchurch main round about onto Sopers Lane, establishment on the left. Christchurch train station 10 min walk and Bournemouth International Airport 3 miles.

Bedrooms: 1 single, 4 double, 2 twin, 2 family
Open: All year

Site: P **Payment:** £ **Leisure:** **Property:** **Children:** **Catering:**
Room: TV DVD

CRANBORNE, Dorset Map ref 2B3 SatNav BH21 5PR B

enjoyEngland.com ★★★★ GUEST ACCOMMODATION

B&B PER ROOM PER NIGHT
S: £65.00
D: £115.00

EVENING MEAL PER PERSON
£22.00 - £27.50

La Fosse at Cranborne

London House, The Square, Cranborne, Wimborne BH21 5PR **T:** (01725) 517604
E: lafossemail@gmail.com
W: www.la-fosse.com **£ BOOK ONLINE**

Mark and Emmanuelle invite you to experience our homely Restaurant with Rooms in beautiful Dorset. Providing six quality accommodations, as well as delicious home cooked dinners with friendly and efficient service. The perfect base for exploring Dorset, Wiltshire and Hampshire. **Directions:** M27 towards Bournemouth, Ringwood. Exit to Verwood. Through Verwood, signs for Cranborne. We are on right in the Square. **Bedrooms:** 2 double, 2 twin, 1 family, 1 suite **Open:** All Year

WALKERS WELCOME CYCLISTS WELCOME
Site: **Payment:** £ **Leisure:** **Property:** **Children:** **Catering:**
Room: TV

DORCHESTER, Dorset Map ref 2B3 SatNav DT1 1UP H

enjoyEngland.com ★★★ HOTEL

B&B PER ROOM PER NIGHT
S: £85.00 - £109.00
D: £99.00 - £185.00

HB PER PERSON PER NIGHT
£74.50 - £104.50

Wessex Royale Hotel

32 High West Street, Dorchester DT1 1UP **T:** (01305) 262660 **F:** 01305 251941
E: info@wessexroyalehotel.co.uk
W: www.wessexroyalehotel.co.uk **£ BOOK ONLINE**

A delightful Georgian building with 27 comfortable en suite rooms. Guests can relax in the cosy lounge area and our a la carte restaurant is open from 6pm each evening. **Directions:** Please see our website for map and full directions. **Bedrooms:** 2 single, 15 double, 5 twin, 2 family, 3 suite **Open:** All year except Christmas and New Year

Site: **Payment:** £ **Leisure:** **Property:** **Children:** **Catering:**
Room: TV

EYPE, Dorset Map ref 1D2 SatNav DT6 6AL H

enjoyEngland.com ★★★ COUNTRY HOUSE HOTEL

B&B PER ROOM PER NIGHT
S: £80.00 - £105.00
D: £110.00 - £130.00

EVENING MEAL PER PERSON
£26.00 - £28.00

Eype's Mouth Country Hotel

Eype, Bridport, Dorset DT6 6AL **T:** (01308) 423300 **F:** 01308 420033
E: info@eypesmouthhotel.co.uk
W: www.eypesmouthhotel.co.uk **£ BOOK ONLINE**

Picturesque village of Eype, Bridport amidst downland and cliff tops of Heritage Coastline. Stunning sea views, lovely walking nearby, excellent hospitality, food and drink, in peaceful surroundings of family-run hotel. Perfect for relaxing. **Directions:** A35, Bridport bypass, take turning to Eype, also signed to service area, then 3rd right to beach. Hotel 0.5 miles down lane. **Bedrooms:** 1 single, 12 dble, 3 twin, 1 family **Open:** All year

Site: **Payment:** **Leisure:** **Property:** **Children:** **Catering:** **Room:**

SHAFTESBURY, Dorset Map ref 2B3 SatNav SP7 8AE B

enjoyEngland.com ★★★★ GUEST ACCOMMODATION
enjoyEngland.com Silver AWARD

B&B PER ROOM PER NIGHT
S: £55.00 - £60.00
D: £85.00 - £90.00

SPECIAL PROMOTIONS
Special promotions available upon request.

The Retreat

47 Bell Street, Shaftesbury, Dorset SP7 8AE **T:** (01747) 850372 **E:** info@the-retreat.co.uk
W: www.the-retreat.co.uk

Perfectly positioned in a quiet street, this Georgian townhouse has light, airy, individually furnished, en suite bedrooms with flatscreen TV/DVD, hospitality tray and parking. Winner of 2005 'Best B&B Dorset'. Sheena & Bernard are happy to advise you on what to do in the area including Stonehenge, The New Forest, & Longleat park.

Directions: Please contact us for directions.

Bedrooms: 1 single, 3 double, 1 twin, 4 family, 1 guest lounge
Open: End December - End January

Site: P **Payment:** **Property:** **Children:** **Catering:** **Room:**

SWANAGE, Dorset Map ref 2B3 SatNav BH19 1LU

The Grand Hotel

Burlington Road, Swanage BH19 1LU **T:** (01929) 423353 **F:** (01929) 427068
E: reservations@grandhotelswanage.co.uk
W: www.grandhotelswanage.co.uk

B&B PER ROOM PER NIGHT
S: £55.00 - £80.00
D: £75.00 - £160.00
HB PER PERSON PER NIGHT
£73.00 - £98.00

The Grand Hotel, Swanage is a classic Victorian seaside hotel that nestles in the heart of the beautiful Isle of Purbeck and dates back to 1898. The Hotel, The Coast restaurant and Lounge Bar command spectacular views across Swanage Bay and Peveril Point and many of the bedrooms and public areas take advantage of these delightful views. Direct access from the gardens to our private beach. Available for weddings, conferences and exclusive use. Health spa including indoor pool, spa bath, sauna and a large gymnasium. Group accommodation available. Free Wi-Fi available. Prices are based on a standard room. Sea view rooms will incur a supplement.

Directions: Please see the 'Getting Here' page on our website for directions.

Bedrooms: 3 Single, 17 Double, 8 Twin and 2 Family - All en suite
Open: All year

Site: **Payment:** **Leisure:** **Property:** **Children:** **Catering:** **Room:**

SWANAGE, Dorset Map ref 2B3 SatNav BH19 1LT

The Pines Hotel

Burlington Road, Swanage BH19 1LT **T:** (01929) 425211 **F:** 01929 422075
E: reservations@pineshotel.co.uk
W: www.pineshotel.co.uk **£ BOOK ONLINE**

B&B PER ROOM PER NIGHT
S: £72.00
D: £144.00 - £194.00
EVENING MEAL PER PERSON
£6.75 - £33.50

Family-run hotel in Purbeck countryside at quiet end of Swanage Bay. Access to beach for walks encompassing coastal views. Friendly staff, refurbished sea-facing lounges and highly acclaimed seaview restaurant. **Directions:** A351 to seafront. Turn left then 2nd or 3rd turn on your right (either Victoria road or Burlington road). We are at the end of these roads. **Bedrooms:** 2 single, 15 double, 8 twin, 8 family, 8 suite **Open:** All year

Site: P **Payment:** **Leisure:** **Property:** **Children:** **Catering:** **Room:**

WAREHAM, Dorset Map ref 2B3 SatNav BH20 5NU

Bradle Farmhouse

Bradle Farm, Church Knowle, Wareham, Dorset BH20 5NU **T:** (01929) 480712
F: 01929 481144 **E:** info@bradlefarmhouse.co.uk
W: www.bradlefarmhouse.co.uk

B&B PER ROOM PER NIGHT
S: £65.00 - £80.00
D: £82.50 - £90.00

Picturesque farmhouse set in the heart of Purbeck. Fine views of Corfe Castle and surrounding countryside, with many spectacular walks. Large spacious rooms, delicious breakfast with home produce and a warm welcome assured. Local pub 1 mile. **Directions:** A351 from Wareham to Corfe Castle. At Corfe take a right turn at the foot of the castle signed Church Knowle. After Church Knowle turn left 1 mile. **Bedrooms:** Spacious rooms all en suite, TVs and Tea/coffee facilities **Open:** All Year except Christmas

Site: P **Property:** **Room:**

WAREHAM, Dorset *Map ref 2B3* — *SatNav BH20 5LR* B

B&B PER ROOM PER NIGHT
S: £40.00 - £60.00
D: £120.00 - £170.00
HB PER PERSON PER NIGHT
£60.00 - £70.00

Kingston Country Courtyard

Kingston, Nr Corfe Castle, Wareham, Dorset BH20 5LR **T:** (01929) 481066 **F:** 01929 481256
E: relax@kingstoncountrycourtyard.com
W: www.kingstoncountrycourtyard.com

Kingston Country Courtyard gives you a taste of authentic farmstead life in an Area of Outstanding Natural Beauty. Tastefully converted outbuildings, high beamed ceilings, thick Purbeck stone walls. Bed and Breakfast or Self Catering apartments available. Some dog friendly rooms by arrangement. Views of the Castle from the garden. Limited Wi-Fi...enjoy an escape from the city!

Directions: From Wareham, take the A351 towards Swanage. On leaving the village of Corfe Castle, turn right on to the B3069 - signposted to Kingston, up the hill, round a sharp left bend, we are on the left.

Bedrooms: En suite, TVs, tea and coffee, kettles in rooms
Open: All year round except Xmas & New Year

Site: P **Leisure:** **Property:** **Children:** **Catering:** **Room:**

WEYMOUTH, Dorset *Map ref 2B3* — *SatNav DT4 7EY* B

B&B PER ROOM PER NIGHT
S: £40.00 - £55.00
D: £60.00 - £140.00

AcQua Beach Weymouth

131 The Esplanade, Weymouth, Dorset DT4 7EY **T:** (01305) 776900 **F:** 01305 791099
E: info@acquabeachhotel.co.uk
W: www.acquabeachhotel.co.uk **£ BOOK ONLINE**

If you're looking for a funky B&B overlooking Weymouth's beautiful seafront then you've come to the right place. Relax in our rooms; have a coffee overlooking the sea, or when the sun goes down enjoy a cocktail in the gorgeous Bar AcQuA. **Directions:** Located opposite the beach on Weymouth's Esplanade; a mere 5 minute walk from the railway station and the Jubilee Clock. **Bedrooms:** All en suite with flatscreen TV and hospitality tray **Open:** All year

Site: P **Payment:** **Leisure:** **Property:** **Children:** **Catering:** **Room:**

BARNSLEY, Gloucestershire *Map ref 2B1* — *SatNav GL7 5EE* H

B&B PER ROOM PER NIGHT
S: £262.00 - £582.00
D: £280.00 - £600.00

Barnsley House

Barnsley, Cirencester GL7 5EE **T:** (01285) 740000 **E:** reception@barnsleyhouse.com
W: www.barnsleyhouse.com

Luxury 18 bedroom hotel, once the home of the late famous garden designer Rosemary Verey. Beautiful Cotswold house built in 1697 set in stunning gardens, with contemporary bedrooms. We now have a hydrotherapy pool. Weekend prices vary. **Directions:** Centre of Barnsley, on the B4425 (Cirencester to Bibury and Burford road), 4 miles NE of Cirencester. **Open:** All year

Site: P **Payment:** **Leisure:** **Property:** **Children:** 14 **Catering:** **Room:**

BOURTON-ON-THE-WATER, Gloucestershire Map ref 2B1 SatNav GL54 2AZ B

enjoyEngland.com ★★★★ BED & BREAKFAST

B&B PER ROOM PER NIGHT
S: £45.00
D: £65.00 - £70.00

Trevone Bed & Breakfast

Moore Road, Bourton-on-the-Water GL54 2AZ **T:** (07740) 805250
E: trevonebandb@gmail.com
W: www.trevonebb.co.uk **£ BOOK ONLINE**

Cotswold stone house ideally situated for exploring the picturesque and historic delights of the Cotswolds. Within one minute's walk from the village centre. **Directions:** Please contact us for directions. **Bedrooms:** 1 double en suite and one king size en suite **Open:** All year

Site: P **Payment:** £ **Leisure:** **Property:** **Children:** 10 **Catering:** **Room:** TV

CIRENCESTER, Gloucestershire Map ref 2B1 SatNav GL7 1LF B

enjoyEngland.com ★★★★ GUEST ACCOMMODATION

B&B PER ROOM PER NIGHT
S: £55.50 - £65.50
D: £71.00 - £81.00

EVENING MEAL PER PERSON
£10.00 - £21.00

SPECIAL PROMOTIONS
Special group discounts are available at weekends. Ideal for clubs and societies.

Riverside House

Watermoor, Cirencester GL7 1LF **T:** (01285) 647642 **F:** 01285 647615
E: riversidehouse@mitsubishi-cars.co.uk
W: www.riversidehouse.org.uk **£ BOOK ONLINE**

Located 15 minutes walk from the centre of the historic market town of Cirencester with easy access to and from M4/M5 and the Cotswolds. Riverside House is fully licensed and provides superb bed and breakfast for private and corporate guests. Built in the grounds of Mitsubishi UK headquarters.

Directions: Located just off A419 opposite the Tesco superstore.

Bedrooms: 15 double, 9 twin
Open: All year

WALKERS WELCOME CYCLISTS WELCOME

Site: P **Payment:** £ **Leisure:** **Property:** **Children:** **Catering:** **Room:** TV

GLOUCESTER, Gloucestershire Map ref 2B1 SatNav GL12LG

VisitEngland ★★★★ HOTEL BOAT

HB PER PERSON PER NIGHT
£97.50 - £138.00

SPECIAL PROMOTIONS
3 Meals/day included, along with free tea/ coffee, a welcome drink, wine during dinner, outside guided tours and live entertainment on one night. Special low prices apply during April and October.

English Holiday Cruises

The Oliver Cromwell & Edward Elgar, West Quay, Gloucester GL1 2LG **T:** (01452) 410411
F: 01452 357959 **E:** sales@englishholidaycruises.co.uk
W: www.englishholidaycruises.co.uk **£ BOOK ONLINE**

For an unusual holiday in England, book a cruise with English Holiday Cruises in the Cotswolds Severn vale. Board their 4-Star hotel boat Edward Elgar, unpack, relax and sail through glorious countryside to fascinating destinations steeped in history.

The meals are delicious and all cabins are en suite. A miniature Rhine cruise but closer to home. From only £195 incl wine at dinner and outside tours.

Directions: Gloucester is easy to reach by car, train or coach. Passengers board MV Edward Elgar in the Historic Docks of Gloucester and secure parking is available nearby.

Bedrooms: 4-Star Hotel Boat standard. All cabins are twin-bedded, with a window, heating/air conditioning, ample storage and en suite shower, basin and WC
Open: 40 Cruise dates available from April to October

Payment: **Property:** **Catering:** **Room:**

LECHLADE, Gloucestershire Map ref 2B1 SatNav GL7 3AB

enjoyEngland.com ★★ INN

B&B PER ROOM PER NIGHT
S: £45.00 - £65.00
D: £55.00 - £80.00

EVENING MEAL PER PERSON
£8.00 - £20.00

The New Inn Hotel

Market Square, Lechlade-On-Thames, Gloucestershire GL7 3AB **T:** (01367) 252296
F: 01367 252315 **E:** info@newinnhotel.com
W: www.newinnhotel.co.uk **£ BOOK ONLINE**

The New Inn Hotel is where 250-years tradition of hospitality blends with 21st century comfort and Cotswold charm, on the banks of the river Thames. We are a 30 bedroom hotel with good access to Oxford, Cheltenham and Swindon. **Directions:** The New Inn Hotel is situated in the Market Square next to the Church.
Bedrooms: En suite, flatscreen TV, tea and coffee facilities
Open: All year

Site: P **Payment:** € **Leisure:** **Property:** **Children:** **Catering:**
Room:

STROUD, Gloucestershire Map ref 2B1 SatNav GL5 5PA

enjoyEngland.com ★★★★ BED & BREAKFAST

enjoyEngland.com Gold AWARD

B&B PER ROOM PER NIGHT
S: £55.00 - £60.00
D: £80.00 - £85.00

EVENING MEAL PER PERSON
£7.95 - £20.00

1 Woodchester Lodge

Southfield Road, Woodchester, Stroud GL5 5PA **T:** (01453) 872586
E: anne@woodchesterlodge.co.uk
W: www.woodchesterlodge.co.uk

Historic, Victorian timber merchant's property; peaceful village setting near Cotswold Way. Attractive gardens, parking, spacious and comfortable rooms, separate TV lounge/dining room. Meals cooked by qualified chef using our own produce and eggs. **Directions:** From Stroud/M5, take A46 towards Bath. Pass the Old Fleece pub. Right into Selsley Road. 2nd left, Southfield Road. 200yds on left-hand side. **Bedrooms:** 2 double, 1 family
Open: All year except Christmas, New Year and Easter

Site: P **Payment:** **Leisure:** **Property:** **Children:** **Catering:** **Room:**

For **key to symbols** see page 7

STROUD, Gloucestershire Map ref 2B1 *SatNav GL6 9JE* B

enjoyEngland.com ★★★★ BED & BREAKFAST | enjoyEngland.com Silver AWARD

B&B PER ROOM PER NIGHT
S: £55.00 - £65.00
D: £80.00 - £90.00

The Close B&B

The Close, Well Hill, Minchinhampton, Stroud, Gloucestershire GL6 9JE **T:** (01453) 883338
E: theclosebnb@gmail.com
W: www.theclosebnb.co.uk

Historic Town House offering stylish and comfortable accommodation, the perfect place for a short break in the Cotswolds. Set in a charming small market town with shops and cafes nearby. Wonderful walking country with beautiful views. **Directions:** 2nd house on the left, from the top of Well Hill. **Bedrooms:** Spacious rooms with en suites, TVs and tea/coffee making facilities **Open:** All year except mid Jan - end Feb

WALKERS WELCOME | CYCLISTS WELCOME
Site: P **Payment:** £ **Leisure:** **Property:** **Catering:** **Room:** TV

STROUD, Gloucestershire Map ref 2B1 *SatNav GL6 7EA* B

enjoyEngland.com ★★★★ GUEST ACCOMMODATION | enjoyEngland.com Gold AWARD

B&B PER ROOM PER NIGHT
S: £60.00
D: £80.00

EVENING MEAL PER PERSON
£15.00 - £20.00

The Old Coach House

Dr. Crouch's Road, Eastcombe, Stroud GL6 7EA **T:** (01452) 771196
E: admin@oldcoachhousebandb.co.uk
W: www.oldcoachhousebandb.co.uk

The Old Coach House, was originally built as the stabling and coach house for the local doctor. Only four miles from the busy market town of Stroud with its award winning weekly Farmers' Market, and the delightful Market Town of Nailsworth. Also within easy reach of the historic Roman Cirencester. All major credit and debit cards accepted.

Directions: From the London direction, take the M4 to junction 15 Swindon, and then the A417 to Cirencester. Pick up the A419 for Stroud and follow for about 8 miles. From the South West or Midlands, take Junction 13 off the M5 for Stroud. Once on the very outskirts of the Town Centre, pick up the A419 for Cirencester.

Bedrooms: Two en suite, one on ground floor, suitable for guests with mobility issues
Open: All year

Site: P **Payment:** £ **Leisure:** **Property:** **Children:** **Catering:** **Room:** TV

STROUD, Gloucestershire Map ref 2B1 *SatNav GL6 7EE* B

enjoyEngland.com ★★★★ BED & BREAKFAST | enjoyEngland.com Silver AWARD

B&B PER ROOM PER NIGHT
S: £50.00
D: £65.00 - £70.00

Pretoria Villa

Wells Road, Eastcombe, Stroud GL6 7EE **T:** (01452) 770435
E: pretoriavilla@btinternet.com
W: www.bedandbreakfast-cotswold.co.uk **£ BOOK ONLINE**

Enjoy luxurious bed and breakfast in a relaxed family country house, set in peaceful secluded gardens. Spacious bedrooms with many home comforts. Guest lounge with TV. Superb breakfast served at your leisure. An excellent base from which to explore the Cotswolds. Personal service and your comfort guaranteed. **Directions:** At bottom of village green in Eastcombe take the lane with the red telephone box, at first crossroad, very sharp right. 400yds on right. **Bedrooms:** 1 double, 2 twin. All bedrooms are en suite **Open:** All year except Christmas

Site: P **Leisure:** **Property:** **Children:** **Catering:** **Room:**

STROUD, Gloucestershire *Map ref 2B1* — SatNav GL6 6AE B

★★★★ ROOM ONLY

B&B PER ROOM PER NIGHT
D: £60.00 - £100.00

Star Inn

Main Road, Whiteshill, Stroud GL6 6AE **T:** (01453) 765321
E: whiteshillstarinn@btconnect.com
W: www.the-star-inn-whiteshill.co.uk

17th Century Village Inn, Stroud. 'CAMRA 2012 Pub of Year.' Real ales served straight from the barrel. Great views, glorious walks on the doorstep. Annual beer festival. New restaurant opening March 2015. **Directions:** 4 Star accommodation, close to the Cotswold Way. Between Stroud and Gloucester. Easy reach of Cheltenham. 3 miles M5 Junction, easy reach Stroud rail station. **Bedrooms:** 1 double, 1 twin, 1 two room suite **Open:** All year

Site: P **Payment:** **Property:** **Children:** **Catering:** **Room:**

TETBURY, Gloucestershire *Map ref 2B2* — SatNav GL8 8YJ H

★★★★ HOTEL — Gold AWARD

B&B PER ROOM PER NIGHT
S: £225.00 - £440.00
D: £250.00 - £490.00

Calcot Manor Hotel & Spa

Tetbury, Gloucestershire GL8 8YJ **T:** (01666) 890391 **F:** 01666 890394
E: reception@calcotmanor.co.uk
W: www.calcotmanor.co.uk **£ BOOK ONLINE**

A 17th C manor house quietly situated in South Cotswolds with relaxing atmosphere amidst elegant surroundings. **Directions:** 3 miles West of Tetbury on A4135. **Bedrooms:** 7 double, 15 twin, 12 family, 1 suite **Open:** All year

Site: **Payment:** **Leisure:** **Property:** **Children:** **Catering:** **Room:**

BATH, Somerset *Map ref 2B2* — SatNav BA1 5LH B

★★★ HOSTEL

B&B PER ROOM PER NIGHT
S: £32.00 - £36.00
D: £28.00 - £65.00

Bath YMCA

International House, Broad Street Place, Bath BA1 5LH **T:** (01225) 325900
F: (01225) 462065 **E:** stay@bathymca.co.uk
W: www.bathymca.co.uk

The YMCA is centrally located, just a minute away from all the major tourist attractions, we have over 200 beds in the form of dormitories, singles, twins, triples and quad rooms. Dorms from £21 per person per night. **Directions:** From the bus or train station walk north up Manvers Street. Go past Bath Abbey on your left and, keeping the river Avon on you right, continue via Orange Grove (on left) and High Street to Walcot Street or Broad Street. **Open:** All year

Site: **Payment:** **Leisure:** **Property:** **Children:** **Catering:** **Bedroom:**

BATH, Somerset *Map ref 2B2* — SatNav BA2 2AS B

★★★★ GUEST HOUSE

B&B PER ROOM PER NIGHT
S: £79.00 - £90.00
D: £115.00 - £140.00

Bloomfield House

146 Bloomfield Road BA2 2AS **T:** (01225) 420105 **E:** info@ecobloomfield.com
W: www.ecobloomfield.co.uk **£ BOOK ONLINE**

Bloomfield House is a family-run B&B with 6 guest bedrooms, ranging from a cosy single to a king-size four-poster. A beautiful Georgian house, with a relaxed atmosphere, it sits in a quiet elevated position with views across the city (only 20 min walk to city centre and on a regular bus route). Superb farmers' market breakfasts are served until 11 am everyday. Dogs are welcome. **Directions:** Please contact for directions. **Bedrooms:** En suite facilities, TV, tea and coffee, hairdryer **Open:** All year with restrictions over Christmas

Site: P **Payment:** **Property:** **Children:** **Catering:** **Room:**

For **key to symbols** see page 7

BATH (6 MILES), Somerset Map ref 2B2 SatNav SN14 8AZ H

enjoyEngland.com ★★★★★ HOTEL

enjoyEngland.com Gold AWARD

B&B PER ROOM PER NIGHT
D: £325.00 - £1345.00

Lucknam Park Hotel and Spa

Lucknam Park, Colerne, Chippenham SN14 8AZ **T:** (01225) 742777 **F:** (01225) 743536
E: reservations@lucknampark.co.uk
W: lucknampark.co.uk **£ BOOK ONLINE**

Mansion set within 500 acres, 6 miles from Bath. 42 bedrooms & suites, Spa, Well-being House, equestrian centre, fine dining in The Park, informal dining in The Brasserie. Cookery School offering a range of courses. **Directions:** Located 6 miles from Bath and 15 minutes from junction 17 of the M4. Please see website for directions. **Bedrooms:** 29 dble, 13 suite **Open:** All year

Site: **Payment:** **Leisure:** **Property:** **Children:** **Catering:** **Room:**

BATH, Somerset Map ref 2B2 SatNav BA1 2NQ B

enjoyEngland.com ★★★★ GUEST ACCOMMODATION

enjoyEngland.com Gold AWARD

B&B PER ROOM PER NIGHT
S: £95.00 - £145.00
D: £95.00 - £155.00

Marlborough House Guest House

1 Marlborough Lane, Bath BA1 2NQ **T:** (01225) 318175 **F:** 01225 466127
E: mars@manque.dircon.co.uk
W: www.marlborough-house.net

Enchanting Victorian town house in Bath's Georgian centre. Exquisitely furnished, with fully air conditioned en suite rooms, 1 four-poster, king or super-king size beds. Generous and organic breakfast choices. Parking subject to availability. **Directions:** M4 junct 18 to Bath. A4 into city centre via Queen Square and take Charlotte Street exit, continue to Vauxhall garage, Marlborough Lane is opposite. **Bedrooms:** 2 double, 2 twin, 2 family **Open:** All year except Christmas

Site: P **Payment:** **Leisure:** **Property:** **Children:** **Catering:** **Room:**

BATH, Somerset Map ref 2B2 SatNav BA2 4HJ B

enjoyEngland.com ★★★★ BED & BREAKFAST

B&B PER ROOM PER NIGHT
D: £75.00 - £95.00

Membland Guest House

7 Pulteney Terrace, Pulteney Road, Bath BA2 4HJ **T:** (01225) 839847 / 07958 599572
E: memblandguesthouse@sky.com
W: www.memblandguesthouse.co.uk

Warm and friendly accommodation with delicious freshly cooked breakfasts. Great location, only 5 minutes level stroll to the stunning attractions of the City, Thermae Spa, Roman Baths and the magnificent Bath Abbey. Situated below the Kennet and Avon canal with beautiful walks, perfect for exploring the picturesque villages surrounding Bath.

Directions: Membland Guest House is on the corner of Pulteney Terrace and Pulteney Avenue. Under the Railway Bridge of Pulteney Road, opposite the Royal Oak Pub.

Bedrooms: 4 doubles
Open: All year

Site: P **Payment:** € **Property:** **Catering:** **Room:**

BATH, Somerset *Map ref 2B2* — *SatNav BA2 4HA* B

B&B PER ROOM PER NIGHT
S: £50.00 - £90.00
D: £80.00 - £150.00

SPECIAL PROMOTIONS
Reduced rates for stays of 3 nights or more - each booking assessed individually.

Pulteney House

14 Pulteney Road, Bath BA2 4HA **T:** (01225) 460991 **F:** 01225 460991
E: pulteney@tinyworld.co.uk
W: www.pulteneyhotel.co.uk **£ BOOK ONLINE**

Large, elegant, Victorian house in picturesque gardens. Large, private car park with CCTV. 5-10 minutes walk from city centre. An ideal base for exploring Bath and surrounding areas. All rooms (except one) are en suite. All have hairdryer, TV with Freeview/Sat, hospitality tray and radio/alarm clocks. Free Wi-Fi in most rooms.

Directions: Pulteney House is situated on A36, which runs through Bath. For more detailed directions please refer to our website.

Bedrooms: 2 singles, 8 doubles, 4 twins, 3 family
Open: All year except Christmas

Site: P **Payment:** **Property:** **Children:** **Catering:** **Room:**

BATH, Somerset *Map ref 2B2* — *SatNav BA1 1JP* H

B&B PER ROOM PER NIGHT
S: £70.00 - £89.00
D: £120.00 - £140.00

EVENING MEAL PER PERSON
£12.95 - £22.00

SPECIAL PROMOTIONS
Always available - see our website for details.

The Royal Hotel

Manvers Street BA1 1JP **T:** (01225) 463134 **F:** 01225 442931 **E:** info@royalhotelbath.co.uk
W: www.royalhotelbath.co.uk **£ BOOK ONLINE**

The Royal is Grade II listed, designed by Brunel and opened as a hotel in 1846. The present owners (since 1995) have ensured that this lovely property is maintained to a high standard and retains its character.

Our stylish restaurant "Brasserie Brunel" offers French specialities with grills including steaks. We have an excellent reputation for food and a friendly, relaxing atmosphere.

Directions: By car: A46 off M4 (Jct 18) to City Centre. By train: directly opposite Bath Spa railway station.

Bedrooms: En suite, digital TVs and DVD players, modem points, hair dryer, trouser press, tea and cafetiere ground coffee, biscuits and mineral water
Open: All year

Site: P **Payment:** **Property:** **Children:** **Catering:** **Room:**

BATH, Somerset Map ref 2B2 SatNav BA2 4HG B

B&B PER ROOM PER NIGHT
S: £50.00 - £60.00
D: £65.00 - £80.00

The White Guest House

23 Pulteney Gardens, Bath BA2 4HG **T:** (01225) 426075 **F:** 01225 426075
E: enquiries@whiteguesthouse.co.uk
W: www.whiteguesthouse.co.uk

Family-run establishment. Seven-minute walk to all of Bath's famous attractions. En suite rooms, tea/coffee-making facilities, TV, great English or continental breakfast. **Bedrooms:** All rooms en suite, TV, tea and coffee facilities **Open:** All Year

Children: **Room:**

BREAN, Somerset Map ref 1D1 SatNav TA8 2QT B

B&B PER ROOM PER NIGHT
S: £42.50 - £50.00
D: £60.00 - £85.00

Yew Tree House Bed and Breakfast

Hurn Lane, Berrow Nr Brean, Burnham on Sea, Somerset TA8 2QT **T:** (01278) 751382
E: yewtree@yewtree-house.co.uk
W: www.yewtree-house.co.uk **£ BOOK ONLINE**

We warmly welcome visitors to our charming old house. We are easy to reach from the motorway and in the perfect location for a short break or holiday. The house is on a quiet lane just 10 minutes walk from Berrow Beach. **Directions:** M5 jct 22. B3140 to Burnham and Berrow. From Berrow follow signs to Brean. 0.5 miles after church turn right, we are 300yds on left. **Bedrooms:** All en suite with TV, tea and coffee making facilites and heating **Open:** All year except Christmas.

Site: P **Payment:** **Leisure:** **Property:** **Children:** **Catering:** **Room:**

BRIDGWATER, Somerset Map ref 1D1 SatNav TA5 2HW B

B&B PER ROOM PER NIGHT
S: £35.00 - £45.00
D: £70.00 - £80.00

Gurney Manor Mill

Gurney Street, Cannington, Bridgwater TA5 2HW **T:** (01278) 653582
E: gurneymill@yahoo.co.uk
W: www.gurneymill.co.uk

Old watermill and barn conversion, alongside a stream with waterfall, pond and wildlife. Situated in picturesque village at gateway to Quantock Hills. Ideal location for touring the beautiful West Country and South West. Many historical sights. **Directions:** Cannington (Bridgwater). Turn right into East St, turn right into Gurney St. Gurney Manor Mill is after Gurney Manor. **Bedrooms:** 2 double, 1 twin, 1 family **Open:** All year

Site: P **Payment:** **Leisure:** **Property:** **Children:** **Catering:** **Room:**

BRISTOL, Somerset Map ref 2A2 — SatNav BS13 8AG B

enjoyEngland.com ★★★ GUEST ACCOMMODATION

B&B PER ROOM PER NIGHT
S: £55.00
D: £65.00

EVENING MEAL PER PERSON
£9.50 - £19.50

SPECIAL PROMOTIONS
Stay Fri and Sat night and get Sunday night free (incl Bank Holiday weekends).

The Town & Country Lodge

A38 Bridgwater Road, Bristol BS13 8AG **T:** (01275) 392441 **F:** 01275 393362
E: reservations@tclodge.co.uk
W: www.tclodge.co.uk

Highly comfortable lodge offering genuine value for money. Splendid, rural location on the A38 only three miles from central Bristol and handy for airport, Bath, Weston and all major local attractions. Excellent restaurant offering bar menus. Ideal for functions, wedding receptions and conferences.

Directions: Situated on A38 halfway between Airport and city centre. From North M5 exit J18 Avonmouth. A4 Bristol Airport. From South exit M5 J22. A38 Bristol.

Bedrooms: 4 single, 11 double, 14 twin, 7 family
Open: All year except Christmas

Site: P **Payment:** **Leisure:** **Property:** **Children:** **Catering:**
Room:

CHEDDAR, Somerset Map ref 1D1 — SatNav BS28 4SN B

enjoyEngland.com ★★★ BED & BREAKFAST

B&B PER ROOM PER NIGHT
S: £40.00 - £45.00
D: £70.00

EVENING MEAL PER PERSON
£8.95 - £18.95

Yew Tree Farm

Wells Road, Theale, Nr Wedmore, Somerset BS28 4SN **T:** (01934) 712475 **F:** 01934 712475
E: yewtreefarm@yewtreefarmbandb.co.uk
W: www.yewtreefarmbandb.co.uk

17th century farmhouse nr Cheddar, Wells and Wookey. Idyllic walks fishing/golf/cycling. 1, 2, 3 course home cooked and freshly prepared evening meals available, as well as snacks and cream teas. Large secure off street parking area available and free Wi-Fi. **Directions:** From Wells, take B3139 towards Burnham-on-Sea. Drive through Wookey, Henton, Panborough. **Bedrooms:** 1 double, 1 twin, 1 family **Open:** All year

Site: P **Payment:** € **Leisure:** **Property:** **Children:** **Catering:**
Room:

DUNSTER, Somerset Map ref 1D1 SatNav TA24 6SF H

enjoyEngland.com ★★★ HOTEL

B&B PER ROOM PER NIGHT
S: £65.00 - £90.00
D: £90.00 - £140.00

EVENING MEAL PER PERSON
£17.00 - £27.00

SPECIAL PROMOTIONS
Discounted rates for longer stays and midweek bookings. Ring for newsletter with information on special events. Group bookings welcome.

Yarn Market Hotel

25-33 High Street, Dunster TA24 6SF **T:** (01643) 821425 **F:** 01643 821475
E: hotel@yarnmarkethotel.co.uk
W: www.yarnmarkethotel.co.uk **£ BOOK ONLINE**

Within Exmoor National Park, our hotel is ideal for walking, riding, fishing. Family-run with a friendly, relaxed atmosphere. All rooms en suite with colour TV. Four-poster and superior rooms available. Non-smoking. Home-cooked dishes to cater for all tastes. Group bookings welcomed. Conference facilities. Special Christmas and New Year breaks.

Directions: From M5 jct 25 follow signs for Exmoor/Minehead A358/A39. Dunster signed approx 0.5 miles from A39 on left. Hotel in village centre beside Yarn Market.

Bedrooms: 2 single, 12 dble, 7 twin, 2 family
Open: All year

WALKERS WELCOME · CYCLISTS WELCOME · PETS! WELCOME

Site: **Payment:** **Leisure:** **Property:** **Children:**
Catering: **Room:**

FROME, Somerset Map ref 2B2 SatNav BA11 5BW B

enjoyEngland.com ★★★★ GUEST ACCOMMODATION

B&B PER ROOM PER NIGHT
S: £45.00 - £55.00
D: £75.00 - £85.00

EVENING MEAL PER PERSON
£6.00 - £12.00

SPECIAL PROMOTIONS
We are able to offer 1 or 2 day tickets for Longleat Safari & Adventure Park at a discounted rate if ordered 48 hours before your arrival

The Lighthouse

Tytherington, Frome, Somerset BA11 5BW **T:** (01373) 453585
E: reception@lighthouse-uk.com
W: www.lighthouse-uk.com

The Lighthouse is a beautifully restored 17th Century Guest House set in 30 acres of parkland on the outskirts of Frome, Somerset. The stunning grounds and period setting provide the perfect place for a break with friends and family, or as a stopover while working away from home. Guests enjoy the opportunity to rest in the tranquil rural setting, or use it as a base to explore the local area.

Directions: As you come off the A361 and enter the village of Tytherington, The Lighthouse is the first property on the right.

Bedrooms: Modern and tastefully renovated en suite rooms in the courtyard of a C17th Country House, set within 30 acres of stunning parkland
Open: All Year

Site: P **Payment:** **Leisure:** **Property:** **Children:** **Catering:**
Room:

SOUTH PETHERTON, Somerset Map ref 1D2 — *SatNav TA13 5DB* B

enjoyEngland.com ★★★★ GUEST ACCOMMODATION

B&B PER ROOM PER NIGHT
S: £65.00
D: £90.00

Rock House B&B

5 Palmer Street, South Petherton, Somerset TA13 5DB **T:** (01460) 240324
E: enquiries@unwindatrockhouse.co.uk
W: www.unwindatrockhouse.co.uk

Rock House, an unexpected discovery in the heart of South Petherton; an unspoilt Somerset village - a place to unwind. Garden for guests' sole use, secure parking. National Trust nearby. **Directions:** See website for accurate directions. **Bedrooms:** 2 suite **Open:** All year

Site: P **Payment:** **Property:** **Catering:** **Room:**

WELLS, Somerset Map ref 2A2 — *SatNav BA5 3JP* B

enjoyEngland.com ★★★★ GUEST ACCOMMODATION — enjoyEngland.com Gold AWARD

B&B PER ROOM PER NIGHT
S: £80.00 - £100.00
D: £100.00 - £160.00

Beryl

Off Hawkers Lane, Wells, Somerset BA5 3JP **T:** (01749) 678738 **F:** 01749 670508
E: stay@beryl-wells.co.uk
W: www.beryl-wells.co.uk

A small Victorian Gothic mansion in a beautiful part of Somerset, Beryl is just 1 mile from Wells Cathedral. A warm and friendly welcome awaits every guest in this family-run home. Experience a stay for luxury bed and breakfast at 'Beryl'. Byworth and Nowell fine jewellery in the coach house. **Directions:** In Wells, follow signs to the Horringtons until you reach a Budgens BP Garage. Then turn left into Hawkers Lane. We are right at the top of the hill. **Open:** All year except Christmas

Site: P **Payment:** **Leisure:** **Property:** **Children:** **Catering:** **Room:**

CRICKLADE, Wiltshire Map ref 2B2 — *SatNav SN6 6DD* B

enjoyEngland.com ★★★★ GUEST ACCOMMODATION

B&B PER ROOM PER NIGHT
D: £85.00

The Red Lion

74 High Street, Cricklade SN6 6DD **T:** (01793) 750776 **E:** info@theredlioncricklade.co.uk
W: www.theredlioncricklade.co.uk **£ BOOK ONLINE**

Situated on the Thames path, The Red Lion Inn dates back to the 1600s. Roaring log fires, 10 traditional ales including 5 brewed in our own on site micro brewery (Hop Kettle Brewery). A contemporary restaurant serving homemade and seasonal food, a traditional bar area serving pub classics, a garden and 5 recently built en suite bedrooms.

Directions: Located just off the A419 between Swindon and Cirencester, which is minutes from junction 15 of the M4.

Bedrooms: 3 double, 2 twin
Open: All year

Site: **Payment:** **Leisure:** **Property:** **Children:** **Catering:** **Room:**

DINTON, Wiltshire Map ref 2B3 SatNav SP3 5ET B

enjoyEngland.com ★★★★ BED & BREAKFAST

B&B PER ROOM PER NIGHT
S: £45.00 - £60.00
D: £65.00 - £80.00

SPECIAL PROMOTIONS
Discount for stays of 2 consecutive nights or more.

Marshwood Farm B&B

Dinton, Salisbury SP3 5ET **T:** (01722) 716334 **E:** marshwood1@btconnect.com
W: www.marshwoodfarm.co.uk

Come and enjoy the peace and tranquility of the Wiltshire countryside in one of our spacious rooms. We look forward to welcoming you in our farmhouse dating from 17th century. Within easy reach to explore Stonehenge, Salisbury, Bath, Longleat, English Heritage and National Trust Properties. Walkers and cyclists welcome.

Directions: At A303/A36 intersection turn into Wylye, follow the Dinton signs. Marshwood Farm is approx 4 miles.

Bedrooms: 1 twin/double, 1 double/family Wi-Fi in both rooms
Open: All year

Site: P **Payment:** £ € **Leisure:** **Property:** **Children:** **Catering:** **Room:** TV

MANNINGFORD ABBOTS, Wiltshire Map ref 2B2 SatNav SN9 6HZ B

enjoyEngland.com ★★★★ BED & BREAKFAST

B&B PER ROOM PER NIGHT
S: £40.00
D: £60.00 - £85.00
EVENING MEAL PER PERSON
£15.00 - £17.00

Huntly's Farmhouse

Manningford Abbots, Pewsey SN9 6HZ **T:** (01672) 563663 / 07900 211789
E: gimspike@esend.co.uk
W: www.huntlys.co.uk

Peaceful, thatched 17th century farmhouse including horse-stabling/grazing. Good walking country. Heated outdoor swimming pool. Free range and organic food. Family room comprises 1 twin adjoining separate single room. **Directions:** Turn off A345 SW of Pewsey signed Manningford Abbotts. Huntlys is 0.5 mile on RHS just past turn to Sharcott. Opposite post box in wall. **Bedrooms:** 1 double, 1 family **Open:** All year

Site: P **Leisure:** **Property:** **Children:** 5 **Catering:** **Room:** TV

MARLBOROUGH, Wiltshire Map ref 2B2 SatNav SN8 3DP B

enjoyEngland.com ★★★ FARMHOUSE

B&B PER ROOM PER NIGHT
D: £70.00

Suddene Park Farm

Burbage SN8 3DP **T:** (01672) 810296 **E:** peter.devenish@btconnect.com
W: www.suddeneparkfarm.co.uk

Situated in a beautiful secluded Wiltshire farm house, 6 miles South of Marlborough, with spacious room, lovely outlook and easy access to local attractions. **Directions:** From Burbage High Street turn into Taskers Lane, take 3rd left onto Wolf Hall Road, after 1/2 mile follow road through "S" bend. Our drive is on the right. **Bedrooms:** En suite, TV, Wi-Fi, tea and coffee, microwave and fridge **Open:** All year except Christmas and New Year

Site: P **Property:** **Children:** **Room:** TV DVD

MELKSHAM, Wiltshire Map ref 2B2 SatNav SN12 8EF H

enjoyEngland.com ★★ SMALL HOTEL

B&B PER ROOM PER NIGHT
S: £65.00 - £90.00
D: £90.00 - £110.00
HB PER PERSON PER NIGHT
£85.00 - £110.00

Shaw Country Hotel

Bath Road, Shaw, Nr Melksham, Wiltshire SN12 8EF **T:** (01225) 702836 **F:** 01225 790275
E: shawcountryhotel@hotmail.co.uk
W: www.shawcountryhotel.com **£ BOOK ONLINE**

Four hundred year old farmhouse in own grounds, nine miles from Bath. Licensed bar and restaurant, with table d'hote and a la carte menus. All rooms en suite. **Bedrooms:** 3 single, 7 double, 3 twin **Open:** All year

Site: **Payment:** **Property:** **Children:** **Catering:** **Room:**

MONKTON FARLEIGH, Wiltshire Map ref 2B2 SatNav BA15 2QH B

enjoyEngland.com ★★★★ INN
enjoyEngland.com Silver AWARD

Muddy Duck

42 Monkton Farleigh, Monkton Farleigh BA15 2QH **T:** (01225) 858705
E: dishitup@themuddyduckbath.co.uk
W: www.themuddyduckbath.co.uk

Individually styled boutique rooms above a stunning 17th century country pub. Situated in the picturesque village of Monkton Farleigh just 5 miles from Bath. Friendly service, local seasonal food. Please contact us for prices. **Directions:** Junction 18 M4 towards Bath. Just off the A36 Bath to Bradford on Avon road follow signs to Monkton Farleigh Bath Spa Train Station 5m. **Bedrooms:** 3 double **Open:** All year

Site: P **Payment:** **Leisure:** **Property:** **Children:** **Catering:** **Room:**

SALISBURY, Wiltshire Map ref 2B3 SatNav SP5 4LH B

B&B PER ROOM PER NIGHT
S: £37.00 - £40.00
D: £46.00 - £50.00

Evening Hill

Blandford Road, Coombe Bissett, Salisbury, Wiltshire SP5 4LH **T:** (01722) 718561
E: info@eveninghill.com
W: www.eveninghill.com

A quiet village location 10 mins from the city of Salisbury. Ideal for visiting Salisbury city and Cathedral, Stonehenge, New Forest, Bath, Southampton, Portsmouth, Winchester. **Directions:** 2 miles South of Salisbury on the A354. Drive through the village of Coombe Bissett 500 meters past the church on right hand side. **Bedrooms:** 1 double, 1 family **Open:** All year

Site: P **Payment:** **Property:** **Children:** **Catering:** **Room:**

For **key to symbols** see page 7

SALISBURY, Wiltshire Map ref 2B3 SatNav SP5 5LU B

Lodge Farmhouse Bed & Breakfast

Lodge Farmhouse, Broad Chalke, Salisbury SP5 5LU **T:** (01725) 519242
E: info@lodge-farmhouse.co.uk
W: www.lodge-farmhouse.co.uk **£ BOOK ONLINE**

B&B PER ROOM PER NIGHT
S: £40.00
D: £70.00 - £80.00

SPECIAL PROMOTIONS
For bookings of 3 nights, or more, discount of £5 per person per night.

Peaceful brick-and-flint farmhouse with Wiltshire's most stunning views overlooking 1,000 square miles of Southern England. Comfortable and welcoming, the perfect tour base for the South. Lying on the Ox Drove 'green lane', a paradise for walkers. This is perhaps the county's richest heritage seam with historic features and archaeological sites too numerous to mention, as well as modern features.

Directions: A354 from Salisbury (8mls) or Blandford (14mls). Turn to Broad Chalke at crossroads on only stretch of dual carriageway on the A354. One mile signposted.

Bedrooms: 2 double, 1 twin
Open: All year except Christmas to New Year

Site: P **Payment:** **Leisure:** **Property:** **Children:** 12 **Room:**

SALISBURY, Wiltshire Map ref 2B3 SatNav SP2 0AX B

The Wheatsheaf

1 King Street, Wilton, Salisbury SP2 0AX **T:** (01722) 742267
E: mail@thewheatsheafwilton.co.uk
W: www.thewheatsheafwilton.co.uk

B&B PER ROOM PER NIGHT
S: £50.00 - £65.00
D: £70.00 - £90.00

Grade II listed country pub with en suite B&B accommodation. Tasty home-cooked evening meals and lunches. Riverside garden and private car park. Free wireless internet access. Open all day. **Directions:** Wilton is three miles west of Salisbury on the A36 heading towards Bath. The nearest railway station is Salisbury (5-10 minutes by taxi). **Bedrooms:** 3 double, 1 family (from £120 prpn) **Open:** All year

Site: P **Payment:** **Leisure:** **Property:** **Children:** **Catering:**
Room:

TROWBRIDGE, Wiltshire Map ref 2B2 SatNav BA14 6LF B

Newhouse Farm

Littleton, Semington, Trowbridge, Wiltshire BA14 6LF **T:** (01380) 870349
E: stay@newhousefarmwilts.co.uk
W: www.newhousefarmwilts.co.uk

B&B PER ROOM PER NIGHT
S: £44.00 - £60.00
D: £70.00 - £80.00

Former Victorian farmhouse, lovely gardens and grounds with wildflower meadow. Warm welcome, comfortable spacious rooms. Ideal touring centre for Longleat, Bowood, Lacock and Bath. Perfect for walking and cycling along the Kennet and Avon Canal. Great pubs nearby. **Directions:** On A361 between Trowbridge and Devizes. No.49 bus stops outside. **Bedrooms:** 2 double and 1 twin room, all en suite **Open:** All year

Site: P **Property:** **Children:** **Catering:** **Room:**

Walkers and cyclists welcome

Look out for quality-assessed accommodation displaying the Walkers Welcome and Cyclists Welcome signs.

Participants in these schemes actively encourage and support walking and cycling. In addition to special meal arrangements and helpful information, they'll provide a water supply to wash off the mud, an area for drying wet clothing and footwear, maps and books to look up cycling and walking routes and even an emergency puncture-repair kit! Bikes can also be locked up securely undercover.

The standards for these schemes have been developed in partnership with the tourist boards in Northern Ireland, Scotland and Wales, so wherever you're travelling in the UK you'll receive the same welcome.

Don't Miss...

Beaulieu National Motor Museum, House and Garden

Beaulieu, Hampshire SO42 7ZN
(01590) 612345
www.beaulieu.co.uk
In the New Forest, Beaulieu is one of England's top family days out. There's lots to enjoy including the world famous National Motor Museum, home to a stunning and historic collection of automobiles; Palace House, home of the Montagu family; historic Beaulieu Abbey founded in 1204 by Cistercian Monks, and World of Top Gear features vehicles from some of the most ambitious challenges.

Portsmouth Historic Dockyard

Portsmouth, Hampshire PO1 3LJ
(023) 9283 9766
www.historicdockyard.co.uk
Portsmouth Historic Dockyard offers a great day out for all the family and spans over 800 years of British Naval history. The state-of-the-art Mary Rose Museum is home to the remains of Henry VIII's flagship and an astounding collection of 400 year old artefacts recovered from the sea.

The Royal Pavilion Brighton

Brighton, East Sussex BN1 1EE
03000 290900
www.brighton-hove-rpml.org.uk/RoyalPavilion
This spectacularly extravagant seaside palace was built for the Prince Regent, later King George IV, between 1787 and 1823. Housing furniture, works of art and a splendid balconied tearoom overlooking the gardens, it is one the most extraordinary and exotic oriental buildings in the country.

Turner Contemporary Art Gallery

Margate, Kent, CT19 1HG
(01843) 233000
www.turnercontemporary.org
Situated on Margate's seafront, Turner Contemporary is a welcoming space that offers world-class exhibitions of contemporary and historical art, events and activities. Taking inspiration from Britain's best-known painter JMW Turner and designed by internationally acclaimed David Chipperfield Architects, this gleaming structure hovering over the town is the largest exhibtiion space in the South East outside of London and admission to the gallery is free.

Windsor Castle

Windsor, Berkshire SL4 1NJ
(020) 7766 7304
www.royalcollection.org.uk
Built by Edward III in the 14th century and restored by later monarchs, Windsor Castle is the largest and oldest occupied castle in the world and has been the family home of British kings and queens for almost 1,000 years. It is an official residence of Her Majesty the Queen and encapsulates more than 900 years of English history. St George's Chapel within the Castle Precincts is the spiritual home of the Order of the Garter, the oldest order of chivalry in the world.

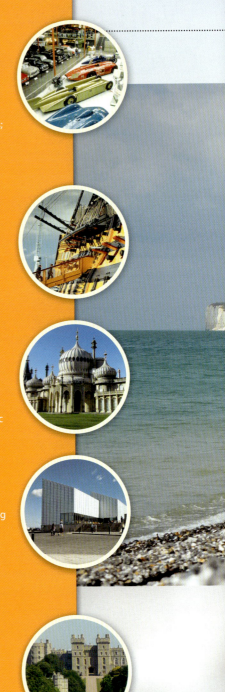

South East

Berkshire, Buckinghamshire, Hampshire, Isle of Wight, Kent, Oxfordshire, Surrey, Sussex

The Thames sweeps eastwards in broad graceful curves, cutting through the beeches of the Chiltern Hills. Miles of glorious countryside and historic cities offer heritage sites, gardens, parks and impressive architecture for you to visit. In the far south, fun-filled resorts and interesting harbours are dotted along 257 miles of delightful coastline and the Isle of Wight is a only a short ferry ride away. The South East of England is an area of great beauty that will entice you to return again and again.

Explore – South East

Berkshire

Renowned for its royal connections, the romantic county of Berkshire counts Windsor Castle as its most famous building. Cliveden House, former seat of the Astor family and now a famous hotel, is nearby. Highclere Castle, the setting for Downton Abbey, as well as Eton College and Ascot Racecourse can be found here too.

Hotspot: LEGOLAND® Windsor Berkshire SL4 4AY (0871) 222 2001 www.legoland.co.uk
With over 55 interactive rides and attractions, there's just too much to experience in one day!

Buckinghamshire

Buckinghamshire, to the north east of the region, is home to the most National Trust properties in the country as well as the magnificent 'Capability Brown' landscape at Stowe, now a famous public school.

The city of Milton Keynes has its infamous concrete cows and the delights of its vast shopping centre but there's plenty more to see and do in the county. Experience a hands-on history lesson at the fascinating Chiltern Open Air Museum or get your adrenalin pumping and test your head for heights with a zip wire adventure at Go Ape Wendover Woods. For a gentler pace, enjoy a tranquil bike ride through beautiful countryside along the meandering Thames.

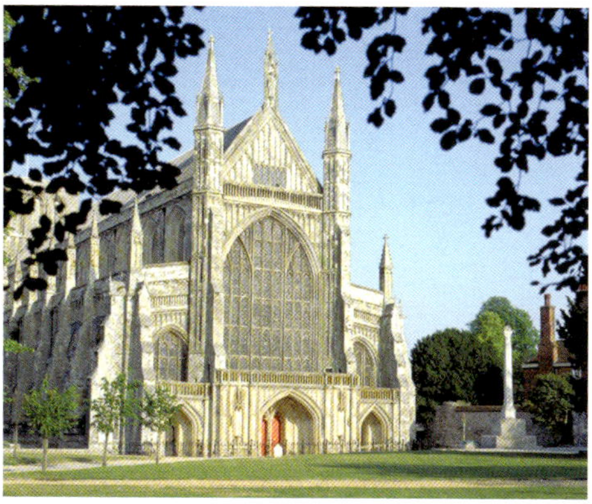

Kent

The Garden of England is a diverse county full of romantic villages and unmissable heritage. The opulent Leeds Castle, surrounded by its shimmering lake and set in 500 acres of spectacular parkland and gardens, has attractions and events aplenty. Take a tour of Kent's rural past with a scenic cruise along the River Medway to Kent Life, a museum and working farm with animals galore and a real sense of nostalgia for bygone days. At the northeast tip of the county, where stunning sea- and sky-scapes famously inspired JMW Turner, Margate is home to the brilliant Turner Contemporary art gallery and the Shell Grotto, a subterranean wonder lined with 4.6 million shells. Broadstairs hosts an acclaimed annual folk festival and Ramsgate is a firm favourite, with its sophisticated café culture, marina and award-winning sandy beach.

Hotspot: Hever Castle in Kent is a romantic 13th century moated castle with magnificently furnished interiors, award winning gardens, miniature Model House Exhibition, Yew Maze and a unique Splashing Water Maze. www.hevercastle.co.uk

Hampshire & Isle Of Wight

Historic Winchester is a must-visit for its charming medieval streets, imposing Cathedral, vibrant galleries and stylish, independent shops. The ancient heaths and woodlands of the New Forest National Park were once a royal hunting ground for William the Conqueror and deer, ponies and cattle continue to roam free. Cycle, walk or go horseriding in this tranquil, car-free environment or visit attractions such as the National Motor Museum at Beaulieu and Exbury Gardens & Steam Railway for a great day out.

Coastal Hampshire, with the Solent, Southampton Water and the Isle of Wight, is one of the sailing playgrounds of England. Nearby Portsmouth Harbour has Nelson's Victory, the Mary Rose and the ironclad HMS Warrior. Stroll gently around the picturesque village of Lymington or explore the cliffs along the coast. The Isle of Wight can be reached by ferry and is a great destination for amazing beaches, exciting events such as Bestival, or a step back in time, counting Osborne House and Carisbrooke Castle among its historic gems.

Oxfordshire

Oxford's dreaming spires, echoing quads and cloistered college lawns have a timeless beauty. The Ashmolean Museum, Britain's oldest public museum, opened in 1683 and contains gold and jewellery believed to have belonged to King Alfred, the lantern carried by Guy Fawkes and riches from ancient Egypt and Greece. The Bodleian Library, founded in 1596, contains over one million volumes, including a copy of every book published in the UK since 1900. Just north of Oxford at Woodstock sits magnificent Blenheim Palace, the birthplace of Sir Winston Churchill. Oxfordshire's quiet paths and roads are perfect for cycling, and charming picture postcard villages like Great Tew make excellent rest points.

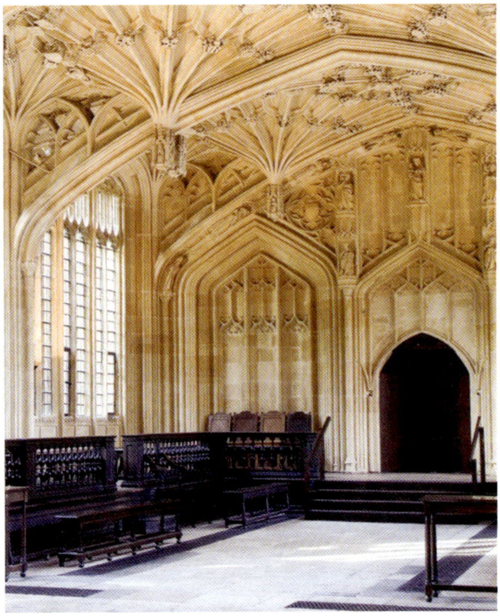

Surrey

Ashdown Forest, now more of a heath, covers 6400 acres of upland, with a large deer, badger and rare bird population. The heights of Box Hill and Leith Hill rise above the North Downs to overlook large tracts of richly wooded countryside, containing a string of well protected villages. The Devil's Punchbowl, near Hindhead, is a two mile long sandstone valley, overlooked by the 900-ft Gibbet Hill. Farnham, in the west of the country, has Tudor and Georgian houses flanking the 12th century castle. Nearby Aldershot is the home of the British Army and county town Guildford is a contemporary business and shopping centre with a modern cathedral and university. The north of the county borders Greater London and includes the 2400 acre Richmond Park, Hampton Court Palace and Kew Gardens.

Sussex

Sussex is a popular county for those wanting a short break from the hustle and bustle of London. Cosmopolitan Brighton, surely the capital of East Sussex, oozes culture, boutique hotels, marina, shops and 'buzz'. The eccentric Royal Pavilion testifies to its history as the Regency summer capital of Britain.

Hotspot: The Brighton Festival in May is a sensational programme of art, theatre, dance, music, literature and family shows starting with a Children's Parade winding its way through the city. www.brightonfestival.org

To the west is the impressive Arundel Castle, with its famous drama festival, nearby popular marinas and Wittering sands. Bognor Regis is a traditional seaside resort with a blue flag beach and the usual attractions. To the east the impressive Beachy Head and Seven Sisters cliffs provide a dramatic backdrop for Eastbourne. The Sussex section of the South Downs National Park stretches from Beachy Head to Harting Down with miles of open chalk grassland, lush river valleys and ancient forests to explore.

If heritage is your thing then Sussex has a plethora of historic houses and gardens and three of the historic cinque ports. Rye in particular, with its cobbled streets, transports the visitor back three centuries. The 1066 Story is told at Battle, near Hastings and Groombridge Place, Great Dixter and Borde Hill all feature stunningly beautiful heritage gardens.

The world famous **Blackbird Tea Rooms** in Brighton is a treat to be savoured, evoking the charm of a bygone era with delicious breakfasts and home-made cakes served on original vintage china in an elegant pre-war setting.
www.blackbirdtearooms.com

For retro-style sweet treats in Kent, **Morelli's ice** cream parlour on Victoria Parade in Broadstairs can't be beaten.

The Grapes in George Street, Oxford is the sole surviving Victorian pub in the city centre and is a fabulous example of a traditional pub with a contemporary approach.

Take a tour of the **Chiltern Brewery**, the oldest independent brewery in the Chiltern Hills and Buckinghamshire, and test its award-winning range of bottle conditioned and draught ales.
www.chilternbrewery.co.uk

For sheer luxury, book a visit to the Elizabethan **Ockenden Manor Hotel & Spa** in Cuckfield near Haywards Heath and enjoy full use of the spa facilities and dinner in the Michelin starred restaurant. Tel (01444) 416111
www.hshotels.co.uk/ockenden-manor-hotel-and-spa

Barefoot Books in Oxford is the perfect place to browse and experience live storytelling, educational games, music, arts, crafts and more.
www.barefootbooks.com

Visit – South East

Attractions with this sign participate in the Visitor Attraction Quality Assurance Scheme.

Berkshire

French Brothers Ltd
Windsor, Berkshire SL4 5JH
(01753) 851900
www.boat-trips.co.uk
Large range of public trips on weather-proof vessels from Windsor, Runnymede and Maidenhead.

Go Ape! Bracknell, Swinley Forest
Berkshire RG12 7QW
(0845) 643 9215
www.goape.co.uk
Go Ape! and tackle a high-wire forest adventure course of rope bridges, Tarzan swings and zip slides up to 35 feet above the forest floor.

Ascot CAMRA Beer Festival
Ascot Racecourse, October
An action packed day of flat racing and an array of over 240 real ales, ciders and perries at the Ascot CAMRA Beer Festival.

Highclere Castle and Gardens
Newbury, Berkshire RG20 9RN
(01635) 253210
www.highclerecastle.co.uk
Visit the spectacular Victorian Castle which is currently the setting for Downton Abbey. Splendid State Rooms, Library and Egyptian Exhibition in the Castle Cellars, plus gardens inspired by Capability Brown.

The Look Out Discovery Centre
Bracknell, Berkshire RG12 7QW
(01344) 354400
www.bracknell-forest.gov.uk
A hands-on, interactive science exhibition with over 80 exhibits, set in 1,000 hectares of Crown woodland.

Reading Festival
August, Reading, Berkshire
www.readingfestival.com
The Reading and Leeds Festivals are a pair of annual music festivals that take place simultaneously.

REME Museum of Technology

Reading, Berkshire RG2 9NJ
(0118) 976 3375
www.rememuseum.org.uk
The museum shows the developing technology used by the Royal Electrical and Mechanical Engineers in maintaining and repairing the army's equipment since 1942.

Buckinghamshire

Aerial Extreme Milton Keynes

Milton Keynes, Buckinghamshire MK15 0DS
0845 652 1736
www.aerialextreme.co.uk/courses/willen-lake
Amaze yourself as you take each of the challenges head on.

Bekonscot Model Village and Railway

Beaconsfield, Buckinghamshire HP9 2PL
(01494) 672919
www.bekonscot.co.uk
Use your imagination in this unique world of make-believe that has delighted generations of visitors.

Gulliver's Land

Milton Keynes, Buckinghamshire MK15 0DT
(01908) 609001
www.gulliversfun.co.uk
Family theme park with 40 rides aimed at children between 2 and 12 years.

Kop Hill Climb

September, Princes Risborough, Buckinghamshire
www.kophillclimb.org.uk
In the 1900s Kop Hill Climb was one of the most popular hill climbs in the country for cars and motorcycles. Now the spirit of the climb is revived.

Marlow Regatta

June, Eton Dorney, Buckinghamshire
www.themarlowregatta.com
Marlow Regatta is one of the multi-lane regattas in the British Rowing calendar.

National Trust Stowe

Buckinghamshire MK18 5DQ
(01280) 817156
www.nationaltrust.org.uk/stowe
Over 40 temples and monuments, laid out against an inspiring backdrop of lakes and valleys.

Reading Real Ale and Jazz Festival

June, Reading, Buckinghamshire
www.readingrealalejazzfest.co.uk
This year's festival is going to be the biggest and best yet, featuring some of the best jazz acts on the circuit.

Roald Dahl Festival

July, Aylesbury Town Centre, Buckinghamshire
www.aylesburyvaledc.gov.uk/dahl
An annual celebration of the famous author, including a 500-strong parade of pupils, teachers and musicians with puppets and artwork based on the Roald Dahl stories.

Roald Dahl Museum and Story Centre

Great Missenden, Buckinghamshire HP16 0AL
(01494) 892192
www.roalddahl.com/museum
Where Roald Dahl (1916-1990) lived and wrote many of his well-loved books.

Waddesdon Manor

Aylesbury, Buckinghamshire HP18 0JH
(01296) 653226
www.waddesdon.org.uk
This National Trust property houses the Rothschild Collection of art treasures and wine cellars. It also features spectacular grounds with an aviary, parterre and woodland playground, licensed restaurants, gift and wine shops.

Xscape

Milton Keynes, Buckinghamshire MK9 3XS
01908 397007
www.xscape.co.uk
Xscape, Milton Keynes offers a unique combination of extreme sports and leisure activities for all ages.

Hampshire & Isle Of Wight

Alton Summer Beer Festival
May, Alton, Hampshire
www.altonbeerfestival.co.uk
Celebrating the cultural heritage of Alton as a traditional area for brewing, based on the clear waters rising from the source of the River Wey, and locally grown hops.

Blackgang Chine
Chale, Isle of Wight PO38 2HN
(01983) 730330
www.blackgangchine.com
Great family fun in over 40 acres of spectacular cliff-top gardens.

Cowes Week
August, Cowes, Isle of Wight
www.aamcowesweek.co.uk
Cowes Week is one of the longest-running regular regattas in the world.

Dinosaur Isle
Sandown, Isle of Wight PO36 8QA
(01983) 404344
www.dinosaurisle.com
In a spectacular pterosaur shaped building on Sandown's blue flag beach walk back through fossilised time and meet life sized replica dinosaurs.

Exbury Gardens and Steam Railway
Beaulieu, Hampshire SO45 1AZ
(023) 8089 1203
www.exbury.co.uk
World famous woodland garden, home to the Rothschild Collection of rhododendrons, azaleas, camellias, rare trees and shrubs, with its own steam railway.

Isle of Wight Festival
June, Newport, Isle of Wight
www.isleofwightfestival.com
Annual music festival featuring some of the UK's top acts and bands.

Isle of Wight Walking Festival
May, Isle of Wight
www.isleofwightwalkingfestival.co.uk
The festival boasts 16 days of unbeatable, informative and healthy walks.

Marwell Zoo
Winchester, Hampshire SO21 1JH
(01962) 777407
www.marwell.org.uk
A chance to get close to the wonders of the natural world – and play a big part in helping to save them.

New Forest and Hampshire Show
July, New Park, Brockenhurst, Hampshire
www.newforestshow.co.uk
The show attracts, on average, 95,000 visitors every year and brings together a celebration of traditional country pursuits, crafts, produce and entertainment.

Osborne House
East Cowes, Isle of Wight PO32 6JX
(01983) 200022
www.english-heritage.org.uk/daysout/properties/osborne-house
Step into Queen Victoria's favourite country home and experience a world unchanged since the country's longest reigning monarch died here just over 100 years ago.

Paultons Family Theme Park
Romsey, Hampshire SO51 6AL
(023) 8081 4442
www.paultonspark.co.uk
A great family day out with over 60 different attractions and rides included in the price!

Shanklin Chine
Shanklin, Isle of Wight PO37 6BW
(01983) 866432
www.shanklinchine.co.uk
Historic gorge with dramatic waterfalls and nature trail.

Southampton Boat Show
September, Southampton, Hampshire
www.southamptonboatshow.com
See the best boats and marine brands gathered together in one fantastic water-based show.

Ventnor Botanic Gardens
St. Lawrence, Isle of Wight PO38 1UL
(01983) 855397
www.botanic.co.uk
The Botanic Garden on the Isle of Wight is a place where the pleasure of plants can be enjoyed to the fullest.

Winchester Hat Fair
July, Winchester, Hampshire
www.hatfair.co.uk
Named after the tradition of throwing donations into performer's hats, it's Britain's longest running festival of street theatre and outdoor arts.

Kent

Bedgebury National Pinetum & Forest
Cranbrook, Kent TN17 2SL
(01580) 879820
www.forestry.gov.uk/bedgebury
Visit the world's finest conifer collection at Bedgebury National Pinetum.

Deal Festival of Music and the Arts
June/July, Deal, Kent
(01304) 370220
www.dealfestival.co.uk
Experience great classical and contemporary music from some of the world's finest music-makers, as well as theatre, opera, cinema and dance – in the beautiful and historic surroundings of Deal and Dover on England's south coast.

The Historic Dockyard Chatham
Kent ME4 4TZ
(01634) 823807
www.thedockyard.co.uk
A unique, award-winning maritime heritage destination with a fantastic range of attractions, iconic buildings and historic ships to explore, plus a fabulous programme of touring exhibitions.

Kent & East Sussex Railway
Tenterden, Kent TN30 6HE
(01580) 765155
www.kesr.org.uk
England's finest rural light railway enables visitors to experience travel and service from a bygone age aboard beautifully restored Victorian coaches and locomotives.

Rochester Castle
Kent ME1 1SW
(01634) 335882
www.visitmedway.org/site/attractions/rochester-castle-p44583
One of the finest keeps in England. Also the tallest, partly built on the Roman city wall. Good views from the battlements over the River Medway.

Oxfordshire

Blenheim Palace
Woodstock, Oxfordshire OX20 1PX
(0800) 849 6500
www.blenheimpalace.com
Birthplace of Sir Winston Churchill and home to the Duke of Marlborough, Blenheim Palace, one of the finest baroque houses in England, is set in over 2,000 acres of landscaped gardens.

Didcot Railway Centre
Oxfordshire OX11 7NJ
(01235) 817200
www.didcotrailwaycentre.org.uk
Living museum recreating the golden age of the Great Western Railway. Steam locomotives and trains, Brunel's broad gauge railway, engine shed and small relics museum.

Henley Royal Regatta
July, Henley, Oxfordshire
www.hrr.co.uk
Attracting thousands of visitors over a five-day period and spectators will be thrilled by over 200 races of international standard.

Oxford Official Guided Walking Tour
owtours@visitoxfordshire.org
The Official Guided Walking Tours are a fascinating and entertaining way to explore and learn about this unique city, its history, University, famous people and odd traditions. Covering a wide range of topics from an introduction to the city and its University to Inspector Morse, Harry Potter, J.R.R. Tolkien and more.

Surrey

British Wildlife Centre
Lingfield, Surrey RH7 6LF
(01342) 834658
www.britishwildlifecentre.co.uk
The best place to see and learn about Britain's own wonderful wildlife, with over 40 different species including deer, foxes, otters, badgers, pine martens and red squirrels.

Guildford Cathedral
Surrey GU2 7UP
(01483) 547860
www.guildford-cathedral.org
New Anglican Cathedral, the foundation stone of which was laid in 1936. Notable sandstone interior and marble floors. Restaurant and shops.

Investec Derby
June, Epsom Racecourse, Surrey
www.epsomderby.co.uk
The biggest horse race in the flat-racing calendar.

Loseley Park
Guildford, Surrey GU3 1HS
(01483) 405120
www.loseleypark.co.uk
A beautiful Elizabethan mansion, set in stunning gardens and parkland. Built in 1562 it has a fascinating history and contains a wealth of treasures.

RHS Garden Wisley
Woking, Surrey GU23 6QB
(0845) 260 9000
www.rhs.org.uk/wisley
Stretching over 240 acres of glorious garden.

RHS Hampton Court Palace Flower Show
July, Hampton Court, Surrey
www.rhs.org.uk
One of the biggest events in the horticulture calendar.

Thorpe Park
Chertsey, Surrey KT16 8PN
(0871) 663 1673
www.thorpepark.com
Thorpe Park Resort is an island like no other, with over 30 thrilling rides, attractions and live events.

Wings & Wheels
August, Dunsfold Aerodrome, Surrey
www.wingsandwheels.net
Outstanding variety of dynamic aviation, motoring displays and iconic cars.

Sussex

1066 Battle Abbey and Battlefield
East Sussex TN33 0AD
(01424) 775705
www.english-heritage.org.uk
An abbey founded by William the Conqueror on the site of the Battle of Hastings.

Arundel Festival
August, Arundel, Sussex
www.arundelfestival.co.uk
Ten days of the best music, theatre, art and comedy.

Arundel Wetland Centre
West Sussex BN18 9PB
(01903) 883355
www.wwt.org.uk/visit/arundel
WWT Arundel Wetland Centre is a 65-acre reserve in an idyllic setting, nestled at the base of the South Downs National Park.

Brighton Digital Festival
September, Brighton, Sussex
www.brightondigitalfestival.co.uk
With a month of exhibitions, performances, workshops and outdoor events, Brighton & Hove is certainly a leading digital destination. There will be workshops, interactive demonstrations and displays throughout the city.

Brighton Fringe
May, Brighton, Sussex
www.brightonfestivalfringe.org.uk
One of the largest fringe festivals in the world, offering cabaret, comedy, classical concerts, club nights, theatre and exhibitions, as well as street performances.

Brighton Marathon
April, Brighton, Sussex
www.brightonmarathon.co.uk
Having grown enormously in just two years, the Brighton Marathon is now one of the top 12 running events in the UK.

Chichester Cathedral
West Sussex PO19 1RP
(01243) 782595
www.chichestercathedral.org.uk
A magnificent Cathedral with treasures ranging from medieval stone carvings to world famous 20th century artworks.

Denmans Garden
Fontwell, West Sussex BN18 0SU
(01243) 542808
www.denmans-garden.co.uk
Beautiful 4 acre garden designed for year round interest through use of form, colour and texture. Beautiful plant centre, award-winning and fully licensed Garden Café.

Eastbourne Beer Festival
October, Winter Gardens, Eastbourne, Sussex
www.visiteastbourne.com/beer-festival
Eastbourne's annual beer festival features over 120 cask ales, plus wines, international bottled beers, ciders and perries. Each session features live music.

Eastbourne Festival
July, Eastbourne, Sussex
www.eastbournefestival.co.uk
Eastbourne Festival is an Open Access Arts Festival which takes place annually for three weeks. It has become recognised as an annual showcase for local professional and amateur talent.

England's Medieval Festival
August, Herstmonceux Castle, Sussex
www.englandsmedievalfestival.com
A celebration of the Middle Ages.

Fishers Adventure Farm Park
Billingshurst, West Sussex RH14 0EG
(01403) 700063
www.fishersfarmpark.co.uk
Award-winning Adventure Farm Park and open all year. Ideally suited for ages 2-11 years. Huge variety of animals, rides and attractions from the skating rink, to pony rides, toboggan run, bumper boats, theatre shows and more!

Glorious Goodwood
July, Chichester, Sussex
www.goodwood.com
Bursting with fabulous fashions, succulent strawberries, chilled Champagne and top horse racing stars, as well as music and dancing.

Glyndebourne Festival
May - August, Lewes, Sussex
www.glyndebourne.com
An English opera festival held at Glyndebourne, an English country house near Lewes.

Great Dixter House and Gardens
Rye, East Sussex TN31 6PH
(01797) 252878
www.greatdixter.co.uk
An example of a 15th century manor house with antique furniture and needlework. The house is restored and the gardens were designed by Lutyens.

London to Brighton Bike Ride
June, Ends on Madeira Drive, Brighton, Sussex
www.bhf.org.uk/london-brighton
The annual bike ride from the capital to the coast in aid of the British Heart Foundation. The UK's largest charity bike ride with 27,000 riders.

Pashley Manor Gardens
Wadhurst, East Sussex TN5 7HE
(01580) 200888
www.pashleymanorgardens.com
Pashley Manor Gardens offer a blend of romantic landscaping, imaginative plantings, fine old trees, fountains, springs and large ponds plus exciting special events.

Petworth House and Park
West Sussex GU28 0AE
(01798) 342207
www.nationaltrust.org.uk/petworth
Discover the National Trust's finest art collection displayed in a magnificent 17th century mansion within a beautiful 700-acre park. Petworth House contains works by artists such as Van Dyck, Reynolds and Turner.

RSPB Pulborough Brooks
West Sussex RH20 2EL
(01798) 875851
www.rspb.org.uk
Set in the scenic Arun Valley with views to the South Downs, the two mile circular nature trail leads around this beautiful reserve.

Tourist Information Centres

When you arrive at your destination, visit the Tourist Information Centre for quality assured help with accommodation and information about local attractions and events, or email your request before you go.

Aldershot	Prince's Hall	01252 320968	aldershotvic@rushmoor.gov.uk
Ashford	Ashford Gateway Plus	01233 330316	tourism@ashford.gov.uk
Aylesbury	The Kings Head, Kings Head Passage	01296 330559	tic@aylesburyvaledc.gov.uk
Banbury	Within Castle Quay Shopping Centre	01295 753752	banbury.tic@cherwell-dc.gov.uk
Battle	Yesterdays World	01797 229049	battletic@rother.gov.uk
Bexley (Hall Place)	Central Library	0208 3037777	touristinfo@bexleyheritagetrust.org.uk
Bicester	Unit 86a Bicester Village	01869 369055	bicestervisitorcentre@valueretail.com
Bracknell	The Look Out Discovery Centre	01344 354409	thelookout@bracknell-forest.gov.uk
Brighton	Brighton Centre Box Office	01273 290337	visitor.info@visitbrighton.com
Buckingham	The Old Gaol Museum	01280 823020	buckinghamtic@touismse.com
Burford	33a High Street	01993 823558	burford.vic@westoxon.gov.uk
Burgess Hill	Burgess Hill Town Council	01444 238202	touristinformation@burgesshill.gov.uk
Canterbury	The Beaney House	01227 378100	canterburyinformation@canterbury.gov.uk
Chichester	The Novium	01243 775888	chitic@chichester.gov.uk
Deal	The Landmark Centre	01304 369576	info@deal.gov.uk
Dover	Dover Museum and VIC	01304 201066	tic@doveruk.com

Eastbourne	Cornfield Road	0871 663 0031	tic@eastbourne.gov.uk
Fareham	Westbury Manor	01329 221342	farehamtic@tourismse.com
Faringdon	The Corn Exchange	01367 242191	tic@faringdontowncouncil.gov.uk
Faversham	Fleur de Lis Heritage Centre	01795 534542	ticfaversham@btconnect.com
Folkestone	20 Bouverier Place Shopping Centre	01303 258594	chris.kirkham@visitkent.co.uk
Fordingbridge	Kings Yard	01425 654560	fordingbridgetic@tourismse.com
Gosportq	Gosport TIC, Bus Station Complex	023 9252 2944	tourism@gosport.gov.uk
Gravesend	Towncentric	01474 337600	info@towncentric.co.uk
Guildford	155 High Street	01483 444333	tic@guildford.gov.uk
Hastings	Queens Square	01424 451111	hic@hastings.gov.uk
Hayling Island	Central Beachlands	023 9246 7111	tourism@havant.gov.uk
Henley-On-Thames	Town Hall,	01491 578034	vic@henleytowncouncil.gov.uk
High Wycombe	High Wycombe Library	01494 421892	tourism_enquiries@wycombe.gov.uk
Horsham	9 The Causeway	01403 211661	visitor.information@horsham.gov.uk
Lewes	187 High Street	01273 483448	lewes.tic@lewes.gov.uk
Littlehampton	The Look & Sea Centre	01903 721866	jo-lhvic@hotmail.co.uk
Lymington	St Barbe Museum	01590 676969	office@stbarbe-museum.org.uk
Lyndhurst & New Forest	New Forest Visitor Centre	023 8028 2269/ 023 8028 5492	info@thenewforest.co.uk
Maidenhead	Maidenhead Library	01628 796502	maidenhead.tic@rbwm.gov.uk
Maidstone	Maidstone Museum	01622 602169	tourism@maidstone.gov.uk
Marlow	55a High Street	01628 483597	tourism_enquiries@wycombe.gov.uk
Midhurst	North Street	01730 812251	midtic@chichester.gov.uk
Newbury	The Wharf	01635 30267	tourism@westberks.gov.uk
Oxford	Oxford Information Centre	01865 252200	info@visitoxfordshire.org
Petersfield	County Library	01730 268829	petersfieldinfo@btconnect.com
Portsmouth	D-Day Museum	023 9282 6722	vis@portsmouthcc.gov.uk
Princes Risborough	Tower Court	01844 274795	risborough_office@wycombe.gov.uk
Ringwood	Ringwood Gateway	01425 473883	town.council@ringwood.gov.uk
Rochester	95 High Street	01634 338141	visitor.centre@medway.gov.uk
Romsey	Museum & TIC	01794 512987	romseytic@testvalley.gov.uk
Royal Tunbridge Wells	Unit 2 The Corn Exchange	01892 515675	touristinformationcentre@ tunbridgewells.gov.uk
Rye	4/5 Lion Street	01797 229049	ryetic@tourismse.com
Sandwich	The Guildhall	01304 613565/ 617197	tourism@sandwichtowncouncil.gov.uk
Seaford	37 Church Street	01323 897426	seaford.tic@lewes.gov.uk
Sevenoaks	Stag Community Arts Centre	01732 450305	tic@sevenoakstown.gov.uk
Swanley	Swanley Library	01322 614660	touristinfo@swanley.org.uk
Tenterden	Tenterden Gateway	08458 247 202	
Thame	Town Hall	01844 212833	oss@thametowncouncil.gov.uk
Thanet	The Droit House	01843 577577	visitorinformation@thanet.gov.uk
Tonbridge	Tonbridge Castle	01732 770929	tonbridge.castle@tmbc.gov.uk
Winchester	Guildhall	01962 840500	tourism@winchester.gov.uk
Windsor	Old Booking Hall	01753 743900	windsor.tic@rbwm.gov.uk
Witney	Welsh Way	01993 775802/ 861780	witney.vic@westoxon.gov.uk
Worthing	The Dome	01903 239868	tic@adur-worthing.gov.uk

Regional Contacts and Information

For more information on accommodation, attractions, activities, events and holidays in South East England, contact one of the following regional or local tourism organisations. Their websites have a wealth of information and many produce free publications to help you get the most out of your visit.

www.visitsoutheastengland.com
email enquiries@tourismse.com or
call (023) 8062 5400.

www.visitnewbury.org.uk
www.visitbuckinghamshire.org
www.visit-hampshire.co.uk
www.visitisleofwight.co.uk
www.visitkent.co.uk
www.visitoxfordandoxfordshire.com
www.visitsurrey.com
www.visitbrighton.com

Entries appear alphabetically by town name in each county. A key to symbols appears on page 7

ASCOT, Berkshire Map ref 2C2 SatNav SL5 7SE H

B&B PER ROOM PER NIGHT
D: £320.00

Coworth Park

Blacknest Road, Ascot, Berkshire SL5 7SE **T:** (01344) 876 600
E: reservations.CPA@dorchestercollection.com
W: www.dorchestercollection.com **£ BOOK ONLINE**

Coworth Park is Dorchester Collection's 70-room luxury country house hotel and spa set in 240 acres of picturesque Berkshire parkland. Seasonal ingredients and exceptional service feature across the three dining experiences - Restaurant Coworth Park, The Barn and The Spatisserie. Relax in the award winning eco-luxury spa with an indoor pool and menu of treatments to refresh and invigorate.

Directions: Coworth Park is just 45 minutes from central London and 20 minutes from London Heathrow airport. Situated near to Ascot and bordering on Windsor Great Park.

Bedrooms: The 70 guestrooms, situated in the Mansion House and in cottages and stables, blend traditional and contemporary design with bespoke furnishings
Open: All year

Site: P **Payment:** **Leisure:** **Property:** **Children:** **Catering:** **Room:**

BRACKNELL, Berkshire Map ref 2C2 SatNav RG12 2JR B

B&B PER ROOM PER NIGHT
S: £70.00 - £85.00
D: £90.00 - £160.00

SPECIAL PROMOTIONS
Complimentary drink of choice on arrival.

Holly House

Goughs Lane, Bracknell RG12 2JR **T:** (01344) 411750 **F:** 01344 411750
E: reservations@hollyhousebracknell.co.uk
W: www.hollyhousebracknell.co.uk

An elegant charming house with a beautiful garden in a quiet leafy lane offering exceptional yet affordable bed and breakfast in a warm and relaxing atmoshphere. Comfort and cleanliness are our bywords. Close to Windsor, Ascot, Henley, Marlow and Reading with London and Gatwick airport an hour away.

Directions: Once along Warfield Road (A3095) turn right by pedestrian traffic lights into Holly Spring Lane then left into Goughs Lane. 350 yards on left entrance.

Bedrooms: 1 single, 2 double, 1 twin
Open: All year except Christmas and New Year

Site: P **Payment:** **Leisure:** **Property:** **Children:** 10 **Catering:** **Room:**

NEWBURY, Berkshire Map ref 2C2 SatNav RG20 8TE B

enjoyEngland.com ★★★★ GUEST ACCOMMODATION
enjoyEngland.com Silver AWARD

B&B PER ROOM PER NIGHT
S: £55.00 - £70.00
D: £75.00 - £90.00

Thatched House B&B

High Street, Chieveley, Newbury, Berks RG20 8TE **T:** (01635) 248295
E: s.malty@btinternet.com
W: www.mychieveley.co.uk/info/thatchedhousebandb

Our B&B offers all the things we like when we stay away - lovely, spacious, self-contained accommodation. Suitable for families (sleeps 5 people). Several good restaurants and pubs close by! **Directions:** From South, at M4 J13 take A34 north to Oxford. Exit Chieveley. From North, exit A34 at Beedon. Thatched House between shop and Village Hall. **Bedrooms:** 1 suite - double room, bathroom + living room + sofabed **Open:** All year

Site: P **Payment:** € **Property:** **Children:** **Catering:** **Room:**

WINDSOR, Berkshire Map ref 2D2 SatNav SL4 5AE B

enjoyEngland.com ★★★ GUEST HOUSE

B&B PER ROOM PER NIGHT
S: £45.00 - £84.00
D: £55.00 - £94.00

Clarence Hotel

9 Clarence Road, Windsor, Berkshire SL4 5AE **T:** (01753) 864436 **F:** 01753 857060
E: clarence.hotel@btconnect.com
W: www.clarencehotelwindsor.co.uk

Characterful budget hotel located in town centre close to restaurants, shopping, Windsor Castle & Eton. Licensed bar, steam sauna. All rooms en suite, TV, beverage trays, hairdryer, radio alarm. Free WiFi Internet. 12m from Heathrow **Directions:** Exit M4 at jct 6 to Windsor. Stay on dual carriageway and turn left at the roundabout onto Clarence Road. **Bedrooms:** 4 single, 4 double, 6 twin, 6 family **Open:** All year except Christmas

Site: P **Payment:** £ **Property:** **Children:** **Catering:** **Room:**

WINDSOR, Berkshire Map ref 2C2 SatNav H

VisitEngland ★★★★★ HOTEL BOAT

SPECIAL PROMOTIONS
Cruises with full board: 3 nights from £405
4 nights from £515
5 nights from £625
6 nights from £735.
Includes wine with 4 course evening meal.

Hotel Boat Kailani

107 High Street, South Milford, Leeds, West Yorkshire LS25 5AQ **T:** 07447 051558
E: info@hotelboatkailani.com
W: www.hotelboatkailani.com **£ BOOK ONLINE**

Luxury 5 star wide beam Hotel Boat cruising Southern England's waterways - Grand Union Canal, River Thames, Kennet and Avon Canal, Central London and Lee & Stort navigations. 3-6 night breaks with all meals freshly prepared on-board. Fully licensed. Two private en suite cabins for 4 guests . Cruises with visits or relax and watch the world go by. You choose!

Directions: Most cruises start and end near to railway stations.

Bedrooms: We have a double cabin and twin cabin both with en suite. Toiletries, hairdryer, fluffy gowns and slippers provided
Open: Spring, Summer & Autumn. Winter charters available

Payment: £ **Leisure:** **Property:** **Children:** **Catering:**
Room:

For **key to symbols** see page 7

WINDSOR, Berkshire Map ref 2D2 SatNav RG42 6LD H

Stirrups Country House Hotel

Maidens Green, Bracknell RG42 6LD **T:** (01344) 882284 **F:** 01344 882300
E: reception@stirrupshotel.co.uk
W: www.stirrupshotel.co.uk **£ BOOK ONLINE**

Stirrups, with its Tudor origins, is located between Bracknell, Ascot and Windsor and is the perfect venue for visits to Legoland Windsor (three miles). Round off your day by relaxing in the oak-beamed bar, by the inglenook fire, prior to dinner. Please contact for prices. **Directions:** Stirrups lies on the B3022, 200 metres south of the crossroads in Maidens Green Village. **Bedrooms:** 19 dbl, 4 twin, 7 family, 5 suite - all en suite **Open:** All year

Site: P **Payment:** **Property:** **Children:** **Catering:** **Room:**

AYLESBURY, Buckinghamshire Map ref 2C1 SatNav HP18 9PD B

The Old School Bed and Breakfast

Ludgershall, Aylesbury, Buckinghamshire HP18 9PD **T:** (01844) 238034
E: aldo.clairetheoldschool@gmail.com
W: www.theoldschool-bandb.co.uk

B&B PER ROOM PER NIGHT
S: £55.00
D: £75.00

Set in a quiet and pretty village, our Bed and Breakfast offers ground floor accommodation including; one double bedroom, private shower room and own sitting room. Own front door, courtyard garden and off road parking. Continental breakfast. **Directions:** The Old School is two miles off the A41 in between the towns of Bicester and Aylesbury. **Bedrooms:** TV and DVD, free Wi-Fi, fridge, microwave and toaster **Open:** All year

Site: P **Payment:** € **Leisure:** **Property:** **Catering:** **Room:**

BUCKINGHAM, Buckinghamshire Map ref 2C1 SatNav MK18 5ND B

Huntsmill Farm B&B

Huntsmill Farm, Shalstone, Nr. Buckingham MK18 5ND **T:** (01280) 704852 / 07970 871104
E: fiona@huntsmill.com
W: www.huntsmill.com

B&B PER ROOM PER NIGHT
S: £45.00
D: £70.00

Home-made bread and preserves welcome you at Huntsmill Farm. Comfortable, en suite rooms adjacent to farmhouse. Quiet location, views over open countryside. Close to National Trust properties and Silverstone. **Directions:** Midway between Buckingham and Brackley on A422. South side, signposted 'Finmere & Mixbury', 1/3 mile on the left. **Bedrooms:** 1 double, 2 twin **Open:** All year except Christmas

Site: P **Payment:** € **Leisure:** **Property:** **Children:** 5 **Catering:** **Room:**

GREAT MISSENDEN, Buckinghamshire Map ref 2C1 SatNav HP16 0AX B

Forge House

Forge House, 10 Church Street, Great Missenden, Buckinghamshire HP16 0AX
T: (01494) 867347 / 07717 949710

B&B PER ROOM PER NIGHT
D: £35.00 - £70.00

Set in the wooded Chiltern Hills, quiet village location - a charming 18th century beamed house traditionally refurbished with three en suite double bedrooms. Set in the home town of Roald Dahl, and a regular film site for Midsummer Murders, Forge House welcomes walkers and cyclists alike and is only a 35 minute trip from Marylebone London station. Prices are based on per person per night with English/continental breakfast included. **Bedrooms:** 2 double rooms and 1 twin, all en suite **Open:** All Year

Site: P **Leisure:** **Property:** **Children:** 5 **Catering:** **Room:**

ANDOVER, Hampshire Map ref 2C2 SatNav SP11 8LZ B

enjoyEngland.com ★★★★ BED & BREAKFAST
enjoyEngland.com Silver AWARD

B&B PER ROOM PER NIGHT
S: £45.00 - £65.00
D: £75.00 - £95.00

May Cottage

Thruxton, Andover SP11 8LZ **T:** (01264) 771241 **E:** maycottagethruxton@gmail.com
W: www.maycottage-thruxton.co.uk

Dating back to 1740, May Cottage is situated in the heart of this picturesque village. All rooms en suite/private bathroom. Guests own sitting/dining room. Secluded garden. Historic attractions nearby. Non-smoking. **Directions:** From Andover take A303 towards Exeter, then take turning for Thruxton (village only). Left at T-junction. May Cottage is on right opposite The George Inn. **Bedrooms:** 2 double, 1 twin **Open:** All year

Site: P **Leisure:** **Property:** **Children:** **Catering:** **Room:**

BEAULIEU, Hampshire Map ref 2C3 SatNav SO45 5TJ B

enjoyEngland.com ★★★★ BED & BREAKFAST
enjoyEngland.com Silver AWARD

B&B PER ROOM PER NIGHT
S: £55.00 - £75.00
D: £80.00 - £110.00

Dale Farm House

Manor Road, Dibden, Southampton SO45 5TJ **T:** (023) 8084 9632
E: chris@dalefarmhouse.co.uk
W: www.dalefarmhouse.co.uk £ BOOK ONLINE

Beautiful 18th century farmhouse in secluded woodland setting. Peaceful garden in which to unwind, a bird watchers paradise. BBC Holiday programme featured B&B. Lovely country views and no road noise. 15 places to eat locally. **Directions:** M3 south - M27 west - exit jct. 2 to A326 for 7 miles - at 5th r'about Dibden go over and turn sharp right, follow Manor Road 250m to our drive on right after the fields. **Bedrooms:** Refreshments, en suite, free WiFi & parking, garden **Open:** All Year

Site: P **Payment:** **Leisure:** **Property:** **Children:** **Catering:** **Room:**

For key to symbols see page 7

BORDON, Hampshire *Map ref 2C2* SatNav GU35 9NA B

Spring Cottage

Main Road, Kingsley, Bordon GU35 9NA **T:** (01420) 472703 **E:** paulineansell@aol.com
W: www.springcottagekingsley.co.uk

B&B PER ROOM PER NIGHT
S: £27.50
D: £55.00

A warm welcome awaits you in an 18th Century family home, in a village and close to pub serving food. Shared guest bathroom, hence two stars. Easy reach Alton, Farnham, Petersfield. Large garden, views of woods and fields. Free Wi-Fi. **Directions:** From 325 take 3004 Alton after 1 mile, 2 bus shelters 50 yds past right hand shelter is a track leading to our house, playground on right as you enter **Bedrooms:** 1 single, 1 double
Open: All year except Christmas

Site: P **Leisure:** **Property:** **Children:** 9 **Catering:** **Room:**

BROCKENHURST, Hampshire *Map ref 2C3* SatNav SO42 7SH

Cottage Lodge New Forest Hotel

Sway Road, Brockenhurst, New Forest National Park SO42 7SH **T:** (01590) 622296
E: enquiries@cottagelodge.co.uk
W: www.cottagelodge.co.uk

B&B PER ROOM PER NIGHT
S: £50.00 - £150.00
D: £60.00 - £160.00
EVENING MEAL PER PERSON
£20.00 - £40.00

94% Trip Advisor rating. 17thC New Forest cottage, oak beams and character. Superb local breakfasts. Great location for exploring the New Forest National Park. Bike hire available. Reserved parking for each room. Free cake. Honesty bar. **Directions:** From Carey's manor, Brockenhurst take Grigg Lane signposted 'village centre'. At Lloyds bank xroads go ahead into Sway Rd. CL is 110 yds on right. **Bedrooms:** Beautiful handmade four poster bedded rooms
Open: All year except a week over Christmas

Site: P **Payment:** **Leisure:** **Property:** **Children:** **Catering:** **Room:**

EASTLEIGH, Hampshire *Map ref 2C3* SatNav SO50 9HQ H

Concorde Club & Ellington Lodge Hotel

Stoneham Lane, Eastleigh SO50 9HQ **T:** (023) 8065 1478 **F:** 023 8065 1479
E: reservations@theconcordeclub.com
W: www.theconcordeclub.com **£ BOOK ONLINE**

SPECIAL PROMOTIONS
Special jazz/ entertainment breaks at the award winning Concorde Club. Short term airport and cruise parking available to residents.

Comfortable air-conditioned bedrooms, just two minutes from Southampton International Airport/ Parkway railway station. In quiet woodland setting with ample free parking. The atmospheric Moldy Fig Wine Bar is open all day and offers excellent food and fine wines. Room rates from £65 prpn B&B.

Directions: Situated on the outskirts of Southampton in Eastleigh, near Southampton International Airport. Exit M27 junction 5, follow signs to Concorde Club & Hotel.

Bedrooms: 29 double, 6 twin
Open: All year

Site: **Payment:** **Leisure:** **Property:** **Catering:** **Room:**

FAREHAM, Hampshire Map ref 2C3 SatNav PO16 7BG B

Trafalgar Guest House

63 High Street, Fareham PO16 7BG **T:** (01329) 235010
E: enquiries@trafalgarguesthouse.co.uk
W: www.trafalgarguesthouse.co.uk

B&B PER ROOM PER NIGHT
S: £57.00
D: £79.00

Trafalgar Guest House has accommodation for singles, doubles or twins and families. All rooms are en suite including hospitality trays, digital TV, iron and hairdryer. Rated at 3* by VisitEngland.
Directions: 63 High Street, Fareham, Hants, PO16 7BG.
Bedrooms: 4 double, 4 twin, 1 family **Open:** All year

Site: P **Payment:** **Leisure:** **Property:** **Children:** **Catering:** **Room:** TV

FORDINGBRIDGE, Hampshire Map ref 2B3 SatNav SP6 2HF H

The Three Lions

Stuckton, Fordingbridge SP6 2HF **T:** (01425) 652489 **F:** 01425 656144
E: the3lions@btinternet.com
W: www.thethreelionsrestaurant.co.uk

B&B PER ROOM PER NIGHT
S: £79.00
D: £125.00

HB PER PERSON PER NIGHT
£70.00 - £85.00

SPECIAL PROMOTIONS
Weekend Two Day Break £235 incl continental breakfast £360 with 3 course dinners Mid Week £215 to £340 respectively.

A restaurant with rooms in the New Forest. Come and stay, relax and enjoy English/French cuisine cooked by Mike a constantly hands on (former) Michelin starred chef. Cosy informal bar, log fire, conservatory and gardens with sauna and hot tub. Three times Hampshire Restaurant of the Year, Good Food Guide. National Newcomer of the Year, Good Hotel Guide. We are family, cyclist and walker friendly & accept pets.

Directions: 15 mins M27 jct 1. 15 mins Salisbury. Locate Total garage east of Fordingbridge, follow brown tourist signs to the Three Lions.

Bedrooms: 2 dble, 2 twin, 3 family
Open: All year

Site: **Payment:** € **Leisure:** **Property:** **Children:** **Catering:** **Room:** TV

NEW MILTON, NEW FOREST, Hampshire Map ref 2B3 SatNav BH23 5QL

Chewton Glen

New Milton, New Forest, Hampshire BH25 6QS **T:** (01425) 282212 **F:** 01425 272310
E: reservations@chewtonglen.com
W: www.chewtonglen.com

enjoyEngland.com ★★★★★ HOTEL — enjoyEngland.com Gold Award

B&B PER ROOM PER NIGHT
D: £377.00 - £1652.00

SPECIAL PROMOTIONS
Two night minimum stay at weekends.

An English Original. Chewton Glen is a luxury countryhouse hotel and spa set in 130 acres of Hampshire countryside on the edge of the New Forest National Park, and just a few minutes walk from the sea. A very special place, Chewton Glen is a proud member of Relais & Châteaux, is one of the finest luxury hotels in the UK and has been voted 'Best Hotel for Service in the UK' and listed as one of the 'World's Best Hotels' by Conde Nast Traveller readers. The unsurpassed heritage of effortlessly gracious English hospitality and the balance between heritage and evolution is what makes Chewton Glen a 5 star, luxury country house hotel and spa that constantly surprises.

Directions: Please contact us for directions.

Bedrooms: 35 Double, 23 Suites, 12 Treehouse Suites.
Open: All year

Site: **Payment:** **Leisure:** **Property:** **Children:** **Catering:** **Room:**

PORTSMOUTH, Hampshire Map ref 2C3 SatNav PO1 3HS

Royal Maritime Club

75-80 Queen Street, Portsmouth PO1 3HS **T:** (023) 9282 4231 **F:** 023 9229 3496
E: info@royalmaritimeclub.co.uk
W: www.royalmaritimeclub.co.uk **£ BOOK ONLINE**

enjoyEngland.com ★★ HOTEL

B&B PER ROOM PER NIGHT
S: £53.00 - £70.00
D: £92.00 - £140.00

EVENING MEAL PER PERSON
£14.75 - £18.50

SPECIAL PROMOTIONS
Minimum 3 night breaks Sunday to Thursday from £56.00 pp per night. Friday and Saturday from £62 pp per night.

Situated at the heart of Portsmouth's unique naval heritage area. Within walking distance of HMS Victory, HMS Warrior, the Mary Rose, Gunwharf Quays shopping complex. Rail, coach, ferry links nearby.

Directions: Take the M275 Portsmouth(W) and then follow signs to Historic Waterfront/Historic Dockyard.

Bedrooms: 20 single, 33 dble, 19 twin, 8 family, 20 superior
Open: All year except Christmas and New Year

Payment: **Leisure:** **Property:** **Children:** **Catering:** **Room:**

SOUTHAMPTON, Hampshire Map ref 2C3 SatNav SO31 5DQ

The Prince Consort

Victoria Road, Netley Abbey, Southampton, Hampshire SO31 5DQ **T:** (023) 8045 2676
E: info@theprinceconsortpub.co.uk
W: www.theprinceconsortpub.co.uk

B&B PER ROOM PER NIGHT
S: £50.00 - £60.00
D: £65.00 - £80.00

Grade 2 listed Victorian Pub with separate annexe B&B in the Heart of Netley Abbey. Close to Hamble, Southampton, Winchester and Portsmouth. Rates include breakfast. **Directions:** Situated near A27 & M27 and mainline train links to and from Southampton and Portsmouth. Within easy walking distance of Hamble. **Bedrooms:** 4 double, 3 twin **Open:** All year

Site: P **Payment:** **Leisure:** **Property:** **Children:** **Catering:** **Room:**

SWAY, Hampshire Map ref 2C3 SatNav SO41 6DJ

The Mill At Gordleton

Silver Street, Hordle, Lymington SO41 6DJ **T:** (01590) 682219
E: info@themillatgordleton.co.uk
W: www.themillatgordleton.co.uk

B&B PER ROOM PER NIGHT
S: £115.00 - £245.00
D: £150.00 - £275.00
EVENING MEAL PER PERSON
£23.95 - £47.00

A beautiful individual privately owned small restaurant with rooms, wonderful river, gardens. Homemade, local and organic food. We care passionately about the environment which is reflected in everything we do. **Directions:** A337 Lyndhurst to Brockenhurst to Lymington. Over two mini roundabouts first right Sway Road. The Mill at Gordleton Hotel 2m. **Bedrooms:** 3 kings, 3 twins, 2 suite **Open:** All year except Christmas day

Site: **Payment:** **Leisure:** **Property:** **Children:** **Catering:** **Room:**

WINCHESTER, Hampshire Map ref 2C3 SatNav SO23 9SR

12 Christchurch Road

12 Christchurch Road, Winchester SO23 9SR **T:** (01962) 854272 / 07879 850076
E: pjspatton@yahoo.co.uk

B&B PER ROOM PER NIGHT
S: £55.00 - £60.00
D: £65.00 - £70.00

Elegant Victorian house furnished with style. Easy, pleasant walk to city centre, cathedral, museums, shops and water meadows. Breakfast in conservatory, overlooking beautiful gardens (NGS), with home-made bread, preserves and local produce. **Directions:** Please contact us for directions. **Bedrooms:** 1 double, 1 twin. Comfortable and well furnished **Open:** All year except Christmas and New Year

Property: **Children:** **Catering:** **Room:**

FRESHWATER, Isle of Wight Map ref 2C3 SatNav PO40 9PP

Seahorses

Victoria Road, Freshwater, Isle of Wight PO40 9PP **T:** (01983) 752574 **F:** 01983 752574
E: seahorses-iow@tiscali.co.uk
W: www.seahorsesisleofwight.com **£ BOOK ONLINE**

B&B PER ROOM PER NIGHT
S: £37.00 - £39.00
D: £74.00 - £78.00

A charming early 19th century rectory, standing in 2.5 acres of lovely gardens with direct footpath access to Yarmouth and Freshwater Bay. Art courses available in our studio. Pets welcome. **Directions:** From the Freshwater Co-op (large), go up Stroud Road becoming Victoria Road, just past St. Andrews Village Hall, turn left into our driveway. Ample off-road parking. **Bedrooms:** 1 double, 2 twin, 2 family **Open:** All year

Site: P **Leisure:** **Property:** **Children:** **Catering:** **Room:**

SANDOWN, Isle of Wight Map ref 2C3 SatNav PO36 8JR

The Montpelier

5 Pier Street, Sandown PO36 8JR **T:** (01983) 403964 / 07092 212734
E: steve@themontpelier.co.uk
W: www.themontpelier.co.uk

B&B PER ROOM PER NIGHT
S: £28.00 - £34.00
D: £56.00 - £68.00

The Montpelier is situated opposite the pier and beaches with the High St just around the corner. We offer B&B, room-only and ferry-inclusive from Southampton. Rooms are en suite, most with sea views and all have a fridge. Room only £4pn less. **Directions:** Make your way to Sandown Pier and Esplanade and as you come into Pier Street we are the blue building 15 metres down on your left. **Bedrooms:** 1 single, 3 double, 2 twin, 2 family **Open:** All year

Payment: € **Leisure:** **Property:** **Children:** **Catering:** **Room:**

ASHFORD, Kent Map ref 3B4 SatNav TN25 5NB

Bulltown Farmhouse Bed & Breakfast

Bulltown Lane, West Brabourne, Ashford, Kent TN25 5NB **T:** (01233) 813505
E: lily.wilton@bulltown.co.uk
W: www.bulltown.co.uk

B&B PER ROOM PER NIGHT
S: £45.00 - £50.00
D: £80.00 - £90.00

Stunning 15th Century timber framed farmhouse with wealth of beams surrounded by cottage garden in Area of Outstanding Natural Beauty. Rooms have unspoilt views. All en suite. Guest lounge with large inglenook fireplace. Local produce used. **Directions:** See website for directions but under 4 miles from Junction 10 M20. **Bedrooms:** 1 double, 1 twin, 1 family **Open:** All year

Site: P **Payment:** € **Leisure:** **Property:** **Children:** **Catering:** **Room:**

BROADSTAIRS, Kent Map ref 3C3 SatNav CT10 1EY

Bleak House

Fort Road, Broadstairs, Kent CT10 1EY **T:** (01843) 865338 **F:** 01843 579619
E: enquiries@bleakhousebroadstairs.co.uk
W: www.bleakhousebroadstairs.co.uk **£ BOOK ONLINE**

B&B PER ROOM PER NIGHT
S: £70.00 - £80.00
D: £100.00 - £250.00
EVENING MEAL PER PERSON
£12.95 - £30.00

Bleak House, former home of famous author Charles Dickens, built in 1801, with private gardens and Viking bay just 2 mins walk away. Luxurious bedrooms with Wi-Fi and mini fridges, all with stunning sea views, private dining and afternoon tea available. **Directions:** 10 mins walk from train station, by car Albion street, take right turn in to Church Rd, drive straight ahead to Bleak House. **Bedrooms:** En suite, mini fridge, tea and coffee and flat screen TV **Open:** All year

Site: P **Payment:** € **Leisure:** **Property:** **Children:** **Catering:** **Room:**

CANTERBURY (4 MILES), Kent Map ref 3B3 SatNav CT4 6NY

enjoyEngland.com ★★★ INN

B&B PER ROOM PER NIGHT
S: £50.00
D: £70.00 - £80.00

The Duke of Cumberland

The Street, Barham, Canterbury CT4 6NY **T:** (01227) 831396
E: info@dukeofcumberland.co.uk
W: www.dukeofcumberland.co.uk **£ BOOK ONLINE**

The Duke of Cumberland is first and foremost, a traditional English Country Inn built in 1749. All our rooms are well presented. Newly refurbished and sensitively designed to echo a bygone age they provide warm, comfortable and pleasant accommodation. Each room has an en suite shower room and WC facilities. In addition each room has an LCD TV with freeview, Wi-Fi internet access, tea and coffee making facilities, hairdryer and alarm clock.

Directions: Please contact us for directions or visit our website for map.

Bedrooms: 2 double, 1 family
Open: All year

Site: P **Payment:** **Leisure:** **Property:** **Children:** **Catering:** **Room:**

CANTERBURY, Kent Map ref 3B3 SatNav CT1 3JT

enjoyEngland.com ★★★ BACKPACKERS

B&B PER ROOM PER NIGHT
S: £25.00 - £35.00
D: £20.00 - £30.00
BED ONLY PER NIGHT
£10.00 - £24.50

Kipps Independent Hostel

40 Nunnery Fields, Canterbury CT1 3JT **T:** (01227) 786121 **E:** kippshostel@gmail.com
W: www.kipps-hostel.com **£ BOOK ONLINE**

Self-catering backpackers hostel only a short walk from the Cathedral and City Centre. We offer accommodation for individuals and Groups . Excellent facilities including kitchen, garden, lounge free Wifi, and nightly events. **Directions:** Please go to our website www.kipps-hostel.com for directions. **Bedrooms:** Private/family and dormitory rooms **Open:** All year

WALKERS WELCOME CYCLISTS WELCOME **Site:** **Payment:** € **Leisure:** **Property:** **Catering:** **Bedroom:**

CRANBROOK, Kent Map ref 3B4 SatNav TN17 2BP

enjoyEngland.com ★★★★ GUEST ACCOMMODATION

B&B PER ROOM PER NIGHT
S: £45.00
D: £60.00 - £70.00

Tolehurst Barn

Cranbrook Road, Frittenden, Cranbrook, Kent TN17 2BP **T:** (01580) 714385
E: info@tolehurstbarn.co.uk
W: www.tolehurstbarn.co.uk

Quietly situated, set in 1 acre of garden, near Sissinghurst, Leeds, and Scotney Castles. Good walking area, TV, tea and coffee making facilities in all rooms and ample parking. For more info visit our website. **Directions:** A229 between staplehurst and Cranbrook, behind Bumbles Garden centre. **Bedrooms:** 2 doubles en suite, 1 family room with bathroom **Open:** All year

Site: P **Payment:** € **Leisure:** **Property:** **Children:** 1 **Room:**

For key to symbols see page 7

DOVER, Kent Map ref 3C4 SatNav CT15 4LQ B

Farthingales Bed and Breakfast

Old Court Hill, Nonington, Dover, Kent CT15 4LQ **T:** 07599 303494
E: farthingalesbandb@yahoo.co.uk
W: www.farthingales.co.uk

enjoyEngland.com ★★★★ BED & BREAKFAST

B&B PER ROOM PER NIGHT
S: £65.00 - £95.00
D: £75.00 - £85.00

SPECIAL PROMOTIONS
Local pub 5 minutes walk away.

Truly a rural retreat. Farthingales offers a unique blend of history and the comforts of 21st Century living in a beautiful Victorian building which was once the village shop. For those who enjoy living through medieval times, we offer rooms in our 15th century Kentish hall house. A secluded venue for those travelling alone, as couples, families or groups.

Directions: Via A2 towards Dover, turn off at Wingham/Aylesham exit and follow signs for Nonington. Left at The Royal Oak pub into Vicarage Lane under the tunnel of trees. We're opposite St Mary's Church.

Bedrooms: Twin and double in converted village shop. Lounge and en suites, plus a 15th century suite with lounge, dining room and large en suite. £95 per night
Open: All year

Site: P **Payment:** £ **Leisure:** **Property:** **Room:** TV DVD

DOVER, Kent Map ref 3C4 SatNav CT16 1QW B

Hubert House Guesthouse

9 Castle Hill Road, Dover CT16 1QW **T:** (01304) 202253 **F:** 01304 210142
E: stay@huberthouse.co.uk
W: www.huberthouse.co.uk

enjoyEngland.com ★★★★ GUEST HOUSE
enjoyEngland.com Gold AWARD

B&B PER ROOM PER NIGHT
S: £45.00 - £55.00
D: £65.00 - £100.00

Hubert house is a Georgian grade 2 listed building, our rooms are decorated a bit to suit the age of the building and we do not have an elevator. Our continental buffet breakfast is included in our price, cooked breakfast is an optional extra (porridge and full monty etc). **Directions:** Easy walking distance to town centre, castle, bus stop, ferry port and train station. **Bedrooms:** 6 bedrooms all en suite, parking available on site **Open:** All year except Christmas and New Year

Site: P **Payment:** £ **Leisure:** **Property:** **Children:**
Catering: **Room:** TV

EDENBRIDGE, Kent Map ref 2D2 SatNav TN8 7NG B

The Astor Wing at Hever Castle

Hever Castle, Hever, Edenbridge TN8 7NG **T:** (01732) 861800 **F:** 01732 867860
E: stay@hevercastle.co.uk
W: www.hevercastle.co.uk/stay/bed-breakfast **£ BOOK ONLINE**

enjoyEngland.com ★★★★★ GUEST ACCOMMODATION — enjoyEngland.com Gold AWARD

B&B PER ROOM PER NIGHT
S: £105.00 - £180.00
D: £160.00 - £255.00

SPECIAL PROMOTIONS
Please contact for the latest offers.

Surrounded by glorious Kent countryside, Hever Castle in Kent offers luxury Bed and breakfast in the Astor Wing of Hever Castle, an Edwardian Wing created by William Waldorf Astor, designed in Tudor style. This period property boasts a fine collection of 28, stunning five-star Gold graded bedrooms. On offer you will find an abundance of rich fabrics, crisp linens, panelled walls, perhaps a golden chaise longue or a glimpse of the castle through leaded windows.

All bedrooms are en suite and individually styled, some offering four poster beds, some roll top baths and some walk in showers. All rooms blend modern day comforts with antique furnishings and original features. The fine collection of bedrooms offers a selection of double rooms, twin rooms, single rooms and some rooms that are suitable for families with young children.

Directions: Please see website.

Bedrooms: Luxurious toiletries, Wi-Fi, flat screen TV's and direct-dial telephones
Open: All year

Site: P **Payment:** **Leisure:** **Property:** **Children:** **Catering:**
Room:

GILLINGHAM, Kent Map ref 3B3 SatNav ME7 5QT H

King Charles Hotel

Brompton Road, Gillingham ME7 5QT **T:** (01634) 830303 **F:** 01634 829430
E: reservations@kingcharleshotel.co.uk
W: www.kingcharleshotel.co.uk **£ BOOK ONLINE**

enjoyEngland.com ★★★ HOTEL

B&B PER ROOM PER NIGHT
S: £49.00
D: £59.00

SPECIAL PROMOTIONS
Special Sunday night rates.
Please see website for details.

A privately owned, modern hotel, situated in the heart of Medway. All bedrooms have en suite bathroom, tea/coffee facilities, hairdryer, telephone, TV and wireless internet. We offer extremely competitive group rates.

Directions: M2 jct 4 to Gillingham/Medway Tunnel. Turn left to Brompton before tunnel. We are on left.

Bedrooms: 4 single, 33 dble, 33 twin, 26 family, 2 suite
Open: All year

Site: **Payment:** € **Leisure:** **Property:** **Children:** **Catering:**
Room:

HERNHILL, Kent Map ref 3B3 SatNav ME13 9JW B

B&B PER ROOM PER NIGHT
S: £45.00 - £55.00
D: £75.00 - £85.00

Church Oast

Church Oast, Hernhill, Faversham ME13 9JW T: (01227) 750974 E: jill@geliot.plus.com
W: www.churchoast.co.uk

A warm welcome and luxury accommodation in converted Oast House in quiet picturesque village. Lovely views. Award winning breakfasts. Guest lounge. Special winter breaks. Meals available in nearby pub. **Directions:** From London M2 then A299 Margate first exit and follow signs to Hernhill. From Dover A2 to M2 roundabout 4th exit A299 then as above. **Bedrooms:** 1 double, 1 twin, 1 family **Open:** All year

Site: P Payment: € Leisure: Property: Children: Catering: Room:

MAIDSTONE, Kent Map ref 3B3 SatNav ME17 1RQ B

B&B PER ROOM PER NIGHT
S: £62.00 - £75.00
D: £82.00 - £98.00

SPECIAL PROMOTIONS
Seasonal special offers available, please see website.

Ash Cottage

Penfold Hill, Leeds Village, Nr Maidstone, Kent ME17 1RQ T: (01622) 863142
E: rayne@ashcottagekent.co.uk
W: www.ashcottagekent.co.uk

Hot tea, fresh cake, a good nights sleep, hearty breakfast, candlelight and home made jam. Welcome to Ash Cottage, a Channel 4 Four in a Bed winner for 2014, adjacent to Leeds Castle. Enjoy a relaxed breakfast in front of the inglenook, explore all Kent has to offer, recharge your batteries in our cottage garden or snug, stroll to a country pub. Sleep in goose feather and duck down in crisp cotton sheets and enjoy.

Directions: At M20 Junction 8 follow sign for Leeds Castle. Pass castle entrance, Ash Cottage on right after bridge and 30 mph sign before bend.

Bedrooms: 2 king en suite, 1 twin with private bathroom
Open: All year

Site: P Leisure: Property: Children: 10 Catering: Room:

MAIDSTONE, Kent Map ref 3B3 SatNav ME14 2BD B

B&B PER ROOM PER NIGHT
S: £45.00
D: £85.00

The Limes

118 Boxley Road, Maidstone ME14 2BD T: (01622) 750629 / 07889 594700
E: info@thelimesmaidstone.co.uk
W: www.thelimesmaidstone.co.uk £ BOOK ONLINE

Large Georgian house, 2 star guest accommodation. Close to town centre, motorways, railway stations and shopping centres. Good location for walkers and cyclists. Off-road parking. Silver award for breakfast. **Directions:** From M2 Junction 3 take A229 to Maidstone. From M20 Junction 6 A229 Signposted Penenden Heath. Turn right at roundabout for town centre. **Bedrooms:** 3 single, 1 twin **Open:** All year

Site: P Leisure: Property: Children: 12 Catering: Room:

MAIDSTONE, Kent Map ref 3B3 SatNav ME14 1BH

The Townhouse Hotel

74 King Street, Maidstone, Kent ME14 1BH **T:** (01622) 663266 **E:** reservations@tthh.co.uk
W: www.tthh.co.uk **£ BOOK ONLINE**

★★ METRO HOTEL

B&B PER ROOM PER NIGHT
S: £80.00 - £90.00
D: £90.00 - £100.00
EVENING MEAL PER PERSON
£15.95 - £55.00

Located in the heart of Maidstone, the hotel was built as a vicarage in 1802, retaining may original features. On site restaurant and bar. All rooms en suite. Wireless internet connection. English breakfast cooked to order. **Bedrooms:** All rooms are en suite **Open:** All year

Payment: **Property:** **Children:** **Catering:** **Room:**

RAMSGATE, Kent Map ref 3C3 SatNav CT11 8DT

Comfort Inn Ramsgate

Victoria Parade, Ramsgate, Kent CT11 8DT **T:** (01843) 592345 **F:** 01843 580157
E: reservations@comfortinnramsgate.co.uk
W: www.comfortinnramsgate.co.uk **£ BOOK ONLINE**

★★★ HOTEL

B&B PER ROOM PER NIGHT
S: £35.00 - £50.00
D: £40.00 - £120.00

SPECIAL PROMOTIONS
Promotional rate available mid week and weekends, ring 01843 592345 for details.

Victorian Grade 2 Listed building with modern facilities situated on the cliff top with panoramic views of English Channel. Free Wi-Fi, well stocked bar selling local ale, restaurant offering wide variety of dishes, Beauty Salon. Sea view rooms, some with enclosed balcony, Garden. Free parking. Live Entertainment fortnightly.

Directions: From M2 take the A299 then A253 to Ramsgate. Follow signs for East Cliff. From Victoria Road turn left, hotel is on the left.

Bedrooms: 7 single, 14 double, 9 twin, 7 family, 7 suite
Open: All year

Site: **Payment:** € **Leisure:** **Property:** **Children:** **Catering:**
Room:

RAMSGATE, Kent Map ref 3C3 SatNav CT11 8DB

Glendevon Guest House

8 Truro Road, Ramsgate CT11 8DB **T:** 0800 035 2110 **F:** 01843 570909
E: info@glendevonguesthouse.co.uk
W: www.glendevonguesthouse.co.uk

★★★★ GUEST HOUSE · Silver AWARD

B&B PER ROOM PER NIGHT
S: £50.00 - £60.00
D: £70.00 - £85.00

Victorian house near beach, harbour and town. All rooms have en suite, modern kitchen/dining area. Some rooms with sea views. Free Wi-Fi TV/VCR/Freeview, Fairtrade tea, coffee & hot chocolate. Excellent full English breakfast. **Directions:** We are situated on the East Cliff, directly behind The Granville Building (the large building with a castle turret that overlooks The Granville Cinema). **Bedrooms:** 3 double, 1 twin, 2 family **Open:** All year

Payment: **Leisure:** **Property:** **Children:** **Catering:** **Room:**

For **key to symbols** see page 7

ROYAL TUNBRIDGE WELLS, Kent Map ref 2D2 SatNav TN4 9SS

Badgers End Bed & Breakfast

47 Thirlmere Road, Royal Tunbridge Wells, Kent TN4 9SS **T:** (01892) 533176

B&B PER ROOM PER NIGHT
S: £30.00 - £35.00
D: £50.00

Modern house in quiet cul-de-sac with large garden backing onto woodland. Close to A26. Full English breakfast. Freeview TV plus broadband. Tea and coffee making facilities. Non smoking establishment throughout. **Directions:** 1.5 miles from Tunbridge Wells station. 1 mile from shopping centre. Varying directions, given upon request. **Bedrooms:** 1 single, 1 double **Open:** All year except Christmas

Leisure: **Property:** **Catering:** **Room:**

ROYAL TUNBRIDGE WELLS, Kent Map ref 2D2 SatNav TN3 9TB

Manor Court Farm Bed & Breakfast

Ashurst Road, Ashurst, Tunbridge Wells, Kent TN3 9TB **T:** (01892) 740279 **F:** 01892 740919
E: julia@stonecross.org
W: www.manorcourtfarm.co.uk

B&B PER ROOM PER NIGHT
S: £47.50 - £50.00
D: £75.00 - £80.00

SPECIAL PROMOTIONS
Reductions for longer and room only stays. Reductions for children.

250 year old farmhouse on 300-acre farm stretching to the banks of the River Medway, in a designated Area of Outstanding Natural Beauty. Spacious comfortable rooms, guest lounge with log fires in winter. Ideal centre for exploring a wealth of historical and leisure attractions in the south-east. London 45-55 mins by train. There are various pets including rabbits, chickens , etc. See Tripadvisor.

Directions: On A264 road 5 miles west of Tunbridge Wells, towards East Grinstead/ Gatwick etc. ½ mile east of Ashurst village, in hamlet of Stone Cross.

Bedrooms: 2 twin, 1 double, each with washbasin, flat screen TV, tea and coffee facilities **Open:** All year except Christmas and New Year

Site: P **Payment:** € **Leisure:** **Property:** **Children:** **Catering:** **Room:**

SHORNE, Kent Map ref 3B3 SatNav DA12 3HB

The Inn on the Lake Hotel

Watling Street, Shorne, Gravesend DA12 3HB **T:** (01474) 823333 **F:** 01474 823175
E: reservations@innonlake.co.uk
W: www.innonlake.co.uk **£ BOOK ONLINE**

enjoyEngland.com ★★ HOTEL

B&B PER ROOM PER NIGHT
S: £59.50 - £69.50
D: £69.50 - £79.50

Set in 12 acres of woodland, the Inn on the Lake offers a friendly and comfortable stay in a modern, family run establishment. We have 80 bedrooms, many of them with direct access to the 2 beautiful lakes, offering en suite bathrooms, television, telephone, tea & coffee making facilities and hairdryer.

Directions: The hotel is situated on the A2 midway between Rochester and Dartford, just past Gravesend.

Bedrooms: 35 dble, 35 twin, 8 family
Open: All year

Site: **Payment:** **Leisure:** **Property:** **Children:** **Catering:** **Room:**

STELLING MINNIS, Kent Map ref 3B4 SatNav CT4 6DE

Great Field Farm B&B

Misling Lane, Stelling Minnis, Canterbury CT4 6DE **T:** (01227) 709223 **F:** 01227 709223
E: greatfieldfarm@aol.com
W: www.great-field-farm.co.uk

enjoyEngland.com ★★★★ FARMHOUSE — enjoyEngland.com Silver AWARD

B&B PER ROOM PER NIGHT
S: £40.00 - £100.00
D: £80.00 - £120.00

Delightful farmhouse set amidst lovely gardens and countryside. Spacious, private suites; B&B or self-catering. Hearty breakfasts with home-grown fruits and eggs. Ten minutes to Canterbury/Channel Tunnel. **Directions:** From M20 exit J11 onto B2068 to Canterbury. Look out for brown B & B signs after about 6 miles. **Bedrooms:** 3 double, 2 twin **Open:** All year

Site: P **Payment:** **Leisure:** **Property:** **Children:** **Room:**

ABINGDON, Oxfordshire Map ref 2C1 SatNav OX14 3BT

The Railway Inn

Station Road, Culham, Abingdon, Oxon OX14 3BT **T:** (01235) 528046 **F:** 01235 525183
E: info@railwayinnculham.co.uk
W: www.railwayinnculham.co.uk

enjoyEngland.com ★★★ INN

B&B PER ROOM PER NIGHT
S: £60.00
D: £78.00
EVENING MEAL PER PERSON
£5.50 - £16.00

Bed and breakfast. Evening meals range from home made pies to steaks. Free house. Cask ales. Free parking. Friendly staff. No Sunday evening meals. **Directions:** A415 2 miles East of Abingdon. Adjacent to main rail, London Paddington to Oxford. Close to A34, M40 and M4. 1 mile from Thames Path. **Bedrooms:** 4 double, 3 twin, 2 family **Open:** All year except Christmas

Site: P **Payment:** **Leisure:** **Property:** **Children:** **Catering:** **Room:**

For **key to symbols** see page 7

ABINGDON-ON-THAMES, Oxfordshire Map ref 2C1 SatNav OX14 2BE B

enjoyEngland.com ★★★★ GUEST HOUSE
enjoyEngland.com Gold AWARD

B&B PER ROOM PER NIGHT
S: £50.00 - £66.00
D: £90.00 - £99.00

Abbey Guest House

136 Oxford Road, Abingdon-on-Thames OX14 2AG T: (01235) 537020 / 07976 627252
F: 01235 537020 E: info@abbeyguest.com
W: www.abbeyguest.com £ BOOK ONLINE

We are a quiet, 'Home from Home', non smoking, multi-award winning, highly accessible B&B, in the historic town of Abingdon-on-Thames. Guests enjoy private parking, excellent bus services and local amenities, Fair Trade items + Free Wi-Fi. **Directions:** Oxford Road is the A4183. Detailed walking & driving directions, and information if travelling by bus, train or plane is available on the website. **Bedrooms:** 7 en suite rooms inc easy access, allergy friendly **Open:** All Year - Add. Chge for Xmas & New Year

WALKERS WELCOME · FAMILIES WELCOME · CYCLISTS WELCOME

Site: P Payment: Property: Children: Catering: Room:

BANBURY, Oxfordshire Map ref 2C1 SatNav OX17 2SQ B

enjoyEngland.com ★★★★ GUEST ACCOMMODATION

B&B PER ROOM PER NIGHT
S: £33.00
D: £66.00

Stone Court

Helmdon Road, Sulgrave, Nr. Banbury, Oxon OX17 2SQ T: (01295) 760818 / 07771 524566
E: ronnie@stonecourtsulgrave.co.uk
W: www.stonecourtsulgrave.co.uk

Stone Court's aim is for you to enjoy your stay whether on a business or leisure visit and offers warm, friendly hospitality with excellent breakfast, catering for all diets. Provides easy access to the Cotswolds, Stratford, Warwick, Oxford, Northampton, Sulgrave Manor, ancestral home of George Washington, plus events at Silverstone, Cropredy, Towcester. **Directions:** 10 mins M40/J11 and 25 mins M1/J15a. **Bedrooms:** 2 cosy en suite rooms on ground floor + 1 family room on 1st floor with private facilities
Open: All year except between 23rd and 31st Dec

Site: P Property: Children: Room:

BICESTER, Oxfordshire Map ref 2C1 SatNav OX26 1TE H

enjoyEngland.com ★★★★ HOTEL

B&B PER ROOM PER NIGHT
S: £85.00 - £169.00
D: £95.00 - £189.00

Bicester Hotel Golf and Spa

Bicester Hotel Golf and Spa, Akerman Street, Chesterton, Bicester, Oxfordshire OX26 1TE
T: (01869) 241204 F: 01869 240754 E: carol.barford@bicesterhgs.com
W: www.bicesterhotelgolfandspa.com £ BOOK ONLINE

A unique, independently run 52 bedroomed hotel with extensive leisure and spa facilities and an 18 hole golf course, set in 134 acres. Close to Bicester Village and other local attractions. **Directions:** Just minutes from J9 of M40 motorway. Direct rail links into London and Birmingham from Bicester North. **Bedrooms:** 19 Standard Double, 13 Standard Twin, 14 Superior Double, 4 Feature Rooms, 2 suite.
Open: All year except Christmas day

Site: P Payment: Leisure: Property: Children: Catering: Room:

CHIPPING NORTON, Oxfordshire Map ref 2C1 SatNav OX7 6DQ B

enjoyEngland.com ★★★★ INN
enjoyEngland.com Silver AWARD

B&B PER ROOM PER NIGHT
S: £90.00 - £120.00
D: £110.00 - £140.00

EVENING MEAL PER PERSON
£11.95 - £21.95

The Lamb Inn

High Street, Shipton under Wychwood, Oxon OX7 6DQ T: (01993) 830465
E: info@shiptonlamb.com
W: www.shiptonlamb.com £ BOOK ONLINE

Perfectly situated for exploring the endless attractions the Cotswolds has to offer, historic towns and villages lie side by side, with pursuits in golf, fishing, riding and walking. Cheltenham Racecourse is only 20 miles away. **Directions:** Just off the A361 about 4 miles northeast of Burford, about 23 miles from Oxford. **Bedrooms:** En suite, TV and tea & coffee facilities **Open:** All year except Christmas

Site: P Payment: Leisure: Property: Children: Catering: Room:

HENLEY-ON-THAMES, Oxfordshire Map ref 2C2 SatNav RG9 3NY

B&B PER ROOM PER NIGHT
S: £95.00
D: £105.00

The Baskerville

Station Road, Lower Shiplake, Henley-on-Thames RG9 3NY T: (01189) 403332
E: enquiries@thebaskerville.com
W: www.thebaskerville.com £ BOOK ONLINE

Quality village pub close to the River Thames and minutes from Henley-on-Thames. Outstanding food with menus that change frequently using fresh local produce. Excellent wine list, cosy, comfortable bar with a good choice of cask-conditioned ales. 50 cover restaurant and a garden with seating for 100.

Directions: From Henley-on-Thames, take Reading road for 2 miles, turn left down Station Road for 0.5 mile. Baskerville is on right after cross roads before station.

Bedrooms: 2 double, 1 twin, 1 family
Open: All year

Site: Payment: Leisure: Property: Children: Catering: Room:

MILTON-UNDER-WYCHWOOD, Oxfordshire Map ref 2B1 SatNav OX7 6JH

B&B PER ROOM PER NIGHT
S: £50.00 - £60.00
D: £70.00 - £80.00

Hillborough House

The Green, Shipton Road, Burford OX7 6JH T: (01993) 832352 F: 01993 832352
E: hillboroughhouse@btinternet.com
W: www.hillboroughhouse.co.uk £ BOOK ONLINE

A Victorian village house with spacious en suite rooms overlooking the green with views to distant hills. You will be assured of a warm welcome and a great breakfast. **Directions:** Please contact us for directions. **Bedrooms:** 1 double, 1 twin, 1 family, all en suite **Open:** All year

Site: Leisure: Property: Children: Catering: Room:

MOULSFORD, Oxfordshire Map ref 2C2 SatNav OX10 9JF

B&B PER ROOM PER NIGHT
S: £75.00
D: £90.00 - £100.00

Beetle & Wedge Boathouse

Ferry Lane, Moulsford, Wallingford OX10 9JF T: (01491) 651381 F: 01491 651376
E: boathouse@beetleandwedge.co.uk
W: www.beetleandwedge.co.uk

Riverside restaurant with rooms offering charming accommodation, delicious food and great wines. Boat hire and picnics also available. **Directions:** Located on the River Thames between Reading and Oxford, 15 minutes from the M4 & M40, convenient for Heathrow. **Bedrooms:** 3 double/twin rooms **Open:** All year

Site: Payment: Leisure: Property: Children: Catering: Room:

OXFORD, Oxfordshire Map ref 2C1 SatNav OX2 8DX B

enjoyEngland.com ★★★ GUEST ACCOMMODATION

B&B PER ROOM PER NIGHT
S: £40.00 - £50.00
D: £60.00 - £70.00

Arden Lodge

34 Sunderland Avenue, Oxford OX2 8DX **T:** (01865) 552076 **F:** 01865 512265
E: ardenlodge34@googlemail.com
W: www.ardenlodgeoxford.co.uk

Arden Lodge is a modern, detached house set in a tree-lined avenue, in one of Oxford's most select areas. It offers 3 attractively furnished bedrooms, with private facilities, colour TV and beverage tray. An excellent base for touring: within easy reach of the Cotswolds, London, Stratford and Warwick. The position is convenient for Oxford City Centre, parks, river, meadows, golf course and country inns, including the world famous Trout Inn as featured in 'Inspector Morse'. Ample parking is available, and there is an excellent bus service, with Oxford City Centre about 10 minutes away.

Directions: Please contact us for directions.

Bedrooms: 1 single, 1 double, 1 twin
Open: All year except Christmas

Site: P **Leisure:** **Property:** **Children:** **Catering:** **Room:**

OXFORD, Oxfordshire Map ref 2C1 SatNav OX1 3AP B

enjoyEngland.com ★★★★ GUEST ACCOMMODATION

B&B PER ROOM PER NIGHT
S: £69.00 - £115.00
D: £99.00 - £149.00

The Buttery

11 Broad Street, Oxford OX1 3AP **T:** (01865) 811950 **F:** 01865 811951
E: enquiries@thebutteryhotel.co.uk
W: www.thebutteryhotel.co.uk **£ BOOK ONLINE**

Set on Broad Street, surrounded by historic Oxford colleges and museums, The Buttery welcomes you to explore the wonders of Oxford from its central location. Spacious well-furnished en suite rooms. **Directions:** Please contact us for directions.
Bedrooms: 1 single, 9 double, 3 twin, 3 family **Open:** All year

Payment: **Property:** **Children:** **Catering:** **Room:**

OXFORD, Oxfordshire Map ref 2C1 SatNav OX2 7PL B

enjoyEngland.com ★★★★ GUEST ACCOMMODATION

B&B PER ROOM PER NIGHT
S: £69.00 - £85.00
D: £110.00 - £150.00

Cotswold House

363 Banbury Road, Oxford OX2 7PL **T:** (01865) 310558 **F:** 08721 107068
E: d.r.walker@talk21.com
W: www.cotswoldhouse.co.uk **£ BOOK ONLINE**

A well-situated and elegant property, offering excellent accommodation and service. Cotswold House is in a most desirable part of Oxford. Free parking and Wi-Fi. **Directions:** Exit Oxford ring road on North side, following sign to Summertown. We are half a mile on right as you head towards city centre. **Bedrooms:** 2 single, 2 double, 1 twin, 2 family, 1 deluxe suite **Open:** All year

Site: P **Payment:** **Property:** **Children:** 3 **Room:**

OXFORD, Oxfordshire Map ref 2C1 SatNav OX2 6JP H

Cotswold Lodge Hotel

66A Banbury Road, Oxford OX2 6JP **T:** (01865) 512121 **F:** 01865 512490
E: enquiries@cotswoldlodgehotel.co.uk
W: www.cotswoldlodgehotel.co.uk **£ BOOK ONLINE**

enjoyEngland.com ★★★★ HOTEL

enjoyEngland.com Silver AWARD

B&B PER ROOM PER NIGHT
S: £75.00 - £165.00
D: £115.00 - £220.00

EVENING MEAL PER PERSON
£25.00 - £45.00

SPECIAL PROMOTIONS
Dinner, Bed and Breakfast offers from £60.00 - £130.00 pp based on 2 people sharing.

An elegant 4 Star retreat set in a peaceful conservation area 0.5 miles from Oxford's city centre. The hotel is known for its individuality and excellent levels of service. The Restaurant 66A welcomes non-residents for breakfast, lunch and dinner daily. Please contact us for prices.

Directions: Located in North Oxford. 2 minutes drive from A34.

Bedrooms: 6 single, 27 dble, 6 twin, 10 feature room. All rooms en suite, flat screen tv, tea and coffee facilities, toiletries
Open: All year

Site: P **Payment:** **Leisure:** **Property:** **Children:**
Catering: **Room:**

OXFORD, Oxfordshire Map ref 2C1 SatNav OX1 3PG B

Keble College

Parks Road, Oxford OX1 3PG **T:** (01865) 272789 **F:** 01865 272729
E: conference@keble.ox.ac.uk
W: www.keble.ox.ac.uk/conferences **£ BOOK ONLINE**

enjoyEngland.com 3★-4★ CAMPUS ACCOMMODATION

Keble College, one of Oxford's leading college conference venues, offers high quality facilities and service in a unique and beautiful range of historic and modern buildings. Located in the heart of the city, it is the self-contained world of Keble which is the real attraction for conference organisers and delegates. Please contact for 2015 rates.

Victorian architecture and beautiful Quads, tiered lecture theatre seating 250, 200 sqm area for exhibits and refreshments, Victorian Gothic Dining Hall seating up to 300 guests, 245 en suite bedrooms, support of a dedicated Conference Team both before and during your conference, free Wi-Fi in all meeting rooms.

Directions: Keble College is situated on the northern edge of Oxford city centre, just off Banbury Road and the northern end of St Giles. It is directly opposite the Natural History Museum and University Parks.

Bedrooms: Simple comfortable bedrooms that have tea & coffee making facilities, toiletries and internet access. There is a daily housekeeping service
Open: During student vacations

Site: **Property:** **Children:** **Catering:** **Bedroom:**

OXFORD, Oxfordshire Map ref 2C1 SatNav OX1 4PL B

Newton House Guest House B&B Oxford

82-84 Abingdon Road, Oxford OX1 4PL **T:** (01865) 240561 **F:** 01865 244647
E: stay@newtonhouseoxford.co.uk
W: www.newtonhouseoxford.co.uk **£ BOOK ONLINE**

enjoyEngland.com ★★★ GUEST ACCOMMODATION

B&B PER ROOM PER NIGHT
S: £66.00 - £99.00
D: £74.00 - £110.00

SPECIAL PROMOTIONS
Ask about special offers.

Close to Oxford's city centre, on foot, bus, coach, train or car. A perfect opportunity to visit Oxford's university central city attractions, research facilities, museums, hospitals. Family-run with a personal touch, free Wi-Fi, car park, English traditional breakfast, vegetarian and continental. Special diets catered for.

Directions: Situated on A4144 (OX1 4PL) Postal code 1/2 mile (800 mtrs) from the city centre 10 to 15 min walk see us on google maps.

Bedrooms: 8 double, 4 twin, 2 family, all en suite
Open: All year

Site: P **Payment:** £ € **Leisure:** **Property:** **Children:** **Catering:**
Room: TV

OXFORD, Oxfordshire Map ref 2C1 SatNav OX2 6EH B

Park House

7 St Bernards Road, Oxford OX2 6EH **T:** (01865) 310824 **E:** krynpark@hotmail.com

enjoyEngland.com ★★ BED & BREAKFAST

B&B PER ROOM PER NIGHT
S: £40.00 - £45.00
D: £60.00 - £70.00

Traditional Victorian terraced house in north Oxford, ten minutes walk from city centre and within easy reach of all amenities. Friendly and relaxed atmosphere. Single night bookings carry £5 surcharge. **Directions:** Please contact us for directions. **Bedrooms:** 1 single, 2 double **Open:** All year except Christmas

Site: P **Payment:** € **Leisure:** **Property:** **Children:** **Catering:** **Room:** TV

WOODSTOCK, Oxfordshire Map ref 2C1 SatNav OX20 1SY B

The Blenheim Buttery

7 Market Place, Woodstock OX20 1SY **T:** (01993) 813660 **F:** 01993 811212
E: contact@theblenheimbuttery.co.uk
W: www.theblenheimbuttery.co.uk

enjoyEngland.com ★★★★ INN
enjoyEngland.com Silver AWARD

B&B PER ROOM PER NIGHT
S: £59.00 - £125.00
D: £69.00 - £135.00

Comprising of 6 en suite rooms and a ground floor restaurant, The Blenheim Buttery offers clean and comfortable accommodation refurbished to reflect the traditional charm and warmth of this 17th century building. Latest check-in is at 8pm. **Directions:** Please see our website for directions. **Bedrooms:** 6 en suite- 4 double, 2 twin
Open: All year

Site: **Property:** **Children:** **Catering:** **Room:** TV

WOODSTOCK, Oxfordshire Map ref 2C1 SatNav OX20 1HT B

enjoyEngland.com ★★★★ INN

B&B PER ROOM PER NIGHT
S: £67.50 - £100.00
D: £85.00 - £140.00
EVENING MEAL PER PERSON
£9.95 - £25.00

The Duke of Marlborough

A44 Woodleys, Woodstock, Oxford OX20 1HT **T:** (01993) 811460 **F:** 01993 810165
E: sales@dukeofmarlborough.co.uk
W: www.dukeofmarlborough.co.uk

Family-run and friendly and well known locally for its good food. Situated close to Woodstock. Nearby Blenheim Palace and Oxford. Ideally situated for exploring the surrounding countryside. **Directions:** We are positioned on the A44 Oxford to Stratford road just 2 mile north of Woodstock at the junction with the B4437. **Bedrooms:** 4 double, 2 twin, 5 family, 2 suites **Open:** All year

Site: P **Leisure:** **Property:** **Children:** **Catering:** **Room:**

WOODSTOCK, Oxfordshire Map ref 2C1 SatNav OX29 8HQ B

enjoyEngland.com ★★★ GUEST HOUSE

B&B PER ROOM PER NIGHT
S: £35.00
D: £50.00

SPECIAL PROMOTIONS
Please add £5 on top of above prices for breakfast.

Shepherds Hall

Witney Road, Freeland, Witney OX29 8HQ **T:** (01993) 881256 **F:** 01993 883455
W: www.shepherdshall.co.uk

Well-appointed licensed guest house offering excellent Bed and Breakfast accommodation. All rooms en suite. Ideally situated for Oxford, Woodstock, Blenheim Palace and the Cotswolds.

Directions: About 18 miles north west of Oxford on the A4095 Woodstock to Witney road, just outside the village of Long Hanborough.

Bedrooms: 1 single, 2 double, 2 twin
Open: All year except Christmas

Site: P **Payment:** **Property:** **Children:** **Catering:** **Room:**

GUILDFORD, Surrey Map ref 2D2 SatNav GU1 4SB B

enjoyEngland.com ★★★★ HOSTEL

B&B PER ROOM PER NIGHT
S: £47.59 - £55.15

Guildford YMCA

Bridge Street, Guildford, Surrey GU1 4SB **T:** (01483) 532555 **F:** 01483 537161
E: accom@guildfordymca.org.uk
W: www.guildfordymca.org.uk

Guildford YMCA offers excellent value for money B&B accommodation in central Guildford. It is close to the railway station and features comfortable en suite bedrooms. Generous breakfasts are prepared by our own team of chefs. **Directions:** Guildford YMCA is diagonally opposite the railway station across the main road and accessed by an underpass beneath the road. **Bedrooms:** Single en suites, some twin rooms available **Open:** All year

Payment: **Property:** **Children:** **Catering:** **Bedroom:**

ARUNDEL, Sussex Map ref 2D3 SatNav RH20 1PA

The Barn at Penfolds

The Street, Bury, West Sussex RH20 1PA **T:** (01798) 831496
E: susiemacnamara@hotmail.co.uk
W: www.thebarnatpenfolds.co.uk

B&B PER ROOM PER NIGHT
S: £55.00
D: £70.00 - £85.00

The accommodation comprises two double rooms in the main house, a double and a single in the thatched-roof barn as well as a double in the Shepherds Hut. All rooms en suite. Use of the garden room for breakfast and relaxation. Our own chickens provide the eggs for breakfast. **Directions:** Just off the A29. From Arundel turn right past the Squire & Horse, 300 yards, turn left. From Pulborough turn left after Turners garage. **Bedrooms:** 3 double rooms
Open: All year

Site: P **Payment:** € **Property:** **Children:** 12 **Catering:** **Room:**

BATTLE (4.7 MILES), Sussex Map ref 3B4 SatNav TN32 5SG

Woodside Luxury B&B, Spa and Glamping

Woodside, Junction Road, Staplecross, Robertsbridge, Nr Rye and Battle TN32 5SG
T: (01580) 830903 **F:** 0844 804 0390 **E:** reservations@woodsidebandb.com
W: www.luxuryaccommodationsussex.com / www.yurtandbreakfast.co.uk; www.woodsidebandb.com **£ BOOK ONLINE**

B&B PER ROOM PER NIGHT
S: £70.00 - £95.00
D: £110.00 - £175.00

SPECIAL PROMOTIONS
Private Health Suite £10pp; See websites for Beauty and Spa therapies, glamping/group prices, catering. We also offer 2 self catering apartments 8 minutes drive away see www.robertsbridgeretreat.com

Luxury B&B set in 10 acres of gardens, paddock and ancient bluebell woods. WOW factor suites, en suite bathrooms bath + shower; 3 x luxury themed Yurts 7 x Bell Tents/Tipis. Health Suite/Beauty Spa + massage therapies. Home Cinema (9ft screen). Award winning breakfast. Licensed. Marquee available. Aim to pamper our guests. In AONB near National Trust/English Heritage properties. 15 mins to coast/beach.

Directions: Please see our websites which will produce a bespoke route and map from your home. 1 hour car/train from London/M25; 15 minutes drive to Coast/Beaches (Hastings/Camber Sands); 5 minutes Bodiam Castle.

Bedrooms: 1 Italian King suite; 1 7ft waterbed suite (+singles for family); yurt with 7ft round bed; 2 group yurts 7 tipis/bell tents with double bed + futons
Open: All year

Site: P **Payment:** £ € **Leisure:** **Property:** **Children:** **Catering:** **Room:**

BEXHILL-ON-SEA, Sussex Map ref 3B4 SatNav TN39 4TT

The Cooden Beach Hotel

Cooden Sea Road, Bexhill-on-Sea, East Sussex TN39 4TT **T:** (01424) 842281
F: 01424 846142 **E:** rooms@thecoodenbeachhotel.co.uk
W: www.thecoodenbeachhotel.co.uk

Set directly on the beach, Beachside Restaurant with sea views. The Cooden Tavern, good food served all day with daily specials board all prepared in open kitchen. Seasonal Beachside Bar and Terrace with summer alfresco dining. 5 events and conference rooms, wedding specialists with license for all wedding both inside and in the gardens. From £60 bed and breakfast per person per night. **Bedrooms:** 41 en suite bedrooms, some with sea views
Open: All year

Site: P **Payment:** £ **Leisure:** **Property:** **Children:** **Catering:** **Room:**

BEXHILL-ON-SEA, Sussex Map ref 3B4 SatNav TN40 2HH B

enjoyEngland.com ★★★★ GUEST ACCOMMODATION

B&B PER ROOM PER NIGHT
S: £35.00 - £45.00
D: £65.00 - £90.00

Eve's Bed & Breakfast

20 Hastings Road, Bexhill-on-Sea, East Sussex TN40 2HH **T:** (01424) 733268
E: evesbandb@gmail.com
W: www.evesbandb.co.uk

Bexhill's Old Town is a gentle stroll from our friendly, family run Victorian 4 star B&B. We have 5 en suite bedrooms (2 double, 3 family, single occupancy available) that are spacious but cosy for you to relax in. Special offers available. **Bedrooms:** Ground floor room with wet room available. **Open:** All year

Site: P **Payment:** **Property:** **Children:** **Catering:** **Room:**

BOGNOR REGIS, Sussex Map ref 2C3 SatNav PO22 7AH H

enjoyEngland.com ★★★ HOTEL

B&B PER ROOM PER NIGHT
S: £56.00 - £101.00
D: £77.00 - £122.00
HB PER PERSON PER NIGHT
£61.50 - £84.50

Best Western Beachcroft Hotel

Clyde Road, Felpham, Bognor Regis PO22 7AH **T:** (01243) 827142
F: 01243 863500 **E:** reservations@beachcroft-hotel.co.uk
W: www.beachcroft-hotel.co.uk **£ BOOK ONLINE**

Situated on seafront in Felpham village, within 0.5 miles of restaurants, shops, pubs, tennis, putting. En suite bedrooms with telephone, TV, hospitality tray. Renowned restaurant, indoor heated pool. Within ten miles Chichester Cathedral and theatre, Arundel Castle and Goodwood horse-racing. Seven golf courses. **Directions:** Signposted from A29 in both directions, follow signs to Felpham Village & brown bed signs until Beachcroft hotel sign. **Bedrooms:** 2 single, 16 dble, 12 twin, 4 family **Open:** All year

Site: **Payment:** **Leisure:** **Property:** **Children:** **Catering:** **Room:**

BOGNOR REGIS, Sussex Map ref 2C3 SatNav PO22 7AH B

enjoyEngland.com ★★★★ GUEST ACCOMMODATION

B&B PER ROOM PER NIGHT
S: £45.00 - £50.00
D: £75.00 - £80.00

White Horses Bed & Breakfast

Clyde Road, Felpham, Bognor Regis, West Sussex PO22 7AH **T:** (01243) 824320
E: whitehorsesbandb@btinternet.com
W: www.whitehorsesfelpham.co.uk

White Horses is located in a quiet cul-de-sac overlooking the sea and Felpham beach. A modernised flint and brick house offering quality accommodation. A 3 mile promenade adjacent affords easy sea-side walking. **Directions:** Please see website. **Bedrooms:** En suite, flat screen TV, hairdryer & tea/coffee tray **Open:** All year

WALKERS WELCOME CYCLISTS WELCOME **Site:** P **Payment:** € **Leisure:** **Property:** **Children:** **Room:**

BOGNOR REGIS, Sussex Map ref 2C3 SatNav PO22 9AG B

enjoyEngland.com ★★★★ GUEST ACCOMMODATION

B&B PER ROOM PER NIGHT
S: £40.00
D: £70.00

Willow Rise

131 North Bersted Street, Bognor Regis, West Sussex PO22 9AG
T: (01243) 829544 / 07713 427224 **E:** gillboon@aol.com

Willow rise is a comfortable family B&B built in the 1930's with panoramic views of the south downs and Goodwood. Situated in a conservation area on the outskirts of the town, with execellent access to all amenities. **Directions:** Follow the A259 from Chichester to Bognor Regis, Turn left at Royal Oak Public House into North Bersted Street. Continue along, B&B on left hand side. **Bedrooms:** En suite twin room and double room with private bathroom **Open:** All Year excluding Christmas and New Year

Site: P **Payment:** **Leisure:** **Property:** **Children:** **Catering:** **Room:**

For **key to symbols** see page 7

BOGNOR REGIS, Sussex Map ref 2C3 SatNav PO22 7EG

B&B PER ROOM PER NIGHT
S: £60.00 - £75.00
D: £70.00 - £95.00

Willow Tree Cottage B&B

35 Bereweeke Road, Felpham, Bognor Regis, West Sussex PO22 7EG **T:** (01243) 828000
E: bookings@willowtreecottage.org.uk
W: www.willowtreecottage.org.uk

Minutes from the sea and the busy little village of Felpham, you'll find a warm welcome, a peaceful stay and sumptuous breakfasts. The homely accommodation ensures your stay is undisturbed by other guests. **Directions:** From the centre of Felpham Village head towards the Fox Public House & go down Blakes Road, take the first turn left to the end of Bereweeke Rd. **Bedrooms:** 1 king-sized double room and 1 twin bedded room **Open:** All year except Christmas and New Year

Site: P **Property:** **Catering:** **Room:**

BRIGHTON, Sussex Map ref 2D3 SatNav BN2 1TL

B&B PER ROOM PER NIGHT
D: £85.00 - £295.00

Amsterdam Hotel

11-12 Marine Parade, Brighton BN2 1TL **T:** (01273) 688825 **F:** 01273 688828
E: info@amsterdam.uk.com
W: www.amsterdam.uk.com **£ BOOK ONLINE**

Hotel with modern, fully equipped rooms, bar, restaurant and sun terrace. The hotel is in a prime location on Brighton's seafront and everyone is welcome. **Directions:** Hotel is situated on Brighton Sea front opposite The Palace Pier. **Bedrooms:** 21 double, 3 twin, 1 suite **Open:** All year

Site: **Payment:** **Leisure:** **Property:** **Catering:** **Room:**

BRIGHTON, Sussex Map ref 2D3 SatNav BN2 9JA

BED ONLY PER NIGHT
£15.00 - £80.00

Kipps Brighton

76 Grand Parade, Brighton BN2 9JA **T:** (01273) 604182 **E:** kippshostelbrighton@gmail.com
W: www.kipps-brighton.com **£ BOOK ONLINE**

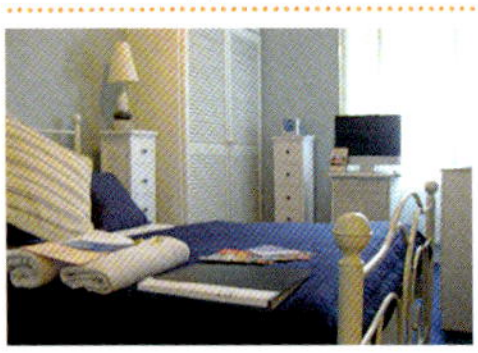

Award winning hostel situated in the heart of Brighton. We offer private rooms as well as dormitory rooms. Excellent facilities, including a self catering kitchen, lounge & outside patio. Views overlooking the historic Royal Pavillion. **Directions:** We are situated in the centre of Brighton. Visit our website to print off a map. **Bedrooms:** 1 single, 6 doubles, 4 twins, & dormitory rooms **Open:** All year

Site: **Payment:** € **Leisure:** **Property:** **Catering:** **Room:** **Bedroom:**

CHICHESTER, Sussex Map ref 2C3 SatNav PO19 7HW

B&B PER ROOM PER NIGHT
S: £45.00
D: £65.00

The Cottage

22B Westhampnett Road, Chichester, W. Sussex PO19 7HW **T:** (01243) 774979
E: thecottagechichester@gmail.com
W: www.chichester-bedandbreakfast.co.uk

Just off the A27. A short walk from the town centre with its Cathedral, cinema, bowling, shops, rail & bus stations, restaurants & pubs. Goodwoods Festival of Speed & Revival, Airfield, golfing & horse racing. The Tangmere Aviation Museum. **Directions:** Westhampnett Road is located on the eastern side of Chichester and is close to Portfield Retail park and Goodwood just off the A27. **Bedrooms:** 1 double, 1 twin with complimentary tea tray, TV **Open:** All year except Christmas and New Year

Site: P **Property:** **Children:** **Catering:** **Room:**

CHICHESTER, Sussex Map ref 2C3 SatNav PO19 1PX B

George Bell House

4 Canon Lane, Chichester, West Sussex PO19 1PX T: (01243) 813586
E: bookings@chichestercathedral.org.uk
W: www.chichestercathedral.org.uk / www.cathedralenterprises.co.uk

enjoyEngland.com ★★★★ GUEST ACCOMMODATION

B&B PER ROOM PER NIGHT
S: £79.00
D: £117.00 - £138.00

SPECIAL PROMOTIONS
Winter Break Offer- 40% discount on room rates in January & February 2015 then 30% discount on room rates from 1st March - 12th April 2015 (not including breakfast)

George Bell House is a beautifully restored eight bedroom house situated in the historic precincts of Chichester Cathedral. All bedrooms are en suite and offer stunning views of the Cathedral or gardens. Breakfast is available in the dining room of the house which looks out over the private, walled garden. Free Wi-Fi and parking are available. Rooms are to be booked in advance.

Directions: Turn though the archway into Canon Lane off South Street and George Bell House is the last house on the left before the next archway.

Bedrooms: 4 x large double / twins, 3 x standard doubles & 1 x single room with disabled access. All rooms en suite with tea & coffee facilities
Open: All Year excluding Christmas and New Year

Site: P Payment: Property: Children: Catering: Room:

CHICHESTER, Sussex Map ref 2C3 SatNav PO18 8HL H

Millstream Hotel

Bosham Lane, Bosham Nr Chichester, West Sussex PO18 8HL T: (01243) 573234
F: 01243 573459 E: info@millstreamhotel.com
W: www.millstreamhotel.com £ BOOK ONLINE

enjoyEngland.com ★★★ HOTEL

B&B PER ROOM PER NIGHT
S: £99.00 - £139.00
D: £159.00 - £229.00
EVENING MEAL PER PERSON
£35.50

This charming English country hotel is situated in picturesque Bosham, just 4 miles west of Chichester. The bright and airy en suite bedrooms are all individually decorated. The Millstream Restaurant serves modern British cuisine and has 2 AA Rosettes. Alternatively, Marwick's Brasserie provides a contemporary and relaxed eating environment. Guests can enjoy afternoon tea in the gardens or lounge.

Bedrooms: Bedrooms are individually decorated, en suite, with fresh milk and water in the fridge, tea & coffee making facilities and dressing gowns
Open: All Year

Site: P Payment: Property: Catering: Room:

EASTBOURNE, Sussex Map ref 2D3 SatNav BN21 4EE

Best Western Lansdowne Hotel

King Edward's Parade, Eastbourne BN21 4EE **T:** (01323) 725174
F: 01323 739721 **E:** sales@lansdowne-hotel.co.uk
W: www.bw-lansdownehotel.co.uk **£ BOOK ONLINE**

Traditional, privately owned seafront hotel overlooking the Western Lawns. Theatres, shops and conference centre nearby. Elegant lounges and foyer facing sea. Lunchtime bar and lounge menu. Traditional lunch on Sunday. Lock-up garages.

Directions: M23/A23/A27, A22 London or A259 from channel ports. Hotel at west end of seafront facing Western Lawns.

Bedrooms: 29 single, 42 double, 23 twin, 8 family
Open: All year

Payment: **Leisure:** **Property:** **Children:** **Catering:**
Room:

★★★ HOTEL

B&B PER ROOM PER NIGHT
S: £45.00
D: £75.00 - £154.00

EVENING MEAL PER PERSON
£24.95

SPECIAL PROMOTIONS
Golf breaks, Christmas, New Year and Easter programme also available.

EASTBOURNE, Sussex Map ref 3B4 SatNav BN21 4DH

Cavendish Hotel

Grand Parade, Eastbourne, East Sussex BN21 4DH **T:** (01323) 410222 **F:** 01323 410941
E: info@cavendishhotel.co.uk
W: www.cavendishhotel.co.uk

A large 4* hotel on the English South Coast, stylish and unpretentious, elegant but relaxed. En suite bedrooms and fine dining complemented by the welcoming friendly and professional service. **Directions:** Located in Eastbourne on the South Coast, regular trains from London Victoria, Gatwick Airport is 43 miles away and good road links from M25. **Bedrooms:** 23 single, 27 dble, 64 twin, 5 suite **Open:** All year

Site: P **Payment:** **Leisure:** **Property:** **Children:** **Catering:**
Room:

★★★★ HOTEL — Silver Award

B&B PER ROOM PER NIGHT
S: £58.00 - £107.00
D: £99.00 - £168.00

EVENING MEAL PER PERSON
£18.95 - £23.00

GATWICK, Sussex *Map ref 2D2* — *SatNav RH6 7DS* B

Southbourne Guest House Gatwick

34 Massetts Road, Horley RH6 7DS **T:** (01293) 771991 **F:** 01293 820112
E: reservations@southbournegatwick.com
W: wwww.southbournegatwick.com **£ BOOK ONLINE**

enjoyEngland.com ★★★★ GUEST ACCOMMODATION — enjoyEngland.com Silver AWARD

B&B PER ROOM PER NIGHT
S: £49.00 - £60.00
D: £69.00 - £80.00

A warm welcome awaits you in our family-run guesthouse. Ideally located for Gatwick Airport, and exploring Surrey, Sussex and London. Five minutes walk from Horley train station, restaurants, shops and pubs and 30 minutes by train from London. Five minutes drive from Gatwick with free courtesy transport from 0930-2130.

Directions: M23 jct 9, follow the A23 through 3 roundabouts. At 3rd roundabout take 3rd exit and continue to the 2nd right-hand turn into Massetts Road.

Bedrooms: 2 single, 3 double, 3 twin, 4 family
Open: All year

Site: **Payment:** **Property:** **Children:** **Catering:** **Room:**

HASTINGS, Sussex *Map ref 3B4* — *SatNav TN37 6DB* B

Seaspray Bed and Breakfast

54 Eversfield Place, St. Leonards-on-Sea, Hastings TN37 6DB **T:** (01424) 436583
E: jo@seaspraybb.co.uk
W: www.seaspraybb.co.uk **£ BOOK ONLINE**

enjoyEngland.com ★★★★ GUEST ACCOMMODATION — enjoyEngland.com Silver AWARD

B&B PER ROOM PER NIGHT
S: £30.00 - £45.00
D: £65.00 - £85.00

Seafront extra special home from home. High standard refurbishment. Quiet location 5mins to amenities. Superking, Wi-Fi, plasma Freeview, fridge. Complimentary parking. Extensive breakfast menu, all diets catered. Silver award. **Directions:** M25 jct 5 onto A21 Hastings. Follow signs to seafront to A259. Located on promenade 100m west of pier. **Bedrooms:** 3 single, 3 double, 3 twin, 1 family **Open:** March-end November

Site: P **Leisure:** **Property:** **Children:** **Catering:** **Room:**

HAYWARDS HEATH, Sussex *Map ref 2D3* — *SatNav RH16 1JH* B

The Old Forge

16 Lucastes Avenue, Haywards Heath RH16 1JH **T:** (01444) 451905 / 07884 408618
F: 01444 451905 **E:** rowlandandhelen@hotmail.com

enjoyEngland.com ★★★ BED & BREAKFAST

B&B PER ROOM PER NIGHT
S: £40.00 - £50.00
D: £65.00 - £75.00

The Old Forge is a charming, late-Victorian home set in delightful conservation area within easy reach of the mainline station. Friendly owners, warm welcome. Delicious cooked breakfast. Centrally heated rooms with TV. Wi-fi access. **Directions:** Please contact us for directions. **Bedrooms:** 2 double en suite rooms, plus attic room for children **Open:** All year except Christmas

Site: P **Property:** **Children:** **Room:**

HENFIELD, Sussex Map ref 2D3 SatNav BN5 9RQ B

No1 The Laurels B&B

1 The Laurels, Martyn Close, Henfield, West Sussex BN5 9RQ **T:** (01273) 493518
E: bookings@no1thelaurels.co.uk
W: www.no1thelaurels.co.uk

B&B PER ROOM PER NIGHT
S: £42.50 - £50.00
D: £75.00 - £90.00

A detached house faced with traditional knapped Sussex flint stones. Comfortable rooms, a warm welcome, easy access to Brighton. Many places of interest nearby. **Directions:** Please refer to website. **Bedrooms:** 1 single, 2 double and 1 twin **Open:** All year

Site: P **Payment:** **Property:** **Children:** **Catering:** **Room:**

LEWES, Sussex Map ref 2D3 SatNav BN7 1UW H

Pelham House

St. Andrews Lane, Lewes, East Sussex BN7 1UW **T:** (01273) 488600 **F:** 01273 470377
E: reservations@pelhamhouse.com
W: www.pelhamhouse.com **£ BOOK ONLINE**

B&B PER ROOM PER NIGHT
S: £69.00 - £179.00
D: £79.00 - £319.00
EVENING MEAL PER PERSON
£15.00 - £30.00

Pelham House Hotel in Lewes is a beautiful 16th century town house hotel near Brighton in East Sussex, that has been exquisitely restored to create a stylish venue, which combines elegance and history. **Directions:** We're located just off the main high street in Lewes, East Sussex. Please feel free to contact us on 01273 488 600 for further information. **Bedrooms:** En suite, tea & coffee, free wifi, Ipod docking **Open:** All year

Property: **Room:**

PETWORTH, Sussex Map ref 2D3 SatNav RH20 1PQ B

Stane House

Bignor, Pulborough, West Sussex RH20 1PQ **T:** (01798) 869454
E: angie@stanehouse.co.uk
W: www.stanehouse.co.uk

B&B PER ROOM PER NIGHT
S: £65.00
D: £80.00

B&B in one of the most beautiful and peaceful parts of Sussex. Country house set in 1 acre of formal garden. Lovely Downland views. Walks (inc. South Downs Way & W. Sussex Literary Trail). Pubs nearby, Coast 20mins, Chichester 30mins. **Directions:** From A29 turn opposite Squire & Horse pub & follow signs to Bignor Roman Villa. House just beyond. From A285 just south of Petworth follow Villa signs. **Bedrooms:** Quality en suite facilities, tea & coffee making and TV **Open:** All year except Christmas and New Year

Site: P **Property:** **Catering:** **Room:**

RINGMER, Sussex Map ref 2D3 SatNav BN8 5RU B

Bryn Clai

Uckfield Road (A26), Ringmer, Lewes BN8 5RU **T:** (01273) 814042
E: daphne@brynclai.co.uk
W: www.brynclai.co.uk **£ BOOK ONLINE**

B&B PER ROOM PER NIGHT
S: £65.00 - £80.00
D: £80.00 - £90.00

Set in seven acres with beautiful garden. Parking. Comfortable interior. Large bedrooms (ground-floor rooms), views over farmland. Walking distance country pub with excellent food. Glyndebourne, South Downs and Brighton nearby. **Directions:** From A26, 2 miles north of Lewes, 5 miles south of Uckfield. **Bedrooms:** 1 double, 1 twin, 2 family **Open:** All year

Site: P **Payment:** **Leisure:** **Property:** **Children:** **Catering:** **Room:**

RYE, Sussex Map ref 3B4 SatNav TN31 7DB B

enjoyEngland.com ★★★★ GUEST HOUSE

B&B PER ROOM PER NIGHT
S: £60.00 - £79.00
D: £79.00 - £115.00

Old Borough Arms

The Strand, Rye, East Sussex TN31 7DB **T:** (01797) 222128 **E:** info@oldborougharms.co.uk
W: www.oldborougharms.co.uk

There are nine tastefully decorated en suite rooms at The Old Borough Arms which is located in the heart of Rye. Clean and comfortable rooms and an excellent breakfast are guaranteed. Free Wi-Fi throughout the building. **Directions:** We are located at the foot of the famous Mermaid Street in the centre of the historic town of Rye. **Bedrooms:** 1 single, 6 double, 1 twin, 1 family
Open: All year

Site: **Payment:** **Leisure:** **Property:** **Children:** **Catering:**
Room:

RYE, Sussex Map ref 3B4 SatNav TN31 7EL H

enjoyEngland.com ★★★ HOTEL

B&B PER ROOM PER NIGHT
S: £60.00 - £85.00
D: £80.00 - £110.00
HB PER PERSON PER NIGHT
£58.50 - £73.50

The River Haven Hotel

Quayside, Winchelsea Road, Rye TN31 7EL **T:** (01797) 227982 **F:** 01797 227983
E: info@riverhaven.co.uk
W: www.riverhaven.co.uk **£ BOOK ONLINE**

Family-run hotel with restaurant. English breakfast, flat screen Freeview TVs, en suite bathrooms. Standard, superior & garden rooms with river views. Special breaks. Disability-friendly. Large car park free parking for guests. **Directions:** From Channel Ports & London M20 to exit 10 to Brenzett. Take A259 to Rye and follow ring road. Hotel is adjacent to the Quay. **Bedrooms:** 13 dble, 3 twin, 6 family **Open:** All year except Christmas

Site: **Payment:** **Leisure:** **Property:** **Children:** **Catering:** **Room:**

RYE, Sussex Map ref 3B4 SatNav TN31 7LD H

enjoyEngland.com ★★★ TOWN HOUSE HOTEL
enjoyEngland.com Gold AWARD

B&B PER ROOM PER NIGHT
D: £130.00 - £250.00

SPECIAL PROMOTIONS
Champagne Celebreak! One night stay in the Champagne room with fruit, flowers, chocolates and Champagne in your room and enjoy dinner at the famous Mermaid Inn. The cost is £295.00.

Rye Lodge Hotel

Hilders Cliff, Rye, East Sussex TN31 7LD **T:** (01797) 223838 **F:** 01797 223585
E: info@ryelodge.co.uk
W: www.ryelodge.co.uk **£ BOOK ONLINE**

Staying at Rye Lodge is always an enjoyable experience at any time of the year. The surroundings are elegant, the atmosphere relaxed - and the service second to none! Luxurious rooms and suites furnished to the highest standards with all the little extras that make such a difference. Room Service. Champagne Bar and Terrace, Leisure Centre with swimming pool and Sauna.
Private car park.

Directions: Please contact for directions.

Bedrooms: All rooms en suite with shower or bath
Open: All year

Site: P **Payment:** **Leisure:** **Property:** **Children:** **Catering:**
Room:

Don't Miss...

Buckingham Palace

London, SW1A 1AA
(020) 7766 7300
www.royalcollection.org.uk
Buckingham Palace is the office and London residence of Her Majesty The Queen. It is one of the few working royal palaces remaining in the world today. The State Rooms are used extensively by The Queen and Members of the Royal Family and during August and September, when The Queen makes her annual visit to Scotland, the Palace's nineteen state rooms are open to visitors.

Houses of Parliament

Westminster, London SW1A 0AA
020 7219 4565
www.parliament.uk/visiting
Tours of the Houses of Parliament offer a unique combination of one thousand years of history, modern day politics, and stunning art and architecture. Visit the Queen's Robing Room, the Royal Gallery and the Commons Chamber, scene of many lively debates.

Madame Tussauds

Marylebone Road, London, NW1 5LR
(0871) 894 3000
www.madametussauds.com/London/
Experience the legendary history, glitz and glamour of Madame Tussauds London. Visit the 14 exciting, interactive zones and the amazing Marvel Super Heroes 4D movie experience. Strike a pose with your favourite movie star, enjoy an audience with the Queen or plant a cheeky kiss on Prince Harry's cheek.

National Gallery

Westminster WC2N 5DN
(020) 7747 2888
www.nationalgallery.org.uk
The National Gallery houses one of the greatest collections of Western European painting in the world. Discover inspiring art by Botticelli, Caravaggio, Leonardo da Vinci, Monet, Raphael, Rembrandt, Titian, Vermeer and Van Gogh.

Natural History Museum

Kensington and Chelsea SW7 5BD
(020) 7942 5000
www.nhm.ac.uk
The Natural History Museum reveals how the jigsaw of life fits together. Animal, vegetable or mineral, the best of our planet's most amazing treasures are here for you to see - for free.

London

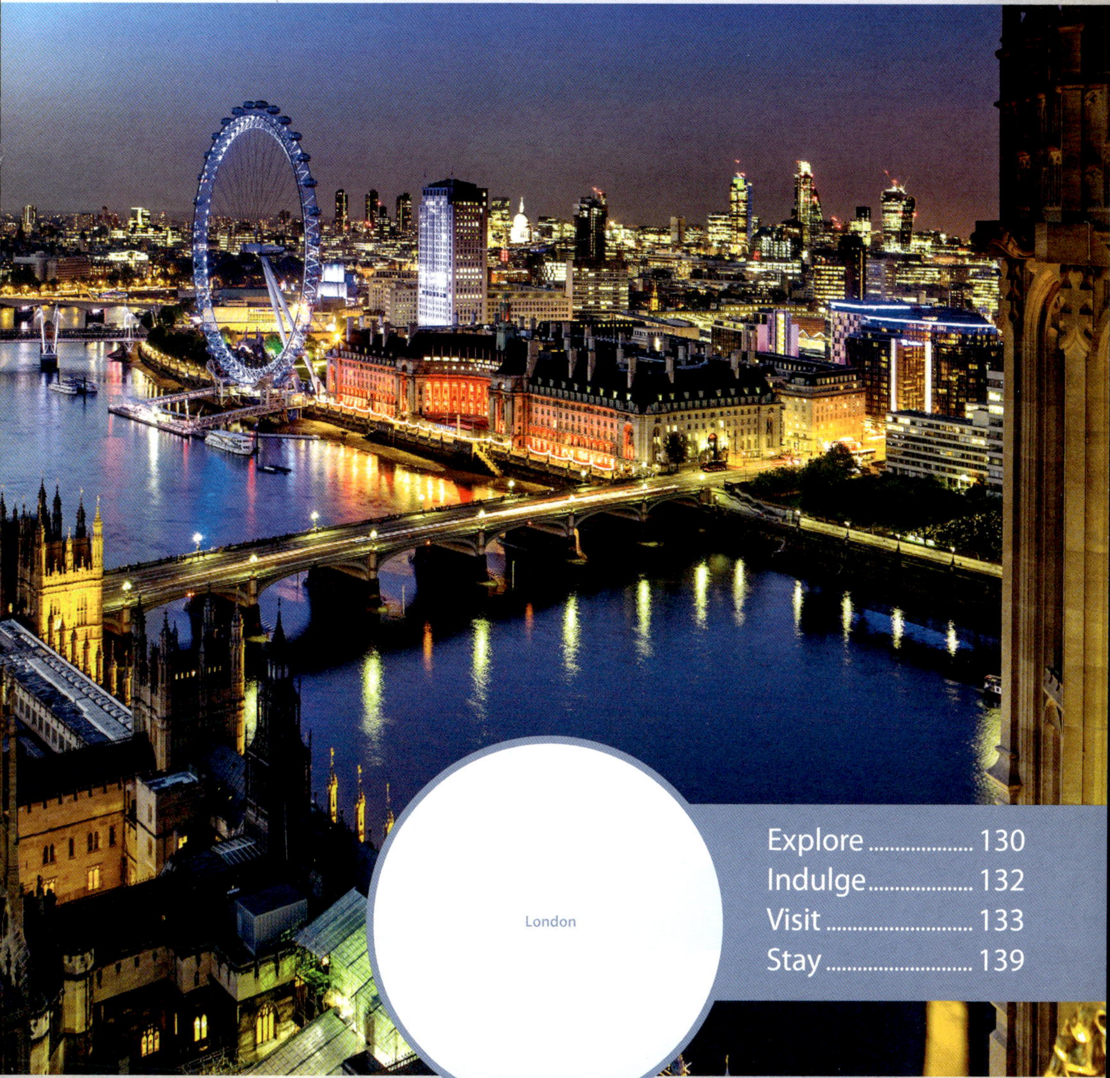

Grand landmarks, gorgeous gardens, spectacular shopping, exciting attractions, museums, galleries, theatres, sporting venues and all the buzz and history of the capital - London's treasures are beyond measure. A single trip is never enough and you'll find yourself returning time and again to take in the many unforgettable sights and experiences on offer.

Explore – London

In the Central/West End area the most visited sights are the now public rooms of Buckingham Palace, the National Gallery in Trafalgar Square, Tate Britain on Millbank, Westminster Abbey, Houses of Parliament and Cabinet War Rooms.

Hotspot: Watch the Changing the Guard ceremony at Buckingham Palace for an impressive display of British pomp and ceremony at 11.30am every day.

Westminster Abbey, nearly a thousand years old, has tombs of many English kings, queens, statesmen and writers. The British Museum in Bloomsbury houses one of the world's largest selections of antiquities, including the Magna Carta, the Elgin Marbles and the first edition of Alice in Wonderland. This entire area can be well viewed from The London Eye on the South Bank.

No visit to London is complete without a spot of shopping. Head for bustling Oxford Street and the stylish shops on Regent Street and Bond Street, or check out the trendy boutiques around Carnaby Street.

For entertainment, enjoy a wide range of theatre, bars, restaurants and culture in Covent Garden and don't forget to take in a musical or an off-beat play and the amazing nightime atmosphere around Leicester Square. Madame Tussauds features all your favourite celebrities and super heroes, or if you fancy an historical fright, visit the London Dungeon near Tower Bridge or explore the streets of old London on a Jack the Ripper tour.

London's parks are its lungs. St James, the oldest, was founded by Henry VIII in 1532. Hyde Park, bordering Kensington, Mayfair and Marylebone, is the largest at 630 acres and one of the greatest city parks in the world. You can enjoy any number of outdoor activities, visit the Serpentine Galleries for contemporary art or Speakers' Corner, the most famous location for free speech in the world. Regents Park, with its zoo, lies north of Oxford Circus and was given to the nation by the Prince Regent.

Hotspot: Come face to face with some of the hairiest, scariest, tallest and smallest animals on the planet - right in the heart of the capital at the ZSL London Zoo.
T: (020) 7722 3333
www.zsl.org/zsl-london-zoo

In the North of the capital, trendy Camden is an eclectic mix of intriguing and unique experiences. Locals and visitors alike hunt for vintage treasures in the open air markets at Camden Lock and far-out attire in the alternative shops that line the high street, or spend time celebrity spotting or strolling along Regent's Canal. There's a different kind of food at every turn, from street vendors to swanky sushi restaurants, and Camden is also home to an extraordinary array of bars, live music and arts venues including the Roundhouse.

Heading East, St Pauls Cathedral in the city of London was redesigned by Sir Christopher Wren and the nearby the Tower of London, a medieval fortress dominated by the White Tower and dating from 1097, houses The Crown Jewels, guarded by the famous Beefeaters. Even further East, the Queen Elizabeth Olympic Park is the exciting legacy of the 2012 Olympic Games and is situated at the heart of a new, vibrant East London. The main stadium re-opens in October 2015 for the Rugby World Cup, before being permanently transformed into the national centre for athletics in the UK and the new home of West Ham United Football Club.

To the South East of the capital, Canary Wharf is one of Londons main financial centres and on the south bank, opposite Docklands, attractions include the National Maritime Museum incorporating the Royal Greenwich Observatory, the Cutty Sark and The O2, one of London's premier entertainment venues.

On Saturday 14th November 2015, the 800th Lord Mayors Show will feature a parade of over 6,000 people, military marching bands, acrobats, a procession of decorated floats, a gilded State Coach that the Lord Mayor travels and starts with an RAF flypast. After the procession London's City Guides will be on hand to lead free guided tours of the City's more strange and wonderful corners, and in the evening fireworks will light up the sky over the river. Visit their website for more information. www.lordmayorsshow.org.

Hotspot: The Globe Theatre, Globe Exhibition & Tour and Globe Education seek to further the experience and international understanding of Shakespeare in performance.
www.shakespearesglobe.com

Indulge – London

Relax and take in the breathtaking views of London while you enjoy a glass of chilled champagne on the **London Eye** with a Champagne Experience, perfect for couples and celebrations.
www.londoneye.com

Head to the stunning open-air Vista bar on the rooftop of **The Trafalgar Hotel** for cheeky cocktails. Relax and enjoy the view as you sip on something delicious. 2 Spring Gardens, Trafalgar Square SW1A 2TS www.thetrafalgar.com.

For a well earned pampering, head to the opulent **St Pancras Spa** in the basement of the beautifully renovated St Pancras Renaissance hotel. This subterranean haven has a stunning pool area bedecked in Victorian tiles, steam room, sauna and luxurious treatment rooms offering exotic sounding treatments like Balinese massage and a Creme de Rassoul Moroccan body wrap.
www.stpancrasspa.co.uk

Porters has served mouth watering food in the heart Covent Garden since 1979. World renowned for traditional dinners like Steak and Kidney Pudding and Fisherman's Pie, not to mention the heavenly steamed syrup sponge pudding and homemade ice creams, this is a treat not to be missed.
www.porters.co.uk T: 020 7836 6466

Since its foundation in 1707, **Fortnum & Mason** has been supplying Londoners and visitors with the very finest goods and services. Enjoy a thoroughly delightful English tradition in elegant surroundings with afternoon tea in the Diamond Jubilee Tea Salon.
www.fortnumandmason.com

Attractions with this sign participate in the Visitor Attraction Quality Assurance Scheme.

Apsley House
Westminster W1J 7NT
(020) 7499 5676
www.english-heritage.org.uk/daysout/properties/apsley-house/
This great 18th century town house pays homage to the Duke's dazzling military career, which culminated in his victory at Waterloo in 1815.

Bateaux London Restaurant Cruisers
Westminster WC2N 6NU
(020) 7695 1800
www.bateauxlondon.com
Bateaux London offers lunch and dinner cruises, combining luxury dining, world-class live entertainment and five-star customer care.

The Boat Race
April, Putney Bridge
www.theboatrace.org
Boat crews from the universities of Oxford and Cambridge battle it out on the Thames.

British Museum
Camden WC1B 3DG
(020) 7323 8299
www.britishmuseum.org.uk
Founded in 1753, the British Museum's remarkable collections span over two million years of human history and culture, all under one roof.

Chessington World of Adventures
Kingston upon Thames KT9 2NE
0870 444 7777
www.chessington.com
Explore Chessington - it's a whole world of adventures! Soar on the Vampire rollercoaster, discover the mystery of Tomb Blaster or visit the park's own SEA LIFE Centre.

Chinese New Year
February, Various venues
www.visitlondon.com
London's Chinese New Year celebrations are the largest outside Asia, with parades, performances and fireworks.

Chiswick House
Hounslow W4 2RP
(020) 8995 0508
www.english-heritage.org.uk/daysout/properties/chiswick-house/
The celebrated villa of Lord Burlington with impressive grounds featuring Italianate garden with statues, temples, obelisks and urns.

Churchill Museum and Cabinet War Rooms
Westminster SW1A 2AQ
(020) 7930 6961
www.iwm.org.uk
Learn more about the man who inspired Britain's finest hour at the highly interactive and innovative Churchill Museum, the world's first major museum dedicated to life of the 'greatest Briton'. Step back in time and discover the secret.

City of London Festival
June-July, Various venues
www.visitlondon.com
The City of London Festival is an annual extravaganza of music, dance, art, film, poetry, family and participation events that takes place in the city's Square Mile.

Eltham Palace
Greenwich SE9 5QE
(020) 8294 2548
www.elthampalace.org.uk
A spectacular fusion of 1930s Art Deco villa and magnificent 15th century Great Hall. Surrounded by period gardens.

Greenwich Heritage Centre
Greenwich SE18 4DX
(020) 8854 2452
www.royalgreenwich.gov.uk
Local history museum with displays of archaeology, natural history and geology. Also temporary exhibitions, schools service, sales point and Saturday club.

Hampton Court Palace
Richmond upon Thames KT8 9AU
(0870) 752 7777
www.hrp.org.uk
This magnificent palace set in delightful gardens was famously one of Henry VIII's favourite palaces.

HMS Belfast
Southwark SE1 2JH
(020) 7940 6300
www.iwm.org.uk
HMS Belfast, launched 1938, served throughout WWII, playing a leading part in the destruction of the German battle cruiser Scharnhorst and in the Normandy Landings.

Imperial War Museum
Southwark SE1 6HZ
(020) 7416 5000
www.iwm.org.uk
This award-winning museum tells the story of conflict involving Britain and the Commonwealth since 1914. See thousands of imaginatively displayed exhibits, from art to aircraft, utility clothes to U-boats.

Kensington Palace State Apartments
Kensington and Chelsea W8 4PX
(0844) 482 7777
www.hrp.org.uk
Home to the Royal Ceremonial Dress Collection, which includes some of Queen Elizabeth II's dresses worn throughout her reign, as well as 14 of Diana, Princess of Wales' evening dresses.

Kenwood House
Camden NW3 7JR
(020) 8348 1286
www.english-heritage.org.uk/daysout/properties/kenwood-house/
Beautiful 18th century villa with fine interiors, and a world class collection of paintings. Also fabulous landscaped gardens and an award-winning restaurant.

London Eye River Cruise Experience
Lambeth E1 7PB
0870 500 0600
www.londoneye.com
See London from a different perspective and enjoy a unique 40 minute circular sightseeing cruise on the river Thames.

London Festival of Architecture
June - July
www.londonfestivalofarchitecture.org
See London's buildings in a new light during the Festival of Architecture.

London Film Festival
October, Various venues
www.bfi.org.uk/lff
A two-week showcase of the world's best new films, the BFI London Film Festival is one of the most anticipated events in London's cultural calendar.

London Transport Museum
Westminster WC2E 7BB
(020) 7379 6344
www.ltmuseum.co.uk
The history of transport for everyone, from spectacular vehicles, special exhibitions, actors and guided tours to film shows, gallery talks and children's craft workshops

London Wetland Centre
Richmond upon Thames SW13 9WT
(020) 8409 4400
www.wwt.org.uk
The London Wetland Centre is a unique wildlife visitor attraction just 25 minutes from central London. Run by the Wildfowl and Wetlands Trust (WWT), it is acclaimed as the best urban site in Europe to watch wildlife.

Lord's Tour
Westminster NW8 8QN
(020) 7616 8595
www.lords.org/history/tours-of-lords/
Guided tour of Lord's Cricket Ground including the Long Room, MCC Museum, Real Tennis Court, Mound Stand and Indoor School.

Museums At Night
May, Various venues
www.visitlondon.com
Explore arts and heritage after dark at museums across London. Packed with special events, from treasure trails to pyjama parties, Museums at Night is a great opportunity to explore culture in a new light.

Museum of London
City of London EC2Y 5HN
(020) 7001 9844
www.museumoflondon.org.uk
Step inside Museum of London for an unforgettable journey through the capital's turbulent past.

National Maritime Museum
Greenwich SE10 9NF
(020) 8858 4422
www.nmm.ac.uk
Britain's seafaring history housed in an impressive modern museum. Themes include exploration, Nelson, trade and empire, passenger shipping, luxury liners, maritime London, costume, art and the sea, the future and environmental issues.

National Portrait Gallery
Westminster WC2H 0HE
(020) 7306 0055
www.npg.org.uk
The National Portrait Gallery houses the world's largest collection of portraits. Visitors come face to face with the people who have shaped British history from Elizabeth I to David Beckham. Entrance is free.

Notting Hill Carnival
August, Various venues
www.thenottinghillcarnival.com
The streets of West London come alive every August Bank Holiday weekend as London celebrates Europe's biggest street festival.

RHS Chelsea Flower Show
May, Royal Hospital Chelsea
www.rhs.org.uk/Chelsea-Flower-Show
Experience the greatest flower show in the world at London's Royal Hospital Chelsea.

Royal Air Force Museum Hendon
Barnet NW9 5LL
(020) 8205 2266
www.rafmuseum.org
Take off to the Royal Air Force Museum and flypast the history of aviation with an exciting display of suspended aircraft, touch screen technology, simulator rides, hands-on section, film shows, licensed restaurant.

Royal Observatory Greenwich
Greenwich SE10 9NF
(020) 8858 4422
www.rmg.co.uk
Stand on the Greenwich Meridian Line, Longitude Zero, which divides East and West. Watch the time-ball fall at 1 o'clock. Giant refracting telescope.

Science Museum
Kensington and Chelsea SW7 2DD
0870 870 4868
www.sciencemuseum.org.uk
The Science Museum is world-renowned for its historic collections, awe-inspiring galleries, family activities and exhibitions - and it's free!

Somerset House
Westminster WC2R 1LA
(020) 7845 4670
www.somersethouse.org.uk
This magnificent 18th century building houses the celebrated collections of the Courtauld Institute of Art Gallery, Gilbert Collection and Hermitage Rooms.

Southbank Centre
Lambeth SE1 8XX
(020) 7960 4200
www.southbankcentre.co.uk
A unique arts centre with 21 acres of creative space, including the Royal Festival Hall, Queen Elizabeth Hall and The Hayward.

Southwark Cathedral
Southwark SE1 9DA
(020) 7367 6700
http://cathedral.southwark.anglican.org
Oldest Gothic church in London (c.1220) with interesting memorials connected with the Elizabethan theatres of Bankside.

Tate Britain
Westminster SW1P 4RG
(020) 7887 8888
www.tate.org.uk
Tate Britain presents the world's greatest collection of British art in a dynamic series of new displays and exhibitions.

Tate Modern
Southwark SE1 9TG
(020) 7887 8888
www.tate.org.uk/modern
The national gallery of international modern art and is one of London's top free attractions. Packed with challenging modern art and housed within a disused power station on the south bank of the River Thames.

Tower Bridge Exhibition
Southwark SE1 2UP
(020) 7403 3761
www.towerbridge.org.uk
Inside Tower Bridge Exhibition you will travel up to the high-level walkways, located 140 feet above the Thames and witness stunning panoramic views of London before visiting the Victorian Engine Rooms.

Tower of London
Tower Hamlets EC3N 4AB
0844 482 7777
www.hrp.org.uk
The Tower of London spans over 900 years of British history. Fortress, palace, prison, arsenal and garrison, it is one of the most famous fortified buildings in the world, and houses the Crown Jewels, armouries, Yeoman Warders and ravens.

Victoria and Albert Museum
Kensington and Chelsea SW7 2RL
(020) 7942 2000
www.vam.ac.uk
The V&A is the world's greatest museum of art and design, with collections unrivalled in their scope and diversity.

Virgin London Marathon
April, Various venues
www.virginlondonmarathon.com
Whether you run, walk or cheer from the sidelines, this is a London sporting institution you won't want to miss.

Vodafone London Fashion Weekend
www.londonfashionweekend.co.uk
London's largest and most exclusive designer shopping event.

Wembley Stadium Tours
Brent HA9 0WS
0844 847 2478
www.wembleystadium.com
Until your dream comes true, there's only one way to experience what it's like winning at Wembley - take the tour.

William Morris Gallery
Lloyd Park, Forest Road, Walthamstow E17 4PP
(020) 8496 4390
www.wmgallery.org.uk
The William Morris Gallery is devoted to the life and legacy of one of Britain's most remarkable designers and is housed in the grade II listed Georgian house that was his family home in north-east London from 1848 to 1856.*

Wimbledon Lawn Tennis Championships
June - July, Wimbledon
www.wimbledon.com
The world of tennis descends on Wimbledon in South West London every summer for two weeks of tennis, strawberries and cream, and good-natured queuing.

Wimbledon Lawn Tennis Museum
Merton SW19 5AG
(020) 8944 1066
www.wimbledon.com
A fantastic collection of memorabilia dating from 1555, including Championship Trophies, Art Gallery, and special exhibitions, reflecting the game and championships of today.

Tourist Information Centres

When you arrive at your destination, visit a Tourist Information Centre for quality assured help with accommodation and information about local attractions and events, or email your request before you go.

City of London
St Paul's Churchyard
(020) 7606 3030
stpauls.informationcentre@cityoflondon.gov.uk

Greenwich
2 Cutty Sark Gardens
(0870) 608 2000
tic@greenwich.gov.uk

Harrow
Gayton Library
(0208) 427 6012
gayton.library@harrow.gov.uk

Regional Contacts and Information

For more information on accommodation, attractions, activities, events and holidays in London, contact Visit London.

Go to visitlondon.com for all you need to know about London. Look for inspirational itineraries with great ideas for weekends and short breaks.

Or call 0870 1 LONDON (0870 1 566 366) for:

- A London visitor information pack
- Visitor information on London
- Accommodation reservations

Speak to an expert for information and advice on museums, galleries, attractions, riverboat trips, sightseeing tours, theatre, shopping, eating out and much more!

Stay – London

Entries appear alphabetically by town name in each county. A key to symbols appears on page 7

LONDON N1, Inner London Map ref 2D2 SatNav N1 3NW B

enjoyEngland.com ★★★ GUEST HOUSE

B&B PER ROOM PER NIGHT
S: £59.00 - £85.00
D: £81.00 - £109.00

SPECIAL PROMOTIONS
Stay 3 nights or more and save up to 25% off our standard one night rate.

Kandara Guest House

68 Ockendon Road, Islington, London N1 3NW T: (020) 7226 5721
E: admin@kandara.co.uk
W: www.kandara.co.uk £ BOOK ONLINE

A family-run guesthouse, providing B&B accommodation for over 60 years!

Situated in a quiet, leafy residential area just minutes from Islington's outstanding theatres and restaurants. Kandara is conveniently located for public transport into both the West End and the City of London. Free overnight street parking.

Directions: From the Angel underground Station: (Northern Line – City branch). From the other side of Upper Street take bus no. 38, 56, 73, 341 or 476 to the last bus stop on Essex Rd. Ockendon Rd is opposite.

Bedrooms: Facilities ie. free WiFI, flat screen TV, tea and coffee in rooms, shared bathrooms with 1 bathroom for every 2 rooms (1 bathroom per 3 guests)
Open: All Year except Christmas (20th to 28th Dec)

Payment: € Property: Children: Catering: Room:

LONDON N4, Inner London Map ref 2D2 SatNav N4 2LX H

enjoyEngland.com ★ METRO HOTEL

B&B PER ROOM PER NIGHT
S: £50.00 - £55.00
D: £60.00 - £70.00

Kent Hall Hotel

414 Seven Sisters Road, Finsbury Park, London N4 2LX T: (020) 8802 0800
F: 020 8802 9070 E: enquiries@kenthallhotel.co.uk
W: www.kenthallhotel.co.uk £ BOOK ONLINE

Budget hotel located next to Manor House Station on the Piccadilly Line (Zone 2). 15 minutes from Central London by Tube. Within walking distance of Arsenal Football Stadium. Direct from Heathrow and Eurostar terminals. **Directions:** Exit 5 from Manor House station- Piccadilly Line. **Bedrooms:** All room have private bathroom, TV, fridge, WiFi **Open:** All year. 24 hours per day

Site: P Payment: € Property: Children: Room:

LONDON SE20, Inner London Map ref 2D2 SatNav SE20 7LY B

enjoyEngland.com ★★★★ GUEST ACCOMMODATION

B&B PER ROOM PER NIGHT
S: £50.00 - £60.00
D: £65.00 - £75.00

Melrose House

89 Lennard Road, London SE20 7LY T: (020) 8776 8884 F: (020) 8778 6366
E: melrosehouse@supanet.com
W: www.uk-bedandbreakfast.com

Superb accommodation in Victorian house with spacious, en suite bedrooms. Easy access to West End. Quiet, respectable, friendly and welcoming. Ground floor rooms opening onto the lovely garden. **Directions:** 15 minutes by train to the centre of London, the train runs every 15 minutes and the station is a 5 minute walk. **Bedrooms:** 1 single, 6 double, 2 twin, 2 family **Open:** All year except Christmas

Site: P Payment: € Property: Children: 8 Room:

LONDON W2, Inner London Map ref 2D2 SatNav W2 3BE H

enjoyEngland.com ★★★★ HOTEL
enjoyEngland.com Silver AWARD

B&B PER ROOM PER NIGHT
S: £320.00
D: £350.00

SPECIAL PROMOTIONS
Please see our website.

The Caesar Hotel

26-33 Queen's Gardens, Hyde Park, London W2 3BE T: (020) 7262 0022 F: 020 7402 5099
E: thecaesar@derbyhotels.com
W: www.thecaesarhotel.com £ BOOK ONLINE

The Caesar is an oasis of tranquillity combining contemporary style with modern thinking. The 140 rooms are designed to ensure maximum comfort. The XO restaurant offers international cuisine and the XO bar Spanish Tapas. The hotel is a few minutes walk from Notting Hill, Hyde Park and Oxford Street.

Directions: Heathrow Express Train (15 min) Paddington Station (10min walk). Underground stations: Paddington - Bakerloo/Circle/District; Lancaster Gate - Central 5min walk.

Bedrooms: 32 single, 66 double / twins, 6 family, 12 suite deluxe
Open: All year

Site: Payment: € Leisure: Property: Children: Catering:
Room:

LONDON W6, Inner London Map ref 2D2 SatNav W6 9QL B

enjoyEngland.com ★★★ GUEST ACCOMMODATION

B&B PER ROOM PER NIGHT
S: £58.00 - £78.00
D: £76.00 - £120.00

SPECIAL PROMOTIONS
Please see website for special promotions.

Temple Lodge Club Ltd

Temple Lodge, 51 Queen Caroline Street, Hammersmith, London W6 9QL
T: (020) 8748 8388 E: templelodgeclub@btconnect.com
W: www.templelodgeclub.com

Hidden away from the hustle and bustle of central Hammersmith, yet a surprisingly short walk from its main transport hub, this listed building provides a quiet and relaxing haven after the exertions of a busy day or night out. Breakfast is hearty, vegetarian and mainly organic. Bedrooms are comfortably furnished, light and airy. Most rooms, including library, look out onto our secluded garden.

Directions: Exit Hammersmith tube towards the Apollo Theatre, turn left towards the river and Hammersmith Bridge, next door but one is Temple Lodge. Enter small courtyard, come to red front door and ring doorbell!

Bedrooms: 5 single with companion bed if needed, 4 double (1 en suite, 1 private bathroom, 1 shower only in room, 1 facilities on corridor) 2 twin-bedded
Open: All year

Site: Payment: Property: Children: 6 Catering: Room:

For key to symbols see page 7

LONDON WC1N, Inner London Map ref 2D2 SatNav WC1N 2AD B

B&B PER ROOM PER NIGHT
S: £118.00 - £175.00
D: £155.00 - £220.00

Goodenough Club

23 Mecklenburgh Square, London WC1N 2AD **T:** (020) 7769 4727
E: reservations@goodenough.ac.uk
W: www.club.goodenough.ac.uk **£ BOOK ONLINE**

Occupies 5 Georgian town houses in the heart of Bloomsbury, walking distance to West End, Covent Garden and the Eurostar. Luxurious Garden Suites are available and guests may attend events at the adjacent Goodenough College. Health club day passes can be purchased. **Bedrooms:** TV, Wi-Fi, hairdryer and hospitality tray **Open:** All year

Site: **Payment:** **Leisure:** **Property:** **Children:** **Room:**

CROYDON, Outer London Map ref 2D2 SatNav CR0 1JR B

B&B PER ROOM PER NIGHT
S: £40.00 - £45.00
D: £60.00

SPECIAL PROMOTIONS
For stays longer than four nights, discounts will be given.

Woodstock Guest House

30 Woodstock Road, Croydon CR0 1JR **T:** (020) 8680 1489 **F:** 020 8680 1489
E: guesthouse.woodstock@gmail.com
W: www.woodstockhotel.co.uk

Victorian house located in a quiet residential area, only a five minute walk to the town centre, local amenities and East Croydon Railway Station. Well-appointed and spacious rooms. High standard of housekeeping and homely atmosphere. Single rooms from £40 to £45 pn, twin/double rooms £60 pn and family rooms £75 pn. Continental breakfast optional extra: £3.00 per person.

Directions: From East Croydon Station via George Street turn left into Park Lane. After roundabout exit A212. Woodstock Road is 2nd left off Park Lane.

Bedrooms: 4 single, 2 twin/double, 2 family
Open: All year except Christmas and New Year

Site: P **Payment:** **Leisure:** **Property:** **Children:** 3 **Catering:** **Room:**

RICHMOND, Outer London Map ref 2D2 SatNav TW9 1YJ B

B&B PER ROOM PER NIGHT
S: £90.00
D: £125.00 - £140.00

EVENING MEAL PER PERSON
£8.00 - £14.95

The Red Cow

59 Sheen Road, Richmond TW9 1YJ **T:** (020) 8940 2511 **F:** 020 8940 2581
E: tom@redcowpub.com
W: www.redcowpub.com

Traditional Victorian inn retaining lovely original features. Short walk from Richmond town centre, river, royal parks, rail links to London. Nearby, Heathrow Airport, Twickenham RFU, Hampton Court, Windsor. **Directions:** Five-minute walk from Richmond town centre and train station. Easily accessed from M25, M4 and M3. **Bedrooms:** 4 double/twin, option for family room **Open:** All year

Site: **Payment:** **Leisure:** **Property:** **Children:** **Catering:** **Room:**

RICHMOND, Outer London Map ref 2D2 SatNav TW10 6UH

Richmond Park Hotel

enjoyEngland.com ★★ METRO HOTEL

B&B PER ROOM PER NIGHT
S: £72.00 - £87.00
D: £82.00 - £99.00

3 Petersham Road, Richmond TW10 6UH T: (020) 8948 4666 F: 020 8940 7376
E: richmdpk@globalnet.co.uk
W: www.therichmondparkhotel.com

Privately owned hotel in the heart of Richmond. All rooms en suite with direct-dial telephone, colour TV, radio and tea/coffee making facilities with Wi-fi. **Directions:** The Richmond Park Hotel is on Petersham Road in the centre of town, where the Petersham Road forks with Hill Rise (leading to the Park). **Bedrooms:** 2 single, 17 double, 3 twin **Open:** All year except Christmas and New Year

Payment: Leisure: Property: Children: Catering: Room:

TEDDINGTON, Outer London Map ref 2D2 SatNav TW11 9NU

Lensbury

enjoyEngland.com ★★★★ HOTEL

B&B PER ROOM PER NIGHT
S: £90.00 - £190.00
D: £105.00 - £210.00
HB PER PERSON PER NIGHT
£110.00 - £230.00

SPECIAL PROMOTIONS
Weekend offer if you stay two or three nights. Best rate available. Prices include Breakfast, Car Parking, Wi-Fi internet and use of extensive leisure facilities including a 25m pool.

Broom Road, Teddington TW11 9NU T: (020) 8614 6400 F: 020 8614 6445
E: accommodation@lensbury.com
W: www.lensbury.com £ BOOK ONLINE

The Lensbury is a 4 Star hotel, situated in 25 acres of grounds on the banks of the River Thames. Located just 35 minutes by train from London Waterloo and within easy reach of London's airports and the M3, M4 and M25 motorways. The Lensbury has 169 en suite bedrooms, each designed to offer maximum comfort and relaxation. Accommodation rates also include use of the extensive leisure facilities.

Directions: Near Heathrow & Gatwick Airports. Motorways: 15 minutes from the M25. 10 minutes from the M3. Rail: 35 minutes to London Waterloo. Complementary shuttle bus to local station Mon to Fri peak times.

Bedrooms: Standard Rooms, Superior, Executive, Deluxe, Disabled room and a Family room. Rooms can take up to a maximum of 4 people
Open: All year

Site: P Payment: € Leisure: Property:
Children: Catering: Room:

Don't Miss

Audley End House & Gardens

Saffron Walden, Essex CB11 4JF
www.english-heritage.org.uk
At Audley End near Saffron Walden, you can discover one of England's grandest stately homes. Explore the impressive mansion house, uncover the story behind the Braybrooke's unique natural history collection, visit an exhibition where you can find out about the workers who lived on the estate in the 1800s and even try dressing the part with dressing up clothes provided.

The Broads

Norfolk
www.broads-authority.gov.uk
The Norfolk Broads with its scenic waterways, rare wildlife and rich history has National Park status. This ancient mosaic of lakes, land and rivers covering 303 square kilometres in the east of England, is the UK's largest protected wetland and boasts a variety of habitats including fen, carr woodland and grazing marshes, as well as pretty villages and no less than 11,000 species of wildlife. Walking, cycling, fishing, boating, wildlife spotting, the list of things to do here is endless and there is something for all ages to enjoy.

The Fitzwilliam Museum

Trumpington Street, Cambridge CB2 1RB
(01223) 332900
http://www.fitzmuseum.cam.ac.uk/
A short walk away from the colleges and the River Cam in the heart of Cambridge, the Fitzwilliam Museum with its imposing neo-classical facade and columns is one of the city's most iconic buildings. Founded in 1816 when the 7th Viscount Fitzwilliam of Merrion left his vast collections of books, art and music to the University of Cambridge, it now has over half a million artworks and artefacts dating back as far as 2500BC in its collection.

Holkham Hall

Wells-next- the-Sea, Norfolk, NR23 1AB
(01328) 710227
www.holkham.co.uk
Steeped in history, magnificent Holkham Hall on the North Norfolk Coast, is a stunning Palladian mansion with its own nature reserve. It is home to many rare species of flora and fauna, a deer park and one of the most beautiful, unspoilt beaches in the country. Step back in time in the Bygones Museum or explore the 18th Century walled gardens which are being restored, while the children have fun in the woodland adventure play area.

ZSL Whipsnade Zoo

Dunstable, Bedfordshire LU6 2LF
(020) 7449 6200
www.zsl.org/zsl-whipsnade-zoo
Set on 600 acres in the rolling Chiltern Hills, Whipsnade is home to more than 2500 species and you can get close to some of the world's hairiest, scariest, tallest and smallest animals here. Meet the animals, take a steam train ride, visit the Hullabazoo Farm or even be a keeper for the day.

East of England

Bedfordshire, Cambridgeshire, Essex, Hertfordshire, Norfolk, Suffolk

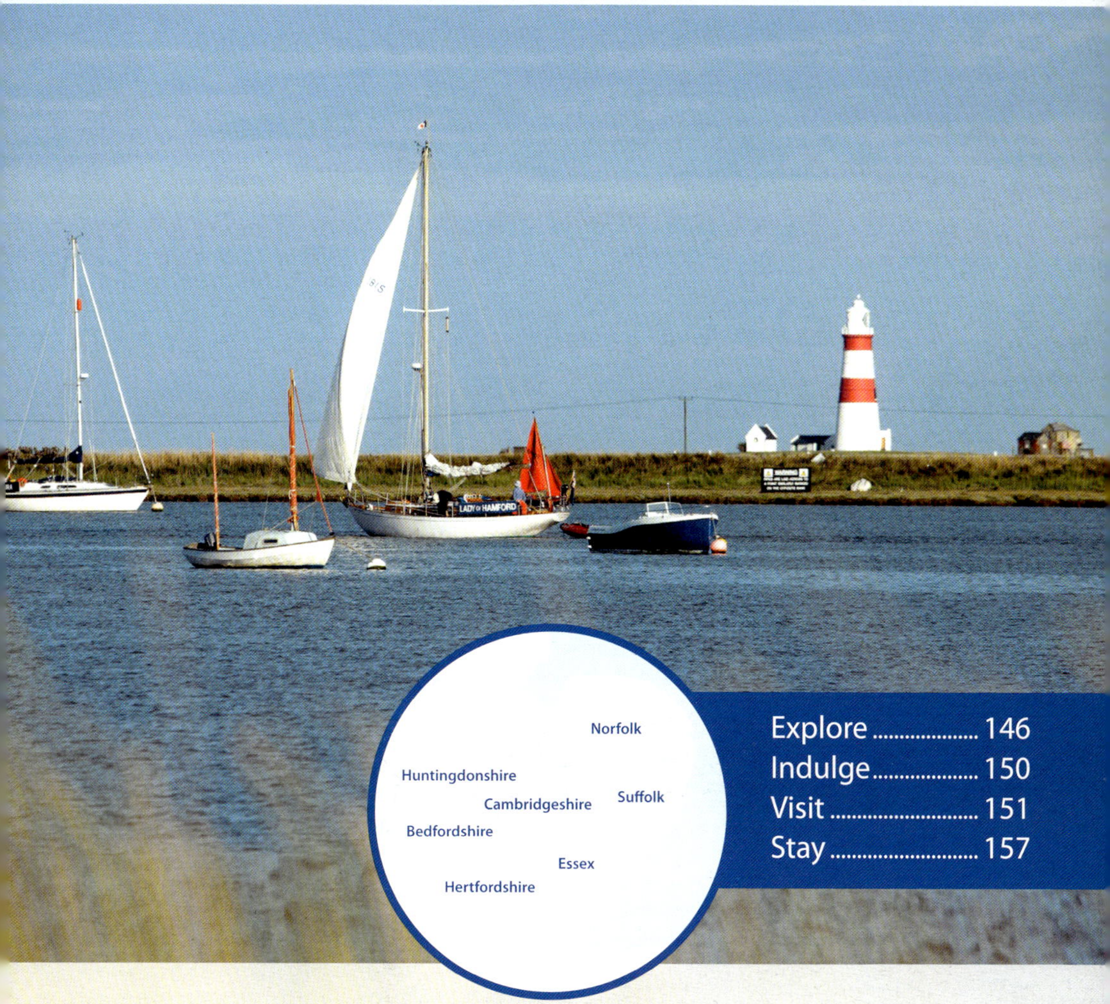

Loved for its unspoiled character, rural landscape, architecture and traditions, the East of England is full of beautiful countryside, idyllic seaside, historic cities and vibrant towns. The Norfolk Broads and Suffolk Coast have always been popular with yachtsmen and the North Norfolk Coast has become a fashionable getaway in recent years. Cambridge is steeped in history and oozes sophistication, while Bedfordshire, Hertfordshire and Essex each have their own charms, with pockets of beauty and fascinating heritage. This is a diverse region where you'll find plenty to keep you busy.

Explore – East of England

Bedfordshire & Hertfordshire

History, the arts, family entertainment and relaxing, unspoilt countryside - this area has it all. Bedfordshire has plenty of attractions, from exotic animals at Whipsnade Zoo to vintage aeroplanes at The Shuttleworth Collection and notable historic houses. Woburn Abbey, the still inhabited home of the Dukes of Bedford, stands in a 3000-acre park and is part of one of Europe's largest drive-through game reserves. The 18th century mansion's 14 state apartments are open to the public and contain an impressive art collection. Luton Hoo is a fine Robert Adam designed house in a 1200-acre Capability Brown designed park.

Hotspot:
Dunstable Downs Kite Festival
July, Dunstable, Bedfordshire
www.dunstablekitefestival.co.uk
Kite enthusiasts from around the UK converge on Dunstable.

Hertfordshire also has its fair share of stately homes, with Hatfield House, built from 1707 by Robert Cecil, first Earl of Salisbury, leading the way. Nearby Knebworth House is the venue for popular summer concerts and events.

Roman walls, mosaic floors and part of an amphitheatre are still visible at Verulanium, St Albans and Much Hadham, where the Bishops of London used to have their country seat, is a showpiece village. Welwyn Garden City, one of Britain's first 20th century new towns retains a certain art deco charm.

Cambridgeshire & Essex

Cambridge is a city of winding streets lined with old houses, world-famous colleges and churches, while the gently flowing Cam provides a serene backdrop to the architectural wonders. Kings College Chapel, started by Henry VI in 1446 should not be missed and the Fitzwilliam Museum is one of Europe's treasure houses, with antiquities from Greece and Rome. First-class shopping can be found in the quirky stores and exquisite boutiques tucked away along cobbled streets, and there's a vast choice of places to eat and drink.

Further afield, Cambridgeshire is a land of lazy waterways, rolling countryside, bustling market towns and quaint villages. Climb grand sweeping staircases in the stately homes of the aristocracy or relax as you chug along in a leisure boat, watching the wildlife in one of the wonderful nature reserves. Peterborough has a fine Norman cathedral with three soaring arches, whilst Ely has had an abbey on its cathedral site since AD 670.

Western Essex is dotted with pretty historic market towns and villages like Thaxted and Saffron Walden and plenty of historic sites. County town Colchester was founded by the Romans and its massive castle keep, built in 1067 on the site of the Roman Temple of Claudius, houses a collection of Roman antiquities. Explore the beautiful gardens and 110ft Norman Keep at Hedingham Castle, which also holds jousting and theatre performances.

Some of the region's loveliest countryside lies to the north, on the Suffolk Border around Dedham Vale where Constable and Turner painted, while further east you can find family seaside resorts such as Walton on the Naze and Clacton-on-Sea. Following the coast south, the Blackwater and Crouch estuaries provide havens for yachts and pleasure craft. Inland, Layer Marney Tower is a Tudor palace with buildings, gardens and parkland dating from 1520 in a beautiful, rural Essex setting. The county city of Chelmsford has a historic 15th century cathedral and Hylands House is a beautiful Grade II* listed neo-classical villa, set in over 500 acres of Hylands Park.

Hotspot: The Essex Way walking route weaves through rural Essex all the way from Epping to Harwich via picturesque Constable Country. Taking in open farmland, ancient woodlands, tranquil river valleys, charming villages and historic sites, it has plenty of country pubs worth a stop along the route.

The county town of Norfolk and unofficial capital of East Anglia is Norwich, a fine city whose cathedral walls are decorated with biblical scenes dating from 1046. There are 30 medieval churches in central Norwich and many other interesting historic sites, but modern Norwich is a stylish contemporary city with first rate shopping and cultural facilities. Sandringham, near Kings Lynn in the north west of the county, is the royal palace bought by Queen Victoria for the then Prince of Wales and where the present Queen spends many a family holiday.

The North Norfolk coast has become known as 'Chelsea-on-Sea' in recent years and many parts of the region have developed a reputation for fine dining. From Hunstanton in the west to Cromer in the east, this stretch of coastline is home to nature reserves, windswept beaches and quaint coastal villages. Wells-next-the-Sea, with its long sweeping beach bordered by pine woodland has a pretty harbour with small fishing boats where children fish for crabs.

Norfolk

Norfolk is not as flat as Noel Coward would have you believe, as any cyclist will tell you, but cycling or walking is still a great way to see the county. In the west Thetford Forest is said to be the oldest in England while in the east, the county is crisscrossed by waterways and lakes known as The Broads - apparently the remains of medieval man's peat diggings!

Hotspot: It's hard to beat Bressingham Steam and Gardens, where world renowned gardener and horticulturist Alan Bloom combined his passion for plants and gardens with his love of steam to create a truly unique experience for all the family. www.bressingham.co.uk

Suffolk

Suffolk is famous for its winding lanes and pastel painted, thatched cottages. The county town of Ipswich has undergone considerable regeneration in recent years, and now boasts a vibrant waterfront and growing arts scene. For history lovers, Framlingham Castle has stood intact since the 13th century and magnificent churches at Lavenham, Sudbury and Long Melford are well worth a visit.

The Suffolk Coast & Heaths Area of Outstanding Natural Beauty has 155 square miles of unspoilt wildlife-rich wetlands, ancient heaths, windswept shingle beaches and historic towns and villages for you to explore. Its inlets and estuaries are extremely popular with yachtsmen. Gems such as Southwold, with its brightly coloured beach huts, and Aldeburgh are home to some excellent restaurants. Snape Maltings near Aldeburgh offers an eclectic programme of events including the world famous Aldeburgh Festival of music.

Hotspot: The Anglo-Saxon burial site at Sutton Hoo is set on a stunning 255 acre estate with breathtaking views over the River Deben and is home to one of the greatest archaeological discoveries of all time. www.nationaltrust.org.uk

The historic market town of Woodbridge on the River Deben, has a working tide mill, a fabulous riverside walk with an impressive view across the river to Sutton Hoo and an abundance of delightful pubs and restaurants.

In the south of the county, the hills and valleys on the Suffolk-Essex border open up to stunning skies, captured in paintings by Constable, Turner and Gainsborough. At the heart of beautiful Constable Country, Nayland and Dedham Vale Area of Outstanding Natural Beauty are idyllic places for a stroll or leisurely picnic.

Indulge – East of England

Punting is quintessentially Cambridge and a great way to see The Backs of seven of the colleges and their beautiful bridges. Relax and enjoy a glass of Champagne on a leisurely chauffered punt tour or hire your own for an afternoon of delightful DIY sightseeing. (01223) 359750 or visit www.scudamores.com

Moored among the pleasure and fishing boats in the harbour at Wells-next-the-Sea, **The Albatros** is a restored Dutch clipper built in 1899. It now serves up delicious sweet and savoury pancakes, real ale and live music, providing an interesting pit stop on the north Norfolk coast. www.albatroswells.co.uk

Pay a visit to **Adnams Brewery** in Southwold where you can explore behind the scenes of one of the most modern breweries in the UK, discover how their award-winning beers and spirits are made, or get creative and make your very own gin! www.adnams.co.uk

Aldeburgh Fish and Chip Shop has been serving up freshly caught, East coast fish since 1967. A tantalisingly tasty treat whether you are enjoying a day at the beach in the height of summer or a brisk walk on a stormy winter day, and especially when you eat them sitting on the sea wall. www.aldeburghfishandchips.co.uk

Indulge every little boy's fantasy with a trip to the **Shuttleworth Collection**, a vast collection of vintage aeroplanes, cars, motorcycles and bicycles at Old Warden Aerodrome, Nr. Biggleswade in Bedfordshire. www.shuttleworth.org

Visit – East of England

Attractions with this sign participate in the Visitor Attraction Quality Assurance Scheme.

Bedfordshire

Bedfordshire County Show
July, Biggleswade, Bedfordshire
www.bedfordshirecountyshow.co.uk
Held in the beautiful grounds of Shuttleworth the Bedfordshire County Show is a showcase of town meets country.

Luton International Carnival
May, Luton, Bedfordshire
www.luton.gov.uk
The highlight is the spectacular carnival parade – an eye-catching, breathtaking procession through the town centre, superbly reflecting the diverse mix of cultures in Luton.

Woburn Safari Park
Bedfordshire MK17 9QN
(01525) 290407
www.woburnsafari.co.uk
Drive through the safari park with 30 species of animals in natural groups just a windscreen's width away, or even closer!

Wrest Park
Silsoe, Luton, Bedfordshire, MK45 4HR
0870 333 1181
www.english-heritage.org.uk
Enjoy a great day out exploring one of Britain's most spectacular French style mansions and 'secret' gardens. With hidden gems including a thatched-roof Bath house, ornate marble fountain, Chinese Temple and bridge and over 40 statues, as well as a kids audio trail and play area, it's popular with families and garden lovers alike.

Cambridgeshire

Cambridge Folk Festival
July/August, Cherry Hinton, Cambridgeshire
www.cambridgefolkfestival.co.uk
Top acts make this a must-visit event for folk fans.

Duxford Air Show
September, Duxford, nr Cambridge, Cambridgeshire
www.iwm.org.uk/duxford
Set within the spacious grounds of the famous former First and Second World War airfield, the Duxford Air Show features an amazing array of aerial displays.

Imperial War Museum Duxford
Cambridge CB22 4QR
(01223) 835000
www.iwm.org.uk/duxford
With its air shows, unique history and atmosphere, nowhere else combines the sights, sounds and power of aircraft quite like Duxford.

Essex

Adventure Island
Southend-on-Sea, Essex SS1 1EE
(01702) 443400
www.adventureisland.co.uk
One of the best value 'theme parks' in the South East with over 60 great rides and attractions for all ages. No admission charge, you only 'pay if you play'.

Central Museum and Planetarium
Southend-on-Sea, Essex SS2 6ES
(01702) 434449
www.southendmuseums.co.uk
An Edwardian building housing displays of archaeology, natural history, social and local history.

Clacton Airshow
August, Clacton Seafront, Essex
www.clactonairshow.com
Impressive aerobatic displays take to the skies while a whole host of exhibition, trade stands, food court and on-site entertainment are available at ground level.

Kings College Chapel
Cambridge CB2 1ST
(01223) 331212
www.kings.cam.ac.uk
It's part of one of the oldest Cambridge colleges sharing a wonderful sense of history and tradition with the rest of the University.

The National Stud
Newmarket, Cambridgeshire CB8 0XE
(01638) 663464
www.nationalstud.co.uk
The beautiful grounds & facilities are a renowned tourist attraction in the eastern region.

Oliver Cromwell's House
Ely, Cambridgeshire CB7 4HF
(01353) 662062
www.olivercromwellshouse.co.uk
Visit the former Lord Protector's family's home and experience an exhibition on 17th Century life.

Peterborough Dragon Boat Festival
June, Peterborough Rowing Lake,
Thorpe Meadows, Cambridgeshire
www.peterboroughdragonboatfestival.com
Teams of up to 11 people, dragon boats and all equipment provided, no previous experience required. Family entertainment and catering stalls.

The Raptor Foundation
Huntingdon, Cambridgeshire PE28 3BT
(01487) 741140
www.raptorfoundation.org.uk
Bird of prey centre, offering 3 daily flying displays with audience participation, gift shop, Silent Wings tearoom, Raptor crafts shop.

Colchester Medieval Festival
June, Lower Castle Park, Colchester, Essex
www.oysterfayre.co.uk
This medieval style fair remembers a time when folk from the countryside and neighbouring villages would travel to the 'Big Fair' in the town.

Colchester Zoo
Essex CO3 0SL
(01206) 331292
www.colchester-zoo.com
Enjoy daily displays, feed elephants and giraffes and see over 260 species in over 60 acres of parkland!

Maldon Mud Race
April, Maldon, Essex
www.maldonmudrace.com
The annual Maldon Mud Race is a wacky fun competition in which participants race to become the first to finish a 400m dash over the bed of the River Blackwater.

RHS Garden Hyde Hall
Chelmsford, Essex CM3 8AT
(01245) 400256
www.rhs.org.uk/hydehall
A garden of inspirational beauty with an eclectic range of horticultural styles from traditional to modern providing year round interest.

Royal Gunpowder Mills
Waltham Abbey, Essex EN9 1JY
(01992) 707370
www.royalgunpowdermills.com
A spectacular 170-acre location for a day of family fun. Special events including Spitfire flypast, award winning Secret History exhibition, tranquil wildlife walks, guided land train tours and rocket science gallery.

Sea-Life Adventure
Southend-on-Sea, Essex SS1 2ER
(01702) 442200
www.sealifeadventure.co.uk
With more than 30 display tanks and tunnels to explore, there are loads of fishy residents to discover at Sea-Life Adventure.

Southend Carnival
August, Southend-on-Sea, Essex
www.southend-on-seacarnival.org.uk
A wide range of events held over eight days.

Hertfordshire

Cathedral and Abbey Church of St Alban
St. Albans, Hertfordshire AL1 1BY
(01727) 860780
www.stalbanscathedral.org
St Alban is Britain's first Christian martyr and the Cathedral, with its shrine, is its oldest place of continuous worship.

Chilli Festival
August, Benington Lordship Gardens, Stevenage, Hertfordshire
www.beningtonlordship.co.uk
A popular family event attracting thousands of visitors over two days, offering a chance to buy Chilli plants, products and sample foods from around the world.

Hertfordshire County Show
May, Redbourn, Hertfordshire
www.hertsshow.com
County show with all the usual attractions.

Knebworth House
Hertfordshire SG1 2AX
(01438) 812661
www.knebworthhouse.com
Historic house, home to the Lytton family since 1490. Knebworth House offers a great day out for all the family with lots to do for all ages.

Norfolk

Banham Zoo
Norwich, Norfolk NR16 2HE
(01953) 887771
www.banhamzoo.co.uk
Wildlife spectacular which will take you on a journey to experience tigers, leopards and zebra plus some of the world's most exotic, rare and endangered animals.

Blickling Hall, Gardens and Park
Norwich, Norfolk NR11 6NF
(01263) 738030
www.nationaltrust.org.uk/blickling-estate
A Jacobean redbrick mansion with a garden, orangery, parkland and lake. Spectacular long gallery, plasterwork ceilings and fine collections of furniture, pictures and books. Walks.

Cromer Pier
Cromer, Norfolk NR27 9HE
www.cromer-pier.com
Cromer Pier is a Grade II listed seaside pier on the north coast of Norfolk. The pier is the home of the Cromer Lifeboat Station and the Pavilion Theatre

Fritton Lake Country World
Great Yarmouth, Norfolk NR31 9HA
(01493) 488288
A woodland and lakeside haven with a children's assault course, putting, an adventure playground, golf, fishing, boating, wildfowl, heavy horses, cart rides, falconry and flying displays.

Great Yarmouth Maritime Festival
September, Great Yarmouth, Norfolk
www.great-yarmouth.co.uk/maritime-festival
A mix of traditional and modern maritime vessels will be moored on South Quay for visitors to admire and go aboard.

King's Lynn May Garland Procession
May, King's Lynn, Norfolk
www.thekingsmorris.co.uk
The King's Morris dancers carry the May Garland around the town.

Norwich Castle Museum and Art Gallery
Norfolk NR1 3JU
(01603) 493649
www.museums.norfolk.gov.uk
Ancient Norman keep of Norwich Castle dominates the city and is one of the most important buildings of its kind in Europe.

Royal Norfolk Show
July, Norwich, Norfolk
www.royalnorfolkshow.co.uk
The Royal Norfolk Show celebrates everything that's Norfolk. It offers 10 hours of entertainment each day from spectacular grand ring displays, traditional livestock and equine classes, to a live music stage, celebrity guests and over 650 stands.

Sainsbury Centre for Visual Arts
UEA, Norwich, Norfolk NR4 7TJ
(01603) 593199
www.scva.ac.uk
Containing a collection of world art, it was one of the first major public buildings to be designed by the architect Norman Foster.

Sandringham
King's Lynn, Norfolk PE35 6EN
(01485) 545400
www.sandringhamestate.co.uk
H.M. The Queen. A fascinating house, an intriguing museum and the best of the Royal gardens.

Suffolk

Aldeburgh Music Festival
June, Snape Maltings, Suffolk IP17 1SP
www.aldeburgh.co.uk
The Aldeburgh Festival of Music and the Arts offers an eclectic mix of concerts, operas, masterclasses, films and open air performances at different venues in the Aldeburgh/Snape area in Suffolk.

Gainsborough's House
Sudbury, Suffolk CO10 2EU
(01787) 372958
www.gainsborough.org
Gainsborough's House is the only museum situated in the birthplace of a great British artist. The permanent collection is built around the works of Thomas Gainsborough.

Go Ape! High Wire Forest Adventure - Thetford, Suffolk
IP27 0AF (0845) 643 9215
www.goape.co.uk
Experience an exhilarating course of rope bridges, tarzan swings and zip slides... all set high in the trees above the forest floor.

Ickworth House, Park and Gardens
Bury St. Edmunds, Suffolk IP29 5QE
(01284) 735270
www.nationaltrust.org.uk/ickworth
Fine paintings, a beautiful collection of Georgian silver, an Italianate garden and stunning parkland.

Latitude Festival
July, Southwold, Suffolk
www.latitudefestival.com
Primarily a music festival but also has a full spectrum of art including film, comedy, theatre, cabaret, dance and poetry.

National Horseracing Museum and Tours
Newmarket, Suffolk CB8 8JH
(01638) 667333
www.nhrm.co.uk
Discover the stories of racing from its early origins at Newmarket to its modern-day heroes

RSPB Minsmere Nature Reserve
Saxmundham, Suffolk IP17 3BY
(01728) 648281
www.rspb.org.uk/minsmere
One of the UK's premier nature reserves, offering excellent facilities for people of all ages and abilities.

Somerleyton Hall and Gardens
Lowestoft, Suffolk NR32 5QQ
(01502) 734901
www.somerleyton.co.uk
12 acres of landscaped gardens to explore including our famous 1864 Yew hedge maze. Guided tours of the Hall.

Suffolk Show
May, Ipswich, Suffolk
www.suffolkshow.co.uk
Animals, food and drink, shopping...there's lots to see and do at this popular county show.

Tourist Information Centres

When you arrive at your destination, visit the Tourist Information Centre for quality assured help with accommodation and information about local attractions and events, or email your request before you go.

Aldeburgh	48 High Street	01728 453637	atic@suffolkcoastal.gov.uk
Aylsham	Bure Valley Railway Station	01263 733903	aylsham.tic@broadland.gov.uk
Beccles	The Quay	01502 713196	admin@beccles.info
Bedford	St Pauls Square	01234 718112	touristinfo@bedford.gov.uk
Bishop's Stortford	2 Market Square	01279 655831	tic@bishopsstortford.org
Brentwood	Town Hall	01277 312500	
Burnham Deepdale	Deepdale Information	01485 210256	info@deepdalefarm.co.uk
Bury St Edmunds	6 Angel Hill	01284 764667	tic@stedsbc.gov.uk
Cambridge	Peas Hill	0871 226 8006	info@visitcambridge.org
Clacton-On-Sea	Town Hall	01255 686633	clactontic@tendringdc.gov.uk
Colchester	1 Queen Street	01206 282920	vic@colchester.gov.uk
Cromer	Louden Road	0871 200 3071	cromerinfo@north-norfolk.gov.uk
Diss	Meres Mouth	01379 650523	dtic@s-norfolk.gov.uk
Dunstable	Priory House	01582 891420	tic@dunstable.gov.uk
Ely	Oliver Cromwell's House	01353 662062	tic@eastcambs.gov.uk
Felixstowe	91 Undercliff Road West	01394 276770	ftic@suffolkcoastal.gov.uk
Great Yarmouth	25 Marine Parade	01493 846346	gab@great-yarmouth.gov.uk
Hertford	10 Market Place	01992 584322	tic@hertford.gov.uk
Holt	3 Pound House	0871 200 3071/ 01263 713100	holtinfo@north-norfolk.gov.uk
Hoveton	Station Road	01603 782281	hovetontic@broads-authority.gov.uk
Hunstanton	Town Hall	01485 532610	info@visithunstanton.info
Ipswich	St Stephens Church	01473 258070	tourist@ipswich.gov.uk
King's Lynn	The Custom House	01553 763044	kings-lynn.tic@west-norfolk.gov.uk
Lavenham	Lady Street	01787 248207	lavenhamtic@babergh.gov.uk
Letchworth Garden City	33-35 Station Road	01462 487868	tic@letchworth.com
Lowestoft	East Point Pavilion	01502 533600	touristinfo@waveney.gov.uk
Luton	Luton Central Library	01582 401579	tourist.information@lutonculture.com
Maldon	Wenlock Way	01621 856503	tic@maldon.gov.uk
Newmarket	63 The Guineas	01638 719749	tic.newmarket@forest-heath.gov.uk
Norwich	The Forum	01603 213999	tourism@norwich.gov.uk
Peterborough	9 Bridge Street	01733 452336	tic@peterborough.gov.uk
Saffron Walden	1 Market Place	01799 524002	tourism@saffronwalden.gov.uk
Sandy	Rear of 10 Cambridge Road	01767 682 728	tourism@sandytowncouncil.gov.uk
Sheringham	Station Approach	01263 824329	sheringhaminfo@north-norfolk.gov.uk
Skegness	Embassy Theatre	0845 6740505	skegnessinfo@e-lindsey.gov.uk
Southend-On-Sea	Pier Entrance	01702 215620	vic@southend.gov.uk
Southwold	69 High Street	01502 724729	southwold.tic@waveney.gov.uk
St Albans	Old Town Hall	01727 864511	tic@stalbans.gov.uk
Stowmarket	The Museum of East Anglian Life	01449 676800	tic@midsuffolk.gov.uk
Sudbury	Sudbury Library	01787 881320/ 372331	sudburytic@sudburytowncouncil.co.uk
Swaffham	The Shambles	01760 722255	swaffham@eetb.info
Waltham Abbey	6 Highbridge Street	01992 660336	tic@walthamabbey-tc.gov.uk
Wells-Next-The-Sea	Staithe Street	0871 200 3071/ 01328 710885	wellsinfo@north-norfolk.gov.uk
Whitlingham	Whitlingham Country Park	01603 756094	whitlinghamtic@broads-authority.gov.uk
Wisbech	2-3 Bridge Street	01945 583263	tourism@fenland.gov.uk
Witham	61 Newland Street	01376 502674	tic@witham.gov.uk
Woodbridge	Woodbridge Library	01394 446510/ 276770	felixstowetic@suffolkcoastal.gov.uk
Wymondham	Market Cross	01953 604721	wymondhamtic@btconnect.com

Regional Contacts and Information

For more information on accommodation, attractions, activities, events and holidays in the East of England, contact the following regional tourism organisation. Their website has a wealth of information.

East of England Tourism (01284) 727470 info@eet.org.uk www.visiteastofengland.com

Stay – East of England

Entries appear alphabetically by town name in each county. A key to symbols appears on page 7

BEDFORD, Bedfordshire Map ref 2D1 SatNav MK44 3RW B

B&B PER ROOM PER NIGHT
S: £80.00 - £95.00
D: £85.00 - £115.00
EVENING MEAL PER PERSON
£8.00 - £15.00

Moggerhanger Park

Park Road, Moggerhanger, Bedford, Bedfordshire MK44 3RW **T:** (01767) 641007
F: 01767 641515 **E:** reception@moggerhangerpark.com
W: www.moggerhangerpark.com **£ BOOK ONLINE**

Country Bed and Breakfast, Bedfordshire. Beautifully situated bedrooms combining modern equipment with period furnishings befitting a Grade 1 listed historic House. Single, double and family room options are available throughout the year and are perfect for wedding guests, corporate attendees or just those looking for a relaxing weekend away.

Directions: Please see map and directions on our website or contact Reception for further details.

Bedrooms: All rooms have Freeview Television, telephone, clothes iron, tea and coffee and hair dryer. Free Wi-Fi and parking
Open: All year except Christmas to December 29th

Site: P **Payment:** € **Leisure:** **Property:** **Children:** **Catering:**
Room:

CAMBRIDGE, Cambridgeshire Map ref 2D1 SatNav CB25 9AF H

B&B PER ROOM PER NIGHT
S: £82.50 - £222.50
D: £95.00 - £255.00
EVENING MEAL PER PERSON
£30.00 - £46.00

Cambridge Quy Mill Hotel and Spa

Best Western PLUS

Church Road, Stow-cum-Quy, Cambridge, Cambridgeshire CB25 9AF
T: (01223) 293383 **F:** 01223 293770 **E:** qmh.reception@cambridgequymill.co.uk
W: www.cambridgequymill.co.uk **£ BOOK ONLINE**

On the outskirts of Cambridge with easy access from the A14. Enjoy award winning 2 AA Rosette food in the informal Mill House Restaurant or bar meals in the Orangery. The Celtic Bar and Lounge features real ales and over 40 whiskies. **Directions:** Please see website. **Bedrooms:** 24 hour reception, 24 hour porter service, express check out, dry cleaning and laundry service, room service menus, wake up calls, overnight shoe shine service **Open:** All year

Site: P **Payment:** **Leisure:** **Property:** **Children:** **Catering:**
Room:

CAMBRIDGE, Cambridgeshire Map ref 2D1 SatNav CB4 1DE B

B&B PER ROOM PER NIGHT
S: £35.00 - £50.00
D: £60.00 - £65.00

Southampton Guest House

7 Elizabeth Way, Cambridge CB4 1DE **T:** (01223) 357780 **F:** 01223 314297
E: southamptonhouse@btinternet.com
W: www.southamptonguesthouse.com

Victorian property with friendly atmosphere, only 15 minutes walk along riverside to city centre, colleges and shopping mall. **Directions:** Please contact us for directions. **Bedrooms:** 1 single, 1 double, 3 family **Open:** All year

Site: P **Payment:** € **Property:** **Children:** **Room:**

CAMBRIDGE, Cambridgeshire Map ref 2D1 *SatNav CB4 3HS* B

B&B PER ROOM PER NIGHT
S: £50.00 - £60.00
D: £80.00

Tudor Cottage

292 Histon Road, Cambridge, Cambridgeshire CB4 3HS **T:** (01223) 565212 / 07736 144496
E: email@tudor-cottage.net
W: www.tudorcottageguesthouse.co.uk

Comfortable, friendly, Tudor-style cottage conveniently situated within 30 minutes walking distance of Cambridge city centre. En suite or shared facilities, Digital TV/DVD, Wi-Fi, tea/coffee-making facilities. Excellent food over looking our picturesque garden. A warm and personal service. Off-street parking. Easy access to bus stop and A14/M11. 5* Health and Hygiene rating.

Directions: Close to A14 and M11. For further details please refer to website.

Bedrooms: 2 single, 2 double, 1 twin
Open: All year

Site: P **Payment:** € **Property:** **Children:** **Catering:** **Room:**

BURNHAM-ON-CROUCH, Essex Map ref 3B3 *SatNav CM0 8BQ* B

B&B PER ROOM PER NIGHT
S: £64.50 - £74.50
D: £82.00

The Railway

12 Station Road, Burnham-on-Crouch, Essex CM0 8BQ **T:** (01621) 786868 **F:** 01621 783002
E: info@therailwayhotelburnham.co.uk
W: www.therailwayhotelburnham.co.uk

Originally built in the late 1800s lovingly restored by Jenny & Colin Newcombe to incorporate 21st century luxuries with Victorian charm. **Bedrooms:** All rooms en suite, dd phone. Tea/coffee facilities and colour TV **Open:** All year

Site: P **Payment:** £ **Property:** **Children:** **Catering:** **Room:**

CHELMSFORD, Essex Map ref 3B3 *SatNav CM2 9AJ* H

Miami Hotel

Princes Road, Chelmsford CM2 9AJ **T:** (01245) 269603 **F:** 01245 259860
E: sales@miamihotel.co.uk
W: www.miamihotel.co.uk

Family-run hotel, one mile from town centre. All rooms have tea-making facilities, trouser press, direct-dial telephone with voice mail and PC access, cable TV and hairdryer. Five conference rooms available. Please contact for prices. **Bedrooms:** 23 dble, 32 twin
Open: All year except Christmas

Payment: £ **Property:** **Children:** **Catering:** **Room:**

CLAVERING, Essex Map ref 2D1 SatNav CB11 4QT B

The Cricketers

Wicken Road, Clavering, Saffron Walden CB11 4QT **T:** (01799) 550442 **F:** 01799 550882
E: info@thecricketers.co.uk
W: www.thecricketers.co.uk

SPECIAL PROMOTIONS
Please contact us for prices and special offers.

A delightful 16th century country Inn with award winning food and accommodation. Very popular for business and pleasure alike, good food being a core ingredient of a stay at The Cricketers. Owners' son, Jamie Oliver, grew up here and supplies vegetables, leaves and herbs from his nearby certified organic garden. Six new double bedrooms have been added this year, now offering twenty double accommodation rooms to guests. Accommodation special offers and menus are shown on the website.

Directions: M11 jct 8. A120 west and B1383 to Newport. B1038 to Clavering.

Bedrooms: 17 double, 3 twin
Open: All year except Christmas Day and Boxing Day

Site: P **Payment:** **Leisure:** **Property:** **Children:** **Catering:** **Room:**

COLCHESTER, Essex Map ref 3B2 SatNav CO6 4PZ H

Stoke by Nayland Hotel, Golf & Spa

Keepers Lane, Leavenheath, Colchester, Essex CO6 4PZ **T:** (01206) 265835
F: 01206 265840 **E:** sales@stokebynayland.com
W: www.stokebynayland.com **£ BOOK ONLINE**

B&B PER ROOM PER NIGHT
S: £73.00
D: £85.00

SPECIAL PROMOTIONS
For current special offers please see our website or call 01206 265835.

In secluded tranquility yet only 10 minutes from Colchester, this multi award-winning, family-owned hotel is situated in 300 acres of stunning "Constable Country". Two championship golf courses, 2 AA Rosette Lakes Restaurant, extensive spa facilities, indoor pool, gym, free car parking and free hi-speed Wi-Fi.

Directions: Situated North of Colchester on the Essex/Suffolk border just off the A134, only an hour from London via the A12.

Bedrooms: 80 en suite bedrooms including luxury honeymoon, executive and family rooms. Flat screen TVs, in-room safes, air conditioning and free hi-speed Wi-Fi
Open: All Year

Site: P **Payment:** **Leisure:** **Property:** **Children:** **Catering:** **Room:**

ORSETT, Essex Map ref 3B3 SatNav RM16 3LJ B

enjoyEngland.com ★★★★ ROOM ONLY

B&B PER ROOM PER NIGHT
S: £35.00 - £47.50
D: £50.00 - £65.00

Jays Lodge

Chapel Farm, Baker Street, Orsett, Grays RM16 3LJ **T:** (01375) 891663
E: info@jayslodge.co.uk
W: www.jayslodge.co.uk

Barn conversion to provide twelve rooms all with en suite, mini kitchen facility, colour television with Freeview and free Wi-Fi access. Ample, free and secure car parking available. **Directions:** Please contact us for directions. **Bedrooms:** 2 single, 2 double, 8 twin **Open:** All year

Site: P **Payment:** **Leisure:** **Property:** **Catering:** **Room:**

WEST MERSEA, Essex Map ref 3B3 SatNav CO5 8LS B

enjoyEngland.com ★★★★ INN

B&B PER ROOM PER NIGHT
S: £65.00 - £90.00
D: £75.00 - £115.00
EVENING MEAL PER PERSON
£12.00 - £22.00

Victory at Mersea

Coast Road, Mersea Island, Colchester CO5 8LS **T:** (01206) 382907
E: info@victoryatmersea.com
W: www.victoryatmersea.com £ BOOK ONLINE

The Victory is situated on the Mersea waterfront. We have 7 really comfortable, superior quality rooms, individually decorated with a personal touch, some with fantastic estuary views. **Directions:** Mersea is clearly signposted from the A12 and you'll find us on the outskirts of the village centre, right on the waterfront. **Bedrooms:** 5 double, 1 twin, 1 family **Open:** All year

Site: P **Payment:** **Leisure:** **Property:** **Children:** **Catering:**
Room:

ST. ALBANS, Hertfordshire Map ref 2D1 SatNav AL3 4RY H

enjoyEngland.com ★★★★ HOTEL — enjoyEngland.com Silver AWARD

B&B PER ROOM PER NIGHT
S: £125.00
D: £135.00 - £305.00
EVENING MEAL PER PERSON
£18.00 - £34.00

SPECIAL PROMOTIONS
Please check website for details.

St Michael's Manor Hotel

St Michael's Village, Fishpool Street, St Albans, Hertfordshire AL3 4RY **T:** (01727) 864444
F: 01727 848909 **E:** reservations@stmichaelsmanor.com
W: www.stmichaelsmanor.com £ BOOK ONLINE

Close to the city centre of St Alban's Hertfordshire, formerly the ancient Roman city of Verulanium, and near the famous Abbey Cathedral you will find this lovely manor house hotel. Set in five acres of beautiful private English country gardens with its own one acre lake this country-style venue is, surprisingly, only 20 minutes by train from London. The original house dates back over 500 years and was converted into a hotel in the early 1960s by the Newling Ward family. They still remain as private owners and managers, which gives the hotel its unique flavour. Bedroom prices start from £125, including breakfast. Evening meal prices based on The Lake Menu. Please see website for A la Carte, Sunday Lunch and Afternoon Tea menus.

Directions: Please contact us for directions.

Bedrooms: Premier, Luxury, Deluxe, Suites & Accessible. Most rooms have garden views. All have tea/coffee making facilities, biscuits/sweets, bottled water
Open: All year

Site: P **Payment:** **Leisure:** **Property:** **Children:** **Catering:**
Room:

WARE, Hertfordshire Map ref 2D1 SatNav SG12 0SD H

B&B PER ROOM PER NIGHT
S: £175.00
D: £160.00 - £220.00

Hanbury Manor, A Marriott Hotel & Country Club

Ware SG12 0SD **T:** (01920) 487722 **F:** 01920 487692
W: www.marriotthanburymanor.co.uk

Hanbury Manor provides the perfect venue for both business and pleasure. Relax in the 200 acres of Hertfordshire countryside, challenge yourself on the world championship golf course or luxuriate in the Romanesque Spa. **Directions:** Only 10 miles north of junction 25 of the M25, Hanbury Manor is located off the A10. For further directions please visit www.MarriottHanburyManor.co.uk **Bedrooms:** 74 dble, 38 twin, 37 family, 12 suite **Open:** All year

Site: P **Payment:** **Leisure:** **Property:** **Children:** **Catering:** **Room:**

AYLSHAM, Norfolk Map ref 3B1 SatNav NR11 6BY B

B&B PER ROOM PER NIGHT
S: £85.00 - £100.00
D: £100.00 - £125.00

The Old Pump House

Holman Road, Aylsham, Norwich NR11 6BY **T:** (01263) 733789
E: theoldpumphouse@btconnect.com
W: www.theoldpumphouse.com

Beautiful Georgian home located a short walk from the market place with 5 tastefully furnished, comfortable bedrooms. Delicious breakfasts served in the Georgian room overlooking the garden. Situated within easy reach of the North Norfolk coast, the cathedral city of Norwich and several National Trust houses, Blickling Hall being just 1.5 miles away. Free Wi-Fi. **Bedrooms:** 1 double (four poster), 2 king size, 2 twin family. All rooms are en suite **Open:** All year except Christmas & New Year.

Site: P **Payment:** **Leisure:** **Property:** **Children:** **Room:**

CROMER, Norfolk Map ref 3C1 SatNav NR27 9HD B

B&B PER ROOM PER NIGHT
S: £43.00
D: £86.00

Cambridge House

Sea Front, East Cliff, Cromer, Norfolk NR27 9HD **T:** (01263) 512085
E: elizabeth.wass@btconnect.com
W: www.cambridgecromer.co.uk

Cambridge house is a charming family run Victorian Guest House quietly situated on the sea front, just off Cromer town centre. We overlook the East Beach and pier, with access to the promenade opposite the front door. Delicious English Breakfast using local produce, homemade marmalade and preserves. Walkers welcome, secure cycle storage. Private car park. **Directions:** Please contact for directions. **Bedrooms:** En suite bedrooms all with uninterrupted panoramic sea view

Site: P **Property:** **Catering:** **Room:**

CROMER, Norfolk Map ref 3C1 SatNav NR27 0AB B

B&B PER ROOM PER NIGHT
D: £30.00 - £42.00

Cliff Cottage

18 High Street, Overstrand, Cromer, Norfolk NR27 0AB **T:** (01263) 578179
E: roymin@btinternet.com
W: www.cliffcottagebandb.com

A quiet, friendly atmosphere invites you to Cliff Cottage. Built in the 18th century, just 2 minutes walk from the sandy beach. We offer use of our secluded garden and private parking to make your stay relaxing and comfortable. Good food. Special Offer: 7 nights for the price of 6 nights. (Saturday to Saturday only). **Directions:** Please contact us for directions. **Bedrooms:** 1 double, 1 twin **Open:** All Year

Site: P **Leisure:** **Property:** **Catering:** **Room:**

CROMER, Norfolk Map ref 3C1 SatNav NR27 0JN H

Northrepps Cottage Country Hotel

Nut Lane, Northrepps, Cromer, Norfolk NR27 0JN **T:** (01263) 579202
E: enquiries@northreppscottage.co.uk
W: www.northreppscottage.co.uk

enjoyEngland.com ★★★ COUNTRY HOUSE HOTEL — enjoyEngland.com Gold AWARD

B&B PER ROOM PER NIGHT
D: £130.00

EVENING MEAL PER PERSON
£50.00

SPECIAL PROMOTIONS
Special offers available, also events packages - please see our website for details.

One of East Anglia's finest bijou hotels from which you'll enjoy beautiful North Norfolk. The atmosphere inside is one of luxurious warmth. Our suites combine classic, stylish decor reflecting their elegant history, the height of modern comfort and luxurious features. Contemporary Humphrys bar and fine-dining in Reptons restaurant.

Directions: Cromer Coast Road, turn left at Overstrand Church.

Bedrooms: 6 dble, 1 twin, 1 family
Open: All year

WALKERS WELCOME — CYCLISTS WELCOME

Site: P **Payment:** **Leisure:** **Property:** **Children:** **Catering:** **Room:**

FAKENHAM, Norfolk Map ref 3B1 SatNav NR21 0AW B

Abbott Farm B&B

Walsingham Road, Binham, Fakenham NR21 0AW **T:** (01328) 830519
E: abbot.farm@btinternet.com
W: www.abbottfarm.co.uk

enjoyEngland.com ★★★ FARMHOUSE

B&B PER ROOM PER NIGHT
S: £30.00 - £35.00
D: £60.00 - £70.00

A 190-acre arable farm. Rural views of North Norfolk including the historic Binham Priory. Liz and Alan offer a warm welcome to their guest house. **Directions:** Please refer to website. **Bedrooms:** 1 double (en suite), 1 twin (en suite) **Open:** All year except Christmas

Site: P **Payment:** € **Leisure:** **Property:** **Children:** **Catering:** **Room:**

GREAT YARMOUTH, Norfolk Map ref 3C1 SatNav NR30 1EG H

enjoyEngland.com ★★★ HOTEL

B&B PER ROOM PER NIGHT
S: £55.00 - £120.00
D: £80.00 - £160.00

EVENING MEAL PER PERSON
£12.95 - £30.50

SPECIAL PROMOTIONS
Nightly discounts for extended stays. Check website for special offers.

Burlington Palm Hotel

North Drive, Great Yarmouth NR30 1EG **T:** (01493) 844568 **F:** 01493 331848
E: enquiries@burlington-hotel.co.uk
W: www.burlington-hotel.co.uk **£ BOOK ONLINE**

Seafront Hotel overlooking Great Yarmouth's Golden Sands. We are a short walk from all the main attractions and 1.5 miles from the train station. We are also the only Hotel in Great Yarmouth with a heated indoor swimming pool.

Directions: From the A12 or A47 follow signs for Seafront turn left, we are on North Drive about 600 Yards north of the Britannia Pier.

Bedrooms: 7 single, 23 double, 21 twin, 18 family
Open: All year except 28th December - 2nd January

Site: P **Payment:** £ **Leisure:** **Property:** **Children:** **Catering:** **Room:**

HEACHAM, Norfolk Map ref 3B1 SatNav PE31 7HB B

enjoyEngland.com ★★★★ GUEST HOUSE — enjoyEngland.com Silver AWARD

B&B PER ROOM PER NIGHT
S: £43.00 - £50.00
D: £75.00 - £80.00

St Anne's Guest House

53 Neville Road, Heacham, Norfolk PE31 7HB **T:** (01485) 570021
E: jeannie@stannesguesthouse.co.uk
W: www.stannesguesthouse.co.uk

A Victorian family-run guest house in the quiet village of Heacham near Hunstanton, we offer a relaxed informal atmosphere for a peaceful enjoyable break. Rooms: 2 single, 1 with en suite, 1 family en suite, 2 twin, 1 en suite, 2 double en suite. Family room available from £100 per night. **Bedrooms:** Flatscreen TV, tea and coffee in rooms **Open:** All Year

WALKERS WELCOME · CYCLISTS WELCOME **Site:** **Payment:** £ **Property:** **Children:** **Catering:** **Room:**

KING'S LYNN, Norfolk Map ref 3B1 SatNav PE30 5PE B

enjoyEngland.com ★★★★ GUEST ACCOMMODATION — enjoyEngland.com Silver AWARD

B&B PER ROOM PER NIGHT
S: £45.00 - £70.00
D: £65.00 - £85.00

Fairlight Lodge

79 Goodwins Road, King's Lynn, Norfolk PE30 5PE **T:** (01553) 762234 / 07981 058370
E: enquiries@fairlightlodge.co.uk
W: www.fairlightlodge.co.uk **£ BOOK ONLINE**

Victorian detached home set in large garden with friendly atmosphere. The 4 star silver award accommodation offers all the convenience of modern facilities whilst maintaining much of the Victorian charm. Near the centre for shops and train. Great reviews on TripAdvisor. **Directions:** From A17/A10/A47 Hardwick roundabout, take signs to King's Lynn. At Southgates Roundabout, take fourth exit signposted Gaywood/College W.Anglia. **Bedrooms:** Flatscreen TV, tea/coffee, home made biscuits **Open:** All year except Christmas and New Year

Site: P **Payment:** £ **Property:** **Children:** **Catering:** **Room:**

KING'S LYNN, Norfolk *Map ref 3B1* *SatNav PE31 8HD*

B&B PER ROOM PER NIGHT
S: £110.00 - £220.00
D: £130.00 - £240.00
EVENING MEAL PER PERSON
£30.00 - £55.00

The Hoste

The Green, Burnham Market, King's Lynn, Norfolk PE31 8HD **T:** (01328) 738777
F: 01328 730103 **E:** reservations@thehoste.com
W: www.thehoste.com £ BOOK ONLINE

The Hoste is a renowned four-star hotel that is popular with those wanting a luxurious and relaxing stay in North Norfolk. 62 Luxury bedrooms, 2AA Rosette restaurants, historic bar and a relaxing Beauty Spa. **Bedrooms:** En suite, plasma TVs with Sky, tea and coffee **Open:** All Year

Site: P **Payment:** **Leisure:** **Property:** **Children:**
Catering: **Room:**

KING'S LYNN, Norfolk *Map ref 3B1* *SatNav PE31 6HQ* B

The White House

44 Hunstanton Road, Dersingham, King's Lynn, Norfolk PE31 6HQ **T:** (01485) 541895
E: aquapure@talktalk.net
W: www.thewhitehousenorfolk.co.uk

Are you looking for relaxing affordable country guest houses in Kings Lynn? When you are looking for affordable accommodation in Norfolk, look no further than The White House. Our bed and breakfast is a well established guest house and only 8 miles from Kings Lynn train station, 6 miles from Hunstanton and 1 mile from royal Sandringham estate. Please contact for 2015 Rates. **Directions:** Please see website. **Bedrooms:** All rooms are en suite with coffee/tea tray, free Wi-Fi hair dryer etc **Open:** All year

Site: P **Payment:** **Property:** **Catering:** **Room:**

MUNDESLEY, Norfolk *Map ref 3C1* *SatNav NR118DB* B

B&B PER ROOM PER NIGHT
S: £50.00 - £60.00
D: £75.00 - £85.00

Overcliff Lodge

46 Cromer Road, Mundesley, Norfolk NR11 8DB **T:** (01263) 720016
E: enquiries@overclifflodge.co.uk
W: www.overclifflodge.co.uk £ BOOK ONLINE

Overcliff Lodge is a large Victorian house, situated just a few minutes walk from Blue Flag sandy beach and village centre. The house offers spacious, comfortable accommodation and has a fully enclosed small rear garden. **Directions:** Overcliff Lodge is situated at the junction of Gimingham Road and Cromer Road just west of Mundesley. **Bedrooms:** All rooms are en suite with tea and coffee **Open:** All year except 3 weeks in January

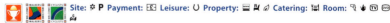

Site: P **Payment:** **Leisure:** **Property:** **Catering:** **Room:**

NORWICH, Norfolk *Map ref 3C1* *SatNav NR10 5NP* B

B&B PER ROOM PER NIGHT
S: £75.00 - £120.00
D: £80.00 - £150.00
EVENING MEAL PER PERSON
£10.95 - £25.00

Marsham Arms Coaching Inn

40 Holt Road, Hevingham, Norwich, Norfolk NR10 5NP **T:** (01603) 754268 **F:** 01603 754839
E: info@marshamarms.co.uk
W: www.marshamarms.co.uk £ BOOK ONLINE

Welcome to one of Norfolk's best loved inns noted for its quiet rooms, country setting, wines & ales and freshly prepared food. **Directions:** 2 miles north of Horsford on B1149. 4 miles from Norwich International Airport. 7 miles from Norwich city centre. **Bedrooms:** 10 double, 4 twin, 2 family **Open:** All year

Site: P **Payment:** **Leisure:** **Property:** **Children:**
Catering: **Room:**

For **key to symbols** see page 7

NORWICH, Norfolk Map ref 3C1 SatNav NR3 1BN B

enjoyEngland.com ★★★★ GUEST HOUSE

B&B PER ROOM PER NIGHT
S: £58.00 - £60.00
D: £90.00 - £100.00

Number 17

17 Colegate, Norwich NR3 1BN **T:** (01603) 764486 **E:** enquiries@number17.co.uk
W: www.number17norwich.co.uk **£ BOOK ONLINE**

This contemporary styled, family run bed and breakfast is close to Norwich city centre making it an ideal location whether your stay is for business or pleasure. Family suite prices £130 per night. **Directions:** Number 17 is located about a 15 minute walk from both Norwich railway station or the bus station and about 10 miles from Norwich airport. **Bedrooms:** 1 single, 2 double, 3 twin, 2 family **Open:** All year except Christmas and New Year

Site: **Payment:** **Property:** **Children:** 2 **Catering:** **Room:**

NORWICH, Norfolk Map ref 3C1 SatNav NR12 7BG H

enjoyEngland.com ★★★ HOTEL

B&B PER ROOM PER NIGHT
S: £60.00 - £65.00
D: £79.00 - £95.00

EVENING MEAL PER PERSON
£9.50 - £35.50

SPECIAL PROMOTIONS
Discounted mid week breaks from £39.50 pppn B&B or £59 pppn Dinner B&B. Min 2 night stay between Mon/Fri. Excluding bank holidays.

Old Rectory Hotel

North Walsham Road, Crostwick, Norwich NR12 7BG **T:** (01603) 738513 **F:** 01603 738712
E: info@oldrectorycrostwick.com
W: www.oldrectorycrostwick.com **£ BOOK ONLINE**

Ideal location for Norwich and Broads. This family run hotel offers excellent facilities and service in a beautiful setting in rural Norfolk. All rooms are ground floor, en suite and very well equipped. It also boasts 3.5 acres of gardens, patio seating, bar, restaurant, heated outdoor pool and ample free parking.

Directions: B1150 North Walsham Rd out of Norwich off the outer ring-road travel 4-miles. The Old Rectory is situated 200m past the Spixworth turning.

Bedrooms: 6 dble, 8 twin, 1 family, 1 suite
Open: All year

WALKERS WELCOME FAMILIES WELCOME CYCLISTS WELCOME

Site: **Payment:** **Leisure:** **Property:** **Children:** **Catering:**
Room:

RACKHEATH, Norfolk Map ref 3C1 SatNav NR13 6NN B

enjoyEngland.com ★★★★ GUEST ACCOMMODATION

B&B PER ROOM PER NIGHT
S: £30.00 - £35.00
D: £55.00 - £65.00

Barn Court

6 Back Lane, Rackheath, Norwich NR13 6NN **T:** (01603) 782536
E: barncourtbb@hotmail.com

Barn Court is a spacious, friendly and comfortable B&B 5 miles from the centre of Norwich, in a traditional barn conversion built around a courtyard. Good variety of breakfasts provided. **Directions:** From Norwich, take A1151 towards Wroxham, Back Lane is 3.5 miles from ring road on left, and Barn Court is first driveway on right. **Bedrooms:** 2 double, 1 twin **Open:** All year except Christmas and New Year

WALKERS WELCOME FAMILIES WELCOME CYCLISTS WELCOME PETS! WELCOME

Site: P **Leisure:** **Property:** **Children:** 1 **Catering:**
Room:

SAHAM TONEY, Norfolk Map ref 3B1 SatNav IP25 7EX

enjoyEngland.com ★★★ COUNTRY HOUSE HOTEL

B&B PER ROOM PER NIGHT
S: £75.00 - £110.00
D: £85.00 - £185.00

EVENING MEAL PER PERSON
£9.15 - £30.00

SPECIAL PROMOTIONS
Two night breaks, dinner B&B, priced per couple for two nights. Winter from £238.00, summer from £272.00.

Broom Hall Country Hotel

Richmond Road, Saham Toney, Thetford IP25 7EX **T:** (01953) 882125 **F:** 01953 885325
E: enquiries@broomhallhotel.co.uk
W: www.broomhallhotel.co.uk **£ BOOK ONLINE**

Family-run, Victorian country house offering peace and tranquillity in 15 acres of garden and parkland. Open fire warms winter evenings. After a swim in heated indoor pool, enjoy a cream tea on the terrace or in the conservatory or relax in the Rose Room Bar. Purpose-built, ground-floor, disabled rooms. Restaurant or bar meals are available lunchtimes and evenings.

Directions: From A11, take A1075 to Watton. Left at lights, 0.5m right at roundabout. From A47, take A1065 Newmarket, left onto B1108, left at roundabout.

Bedrooms: 9 double, 4 twin, 2 family all en suite, ground floor disabled access rooms
Open: All year except Christmas and New Year

Site: **Payment:** **Leisure:** **Property:** **Children:** **Catering:** **Room:**

SHERINGHAM, Norfolk Map ref 3B1 SatNav NR26 8LL

enjoyEngland.com ★★★ HOTEL

B&B PER ROOM PER NIGHT
S: £60.00 - £68.00
D: £120.00 - £136.00

EVENING MEAL PER PERSON
£19.50 - £24.50

The Beaumaris Hotel & Restaurant

15 South Street, Sheringham NR26 8LL **T:** (01263) 822370
E: enquires@thebeaumarishotel.co.uk
W: www.thebeaumarishotel.co.uk **£ BOOK ONLINE**

Family-run hotel established in 1947, with a reputation for personal service and English cuisine. Quietly located close to beach, shops and golf club, National Trust properties, bird-watching, coastal footpath and North Norfolk Railway. We are also AA 3 Star Rated. **Directions:** From the A149 turn towards Sheringham. At the roundabout turn left. Take the next right, then the next left by the church and then left again into South St. **Bedrooms:** 5 single, 8 dble, 8 twin **Open:** March to mid-December

Site: **Payment:** **Leisure:** **Property:** **Children:** **Catering:** **Room:**

THOMPSON, Norfolk Map ref 3B1 SatNav IP24 1PX B

enjoyEngland.com ★★★★ INN

Chequers Inn

Griston Road, Thompson IP24 1PX **T:** (01953) 483360 **F:** 01953 488092
E: richard@thompsonchequers.co.uk
W: www.thompsonchequers.co.uk

The Chequers is a 16th century village inn with a thatched roof, still retaining all of its original character. A true country retreat in the heart of Breckland. Local produce and fresh fish a speciality. Local real ales include Wolf, Wherry, Adnams and Greene King IPA to name a few. Please contact for 2015 Rates.

Directions: Twelve miles north east of Thetford, just off the A1075. Snetterton Race Track just a short drive away.

Bedrooms: 2 double, 1 twin
Open: All year

Site: **Payment:** **Leisure:** **Property:** **Children:** **Catering:**
Room:

WELLS-NEXT-THE-SEA, Norfolk Map ref 3B1 SatNav NR23 1DB B

enjoyEngland.com ★★★★ GUEST ACCOMMODATION

B&B PER ROOM PER NIGHT
D: £70.00 - £100.00

Arch House Bed and Breakfast

50 Mill Road, Wells-Next-The-Sea, Norfolk NR23 1DB **T:** (01328) 710112
E: enquiries@archhouse.co.uk
W: www.archhouse.co.uk **£ BOOK ONLINE**

Arch House is a distinguished Grade II listed Bed & Breakfast with large car park, just a short walk from the centre of Wells-next-the-Sea with its excellent restaurants, pubs, quirky shops and bustling fishing quay. Situated a mile from the stunning Holkham Estate and The Norfolk Coastal Path, Arch House is the perfect base to explore this Area of Outstanding Natural Beauty.
Bedrooms: Accommodates up to twenty four guests
Open: All year except Christmas

Site: **Payment:** **Leisure:** **Property:** **Children:** 4 **Catering:** **Room:**

WIGHTON, Norfolk Map ref 3B1 SatNav NR23 1PF B

B&B PER ROOM PER NIGHT
S: £80.00
D: £95.00

SPECIAL PROMOTIONS
Oct/Nov stay for 3 nights pay for 2 nights

Meadow View Guest House

53 High Street, Wighton, Wells-next-The-Sea, Norfolk NR23 1PF **T:** (01328) 821527
F: 01328 821527 **E:** booking@meadow-view.net
W: www.meadow-view.net **£ BOOK ONLINE**

A 5 star Gold award guest house awaits you with a warm, friendly welcome in the centre of Wighton, 3 miles from Wells, a busy coastal resort on the North Norfolk coast.

Directions: From B1105 Wighton is situated just off the B1105, accessible from the A149 coast road.

Bedrooms: 1 double, 1 twin, 3 suite
Open: All year

Site: P **Payment:** **Leisure:** **Property:** **Catering:** **Room:**

BURY ST. EDMUNDS, Suffolk Map ref 3B2 SatNav IP33 1SZ B

B&B PER ROOM PER NIGHT
S: £45.00 - £50.00
D: £70.00

St Edmunds Guesthouse

35 St Andrews Street North, Bury St. Edmunds IP33 1SZ **T:** (01284) 700144
E: info@stedmundsguesthouse.net
W: www.stedmundsguesthouse.net **£ BOOK ONLINE**

Beautifully restored Victorian town house with 9 luxurious en suite rooms. Central to bus and rail stations. Tea/coffee, power shower, iron, free Wi-Fi and digital Freeview TV. From £45 per room per night. **Directions:** Please contact us for directions. **Bedrooms:** 1 single, 3 double, 5 twin **Open:** All year except Christmas and New Year

Site: P **Payment:** **Leisure:** **Property:** **Children:** **Catering:**
Room:

BURY ST. EDMUNDS, Suffolk Map ref 3B2 SatNav IP28 6EY B

B&B PER ROOM PER NIGHT
S: £60.00 - £75.00
D: £110.00 - £115.00
EVENING MEAL PER PERSON
£15.00 - £30.00

West Stow Hall

Icklingham Road, West Stow, Bury St. Edmunds IP28 6EY **T:** (01284) 728127
E: eileengilbert54@aol.com
W: www.weststowhall.com

Enjoy the tranquility and beauty of this historic hall set in six acres of lovely grounds. Large comfortable bedrooms, great breakfasts and a warm welcome are guaranteed. The Studio, with ground floor access, is ideally suited for less mobile guests. **Directions:** M11 to A11 direction Mildenhall. Before Mildenhall take A1101 to Bury St Edmunds, left turn West Stow. The hall is clearly signposted on the left. **Bedrooms:** 2 double, 1 twin, 1 family **Open:** All year except Christmas

Site: P **Payment:** € **Leisure:** **Property:** **Children:** **Catering:**
Room:

For **key to symbols** see page 7

ELMSWELL, Suffolk Map ref 3B2 SatNav IP30 9QR B

Kiln Farm Guest House

Kiln Lane, Elmswell, Bury St Edmunds, Suffolk IP30 9QR **T:** (01359) 240442
E: davejankilnfarm@btinternet.com

B&B PER ROOM PER NIGHT
S: £40.00 - £50.00
D: £80.00 - £100.00
EVENING MEAL PER PERSON
£12.50

Welcoming Victorian farmhouse with courtyard of converted barns in secluded location just off A14. Licensed bar with conservatory for breakfasts and pre-booked evening meals. Ideal for exploring Suffolk. Businessmen welcome. **Directions:** A14 jct47. Travelling East Kiln Lane is right off exit slip road. From West, turn right over to roundabout, third exit. 50 yards on left. **Bedrooms:** 5 double, 1 twin, 2 family **Open:** All year

Site: P **Payment:** € **Property:** **Children:** **Catering:** **Room:**

FRAMLINGHAM, Suffolk Map ref 3C2 SatNav IP13 9PD B

High House Farm

Cransford, Woodbridge, Suffolk IP13 9PD **T:** (01728) 663461 **E:** info@highhousefarm.co.uk
W: www.highhousefarm.co.uk

B&B PER ROOM PER NIGHT
S: £46.00 - £60.00
D: £70.00 - £95.00

A warm welcome awaits you in our beautifully restored 15th century farmhouse, featuring exposed beams, inglenook fireplaces and attractive gardens. Situated midway between Framlingham and Saxmundham. **Directions:** Please refer to website address. **Bedrooms:** 1 double, 1 family **Open:** All year

Site: P **Leisure:** **Property:** **Children:** **Catering:** **Room:**

HALESWORTH, Suffolk Map ref 3C2 SatNav IP19 8BW B

Fen-Way Guest House

School Lane, Halesworth IP19 8BW **T:** (01986) 873574
W: www.tiscover.co.uk

B&B PER ROOM PER NIGHT
S: £35.00 - £40.00
D: £60.00 - £70.00

Spacious bungalow in seven acres of peaceful meadowland. Five minutes walk from town centre. Convenient for many places, including Southwold (9 miles). **Bedrooms:** 2 double, 1 twin all with en suite or private facilities **Open:** All year

Site: P **Leisure:** **Children:** 8 **Catering:** **Room:**

HITCHAM, Suffolk Map ref 3B2 SatNav IP7 7NY B

Stanstead Hall

Buxhall Road, Hitcham, Ipswich IP7 7NY **T:** (01449) 740270 **E:** stanstead@btinternet.com
W: www.stansteadcamping.co.uk

B&B PER ROOM PER NIGHT
S: £40.00
D: £70.00

Very friendly Moated Farmhouse standing off the road in the quiet open countryside. Large garden to relax in under a glass verandah. In easy reach of Lavenham, Long Melford, Bury St Edmunds and central to many of Suffolk's beauty spots. **Directions:** Directions on website. **Bedrooms:** Large rooms, with shower, TV and tea/coffee **Open:** All year

Site: P **Leisure:** **Property:** **Room:**

NEWMARKET, Suffolk *Map ref 3B2* *SatNav CB8 7BX*

B&B PER ROOM PER NIGHT
S: £109.00 - £350.00
D: £120.00 - £350.00

Bedford Lodge Hotel & Spa

Bury Road, Newmarket, Suffolk CB8 7BX **T:** (01638) 663175 **F:** 01638 667391
E: info@bedfordlodgehotel.co.uk
W: www.bedfordlodgehotel.co.uk **£ BOOK ONLINE**

The four red star Bedford Lodge Hotel & Spa was originally an 18th century Georgian Hunting Lodge. Today, we offer the best in modern comfort. Our stylish hotel retains the charm and character of its country house beginnings. **Directions:** Between Cambridge and Bury St. Edmunds; in Newmarket and is easily accessible by road, rail and air with the A14 and A11 dual carriageways close by. **Bedrooms:** Flat screen tv, tea and coffee, safe and cooler **Open:** All Year

Site: P **Payment:** **Leisure:** **Property:** **Children:** **Catering:** **Room:**

STOWMARKET, Suffolk *Map ref 3B2* *SatNav IP14 5EU*

B&B PER ROOM PER NIGHT
S: £30.00
D: £60.00

Three Bears Cottage

Mulberry Tree Farm, Middlewood Green, Stowmarket IP14 5EU **T:** (01449) 711707
F: 01449 711707 **E:** gbeckett01@aol.com
W: www.3bearscottagesuffolk.co.uk **£ BOOK ONLINE**

Self-contained converted barn offering comfort, privacy & country views. Lounge with TV, kitchenette, a substantial continental breakfast available. Ground floor bedroom, shower/bathroom sleeps 6. Well behaved dogs accepted, many bridalway walks at the back of the cottage. Within easy reach of Bury St Edmunds, Ipswich Cambridge & Suffolk coast. **Directions:** A14, A1120 through Stowupland turn into Saxham St, 1st right 1m, right into Blacksmiths Lane **Bedrooms:** 1 King size, 1 family **Open:** All year

Site: P **Leisure:** **Property:** **Children:** **Catering:** **Room:**

Don't Miss...

Burghley House

Stamford, Lincolnshire PE9 3JY
(01780) 752451
www.burghley.co.uk
Used in films Pride and Prejudice and The Da Vinci Code, the house boasts eighteen magnificent State Rooms and a huge collection of works and art, including one of the most important private collections of 17th century Italian paintings, the earliest inventoried collection of Japanese ceramics in the West and wood carvings by Grinling Gibbons and his followers.

Castle Ashby Gardens

Northamptonshire NN7 1LQ
(01604) 695200
www.castleashbygardens.co.uk
A haven of tranquility and beauty in the heart of Northamptonshire. Take your time to explore these beautiful gardens and enjoy fascinating attractions, from the rare breed farmyard to the historic orangery.

Chatsworth

Bakewell, Derbyshire DE45 1PP
(01246) 565300
www.chatsworth.org
Chatsworth is a spectacular historic house set in the heart of the Peak District in Derbyshire, on the banks of the river Derwent. There are over 30 rooms to explore, including the magnificent Painted Hall and Sculpture Gallery. In the garden, discover water features, giant sculptures and beautiful flowers set in one of Britain's most well-known historic landscapes.

Sherwood Forest

Sherwood Forest Visitor Centre,
Edwinstowe, Nottinghamshire NG21 9HN
www.nottinghamshire.gov.uk
Once part of a royal hunting forest and legendary home of Robin Hood, Sherwood Forest National Nature Reserve covers 450 acres of ancient woodlands where veteran oaks over 500 years old grow, as well as being home to a wide variety of flora and fauna.

Twycross Zoo

Hinckley, Leicestershire CV9 3PX
(01827) 880250
http://twycrosszoo.org
Set in more than 80 acres and renowned as a World Primate Centre, Twycross Zoo has around 500 animals of almost 150 species, including many endangered animals and native species in the Zoo's Nature Reserve. Pay a visit to meet the famous orangutans, gorillas and chimpanzees plus many other mammals, birds and reptiles.

East Midlands

Derbyshire, Leicestershire, Lincolnshire, Northamptonshire, Nottinghamshire, Rutland

The East Midlands is a region of historic castles and cathedrals, lavish houses, underground caves, a rich industrial heritage and spectacular countryside including the Peak District and the Lincolnshire Wolds. Climb to enchanting hilltop castles for breathtaking views. Explore medieval ruins and battlefields. Discover hidden walks in ancient forests, cycle across hills and wolds, or visit one of the regions many events and attractions.

Explore – East Midlands

Derbyshire

'There is no finer county in England than Derbyshire. To sit in the shade on a fine day and look upon verdure is the most perfect refreshment' according to Jane Austen. Derbyshire is the home of the UK's first National Park, the Peak District, which has been popular with holidaymakers for centuries. It forms the beginning of the Pennine Chain and its reservoirs and hills are second to none in beauty. This is excellent walking, riding and cycling country and contains plenty of visitor attractions and historic sites such as Gullivers Theme Park at Matlock Bath and the 17th century Palladian Chatsworth, seat of the Duke of Devonshire.

Hotspot: Speedwell Cavern and Peak District Cavern offer the chance for amazing adventures in the heart of the Peak District, with unusual rock formations, the largest natural cave entrance in the British Isles and an incredible underground boat trip. www.speedwellcavern.co.uk

Hotspot: There's plenty to keep everyone entertained at Rutland Water, with a huge range of watersports, fantastic fishing, an outdoor adventure centre and nature reserves teeming with wildlife. www.rutlandwater.org.uk

Leicestershire & Rutland

Leicester is a cathedral city with a 2000-year history, now host to a modern university and the county's pastures fuel one of its main exports: cheese. Foxton Locks is the largest flight of staircase locks on the English canal system with two 'staircases' of five locks bustling with narrowboats. Belvoir Castle in the east dominates its vale. Rockingham Castle at Market Harborough was built by William the Conqueror and stands on the edge of an escarpment giving dramatic views over five counties and the Welland Valley below. Quietly nestling in the English countryside, England's smallest county of Rutland is an idyllic rural destination with an array of unspoilt villages and two charming market towns, packed with rich history and character.

Hotspot: Stamford is a charming Georgian market town with a pretty riverside and over 600 listed buildings of mellow limestone including five medieval churches. The Arts Centre, built in 1768, is one of the oldest provincial theatres in England.

Lincolnshire

Lincolnshire is said to produce one eighth of Britain's food and its wide open meadows are testament to this. Gothic triple-towered Lincoln Cathedral is visible from the Fens for miles around, while Burghley House hosts the famous annual Horse Trials and is a top tourist attraction. The Lincolnshire Wolds, a range of hills designated an Area of Outstanding Natural Beauty and the highest area of land in eastern England between Yorkshire and Kent, is idyllic walking and cycling country

Northamptonshire

County town Northampton is famous for its shoe making, celebrated in the Central Museum and Art Gallery, and the county also has its share of stately homes and historic battlefields. Silverstone in the south is home to the British Grand Prix. Althorp was the birthplace and is now the resting place of the late Diana Princess of Wales.

Nottinghamshire

Nottingham's castle dates from 1674 and its Lace Centre illustrates the source of much of the city's wealth, alongside other fine examples of Nottinghamshire's architectural heritage such as Papplewick Hall & Gardens. Legendary tales of Robin Hood, Sherwood Forest and historic battles may be what the county is best known for, but it also hosts world class sporting events, live performances and cutting edge art, and there's plenty of shopping and fine dining on offer too. To the north, the remains of Sherwood Forest provide a welcome breathing space and there are plenty of country parks and nature reserves, including the beautiful lakes and landscape of the National Trust's Clumber Park.

Hotspot: The Newark International Antiques and Collectors Fair at Newark & Nottingham Showground is the largest event of its kind in Europe. It is the ultimate treasure hunting ground with 2,500 stands attracting thousands of dealers and buyers from around the globe. www.iacf.co.uk/newark

Dine in style with a four-course lunch aboard one of the **Great Central Railway**'s First Class Restaurant Cars as a steam locomotive takes you on a leisurely journey through the Charnwood's glorious countryside. A pause on Swithland viaduct takes in the magnificent view across the reservoir to Charnwood Forest. www.gcrailway.co.uk

Enjoy a Champagne Sunset hot air balloon flight over the Peak District and the Derbyshire Dales with **Ladybird Balloons**, based in the Vale of Belvoir near Belvoir Castle and Langar Hall. (01949) 877566 or visit www.ladybirdballoons.co.uk

Indulge in lunch or a sumptuous afternoon tea at **The Dining Room at 78 Derngate** in Northampton, the beautifully restored house remodelled by the world-famous designer and architect, Charles Rennie Mackintosh in his iconic Modernist style. www.78derngate.org.uk / www.thediningroom.org

Stamford Cheese Cellar has a mouth-watering range of artisan cheeses, chutneys, jams, crackers, pâtés and sundries to tantalise your taste buds. Treat yourself to a couple of chunks of something delicious for lunch, or even a luxury hamper and a nice bottle from their selection of specialist drinks upstairs at 17 St Mary's Street, Stamford. www.stamfordcheese.com

A stone's throw from Nottingham railway station, cool and quirky **Hopkinson** is three eclectic floors of art, antiques, vintage clothes, and collectibles with a café and tea bar offering a staggering twenty-one varieties of tea. A paradise for treasure seekers, vintage lovers and curators of beautiful home aesthetics, it is housed in a restored historic building that is also home to local artists, designers and makers. www.hopkinson21.co.uk

Attractions with this sign participate in the Visitor Attraction Quality Assurance Scheme.

Derbyshire

Buxton Festival
July, Buxton, Derbyshire
www.buxtonfestival.co.uk
A summer celebration of the best opera, music and literature, at the heart of the beautiful Peak District.

Creswell Crags
Chesterfield, Derbyshire S80 3LH
(01909) 720378
www.creswell-crags.org.uk
A world famous archaeological site, home to Britain's only known Ice Age cave art.

Derby Museum and Art Gallery
Derby DE1 1BS
(01332) 716659
www.derbymuseums.org
Derby Museum and Art Gallery holds collections and displays relating to the history, culture and natural environment of Derby and its region.

Derbyshire Food & Drink Festival
May, Derby, Derbyshire
www.derbyshirefoodfestival.co.uk
Over 150 stalls will showcase the best local produce from Derbyshire and the Peak District region, as well as unique and exotic foods from further afield.

Gulliver's Kingdom Theme Park
Matlock Bath, Derbyshire DE4 3PG
(01629) 580540
www.gulliversfun.co.uk
With more than 40 rides & attractions, Gulliver's provides the complete family entertainment experience. Fun & adventure with Gully Mouse, Dora the explorer, Diego and "The Lost World".

Haddon Hall
Bakewell, Derbyshire DE45 1LA
(01629) 812855
www.haddonhall.co.uk
Haddon Hall is a stunning English Tudor and country house on the River Wye at Bakewell in Derbyshire, Haddon Hall is one of England's finest examples of a medieval manor.

Hardwick Hall
Chesterfield, Derbyshire S44 5QJ
(01246) 850430
www.nationaltrust.org.uk/hardwick
Owned by the National Trust, Hardwick Hall is one of Britain's greatest Elizabethan houses. The water-powered Stainsby Mill is fully functioning and the Park has a fishing lake and circular walks.

Renishaw Hall and Gardens
Dronfield, Derbyshire S21 3WB
(01246) 432310
www.renishaw-hall.co.uk
The Gardens are Italian in design and were laid out over 100 years ago by Sir George Sitwell. The garden is divided into 'rooms' with yew hedges, flanked with classical statues.

Kedleston Hall
Derby DE22 5JH
(01332) 842191
www.nationaltrust.org.uk/main/w-kedlestonhall
A fine example of a neo-classical mansion built between 1759-65 by the architect Robert Adam and set in over 800 acres of parkland and landscaped pleasure grounds. Administered by The National Trust.

The Silk Mill - Museum of Industry and History
Derby DE1 3AF
(01332) 255308
www.derbymuseums.org
The Silk Mill was completed around 1723 and the re built Mill now contains displays on local history and industry.

Sudbury Hall
Ashbourne, Derbyshire DE6 5HT
(01283) 585305
www.nationaltrust.org.uk/sudburyhall/
Explore the grand 17th Century hall with its richly decorated interior and see life below stairs.

Leicestershire & Rutland

Artisan Cheese Fair
May, Melton Mowbray, Leicestershire
www.artisancheesefair.co.uk
A chance to taste the huge range of cheeses that are made locally and further afield.

Ashby-de-la-Zouch Castle
Leicestershire LE65 1BR
(01530) 413343
www.english-heritage.org.uk/daysout/properties/ashby-de-la-zouch-castle
Visit Ashby-de-la-Zouch Castle where you will see the ruins of this historical castle, the original setting for many of the scenes of Sir Walter Scott's classic tale 'Ivanhoe'.

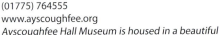

Bosworth Battlefield Heritage Centre
Market Bosworth, Leicestershire CV13 0AD
(01455) 290429
www.bosworthbattlefield.com
Delve into Leicestershire's fascinating history at Bosworth Battlefield Country Park - the site of the 1485 Battle of Bosworth.

Conkers Discovery Centre
Ashby-de-la-Zouch, Leicestershire DE12 6GA
(01283) 216633
www.visitconkers.com/thingstodo/discoverycentre
Enjoy the great outdoors and explore over 120 acres of the award winning parkland.

Easter Vintage Festival
April, Great Central Railway, Leicestershire
www.gcrailway.co.uk
A real treat for all this Easter with traction engines, classic cars and buses, fairground rides, trade stands, a beer tent as well as lots of action on the double track.

Great Central Railway
Leicester LE11 1RW
(01509) 230726
www.gcrailway.co.uk
The Great Central Railway is Britain's only double track main line steam railway. Enjoy an exciting calendar of events, a footplate ride or dine in style on board one of the steam trains.

National Space Centre
Leicester LE4 5NS
(0845) 605 2001
www.spacecentre.co.uk
The award winning National Space Centre is the UK's largest attraction dedicated to space. From the moment you catch sight of the Space Centre's futuristic Rocket Tower, you'll be treated to hours of breathtaking discovery & interactive fun.

Twinlakes Theme Park
Melton Mowbray, Leicestershire LE14 4SB
(01664) 567777
www.twinlakespark.co.uk
Twinlakes Theme Park - packed with variety, fun and endless adventures for every member of your family.

Lincolnshire

Ayscoughfee Hall Museum and Gardens
Spalding, Lincolnshire PE11 2RA
(01775) 764555
www.ayscoughfee.org
Ayscoughfee Hall Museum is housed in a beautiful wool merchant's house built in 1451 on the banks of the River Welland.

Belton House
Belton, Lincolnshire NG32 2LS
(01476) 566116
www.nationaltrust.org.uk/main/w-beltonhouse
Belton, is a perfect example of an English Country House.

Burghley Horse Trials
September, Burghley House, Lincolnshire
www.burghley-horse.co.uk
One of the most popular events in the British equestrian calendar.

Doddington Hall
Lincoln LN6 4RU
(01522) 694308
www.doddingtonhall.com
A superb Elizabethan mansion by the renowned architect Robert Smythson. The hall stands today as it was completed in 1600 with walled courtyards, turrets and gatehouse.

Hardys Animal Farm
Ingoldmells, Lincolnshire PE25 1LZ
(01754) 872267
www.hardysanimalfarm.co.uk
An enjoyable way to learn about the countryside and how a farm works. There are animals for the children to enjoy as well as learning about the history and traditions of the countryside.

Lincolnshire Show
June, Lincolnshire Showground
www.lincolnshireshow.co.uk
Agriculture remains at the heart of the Lincolnshire Show with livestock and equine competitions, machinery displays and the opportunity to find out where your food comes from and to taste it too!

Lincolnshire Wolds Walking Festival
May, Louth, Lincolnshire
www.woldswalkingfestival.co.uk
Over 90 walks, taking place in an Area of Outstanding Natural Beauty and surrounding countryside.

Normanby Hall Museum and Country Park
Scunthorpe, Lincolnshire DN15 9HU
(01724) 720588
www.normanbyhall.co.uk
Normanby Hall is a classic English mansion set in 300 acres of gardens, parkland, deer park, woods, ornamental and wild birds, with a well-stocked gift shop.

RAF Waddington Air Show
July, Waddington, Lincoln, Lincolnshire
www.waddingtonairshow.co.uk
The largest of all RAF air shows, regularly attended by over 150,000 visitors.

Tattershall Castle
Lincolnshire LN4 4LR
(01526) 342543
www.nationaltrust.org.uk/tattershall-castle
Tattershall Castle was built in the 15th Century to impress and dominate by Ralph Cromwell, one of the most powerful men in England. The castle is a dramatic red brick tower.

Northamptonshire

Althorp
Northampton NN7 4HQ
(01604) 770107
www.althorp.com
Come and visit one of England's finest country houses, home of the Spencer family for over 500 years and ancestral home of Diana, Princess of Wales.

British Grand Prix
July, Silverstone, Northamptonshire
www.silverstone.co.uk
The only place in the UK to see the world's best Formula One drivers in action.

Lamport Hall and Gardens
Northamptonshire NN6 9HD
(01604) 686272
www.lamporthall.co.uk
Grade 1 listed building that was home to the Isham family and their collections for over four centuries.

National Waterways Museum - Stoke Bruerne
Towcester, Northamptonshire NN12 7SE
(01604) 862229
www.stokebruernecanalmuseum.org.uk
Stoke Bruerne is an ideal place to explore the story of our waterways.

Northampton Museum & Art Gallery
Northampton NN1 1DP
(01604) 838111
www.northampton.gov.uk/museums
Displays include footwear and related items, paintings, ceramics and glass and the history of Northampton.

Prebendal Manor Medieval Centre
Nassington, Northamptonshire PE8 6QG
(01780) 782575
www.prebendal-manor.co.uk
Visit a unique medieval manor and enjoy the largest recreated medieval gardens in Europe.

Rockingham Castle
Market Harborough, Northamptonshire LE16 8TH
(01536) 770240
www.rockinghamcastle.com
Rockingham Castle stands on the edge of an escarpment giving dramatic views over five counties and the Welland Valley below.

Salcey Forest
Hartwell, Northamptonshire NN17 3BB
(01780) 444920
www.forestry.gov.uk/salceyforest
Get a birds eye view of this wonderful woodland on the tremendous Tree Top Way.

Sulgrave Manor
Northamptonshire OX17 2SD
(01295) 760205
www.sulgravemanor.org.uk
A Tudor manor house and garden, the ancestral home of George Washington's family with authentic furniture shown by friendly guides

Wicksteed Park
Kettering, Northamptonshire NN15 6NJ
(01536) 512475
www.wicksteedpark.co.uk
Wicksteed Park remains Northamptonshire's most popular attraction and entertainment venue.

Nottinghamshire

Armed Forces Weekend
June, Wollaton Park, Nottingham, Nottinghamshire
www.experiencenottinghamshire.com
Nottingham welcomes the annual national event celebrating our Armed Forces past and present.

Festival of Words
Nottingham, Nottinghamshire
www. nottwords.org.uk
Celebrating Nottingham's love of words, this dazzling line up of events and diverse range of host venues pay a fitting tribute to Nottinghamshire's rich literary heritage.

Galleries of Justice Museum
Nottingham NG1 1HN
(0115) 952 0555
www.galleriesofjustice.org.uk
You will be delving in to the dark and disturbing past of crime and punishment.

GameCity
October, Nottingham, Nottinghamshire
www.gamecity.org
GameCity is the largest festival dedicated to the videogame culture in Europe.

Holme Pierrepont Country Park
Newark, Nottinghamshire NG24 1BG
(01636) 655765
www.newark-sherwood.gov.uk
Set in 270 acres of beautiful parkland and home to the National Watersports Centre. With excellent water sports facilities, Family Fun Park, Life Fitness Gym and marvellous nature trails for cycling and walking,

Newark Castle
Holme Pierrepont, Nottinghamshire NG12 2LU
(0115) 982 1212
www.nwscnotts.com
At the heart of the town for many centuries the castle has played an important role in historical events.

Newark Air Museum
Nottinghamshire NG24 2NY
(01636) 707170
www.newarkairmuseum.org
The museum is open to the public every day except December 24th, 25th, 26th and January 1st.

Nottingham Castle
Nottingham NG1 6EL
(0115) 915 3700
www.nottinghamcity.gov.uk/museums
Situated on a high rock, Nottingham Castle commands spectacular views over the city and once rivalled the great castles of Windsor and the Tower of London.

Nottinghamshire County Show
May, Newark Showground, Nottinghamshire
www.newarkshowground.com
A fantastic traditional county show promoting farming, food, rural life and heritage in Nottinghamshire and beyond.

Papplewick Hall & Gardens
Nottinghamshire NG15 8FE
(0115) 963 3491
www.papplewickhall.co.uk
A fine Adam house, built in 1787 and Grade I listed building with a park and woodland garden.

Robin Hood Beer Festival
October, Nottingham Castle, Nottinghamshire
www.beerfestival.nottinghamcamra.org
Set in the stunning grounds of Nottingham Castle, the Robin Hood Beer Festival offers the world's largest selection of real ales and ciders.

Robin Hood Festival
August, Sherwood Forest, Nottinghamshire
www.nottinghamshire.gov.uk/robinhoodfestival
Celebrate our most legendary outlaw in Sherwood Forest's medieval village.

Sherwood Forest Country Park
Nottinghamshire NG21 9HN
(01623) 823202
www.nottinghamshire.gov.uk/sherwoodforestcp
Sherwood Forest Country Park covers 450 acres and incorporates some truly ancient areas of native woodland.

Sherwood Forest Farm Park
Nottinghamshire NG21 9HL
(01623) 823558
www.sherwoodforestfarmpark.co.uk
Meet over 30 different rare farm breeds, plus other unusual species!

Sherwood Pines Forest Park
Edwinstowe, Nottinghamshire NG21 9JL
(01623) 822447
www.forestry.gov.uk/sherwoodpines
The largest forest open to the public in the East Midlands and centre for a wide variety of outdoor activities.

Tourist Information Centres

When you arrive at your destination, visit the Tourist Information Centre for quality assured help with accommodation and information about local attractions and events, or email your request before you go.

Ashbourne	13 Market Place	01335 343666	ashbourneinfo@derbyshiredales.gov.uk
Ashby-de-la-Zouch	North Street	01530 411767	ashby.tic@nwleicestershire.gov.uk
Bakewell	Old Market Hall	01629 813227	bakewell@peakdistrict.gov.uk
Boston	Boston Guildhall	01205 356656/ 720006	ticboston@boston.gov.uk
Buxton	The Pavilion Gardens	01298 25106	tourism@highpeak.gov.uk
Castleton	Buxton Road	01433 620679	castleton@peakdistrict.gov.uk
Chesterfield	Rykneld Square	01246 345777	tourism@chesterfield.gov.uk
Derby	Assembly Rooms	01332 643411	tourism@derby.gov.uk
Glossop	Glossop One Stop Shop	0845 1297777	
Grantham	The Guildhall Centre, Council Offices	01476 406166	granthamtic@southkesteven.gov.uk
Horncastle	Wharf Road	01507 601111	horncastle.info@cpbs.com
Kettering	Municipal Offices	01536 315115	tic@kettering.gov.uk
Leicester	51 Gallowtree Gate	0844 888 5181	info@goleicestershire.com
Lincoln Castle Hill	9 Castle Hill	01522 545458	visitorinformation@lincolnbig.co.uk
Loughborough	Loughborough Town Hall	01509 231914	loughborough@goleicestershire.com
Louth	Cannon Street	01507 601111	louth.info@cpbs.com
Mablethorpe	Louth Hotel, Unit 5	01507 474939	mablethorpeinfo@e-lindsey.gov.uk
Melton Mowbray	The Library, Wilton Road	0116 305 3646	
Newark	Keepers Cottage, Riverside Park	01636 655765	newarktic@nsdc.info
Northampton	Sessions House, County Hall	01604 367997/8	tic@northamptonshire.gov.uk
Nottingham City	1-4 Smithy Row	08444 775 678	tourist.information@nottinghamcity.gov.uk
Retford	40 Grove Street	01777 860780	retford.tourist@bassetlaw.gov.uk
Rutland Water	Sykes Lane	01780 686800	tic@anglianwater.co.uk
Sherwood	Sherwood Heath	01623 824545	sherwoodtic@nsdc.info
Silverstone	Silverstone Circuit	0844 3728 200	Elicia.Bonamy@silverstone.co.uk
Spalding	South Holland Centre	01775 725468/ 764777	touristinformationcentre@sholland.gov.uk
Stamford	Stamford Tourist Information	01780 755611	stamfordtic@southkesteven.gov.uk
Swadlincote	Sharpe's Pottery Museum	01283 222848	gail.archer@sharpespotterymusuem.org.uk
Woodhall Spa	The Cottage Museum	01526 353775	woodhall.spainfo@cpbs.com

Regional Contacts and Information

For more information on accommodation, attractions, activities, events and holidays in the East Midlands, contact one of the following regional or local tourism organisations. Their websites have a wealth of information and many produce free publications to help you get the most out of your visit.

East Midlands Tourism
www.eastmidlandstourism.com

Experience Nottinghamshire
www.experiencenottinghamshire.com

Peak District and Derbyshire
www.visitpeakdistrict.com

Discover Rutland
(01572) 722577
www.discover-rutland.co.uk

Lincolnshire
(01522) 545458
www.visitlincolnshire.com

VisitNorthamptonshire
www.visitnorthamptonshire.co.uk

Leicestershire
0844 888 5181
www.goleicestershire.com

Stay – East Midlands

Entries appear alphabetically by town name in each county. A key to symbols appears on page 7

ASHBOURNE, Derbyshire *Map ref 4B2* *SatNav DE6 1LF*

AA ★★★ Inn

B&B PER ROOM PER NIGHT
S: £50.00 - £90.00
D: £75.00 - £170.00

EVENING MEAL PER PERSON
£10.00 - £25.00

Bentley Brook Inn

Fenny Bentley, Ashbourne, Derbyshire DE6 1LF **T:** (01335) 350278 **F:** 01335 350422
E: all@bentleybrookinn.co.uk
W: www.bentleybrookinn.co.uk

A traditional friendly country inn set in four acres, close to Ashbourne. Standing at the gateway to the National Peak Park and Dove Dale. Well appointed en suite rooms with A la carte restaurant, bar meals & Function Suite. Dog friendly. **Directions:** Just two miles out of Ashbourne, on the A515 Ashbourne to Buxton & B5056 to Bakewell, nestling in the fork of the road. **Bedrooms:** En suite, tv, tea & coffee facilites and toiletries **Open:** All year

Site: P **Payment:** **Property:** **Children:** **Catering:** **Room:** TV DVD

ASHBOURNE, Derbyshire *Map ref 4B2* *SatNav DE6 1QU* B

enjoyEngland.com ★★★★ GUEST ACCOMMODATION

enjoyEngland.com Silver AWARD

B&B PER ROOM PER NIGHT
S: £61.00 - £83.00
D: £66.00 - £88.00

Peak District Spa

Buxton Road, Nr Alsop en le Dale, Ashbourne, Derbyshire DE6 1QU **T:** (01335) 310100
F: 01335 310100 **E:** PeakDistrictSpa@rivendalecaravanpark.co.uk
W: www.peakdistrictspa.co.uk **£ BOOK ONLINE**

Occupying a secluded location on part of Rivendale's 37 acre site with its own parking, terrace and garden with superb views over Eaton Dale. Ideal for cycling, walking & outdoor pursuits (fly fishing lake on site). Convenient Chatsworth, Alton Towers, Carsington Water. All rooms with en suites, oak or travertine floors, under floor heating. Ground floor rooms accessible for wheelchairs.

Directions: Travelling north from Ashbourne towards Buxton on the A515, find Rivendale on the RHS.

Bedrooms: 2 double, 2 twin. Ground floor rooms with wheelchair access & shower room wet rooms en suite. 1st floor rooms with over bath showers en suite
Open: All year except closes 2nd Jan - 31st Jan

WALKERS WELCOME

Site: P **Payment:** **Leisure:** **Property:** **Children:** **Catering:**
Room: TV

BAMFORD, Derbyshire Map ref 4B2 SatNav S33 0AZ B

B&B PER ROOM PER NIGHT
S: £55.00 - £70.00
D: £70.00 - £120.00

EVENING MEAL PER PERSON
£9.95 - £19.95

SPECIAL PROMOTIONS
Go to our website to see the latest offers available. Discounts for 3 or more nights. For those that would like to stay longer we also have 5* self catering apartments. www.ladybowerapartments.co.uk

Yorkshire Bridge Inn

Ashopton Road, Bamford in the High Peak, Hope Valley S33 0AZ **T:** (01433) 651361
F: 01433 651361 **E:** info@yorkshire-bridge.co.uk
W: www.yorkshire-bridge.co.uk **£ BOOK ONLINE**

This famous inn enjoys an idyllic setting near the beautiful reservoirs of Ladybower, Derwent and Howden in the Peak District, and was voted one of the top six freehouses of the year for all-year-round excellence. Superb, en suite rooms, lovely bar and dining areas offering excellent cuisine. Brochure available.

Directions: M1 jct 29, Chesterfield - Baslow - Calver - Hathersage - Bamford. A6013 through Bamford. After 0.5 miles on left-hand side.

Bedrooms: 10 double, 2 twin, 2 family
Open: All year except Christmas

Site: P **Payment:** **Leisure:** **Property:** **Children:** **Catering:**
Room:

BIGGIN-BY-HARTINGTON, Derbyshire Map ref 4B2 SatNav SK17 0DH

Biggin Hall Hotel

Biggin by Hartington, Buxton SK17 0DH **T:** (01298) 84451 **E:** enquiries@bigginhall.co.uk
W: www.bigginhall.co.uk

B&B PER ROOM PER NIGHT
S: £80.00 - £132.00
D: £90.00 - £142.00
EVENING MEAL PER PERSON
£25.00

SPECIAL PROMOTIONS
Available throughout the year. See website www.bigginhall.co.uk

Biggin Hall in the Peak District National Park is the ideal base for cycling and walking and for exploring stunning landscapes and glimpses of past grandeurs – including Chatsworth, Haddon Hall, Kedleston etc - and bold enterprises now preserved as industrial archaeology. The 17th century Grade II* listed main house oozes character and charm. 21st century comforts and Classical English cuisine.

Directions: Half a mile off the A515, midway between Ashbourne and Buxton.

Bedrooms: 1 single, 8 double, 9 twin, 3 suites.
Open: All year

Site: **Payment:** **Leisure:** **Property:** **Children:** 12 **Catering:**
Room:

BUXTON, Derbyshire Map ref 4B2 SatNav SK17 9BA

Alison Park Hotel

3 Temple Road, Buxton, Derbyshire SK17 9BA **T:** (01298) 22473 **F:** 01298 72709
E: reservations@alison-park-hotel.co.uk
W: www.alison-park-hotel.co.uk £ BOOK ONLINE

B&B PER ROOM PER NIGHT
S: £54.00 - £60.00
D: £108.00 - £120.00
EVENING MEAL PER PERSON
£16.00 - £18.50

An Edwardian arts and crafts house, set within its own grounds in quiet location, just out of the town centre. The family management of the hotel ensures a warm welcome. **Bedrooms:** 3 single, 7 double, 3 twin, 2 family **Open:** All year

Site: **Payment:** **Leisure:** **Property:** **Children:** **Catering:** **Room:**

BUXTON, Derbyshire Map ref 4B2 SatNav SK10 5XJ

Common Barn Farm B&B

Common Barn Farm, Smith Lane, Rainow, Macclesfield SK10 5XJ **T:** (01625) 574878
E: g_greengrass@hotmail.com
W: www.cottages-with-a-view.co.uk

B&B PER ROOM PER NIGHT
S: £55.00
D: £75.00

Cosy AA 4* B&B situated on our farm in the Peak District with spectacular views over the Cheshire Plain to the Welsh mountains. **Directions:** Off B5470. **Bedrooms:** 1 ground floor family room. 1 ground floor disabled room with wet room. 1 ground floor double room. 2 twin rooms 1st floor. All en suite, underfloor heating **Open:** All year

Site: P **Payment:** **Leisure:** **Property:** **Children:** **Catering:** **Room:**

BUXTON, Derbyshire Map ref 4B2 SatNav SK17 9DP B

B&B PER ROOM PER NIGHT
S: £40.00 - £55.00
D: £80.00 - £90.00

Kingscroft Guest House

10 Green Lane, Buxton, Derbyshire SK17 9DP **T:** (01298) 22757 **F:** 01298 27858
E: kingscroftbuxton1@btinternet.com
W: www.kingscroftguesthouse.co.uk

Late Victorian luxury guesthouse, in central yet quiet position in heart of Peak District. Comfortable surroundings with period decor. Enjoy our hearty, delicious, home cooked full English or continental breakfasts. **Directions:** Kingscroft is situated only 5 minutes walk from the town's shopping centre, pubs and restaurants, and easy reach at both railway and bus stations. **Bedrooms:** 1 single, 6 double, 1 twin **Open:** All year

Site: P **Payment:** **Leisure:** **Property:** **Catering:** **Room:**

BUXTON, Derbyshire Map ref 4B2 SatNav SK17 6BD H

B&B PER ROOM PER NIGHT
S: £70.00
D: £79.00 - £165.00

EVENING MEAL PER PERSON
£18.00 - £35.00

SPECIAL PROMOTIONS
Chatsworth House Breaks, Theatre Breaks and Special promotions available throughout the year.

Old Hall Hotel

The Square, Buxton SK17 6BD **T:** (01298) 22841 **F:** 01298 72437
E: reception@oldhallhotelbuxton.co.uk
W: www.oldhallhotelbuxton.co.uk £ BOOK ONLINE

This historic hotel, reputedly the oldest in England, offers a warm and friendly service. Ideally located opposite Pavillion Gardens and Edwardian opera house, we serve pre and post theatre dinner in our restaurant and wine bar. Rooms available on B&B and half-board basis. The perfect Peak District base.

Directions: Map available, please see our website for full directions.

Bedrooms: 14 classic double and twin bedrooms, 11 standard doubles, 6 executive doubles and twins, 4 four poster beds, 2 singles and a flat
Open: All year

Site: **Payment:** **Leisure:** **Property:** **Children:**
Catering: **Room:**

CASTLETON, Derbyshire   Map ref 4B2   SatNav S33 8WE B

Causeway House B&B

Back Street, Castleton, Hope Valley S33 8WE **T:** (01433) 623291
E: info@causewayhouse.co.uk
W: www.causewayhouse.co.uk **£ BOOK ONLINE**

B&B PER ROOM PER NIGHT
S: £35.00 - £42.50
D: £75.00 - £85.00

A Former Cruck cottage from the 14th century with oak beams and low ceilings. Heart of the Peak district Castleton is renowned for its Hiking and Cycling trails. **Directions:** Castleton, Hope Valley Derbyshire. Nearest station Hope Derbyshire. Bus depot in the village. **Bedrooms:** 2 single, 1 double, 2 family **Open:** All year

Site: P **Payment:** **Leisure:** **Property:** **Children:** **Catering:** **Room:**

CHESTERFIELD, Derbyshire   Map ref 4B2   SatNav S40 4EE B

Abigails Guest House

62 Brockwell Lane, Chesterfield S40 4EE **T:** (01246) 279391 **F:** 01246 854468
E: gail@abigails.fsnet.co.uk
W: www.abigailsguesthouse.co.uk

B&B PER ROOM PER NIGHT
S: £38.00
D: £56.00

Relax taking breakfast in the conservatory overlooking Chesterfield and surrounding moorlands. Garden with pond, private car park. Best B&B winners 2000. Free Wi-Fi. **Directions:** Please contact us for directions. **Bedrooms:** 2 single, 3 double, 2 twin **Open:** All year

Site: P **Payment:** **Leisure:** **Property:** **Children:** **Catering:** **Room:**

CRESSBROOK, Derbyshire   Map ref 4B2   SatNav SK17 8SY B

Cressbrook Hall

Cressbrook, Buxton SK17 8SY **T:** (01298) 871289 **F:** 01298 871845
E: stay@cressbrookhall.co.uk
W: www.cressbrookhall.co.uk

B&B PER ROOM PER NIGHT
S: £50.00 - £75.00
D: £100.00 - £120.00

Accommodation with a difference. Enjoy this magnificent home built in 1835, set in 23 acres. Spectacular views around the compass. Elegance, simplicity, peace and quiet. Formal gardens by Edward Kemp. **Directions:** Please contact us for directions. **Bedrooms:** 2 double, 1 suite **Open:** All year except Christmas and New Year

Site: P **Payment:** **Leisure:** **Property:** **Children:** **Room:**

HIGH PEAK, Derbyshire Map ref 4B2 — SatNav SK23 6EJ B

enjoyEngland.com ★★★★ INN

B&B PER ROOM PER NIGHT
S: £69.00 - £75.00
D: £79.00 - £105.00
EVENING MEAL PER PERSON
£8.00 - £19.00

The Old Hall Inn

Whitehough, Chinley, High Peak SK23 6EJ **T:** (01663) 750529 **E:** info@old-hall-inn.co.uk
W: www.old-hall-inn.co.uk **£ BOOK ONLINE**

The Old Hall Inn is the quintessential country inn offering a famously warm welcome, excellent local produce menu & with a strong local trade all year round making for a great lively atmosphere any time of the year. The Old Hall has been voted Derbyshire Pub of the Year twice and has won the Great British Pub Awards for 'Best Cask Pub in the East Midlands' for the last four years running.

Directions: Please contact us for directions.

Bedrooms: With eight en suites including a large room with balcony overlooking the garden, we have accommodation choices to suit everyone!
Open: All year

Site: P **Payment:** **Property:** **Children:** **Catering:** **Room:**

HOPE, Derbyshire Map ref 4B2 — SatNav S33 6AF B

enjoyEngland.com ★★★★★ GUEST ACCOMMODATION — enjoyEngland.com Gold AWARD

B&B PER ROOM PER NIGHT
S: £70.00 - £90.00
D: £90.00 - £110.00

Underleigh House

Lose Hill Lane, Off Edale Road, Hope, Hope Valley S33 6AF **T:** (01433) 621372
F: 01433 621324 **E:** info@underleighhouse.co.uk
W: www.underleighhouse.co.uk **£ BOOK ONLINE**

Award-winning and secluded cottage/barn conversion with magnificent countryside views. Ideal for walking and exploring the Peak District. Delicious breakfasts, featuring local and home-made specialities, served in flagstoned dining hall. **Directions:** From Hope, take Edale Road for 0.6 miles. Turn left at de-restriction sign and take Lose Hill Lane for 0.3 miles. **Bedrooms:** 3 double, 2 suite **Open:** All Year Except Christmas, & January

WALKERS WELCOME — CYCLISTS WELCOME

Site: P **Payment:** **Leisure:** **Property:** **Catering:** **Room:**

WESSINGTON, Derbyshire Map ref 4B2 — SatNav DE55 6DU B

enjoyEngland.com ★★★★ FARMHOUSE

B&B PER ROOM PER NIGHT
S: £35.00 - £50.00
D: £70.00 - £100.00

Crich Lane Farm

Moorwood Moor Lane, Wessington, Alfreton, Derbyshire DE55 6DU
T: (01773) 835186 / 07855 510187 **E:** bookings@crichlanefarm.co.uk
W: www.crichlanefarm.co.uk

Stone Farmhouse set in beautiful countryside, a perfect setting for a relaxing break in peaceful surroundings, families very welcome. Meals are served in the village pubs within walking distance. **Directions:** M1 junc 28, A38 towards Derby 3mls, A615 Matlock to Wessington 3 mls, turn opposite church in Wessington, 400yds down lane on left hand side. **Bedrooms:** 1 single, 6 double (includes 2 zip & link), 1 twin, 2 family **Open:** All year except Christmas and New Year

Site: P **Leisure:** **Children:** **Catering:** **Room:**

LOUGHBOROUGH, Leicestershire Map ref 4C3 SatNav LE11 3GR

Burleigh Court Conference Centre & Hotel

Loughborough University, Off Ashby Road, Loughborough, Leicestershire LE11 3GR
T: (01509) 633033 **F:** 01509 211569 **E:** info@welcometoimago.com
W: www.burleigh-court.co.uk **£ BOOK ONLINE**

enjoyEngland.com ★★★★ HOTEL — enjoyEngland.com Silver AWARD

B&B PER ROOM PER NIGHT
S: £65.00 - £110.00
D: £75.00 - £115.00
EVENING MEAL PER PERSON
£22.50

Burleigh Court offers 4 star accommodation ranging from the last word in luxury to unmatched quality and value. The VisitEngland Large Hotel of the Year 2014 Offers award-winning cuisine and an on-site spa and leisure complex. **Directions:** Situated in the Midlands off junction 23 of the M1 motorway, 3 miles from Loughborough's mainline railway station and 8 miles from East Midlands Airport. **Bedrooms:** 40 single, 159 double, 19 twin, 4 family, 4 suite. **Open:** All year except for Christmas day

Payment: **Leisure:** **Property:** **Children:** **Catering:** **Room:**

LOUGHBOROUGH, Leicestershire Map ref 4C3 SatNav LE12 8TD

Bybrook Barn

Leicester Lane, Swithland, Loughborough, Leicestershire LE12 8TD
T: (01162) 357788 / 07973 777395 **E:** info@bybrookbarnbedandbreakfast.co.uk
W: www.bybrookbarnbedandbreakfast.co.uk

enjoyEngland.com ★★★★ BED & BREAKFAST

B&B PER ROOM PER NIGHT
S: £65.00
D: £85.00

Bybrook Barn is a secluded barn conversion set amidst the stunning Charnwood countryside. The ground floor double bedroom with en suite is beatifully furnished with many luxury touches. Breakfast has to be one of the best around. **Directions:** Approximately 15 minutes to M1 J21a, and not much further to East Midlands Airport. **Bedrooms:** Country style of calm colours, light and spacious **Open:** All year except Christmas and New Year

Site: P **Leisure:** **Property:** **Catering:** **Room:**

LOUGHBOROUGH, Leicestershire Map ref 4C3 SatNav LE11 4EX

The Link Hotel

Junction 23/M1, New Ashby Road, Loughborough, Leicestershire LE11 4EX
T: (01509) 633033 **F:** 01509 211569 **E:** info@linkhotel.co.uk
W: www.linkhotelloughborough.co.uk **£ BOOK ONLINE**

AA ★★★ Hotel

B&B PER ROOM PER NIGHT
S: £52.00 - £98.00
D: £72.00 - £108.00
EVENING MEAL PER PERSON
£19.50

The Link is a modern three star hotel which provides outstanding customer service. The venue offers 94 comfortable, en suite bedrooms, including family rooms and suites, bar and dining facilities making it the ideal place to come together. **Directions:** We are located one mile from J23 of the M1. **Open:** All year except Christmas Day

Site: P **Payment:** **Leisure:** **Property:** **Children:** **Catering:** **Room:**

BARKSTON, Lincolnshire Map ref 3A1 SatNav NG32 2NL

Kelling House

17 West Street, Barkston, Nr Grantham NG32 2NL **T:** (01400) 251440
E: sue@kellinghouse.co.uk
W: www.kellinghouse.co.uk

enjoyEngland.com ★★★★ BED & BREAKFAST

B&B PER ROOM PER NIGHT
S: £50.00 - £55.00
D: £85.00 - £95.00
EVENING MEAL PER PERSON
£18.00 - £25.00

In quiet conservation village. C18th cottage with large south facing garden & serving locally sourced food. Perfectly placed to explore Belton House, Belvoir Castle, Burghley House, Lincoln Cathedral, etc **Directions:** A1/Grantham train station 4 miles. **Bedrooms:** 1 single, 1 double, 1 twin **Open:** All year

Site: P **Payment:** € **Leisure:** **Property:** **Children:** **Catering:** **Room:**

BARROW-UPON-HUMBER, Lincolnshire Map ref 4C1 SatNav DN39 6XW B

B&B PER ROOM PER NIGHT
S: £45.95 - £53.95
D: £69.90 - £82.90
EVENING MEAL PER PERSON
£7.95 - £17.95

Thornton Hunt Inn

Thornton Curtis, Near Ulceby, North Lincolnshire DN39 6XW **T:** (01469) 531252
E: thorntonhuntinn@thorntoncurtis.net
W: www.thorntonhuntinn.co.uk **£ BOOK ONLINE**

We are a traditional Freehouse set in an attractive Grade II listed building which dates back to around the Eighteenth Century. The Inn is situated in the quaint village of Thornton Curtis in the glorious North Lincolnshire countryside. **Directions:** M180 (East), Junction 5. Follow the signs to the airport. Take the B1211to Ulceby, then follow the signs for Thornton Curtis. **Bedrooms:** En suite, hairdryer, tea & coffee, TV and Wi-Fi **Open:** All year except Christmas & New Year

Site: P **Payment:** **Leisure:** **Property:** **Children:** **Catering:** **Room:**

BICKER, Lincolnshire Map ref 3A1 SatNav PE20 3AN H

B&B PER ROOM PER NIGHT
S: £60.50 - £68.00
D: £60.50 - £68.00
EVENING MEAL PER PERSON
£12.00 - £25.00

SPECIAL PROMOTIONS
Dinner, Bed & Breakfast £99 based on 2 people sharing

Supreme Inns

Bicker Bar, Bicker, Boston PE20 3AN **T:** (01205) 822804 **E:** enquiries@supremeinns.co.uk
W: www.supremeinns.co.uk **£ BOOK ONLINE**

Situated in Bicker Bar near Boston in Lincolnshire, the Boston Supreme Inn hotel has 55 large and well equipped bedrooms all with en suite facilities. All rooms have internet access, telephone points, flat screen televisions. We have a modern, relaxing bar area, serving homemade bar meals all day, every day. The award winning Haven restaurant is also open in the evenings.

Directions: Located on the junction between the A17/A52.

Bedrooms: 32 dble, 21 twin, 2 suite
Open: All year

Site: **Payment:** **Leisure:** **Property:** **Children:** **Catering:**
Room:

LINCOLN, Lincolnshire Map ref 4C2 SatNav LN41PD

Branston Hall Hotel

Branston Park, Lincoln Road, Branston LN4 1PD **T:** (01522) 793305 **F:** 01522 790549
E: info@branstonhall.com
W: www.branstonhall.com **£ BOOK ONLINE**

AA ★★★ Country House Hotel

B&B PER ROOM PER NIGHT
S: £59.00 - £105.00
D: £79.00 - £139.00

EVENING MEAL PER PERSON
£15.00 - £37.50

SPECIAL PROMOTIONS
For best offers and promotions check our website which is updated constantly with new promotions and offers.

Country house elegance.

Branston Hall is situated just 3 miles away from the centre of Lincoln. It sits within 88 acres of idyllic grounds, has ample free parking and offers luxurious accommodation coupled with award winning food.

It boasts individually styled rooms including 4 posters, family rooms and honeymoon suites as well as an indoor swimming pool, sauna and Jacuzzi and gym.

Directions: GPS: 53.194389, -0.482629. Visit our website for more details.

Bedrooms: A selection of doubles, twins, family rooms, honeymoon suites and 4 poster beds all en suite, sky TV and wifi available at great prices
Open: Every day 24hrs per day

Site: P **Leisure:** **Property:** **Catering:** **Room:**

LINCOLN, Lincolnshire Map ref 4C2 SatNav LN6 9BT B

Redhouse Farm Bed & Breakfast

Thorpe Road, Whisby, Lincoln, Lincolnshire LN6 9BT **T:** (01522) 695513
E: reservations@redhousefarmbnb.com
W: www.redhousefarmbnb.com

enjoyEngland.com ★★★★ BED & BREAKFAST
enjoyEngland.com Silver AWARD

B&B PER ROOM PER NIGHT
S: £43.00 - £48.00
D: £58.00 - £70.00

Redhouse Farm is a delightful old farmhouse with a separate ground floor guest annexe with private parking, overlooking pony paddocks. Situated approx 2 miles off the A46 giving easy access to the historical Cathedral City of Lincoln. **Directions:** At Whisby roundabout on A46 near The Pride of Lincoln pub take exit onto Whisby Road towards Whisby/Eagle, then take the first left onto Thorpe Road. **Bedrooms:** Ground floor, en suite, TV, free Wi Fi and refreshments **Open:** All year

Site: P **Leisure:** **Property:** **Children:** 6 **Room:**

LINCOLN, Lincolnshire Map ref 4C2 SatNav LN6 9PF B

Welbeck Cottage Bed and Breakfast

19 Meadow Lane, South Hykeham, Lincoln LN6 9PF **T:** (01522) 692669
E: maggied@hotmail.co.uk
W: www.welbeckcottagelincoln.com **£ BOOK ONLINE**

enjoyEngland.com ★★★★ BED & BREAKFAST

We offer a warm welcome to our home set in a quiet village location, with access to Lincoln, Newark and many local attractions. Children and pet friendly. Off-road parking. Please contact us for prices. **Directions:** Map and directions supplied on request. **Bedrooms:** 2 double, 1 twin **Open:** All year except Christmas and New Year

WALKERS WELCOME CYCLISTS WELCOME **Site:** P **Leisure:** **Property:** **Children:** **Catering:** **Room:**

RUSKINGTON, Lincolnshire Map ref 3A1 SatNav NG34 9AH B

Sunnyside Farm Bed & Breakfast

Leasingham Lane, Ruskington NG34 9AH **T:** (01526) 833010
E: sunnyside_farm@btinternet.com
W: www.sunnysidefarm.co.uk

enjoyEngland.com ★★★ GUEST ACCOMMODATION

B&B PER ROOM PER NIGHT
S: £32.00
D: £64.00

A family-run farmhouse with en suite guest bedrooms. Warm, friendly welcome. Local golf courses. Coast 40 miles. Boston, Grantham, Lincoln, Newark all within easy reach.

Directions: From A17, take A153 towards Ruskington, B1188 into village. Left at mini roundabout, 400m turn left into Leasingham Lane, follow road 500m to Sunnyside Farm.

Bedrooms: 1 double, 1 twin
Open: All year

Site: **Payment:** € **Leisure:** **Property:** **Children:** **Catering:**
Room:

SKEGNESS, Lincolnshire Map ref 4D2 SatNav PE25 2LA H

Southview Park Hotel

Burgh Road, Skegness PE25 2LA **T:** (01754) 896060 **F:** 01754 896061
E: reception.southviewparkhotel@park-resorts.com
W: www.southviewparkhotel.co.uk **£ BOOK ONLINE**

enjoyEngland.com ★★★ HOTEL

B&B PER ROOM PER NIGHT
S: £55.00 - £154.00
D: £55.00 - £154.00

EVENING MEAL PER PERSON
£7.95 - £30.00

SPECIAL PROMOTIONS
Christmas and New Year packages available. Please contact the hotel for further details.

A hotel where the emphasis is on style, comfort and, above all, relaxation. The hotel offers superior-quality accommodation, food and facilities. All bedrooms are en suite and have TV, internet access, telephone, ironing centre, safe and tea/coffee facilities. One restaurant, two bars, and much, much more. Visit our website to see all the tribute nights at the hotel.

Directions: On the A158, 2 miles from Skegness town centre.

Bedrooms: 24 double, 10 twin, 10 king, 2 family suites, 4 disabled twins, 4 superior doubles, 8 suite
Open: All year

Site: **Payment:** **Leisure:** **Property:** **Children:** **Catering:**
Room:

SKEGNESS, Lincolnshire *Map ref 4D2* *SatNav PE25 2TY* B

enjoyEngland.com ★★★ GUEST ACCOMMODATION

B&B PER ROOM PER NIGHT
D: £50.00 - £55.00
EVENING MEAL PER PERSON
£7.00 - £11.00

Stepping Stones

4 Castleton Boulevard, Skegness PE25 2TY **T:** (01754) 765092
E: info@stepping-stones-hotel.co.uk
W: www.stepping-stones-hotel.co.uk **£ BOOK ONLINE**

Small and friendly we are 50 yards from the prom and all its attractions, including Natureland, bowling greens and the theatre. Within walking distance of town centre. Breakfast menu. **Directions:** A158 head straight through all lights towards sea. A52 south turn left at Ship Inn. A52 north, 2nd right (Scarborough Ave.) until pier, left, left. **Bedrooms:** 3 double, 1 twin, 2 family **Open:** All year except Christmas

Site: P **Payment:** **Children:** **Catering:** **Room:**

SPALDING, Lincolnshire *Map ref 3A1* *SatNav PE11 1SU* H

enjoyEngland.com ★★ HOTEL

B&B PER ROOM PER NIGHT
S: £60.00
D: £80.00

The Red Lion Hotel

Market Place, Spalding, Lincolnshire PE11 1SU **T:** (01775) 722869 **F:** 01775 710074
E: info@redlionhotel-spalding.co.uk
W: www.redlionhotel-spalding.co.uk **£ BOOK ONLINE**

18th century town-centre hotel offering en suite accommodation, friendly local bar, four real ales (CAMRA 2015). Pets Welcome. **Directions:** Five minutes walk from railway/bus station or approx 20 miles east of the A1 via Peterborough or Stamford. **Bedrooms:** 7 double, 8 twin **Open:** All year except Christmas and New Year

Site: P **Payment:** **Leisure:** **Property:** **Children:** **Catering:** **Room:**

STAMFORD, Lincolnshire *Map ref 3A1* *SatNav PE8 6XB* B

enjoyEngland.com ★★★★ BED & BREAKFAST

B&B PER ROOM PER NIGHT
S: £45.00
D: £65.00 - £130.00

19 West Street

King's Cliffe, Peterborough PE8 6XB **T:** (01780) 470365 **E:** kjhl.dixon@gmail.com
W: www.kingjohnhuntinglodge.co.uk

500 year old Grade II Listed rambling stone house clothed with wisteria and roses and a lovely walled garden. Located near Oundle, Stamford, Rutland Water, Rockingham Speedway and Tolethorpe. Many stately homes are located within a 30 minute drive. **Directions:** 4 miles to the west of the A1, at the junction of the A47 **Bedrooms:** 1 Single, 1 Double, 1 Twin and 1 Family **Open:** All Year

Site: P **Property:** **Children:** 10 **Catering:** **Room:**

WOODHALL SPA, Lincolnshire Map ref 4D2 SatNav LN10 6QG H

enjoyEngland.com ★★★ HOTEL

B&B PER ROOM PER NIGHT
S: £70.00
D: £125.00

SPECIAL PROMOTIONS
Book 2 nights Dinner, B&B and get the third night B&B free valid Sunday to Thursday.

Petwood Hotel

Stixwould Road, Woodhall Spa LN10 6QG **T:** (01526) 352411 **F:** 01526 353473
E: reception@petwood.co.uk
W: www.petwood.co.uk **£ BOOK ONLINE**

Friendly service, excellent food and a perfect location for exploring Lincolnshire. Enjoy stunning gardens, cosy log fires and a historical setting linked to the 'Dambusters'. Mid-week special offers available. Rates are from £70 for single rooms and from £125 for double/twin rooms. Upgrade charges apply to executive and four poster rooms.

Directions: From Lincoln take the A15 south to Metheringham (from Sleaford take the A15 north to Metheringham) then take the B1191 to Woodhall Spa. Upon entering Woodhall Spa, continue to the roundabout and turn left (Petwood Hotel is signposted). The hotel is situated 500m on the right.

Bedrooms: 6 singles, 21 doubles, 13 twins, 10 executives, 3 four posters. Half board prices (per room per night) singles £95, doubles £150-£185
Open: All year

Site: P **Payment:** **Leisure:** **Property:** **Children:**
Catering: **Room:**

WOODHALL SPA, Lincolnshire Map ref 4D2 SatNav LN10 6UJ B

Village Limits Country Pub, Restaurant & Motel

Stixwould Road, Woodhall Spa, Lincolnshire LN10 6UJ **T:** (01526) 353312
E: info@villagelimits.co.uk
W: www.villagelimits.co.uk **£ BOOK ONLINE**

B&B PER ROOM PER NIGHT
S: £46.00 - £60.00
D: £70.00 - £90.00

EVENING MEAL PER PERSON
£8.50 - £22.00

SPECIAL PROMOTIONS
15% discount for 4 nights or more. Other low season special offers available.

Select Lincolnshire Food & Accommodation Winners 2006-2013. Free WiFi throughout. All rooms en suite with hairdryers & Sealy mattresses. Peaceful location. Air-conditioning in bar. Delicious, home-cooked pub food available. Ample parking.

Directions: On Stixwould Road, next to Woodhall Country Park. 500m past Petwood Hotel. 1 mile to Woodhall Spa centre. 1.5 miles to Woodhall Spa Golf Club.

Bedrooms: 8 twin
Open: Open all year except New Year

Site: **Payment:** **Property:** **Children:** **Catering:** **Room:**

OUNDLE, Northamptonshire Map ref 3A1 SatNav PE8 5PU B

Lower Farm Bed and Breakfast

Main Street, Barnwell, Nr.Oundle, Northamptonshire PE8 5PU **T:** (01832) 273220
E: lowerfarmbandb@btconnect.com
W: www.lower-farm.co.uk

B&B PER ROOM PER NIGHT
S: £45.00
D: £90.00

10 En suite bedrooms in converted farm buildings in picturesque village of Barnwell, Northamptonshire. **Directions:** Turn off the A605 to Barnwell and turn right at fork,go down hill at bottom turn right before the bridge and follow road until reaching the B&B. **Bedrooms:** All rooms en suite with tv, free wi-fi and tea trays **Open:** All year

Site: **Payment:** **Leisure:** **Property:** **Children:** **Room:**

OAKHAM, Rutland Map ref 4C3 SatNav LE15 8AH H

Barnsdale Lodge Hotel

The Avenue, Rutland Water, Oakham LE15 8AH **T:** (01572) 724678 **F:** 01572 724961
E: reception@barnsdalelodge.co.uk
W: www.barnsdalelodge.co.uk

Enjoy a relaxing break on the beautiful north shore of Rutland Water. We offer you anything from a wedding to an intimate dinner for two. Our informal dining areas are reflected in our seasonal bistro menu. Our bedrooms are all comfortably and individually decorated and have garden or countryside views. **Directions:** Please see our website for map and full directions. **Bedrooms:** 7 single, 27 double, 9 twin, 1 family **Open:** All year

Site: **Payment:** **Leisure:** **Property:** **Children:** **Catering:** **Room:**

For **key to symbols** see page 7

Don't Miss...

Alton Towers

Alton, Staffordshire, ST10 4DB
0871 222 3330
www.altontowers.com
Alton Towers Resort is an exciting destination, with tons of terrific rides, blockbusting attractions, amazing live shows, weird and wonderful costume characters and much more. There's something for the whole family to enjoy!

Dudley Zoological Gardens

Dudley, West Midlands DY1 4QB
(01384) 215313
www.dudleyzoo.org.uk
From lions and tigers to snakes and spiders there's something for all ages. Animal feeding, encounters, face painting, land train and fair rides.

Iron Bridge and Toll House

Telford, Shropshire TF8 7DG
(01952) 433424
www.ironbridge.org.uk
The Ironbridge Gorge is a remarkable and beautiful insight into the region's industrial heritage. Ten award-winning Museums spread along the valley beside the wild River Severn - still spanned by the world's first Iron Bridge, where you can peer through the railings and conjure a vision of sailing vessels heading towards Bristol and the trading markets of the world.

Shakespeare's Birthplace Trust

Stratford-upon-Avon, Warwickshire CV37 6QW
www.shakespeare.org.uk
A unique Shakespeare experience with outstanding archive and library collections, inspiring educational and literary event programmes and five wonderful houses all directly relating to Shakespeare. Shakespeare's Birthplace itself is a fascinating house that offers a tantalising glimpse into Shakespeare's early world.

Warwick Castle

Warwickshire CV34 4QU
0871 265 2000
www.warwick-castle.co.uk
Battlements, towers, turrets, History, magic, myth and adventure - Warwick Castle is a Scheduled Ancient Monument and Grade 1 listed building packed with things to do, inside and out.

Heart of England

Herefordshire, Shropshire, Staffordshire, Warwickshire, West Midlands, Worcestershire

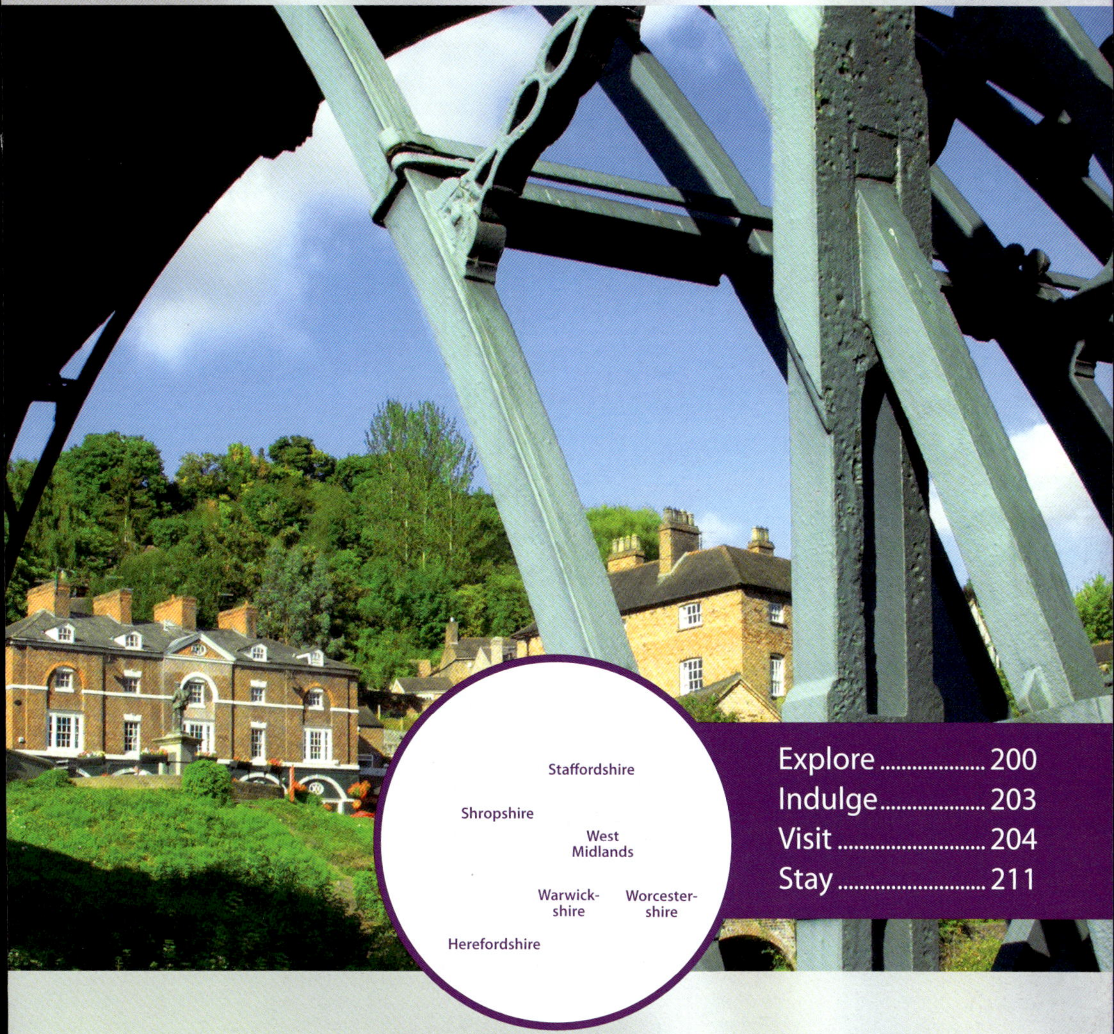

The Heart of England: a name that defines this lovely part of the country so much better than its geographical name: The Midlands. Like a heart it has many arteries and compartments, from the March counties of Shropshire and Herefordshire, through Birmingham and the West Midlands, birthplace of the Industrial revolution. It is a region rich in history and character and you'll find pretty villages, grand castles and plenty of canals and waterways to explore.

Explore – Heart of England

Coventry & Warwickshire

From castles and cathedrals to art galleries, museums and exciting events, this region captivates visitors from all over the world.

A beautifully preserved Tudor town on the banks of the Avon and Warwickshire's most visited, Stratford-upon-Avon is the bard's birthplace with numerous theatres playing Shakespeare and other dramatists' work. The city of Warwick is dominated by its 14th century castle and its museums, and plenty of family activities are staged throughout the year. Historic Coventry has over 400 listed buildings and is most famous for its cathedrals, with the modern Church of St Michael sitting majestically next to the 'blitzed' ruins of its 14th century predecessor.

Herefordshire

Herefordshire's ruined castles in the border country and Iron Age and Roman hill-forts recall a turbulent battle-scarred past. Offa's Dyke, constructed by King Offa of Mercia in the 8th century marks the border with Wales but today the landscape is peaceful, with delightful small towns and villages and Hereford cattle grazing in pastures beside apple orchards and hop gardens.

Hereford has an 11th century cathedral and the Mappa Mundi while in the west, the Wye meanders through meadows and valleys. Hay-on-Wye is now best known for its annual Book Festival and plethora of second hand bookshops.

Staffordshire

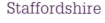

Staffordshire, squeezed between the Black Country to the south and Manchester to the north, is home to the Potteries, a union of six towns made famous by Wedgwood, Spode and other ceramic designers. Lichfield has a magnificent three-spired 13th century cathedral and was birthplace of Samuel Johnson.

The unspoilt ancient heathland of Cannock Chase, leafy woodlands of the National Forest and secluded byways of South Staffordshire all offer the chance to enjoy the great outdoors.

Shropshire

Tucked away on the England/Wales border, Shropshire is another March county that saw much conflict between English and Welsh, hostilities between warring tribes and invading Romans.

The Wrekin and Stretton Hills were created by volcanoes and in the south the Long Mynd rises to 1700 ft with panoramic views of much of the Severn plain. Ironbridge, near the present day Telford, is said to be where the Industrial Revolution started in Britain. County town Shrewsbury was an historic fortress town built in a loop of the river Severn and these days joins Ludlow, with its 11th century castle, as one of the gastronomic high spots of Britain.

Hotspot: The British Ironwork Centre at Oswestry is a treasure trove of magnificent animal sculptures and decorations, including of a 13ft-high gorilla made from an incredible 40,000+ spoons donated by people from all over the world. www.britishironworkcentre.co.uk

West Midlands

The Industrial revolution of the 19th century led to the growth of Birmingham into Britain's second city - the city of a thousand trades. Its prosperity was based on factories, hundreds of small workshops and a network of canals, all of which helped in the production of everything from needles and chocolate to steam engines and bridges. Nowadays the city has one of the best concert halls in Europe, excellent shopping and a regenerated waterside café culture.

The West Midlands is an urban area, criss-crossed by motorways, and still represents the powerhouse of Central Britain. Wolverhampton has been called Capital of the Black Country, made famous through its ironwork and Walsall, birthplace of Jerome K Jerome, has three museums.

Hotspot: Visit the 15 acres of ornamental gardens and glasshouses at Birmingham Botanical Gardens and Glasshouses in Edgbaston. www.birminghambotanicalgardens.org.uk

Affluent Sutton Coldfield and Solihull have proud civic traditions and a number of pretty parks including Sutton Park and Brueton Park. Many of Solihull's rural villages sit along the Stratford-upon-Avon canal and offer plenty of picturesque pubs along the tow path from which to watch the gentle meander of passing narrow boats.

Worcestershire

The beautiful county of Worcestershire has a fantastic selection of historic houses and gardens to discover and Worcester itself has a famous cathedral, cricket ground, and 15th century Commandery, now a Civil war museum.

Hotspot: Ride the Severn Valley Railway for a 16 mile long, steam powered journey through the breathtaking landscape of the Severn Valley from Kidderminister all the way to Bridgnorth in Shropshire. www.svr.co.uk

Great Malvern, still a Spa town, is famous as the birthplace of Sir Edward Elgar, who drew much of his inspiration from this countryside and who is celebrated at the annual Malvern Festival. The old riverside market town of Evesham is the centre of the Vale of Evesham fruit and vegetable growing area which, with the tranquil banks of the river Avon and the undulating hills and peaceful wooded slopes of the Cotswolds, offers some of the prettiest landscapes in the country.

Droitwich, known in Roman times as Salinae, still has briny water in its spa baths and can trace the origins of salt extraction in the area back to prehistoric times, it even holds an annual Salt Festival to celebrate this unique heritage.

Indulge – Heart of England

Enjoy a romantic cruise along the **River Avon** at Stratford-upon-Avon on a traditional Edwardian passenger launch. Cruise downstream from the Bancroft gardens past the Royal Shakespeare Theatre and Holy Trinity Church (the site of Shakespeare's tomb) before turning around and passing under the 15th Century Clopton Bridge to discover quiet river-banks and meadows. www.avon-boating.co.uk

Dine in style at **Harry's Restaurant** at The Chase Hotel, a magnificent georgian country house hotel set in 11 acres of award-winning parkland on the outskirts of Ross-on-Wye. (01989) 768330, www.chasehotel.co.uk

In the quaint, sleepy town of Church Stretton lies one of the best delicatessens in Britain. **Van Doesburg's** deli serves gourmet treats all made on the premises and the desserts are incredible. 3 High Street, Church Stretton, Shropshire. www.vandoesburgs.co.uk

Cadbury World, at the historic Bourneville village near Birmingham, tells the mouth-watering story of Cadbury's chocolate and includes chocolate-making demonstrations with free samples, attractions for all ages, free parking, shop and restaurant. Phone to check availability and book admission. 0845 450 3599 www.cadburyworld.co.uk

Arts and crafts lovers can indulge in a spot of shopping for unusual gifts and artworks at the delightful **Jinney Ring Craft Centre** in Hanbury near Redditch. A range of craftspeople work on site and there's a quirky gift shop and gallery, as well as a daytime restaurant in a rustic old barn, and all set in lovely gardens with duck ponds and stunning views across to the Malvern Hills. www.jinneyring.co.uk

Visit – Heart of England

Attractions with this sign participate in the Visitor Attraction Quality Assurance Scheme.

Coventry & Warwickshire

Coventry Cathedral - St Michael's

West Midlands CV1 5AB
(024) 7652 1257
www.coventrycathedral.org.uk
Glorious 20th century Cathedral, with stunning 1950's art & architecture, rising above the stark ruins of the medieval Cathedral destroyed by German air raids in 1940.

Compton Verney

Stratford-upon-Avon CV35 9HZ
(01926) 645500
www.comptonverney.org.uk
Award-winning art gallery housed in a grade I listed Robert Adam mansion.

Festival of Motoring

August, Stoneleigh, Warwickshire
www.festival-of-motoring.co.uk
This major event takes place at Stoneleigh Park in Warwickshire. In addition to hundreds of fantastic cars to look at, there will be the traditional historic vehicle 'run' through delightful Warwickshire countryside, car gymkhanas and auto tests.

Godiva Festival

July, Coventry, Warwickshire
www.godivafestival.com
The Godiva Festival is the UK's biggest free family festival held over a weekend in the War Memorial Park, Coventry. The event showcases some of the finest local, national and International artists, live comedy, family entertainment, Godiva Carnival, and lots more.

Heart Park

Fillongley, Warwickshire CV7 8DX
(01676) 540333
www.heartpark.co.uk
"We believe that the heart of our Park is the beach and lake. But for those of you who'd like to try out a few 'different' activities - we've got a great assortment for you to try."

Heritage Open Days

September, Coventry, Warwickshire
www.coventry.gov.uk/hod
Heritage Open Days celebrate England's architecture and culture by allowing visitors free access to interesting properties that are either not usually open or would normally charge an entrance fee. Heritage Open Days also include tours, events and activities that focus on local architecture and culture.

Kenilworth Castle and Elizabethan Garden
Warwickshire CV8 1NE
(01926) 852078
www.english-heritage.org.uk/kenilworth
One of the most spectacular castle ruins in England.

Packwood House
Solihull, Warwickshire B94 6AT
0844 800 1895
www.nationaltrust.org.uk/main/w-packwoodhouse
Restored tudor house, park and garden with notable topiary.

Ragley Hall
Stratford-upon-Avon, Warwickshire B49 5NJ
(01789) 762090
www.ragley.co.uk
Ragley Hall is set in 27 acres of beautiful formal gardens.

Ryton Pools Country Parks
Coventry, Warwickshire CV8 3BH
(024) 7630 5592
www.warwickshire.gov.uk/parks
The 100 acres of Ryton Pools Country Park are just waiting to be explored. The many different habitats are home to a wide range of birds and other wildlife.

Stratford River Festival
July, Stratford, Warwickshire
www.stratfordriverfestival.co.uk
The highly successful Stratford-upon-Avon River Festival brings the waterways of Stratford alive, with boatloads of family fun, on the first weekend of July.

Three Counties Show
June, Malvern, Warwickshire
www.threecounties.co.uk
Three jam-packed days of family entertainment and fun, all in celebration of the great British farming world and countryside.

Herefordshire

Eastnor Castle
Ledbury, Herefordshire HR8 1RL
(01531) 633160
www.eastnorcastle.com
Fairytale Georgian Castle dramatically situated in the Malvern Hills.

Goodrich Castle
Ross-on-Wye, Herefordshire HR9 6HY
(01600) 890538
www.english-heritage.org.uk/goodrich
Come and relive the turbulent history of Goodrich Castle with our free audio and then climb to the battlements for breathtaking views over the Wye Valley.

The Hay Festival
May, Hay-on-Wye, Herefordshire
www.hayfestival.com
Some five hundred events see writers, politicians, poets, scientists, comedians, philosophers and musicians come together on a greenfield site for a ten day fesitval of ideas and stories at the Hay Festival.

Hereford Cathedral
Herefordshire HR1 2NG
(01432) 374202
www.herefordcathedral.org
Some of the finest examples of architecture from Norman times to the present day.

Hereford Museum and Art Gallery
Herefordshire HR4 9AU
(01432) 260692
www.herefordshire.gov.uk/leisure/museums_galleries/2869.asp
In the museum, aspects of Herefordshire history and life - in the Gallery, regularly changing exhibitions of paintings, photography and crafts.

Hergest Croft Gardens
Kington, Herefordshire HR5 3EG
(01544) 230160
www.hergest.co.uk
The gardens extend over 50 acres, with more than 4000 rare shrubs and trees. With over 60 champion trees and shrubs it is one of the finest collections in the British Isles.

Ledbury Heritage Centre
Herefordshire, HR8 1DN
(01432) 260692
www.herefordshire.gov.uk/leisure
The story of Ledbury's past displayed in a timber-framed building in the picturesque lane leading to the church.

Shropshire

Darby Houses (Ironbridge)
Telford, Shropshire TF8 7EW
(01952) 433424
www.ironbridge.org.uk
In the Darby houses, Dale House and Rosehill House, you can delve in to the everyday life of Quaker families.

Enginuity
Telford, Shropshire TF8 7DG
(01952) 433424
www.ironbridge.org.uk
At Enginuity you can turn the wheels of your imagination, test your horse power and discover how good ideas are turned in to real things.

English Haydn Festival
June, Bridgnorth, Shropshire
www.englishhaydn.com
An array of the music of Joseph Haydn and his contemporaries, performed in St. Leonards Church, Bridgnorth.

Ludlow Food Festival
September, Ludlow, Shropshire
www.foodfestival.co.uk
More than 160 top quality independent food and drink producers inside Ludlow Castle.

Much Wenlock Priory
Shropshire TF13 6HS
(01952) 727466
www.english-heritage.org.uk/wenlockpriory
Wenlock Priory, with its stunning clipped topiary, has a pastoral setting on the edge of lovely Much Wenlock

RAF Cosford Air Show
June, Shifnal, Shropshire
www.cosfordairshow.co.uk
This RAF-organised show usually features all the airshow favourites, classic and current British and foreign aircraft, exhibits and trade stalls all on this classic RAF airbase.

Royal Air Force Museum Cosford
Shifnal, Shropshire TF11 8UP
(01902) 376200
www.rafmuseum.org
FREE Admission. The award winning museum houses one of the largest aviation collections in the United Kingdom.

Shrewsbury Folk Festival
August, Shrewsbury, Shropshire
www.shrewsburyfolkfestival.co.uk
Shrewsbury Folk Festival has a reputation for delivering the very finest acts from the UK and around the world.

Stokesay Castle
Craven Arms, Shropshire SY7 9AH
(01588) 672544
www.english-heritage.org.uk/stokesaycastle
Stokesay Castle, nestles in peaceful South Shropshire countryside near the Welsh Border. It is one of more than a dozen English Heritage properties in the county.

V Festival
August, Weston Park, Shropshire
www.vfestival.com
Legendary rock and pop festival.

Wenlock Olympian Games
July, Much Wenlock, Shropshire
www.wenlock-olympian-society.org.uk
The games that inspired the modern Olympic Movement.

Wroxeter Roman City
Shrewsbury, Shropshire SY5 6PH
(01743) 761330
www.english-heritage.org.uk/wroxeter
Wroxeter Roman City, or Viroconium, to give it its Roman title, is thought to have been one of the largest Roman cities in the UK with over 200 acres of land, 2 miles of walls and a population of approximately 5,000.

Staffordshire

Abbots Bromley Horn Dance
September, Abbots Bromley, Staffordshire
www.abbotsbromley.com
Ancient ritual dating back to 1226. Six deer-men, a fool, hobby horse, bowman and Maid Marian perform to music provided by a melodian player.

Aerial Extreme Trentham
Staffordshire ST4 8AX
0845 652 1736
www.aerialextreme.co.uk/index.php/courses/trentham-estate
Our tree based adventure ropes course, set within the tranquil grounds of Trentham Estate is a truly spectacular journey.

Etruria Industrial Museum
Staffordshire ST4 7AF
(07900) 267711
www.stokemuseums.org.uk
Discover how they put the 'bone' in bone china at the last working steam-powered potters mill in Britain. Includes a Bone and Flint Mill and family-friendly interactive exhibition.

Lichfield Cathedral
Staffordshire WS13 7LD
(01543) 306100
www.lichfield-cathedral.org
A medieval Cathedral with 3 spires in the heart of an historic City set in its own serene Close.

Midlands Grand National
March, Uttoxeter Racecourse, Staffordshire
www.uttoxeter-racecourse.co.uk
Biggest fixture in Uttoxeter's calendar.

National Memorial Arboretum
Lichfield, Staffordshire DE13 7AR
(01283) 792333
www.thenma.org.uk
150 acres of trees and memorials, planted as a living tribute to those who have served, died or suffered in the service of their Country.

The Roaches
Upper Hulme, Leek, Staffordshire ST13 8UB
www.staffsmoorlands.gov.uk
The Roaches (or Roches) is a wind-carved outcrop of gritstone rocks that rises above the waters or Tittesworth reservoir, between Leek in Staffordshire and Buxton in Derbyshire. It's impressive gritstone edges and craggy rocks are loved by walkers and climbers alike.

Stone Food & Drink Festival
October, Stone, Staffordshire
www.stonefooddrink.org.uk
Staffordshire's biggest celebration of all things gastronomic.

Tamworth Castle
Staffordshire B79 7NA
(01827) 709629
www.tamworthcastle.co.uk
The number one Heritage attraction located in the town. Explore over 900 years of history in the magnificent Motte and Bailey Castle.

Wedgwood Visitor Centre
Stoke-on-Trent, Staffordshire ST12 9ER
(01782) 282986
www.wedgwoodvisitorcentre.com
Enjoy the past, buy the present and treasure the experience. The Wedgwood Visitor Centre offers a unique chance to immerse yourself in the heritage of Britain's greatest ceramics company.

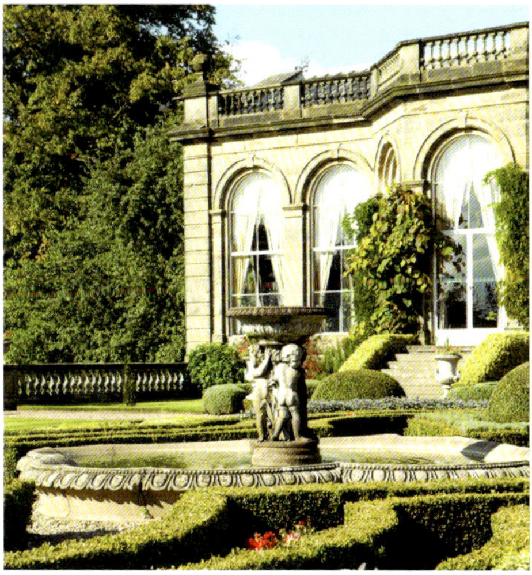

West Midlands

Artsfest
September, Birmingham, West Midlands
www.visitbirmingham.com
Artsfest is one of the UK's biggest free arts festival and showcases work across the performing arts, visual arts and digital arts genres to promote emerging and established talent.

Barber Institute of Fine Arts
Edgbaston, West Midlands B15 2TS
(0121) 414 7333
www.barber.org.uk
British and European paintings, drawings and sculpture from the 13th century to mid 20th century.

Birmingham Literature Festival
October, Birmingham, West Midlands
www.visitbirmingham.com
Celebrating the city's literature scene, the Birmingham Literature Festival takes places every year with its trademark mix of literature events, talks and workshops.

Birmingham International Jazz and Blues Festival
July, Birmingham, West Midlands
www.visitbirmingham.com
Musicians and fans come to the city from every corner of the UK as well as from further afield and significantly, almost all of the events are free to the public.

Black Country Living Museum
Dudley, West Midlands DY1 4SQ
(0121) 557 9643
www.bclm.co.uk
Britain's friendliest open-air museum - visit original shops and houses, ride on fair attractions, take a look down the underground coalmine.

Frankfurt Christmas Market & Craft Fair
November-December, Birmingham, West Midlands
www.visitbirmingham.com
The largest authentic German market outside Germany and Austria and the centrepiece of the city's festive event calendar.

Moseley Folk Festival
September, Birmingham, West Midlands
www.visitbirmingham.com
Offering an inner city Shangri-la bringing together people from all ages and backgrounds to witness folk legends playing alongside their contemporaries.

Thinktank-Birmingham Science Museum
West Midlands B4 7XG
(0121) 202 2222
www.thinktank.ac
Thinktank is Birmingham's science museum where the emphasis is firmly on hands on exhibits and interactive fun.

Worcestershire

The Almonry Museum & Heritage Centre
Evesham, Worcestershire WR11 4BG
(01386) 446944
www.almonryevesham.org
The 14th century house has 12 rooms of exhibits from 2000 years of Evesham history and pleasant gardens to the rear.

Hanbury Hall
Droitwich Spa, Worcestershire WR9 7EA
(01527) 821214
www.nationaltrust.org.uk/hanburyhall
Early 18th century house, garden & park owned by the Vernon family for nearly 300 years.

Worcester Cathedral
Worcestershire WR1 2LA
(01905) 732900
www.worcestercathedral.co.uk
Worcester Cathedral is one of England's most magnificent and inspiring buildings, a place of prayer and worship for 14 centuries.

West Midland Safari and Leisure Park Bewdley,
Worcestershire DY12 1LF
(01299) 402114 www.wmsp.co.uk
Are you ready to SAFARI and come face to face with some of the fastest, tallest, largest and cutest animals around?

Worcester City Art Gallery & Museum
Worcestershire WR1 1DT
(01905) 25371
www.worcestercitymuseums.org.uk
The art gallery & museum runs a programme of exhibitions/events for all the family. Explore the fascinating displays, exhibitions, café, shop and Worcestershire Soldier Galleries.

Tourist Information Centres

When you arrive at your destination, visit the Tourist Information Centre for quality assured help with accommodation and information about local attractions and events, or email your request before you go.

Bewdley	Load Street	0845 6077819	bewdleytic@wyreforestdc.gov.uk
Birmingham Library	Centenary Square	0844 888 3883	visit@marketingbirmingham.com
Bridgnorth	The Library	01746 763257	bridgnorth.tourism@shropshire.gov.uk
Bromyard	The Bromyard Centre	01885 488133	enquiries@bromyard-live.org.uk
Church Stretton	Church Street	01694 723133	churchstretton.scf@shropshire.gov.uk
Droitwich Spa	St Richard's House	01905 774312	heritage@droitwichspa.gov.uk
Ellesmere, Shropshire	The Boathouse Visitor Centre	01691 622981	ellesmere.tourism@shropshire.gov.uk
Evesham	The Almonry	01386 446944	tic@almonry.ndo.co.uk
Hereford	1 King Street	01432 268430	reception@visitherefordshire.co.uk
Ironbridge	Museum of The Gorge	01952 433424/ 01952 435900	tic@ironbridge.org.uk
Kenilworth	Kenilworth Library	0300 5558171	kenilworthlibrary@warwickshire.gov.uk
Ledbury	38 The Homend	0844 5678650	info@vistledbury.info
Leek	1 Market Place	01538 483741	tourism.services@staffsmoorlands.gov.uk
Leominster	1 Corn Square	01568 616460	leominstertic@herefordshire.gov.uk
Lichfield	Lichfield Garrick	01543 412112	info@visitlichfield.com
Ludlow	Castle Street	01584 875053	ludlow.tourism@shropshire.gov.uk
Malvern	21 Church Street	01684 892289	info@visitthemalverns.org
Market Drayton	49 Cheshire Street	01630 653114	marketdrayton.scf@shropshire-cc.gov.uk
Much Wenlock	The Museum - VIC	01952 727679/ 01743 258891	muchwenlock.tourism@shropshire.gov.uk
Newcastle-Under-Lyme	Newcastle Library	01782 297313	tic.newcastle@staffordshire.gov.uk
Nuneaton	Nuneaton Library	0300 5558171	nuneatonlibrary@warwickshire.gov.uk
Oswestry (Mile End)	Mile End	01691 662488	oswestrytourism@shropshire.gov.uk
Oswestry Town	The Heritage Centre	01691 662753	ot@oswestry-welshborders.org.uk
Redditch	Palace Theatre	01527 60806	info.centre@bromsgroveandredditch.gov.uk
Ross-On-Wye	Market House	01989 562768/ 01432 260675	visitorcentreross@herefordshire.gov.uk
Royal leamington spa	Royal Pump Rooms	01926 742762	vic@warwickdc.gov.uk
Rugby	Rugby Art Gallery Museum	01788 533217	visitor.centre@rugby.gov.uk
Shrewsbury	Barker Street	01743 281200	visitorinformation@shropshire.gov.uk
Solihull	Central Library	0121 704 6130	artscomplex@solihull.gov.uk
Stafford	Stafford Gatehouse Theatre	01785 619619	tic@staffordbc.gov.uk
Stoke-On-Trent	Victoria Hall, Bagnall Street	01782 236000	stoke.tic@stoke.gov.uk
Stratford-Upon-Avon	Bridge Foot	01789 264293	tic@discover-stratford.com
Tamworth	Philip Dix Centre	01827 709581	tic@tamworth.gov.uk
Telford	The Telford Shopping Centre	01952 238008	tourist-info@telfordshopping.co.uk
Upton Upon Severn	The Heritage Centre	01684 594200	upton.tic@malvernhills.gov.uk
Warwick	Visit Warwick	01926 492212	info@visitwarwick.co.uk
Whitchurch (Shropshire)	Whitchurch Heritage Centre	01948 664577	heritage@whitchurch-shropshire-tc.gov.uk
Worcester	The Guildhall	01905 726311/ 722561	touristinfo@visitworcester.com
Coventry	St Michael's Tower, Coventry Cathedral Ruins	024 7622 5616	tic@coventry.gov.uk

Regional Contacts and Information

For more information on accommodation, attractions, activities, events and holidays in the Heart of England, contact one of the following regional or local tourism organisations. Their websites have a wealth of information and many produce free publications to help you get the most out of your visit.

Marketing Birmingham
(0844) 888 3883
www.visitbirmingham.com

Visit Coventy & Warwickshire
(024) 7622 5616
www.visitcoventryandwarwickshire.co.uk

Visit Herefordshire
(01432) 268430
www.visitherefordshire.co.uk

Shakespeare Country
(0871) 978 0800
www.shakespeare-country.co.uk

Shropshire Tourism
(01743) 261919
www.shropshiretourism.co.uk

Destination Staffordshire
(01785) 277397
www.enjoystaffordshire.com

Stoke-on-Trent
(01782) 236000
www.visitstoke.co.uk

Destination Worcestershire
(0845) 641 1540
www.visitworcestershire.org

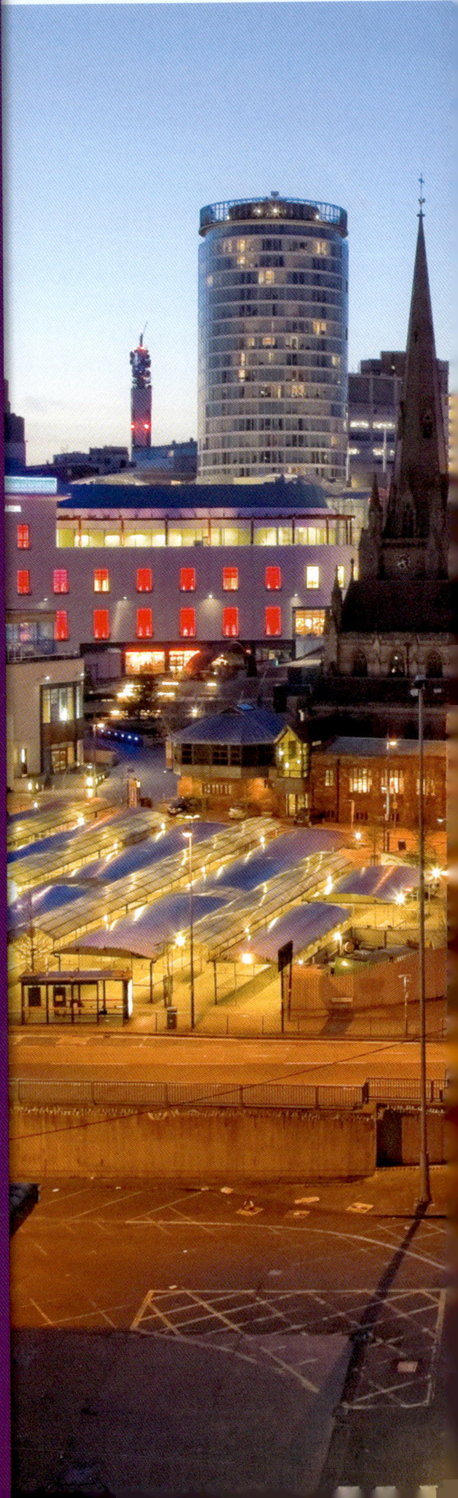

Stay – Heart of England

Entries appear alphabetically by town name in each county. A key to symbols appears on page 7

HEREFORD, Herefordshire *Map ref 2A1* *SatNav HR2 7BP* H

ENJOY ENGLAND ★★★ HOTEL

B&B PER ROOM PER NIGHT
S: £69.00 - £85.00
D: £84.00 - £100.00

EVENING MEAL PER PERSON
£14.95 - £35.00

Three Counties Hotel

Belmont Road, Hereford HR2 7BP **T:** (01432) 299955 **F:** 01432 275114
E: enquiries@threecountieshotel.co.uk
W: www.threecountieshotel.co.uk **£ BOOK ONLINE**

Excellently appointed hotel set in 3.5 acres. Emphasis on traditional, friendly service. Tasteful bedrooms, restaurant and bar offer today's guests all modern comforts. Free Wi-Fi in all public areas and selected bedrooms. Town centre 1.5 miles. **Directions:** Please see website. **Bedrooms:** 18 dble, 42 twin **Open:** All year

Site: **Payment:** **Property:** **Children:** **Catering:** **Room:**

ROSS-ON-WYE, Herefordshire *Map ref 2A1* *SatNav HR9 5LH* H

ENJOY ENGLAND ★★★ HOTEL

B&B PER ROOM PER NIGHT
S: £55.00 - £205.00
D: £75.00 - £205.00

EVENING MEAL PER PERSON
£11.00 - £35.00

SPECIAL PROMOTIONS
Check website for regular special offers.

The Chase Hotel

Gloucester Road, Ross-on-Wye, Herefordshire HR9 5LH **T:** (01989) 763161
F: 01989 768330 **E:** res@chasehotel.co.uk
W: www.chasehotel.co.uk **£ BOOK ONLINE**

Whether on business or pleasure the Chase is the perfect rural location. Concessionary golf arrangements are available. Award-winning cuisine within our fine-dining restaurant and conference and events facility, catering for up to 300 guests, provide good quality of service and product within a country-house venue.

Directions: M50 jct 4, take the A449. Turn left onto the A40 for Gloucester. Carry on across the roundabout past the new houses on the right. Turn right at next roundabout, the Chase is 0.5 miles on your left.

Bedrooms: 28 dble, 9 twin, 1 single
Open: All year except Christmas

Site: **Payment:** **Leisure:** **Property:** **Children:** **Catering:**
Room:

BROSELEY, Shropshire *Map ref 4A3* *SatNav TF12 5EW* B

ENJOY ENGLAND ★★★★ GUEST ACCOMMODATION — Silver AWARD

B&B PER ROOM PER NIGHT
S: £45.00 - £55.00
D: £75.00 - £90.00

Broseley House

1 The Square, Broseley, Ironbridge TF12 5EW **T:** (01952) 882043
E: info@broseleyhouse.co.uk
W: www.broseleyhouse.co.uk

Period townhouse, one mile Ironbridge. Unique, comfortable bedrooms with Wi-Fi, freeview, plus many thoughtful extras and close good local amenities. Walkers, cyclists welcome. Self catering also available. **Directions:** Refer to the website or call for directions. **Bedrooms:** 3 double, 1 twin, 2 family **Open:** All year

Site: **Payment:** **Property:** **Children:** 5 **Catering:** **Room:**

CLUN, Shropshire Map ref 4A3 SatNav SY7 8JA B

The White Horse Inn

The Square, Clun, Shropshire SY7 8JA **T:** (01588) 640305 **E:** room@whi-clun.co.uk
W: www.whi-clun.co.uk **£ BOOK ONLINE**

enjoyEngland.com ★★★ INN

B&B PER ROOM PER NIGHT
S: £40.00 - £42.50
D: £65.00 - £70.00
EVENING MEAL PER PERSON
£7.95 - £18.95

Small, friendly, 'Good Pub Guide' listed pub with well-appointed, en suite family bedrooms in traditional style. Wide-ranging menu available in dining room. Specialising in Real Ales with own micro-brewery **Directions:** In the centre of Clun. **Bedrooms:** 2 twin, 2 double **Open:** All year except Christmas

Site: **Payment:** **Leisure:** **Property:** **Children:** **Catering:** **Room:**

LUDLOW, Shropshire Map ref 4A3 SatNav SY8 3DP B

Elm Lodge B&B

Elm Lodge, Fishmore, Ludlow SY8 3DP **T:** (01584) 872308 **F:** 01584 877397
E: info@elm-lodge.org.uk
W: www.elm-lodge.org.uk

enjoyEngland.com ★★★★ BED & BREAKFAST

B&B PER ROOM PER NIGHT
S: £57.50
D: £70.00 - £90.00

Elm Lodge a Georgian property offering 5 B&B rooms and a Suite in a parkland setting 1 mile from town centre boasting a 9 hole golf course on site. Sleeps 12, free WiFi and ample parking. **Directions:** Please look out for our brown and white Golf and Accommodation signs. **Bedrooms:** All our rooms are located on the first floor **Open:** All year except Christmas

Site: P **Payment:** **Leisure:** **Property:** **Room:**

LUDLOW, Shropshire Map ref 4A3 SatNav SY8 1AA H

The Feathers Hotel

Bull Ring, Ludlow SY8 1AA **T:** (01584) 875261 **F:** 01584 876030
E: enquiries@feathersatludlow.co.uk
W: www.feathersatludlow.co.uk **£ BOOK ONLINE**

enjoyEngland.com ★★★ HOTEL

B&B PER ROOM PER NIGHT
S: £85.00 - £95.00
D: £115.00 - £200.00
EVENING MEAL PER PERSON
£32.00 - £39.95

At the heart of the ancient market town of Ludlow with Jacobean architecture and a medieval heritage. Recently refurbished. Award winning restaurant. High standard of food and service. **Directions:** From A49 follow signs to Ludlow town centre. We are situated on the brow of the hill, near a pedestrian crossing. **Bedrooms:** 3 single, 23 dble, 12 twin, 2 family **Open:** All year

Site: **Payment:** **Leisure:** **Property:** **Children:** **Catering:** **Room:**

NEWPORT, Shropshire Map ref 4A3 SatNav TF10 9LQ B

Lilleshall National Sports and Conferencing Centre

Near Newport, Shropshire TF10 9AT **T:** (01952) 603003 **E:** enquiries.lilleshall@serco.com
W: www.lilleshallnsc.co.uk

enjoyEngland.com ★★★★ CAMPUS ACCOMMODATION

B&B PER ROOM PER NIGHT
S: £60.20
D: £86.70

Built in 1831 as the family retreat of the Duke of Sutherland, Lilleshall is set in spectacular and secluded surroundings with an extensive range of on site facilities. (Rooms are available in adjacent accommodation, not in the main house). **Bedrooms:** En suite, flat screen TV, tea and coffee and Wi-Fi. **Open:** All year except 24th Dec - 2nd Jan.

Site: P **Payment:** **Leisure:** **Property:** **Children:** **Catering:** **Bedroom:**

SHREWSBURY, Shropshire Map ref 4A3 SatNav SY5 6LE B

Brompton Farmhouse

Nr Cross Houses, Shrewsbury, Shropshire SY5 6LE **T:** (01743) 761629
E: info@bromptonfarmhouse.co.uk
W: www.bromptonfarmhouse.co.uk **£ BOOK ONLINE**

Our delightful Georgian farmhouse, set in extensive lawns and gardens, is a haven of peace, comfort and tranquillity. Ideally situated to explore Shropshire. Please contact for 2015 Rates. **Directions:** B4380 at Atcham take turn to X-Houses. Follow signs to Brompton Bed and Breakfast and Brompton Cookery School. **Bedrooms:** 1 double/twin with en suite bath and shower over, 1 double/twin with en suite shower room, 1 family suite containing 2 double rooms & shared bathroom **Open:** All year

Site: **Payment:** **Leisure:** **Property:** **Children:** **Catering:** **Room:**

TELFORD, Shropshire Map ref 4A3 SatNav TF6 6BE B

The Mill House B&B

Shrewsbury Road, High Ercall, Telford TF6 6BE **T:** (01952) 770394 **E:** Judy@ercallmill.co.uk
W: www.ercallmill.co.uk

B&B PER ROOM PER NIGHT
S: £45.00 - £50.00
D: £60.00 - £70.00

The Mill House; an 18th Century converted water mill, is situated beside the River Roden. Located in the village of High Ercall, it is halfway between the historic county town of Shrewsbury and the new town of Telford. Wi-Fi and EV charging. **Directions:** 1 mile South West of High Ercall on B5062 **Bedrooms:** All rooms en suite, Wi-Fi,TV tea & coffee in rooms. **Open:** All Year

Site: **Payment:** **Leisure:** **Property:** **Children:** **Catering:** **Room:**

TELFORD, Shropshire Map ref 4A3 SatNav TF1 2HA B

The Old Orleton Inn

378 Holyhead Road, Wellington, Telford, Shropshire TF1 2HA **T:** (01952) 255011
E: info@theoldorleton.com
W: www.theoldorleton.com **£ BOOK ONLINE**

B&B PER ROOM PER NIGHT
S: £65.00 - £125.00
D: £89.00 - £145.00

EVENING MEAL PER PERSON
£12.00 - £35.00

SPECIAL PROMOTIONS
Stay & Eat offer (DBB for £125 per couple)

Wrekin Weekend (3 nights DBB plus extras £325).

Contemporary Styled 17th Century Coaching Inn facing the famous Wrekin Hill. The Old Orleton Inn, Wellington, Shropshire is a charming retreat for both work and pleasure.

Directions: 7 miles from Shrewsbury, 4 miles from Ironbridge, M54 (exit 7), 400yds on the left towards Wellington.

Bedrooms: 1 single, 7 double, 2 twin.
Open: Closed for two weeks in January

Site: **Payment:** **Leisure:** **Property:** **Catering:** **Room:**

CHEADLE, Staffordshire *Map ref 4B2* — *SatNav ST10 1RA* B

enjoyEngland.com ★★★★ FARMHOUSE

B&B PER ROOM PER NIGHT
S: £30.00
D: £55.00

Rakeway House Farm B&B

Rakeway Road, Cheadle, Alton Towers Area ST10 1RA **T:** (01538) 755295
E: rakewayhousefarm@btinternet.com
W: www.rakewayhousefarm.co.uk

Charming farmhouse and gardens. Fantastic views over Cheadle and surrounding countryside. Alton Towers 15 minutes drive. Good base for Peak District and Potteries. First-class accommodation, excellent menu, superb hospitality. **Bedrooms:** 1 double, 1 family **Open:** All year

Site: P **Leisure:** **Property:** **Children:** **Catering:** **Room:**

LEEK, Staffordshire *Map ref 4B2* — *SatNav ST13 8TW* H

enjoyEngland.com ★★★ HOTEL — enjoyEngland.com Silver AWARD

B&B PER ROOM PER NIGHT
S: £50.00 - £180.00
D: £50.00 - £180.00

EVENING MEAL PER PERSON
£9.95 - £26.00

SPECIAL PROMOTIONS
See website for special promotions.

Three Horseshoes Country Hotel & Spa

Blackshaw Moor, Leek ST13 8TW **T:** (01538) 300296 **E:** enquiries@threeshoesinn.co.uk
W: www.3shoesinn.co.uk **£ BOOK ONLINE**

Set within picturesque Staffordshire Peak District. Bedrooms ranging from classic to garden rooms with cedar hot tub. Two Dining options "Bar & Grill" and 2 AA Rosette Brasserie offering delicious local food from an imaginative menu. The Millwheel Spa provides an experience for guests with wellbeing benefits and relaxation. Guests can enjoy local walks. Chatsworth House, Buxton, Alton Towers.

Directions: 10 miles from Stoke-on-Trent on the A53 Leek-Buxton road.

Bedrooms: 21 dble, 3 twin, 2 family
Open: All year

Site: P **Payment:** £ **Leisure:** **Property:** **Children:** **Catering:**
Room:

LICHFIELD, Staffordshire *Map ref 4B3* — *SatNav WS14 0BG* B

enjoyEngland.com ★★★★ GUEST HOUSE

B&B PER ROOM PER NIGHT
S: £40.00 - £50.00
D: £60.00 - £70.00

Copper's End Guest House

Walsall Road, Muckley Corner, Lichfield, Staffordshire WS14 0BG **T:** (01543) 372910
F: 01543 360423 **E:** info@coppersendguesthouse.co.uk
W: www.coppersendguesthouse.co.uk **£ BOOK ONLINE**

Detached guesthouse, character and charm in own grounds. Wide screen TVs in all bedrooms. Conservatory dining room, large walled garden with patio, guests' lounge. Vegetarians catered for. 4 en suite rooms, 2 ground floor rooms, parking, Motorcyclist, cyclist & walker friendly. **Directions:** 100 yds from Muckley Corner roundabout off the A5, 3 miles south of Lichfield, Walsall 5 miles. Ordnance Survey ref. SK083067. **Bedrooms:** 3 double, 3 twin **Open:** All year except Christmas and New Year

Site: P **Payment:** £ **Leisure:** **Property:** **Children:** **Catering:** **Room:**

STAFFORD, Staffordshire Map ref 4B3 SatNav ST16 3LQ

Wyndale Guest House

199 Corporation Street, Stafford ST16 3LQ **T:** (01785) 223069 **E:** wyndale@aol.com
W: www.wyndaleguesthouse.co.uk **£ BOOK ONLINE**

enjoyEngland.com ★★★ GUEST HOUSE

B&B PER ROOM PER NIGHT
S: £37.00 - £48.00
D: £60.00 - £70.00

EVENING MEAL PER PERSON
£7.00 - £20.00

SPECIAL PROMOTIONS
Offers are available, please ring 01785 223069 for more information.

Wyndale is a comfortable Victorian house conveniently Situated 0.25 miles from town centre, with easy access to Stafford university, the M6, Stafford train station and Stafford record office. We are on route to county show ground, hospitals & business parks. Local attractions including Shugborough, Trentham Gardens & Amerton Farm. Enjoy home made preserves and locally sourced meat for breakfast.

Directions: Please go to our web site where we have full direction & maps. www.wyndaleguesthouse.co.uk.

Bedrooms: We offer 2 single, 2 double, 2 twin and 2 family rooms. Twin rooms have the capability of being used as double rooms. 5 en suite rooms
Open: All year except Christmas

Site: P **Payment:** **Property:** **Children:** **Catering:** **Room:**

LEAMINGTON SPA, Warwickshire Map ref 4B3 SatNav CV31 3PW

Victoria Park Lodge

12 Adelaide Road, Royal Leamington Spa, Warwick CV31 3PW **T:** (01926) 424195
F: 01926 421521 **E:** info@victoriaparkhotelleamingtonspa.co.uk
W: www.victoriaparkhotelleamingtonspa.co.uk **£ BOOK ONLINE**

enjoyEngland.com ★★★★ GUEST HOUSE

B&B PER ROOM PER NIGHT
S: £60.00
D: £70.00 - £80.00

29 en suite bedrooms with free Wi-Fi and free parking. Spacious serviced apartment nearby for short/long stays. 4 mins walk from the town centre and 5 mins drive from Warwick Castle. **Bedrooms:** 8 single, 10 double, 2 twin, 9 family **Open:** All year except Christmas and New Year

Site: P **Payment:** **Leisure:** **Property:** **Children:** **Catering:** **Room:**

STRATFORD-UPON-AVON, Warwickshire Map ref 2B1 SatNav CV37 6PB

Adelphi Guest House

39 Grove Road, Stratford-upon-Avon, Warwickshire CV37 6PB **T:** (01789) 204469
E: info@adelphi-guesthouse.com
W: www.adelphi-guesthouse.com

enjoyEngland.com ★★★★ GUEST HOUSE

enjoyEngland.com Silver AWARD

B&B PER ROOM PER NIGHT
S: £40.00 - £65.00
D: £80.00 - £95.00

Breakfasts are popular, as are the home baked cakes. The rooms are decorated in period style. The bedding is pure cotton. The house over looks the Fir Gardens and is minutes from the train station, town centre, Shakespeare sites, and theatres. **Directions:** From the A3400 turn onto the A4390 which becomes Grove Road at the next crossroads. The Adelphi is approx 200m on the right as is a lane to parking. **Bedrooms:** Rooms have luxury toiletries and hospitality tray **Open:** All year

Site: P **Payment:** **Property:** **Catering:** **Room:**

STRATFORD-UPON-AVON, Warwickshire Map ref 2B1 SatNav CV37 7LN B

enjoyEngland.com ★★★★ GUEST HOUSE

B&B PER ROOM PER NIGHT
S: £45.00 - £55.00
D: £70.00 - £85.00

SPECIAL PROMOTIONS
£5 Discount on stays of 4 or more nights. 50% off Sunday when booking 3 or more nights, subject to T&C.

Avonlea

47 Shipston Road, Stratford-Upon-Avon CV37 7LN **T:** (01789) 205940
E: enquiries@avonlea-stratford.co.uk
W: www.avonlea-stratford.co.uk

This is a stylish Victorian town house situated only five minutes walk from the theatre and Stratford town centre. All rooms are en suite and furnished to the highest quality with comfy beds. Guests are assured of a warm welcome and friendly atmosphere, with a fantastic breakfast the following morning.

Directions: A3400 Shipston Road, 100m from Clopton Bridge.

Bedrooms: 2 single, 2 double, 2 twin/superking, 2 family (1 Double 1 Single bed)
Open: All year except December & January

Site: P **Payment:** **Leisure:** **Property:** **Children:** **Catering:** **Room:**

STRATFORD-UPON-AVON, Warwickshire *Map ref 2B1* SatNav CV37 9DR B

enjoyEngland.com ★★★★ GUEST HOUSE — enjoyEngland.com Silver AWARD

B&B PER ROOM PER NIGHT
S: £45.00 - £52.00
D: £66.00 - £70.00

Brook Lodge Guest House

192 Alcester Road, Stratford-upon-Avon CV37 9DR **T:** (01789) 295988
E: brooklodgeguesthouse@btinternet.com
W: www.brook-lodge.co.uk **£ BOOK ONLINE**

Within an easy walk of all the town's major attractions, Brook Lodge offers first class accommodation and facilities with a personal touch. Your home away from home. **Bedrooms:** 3 double, 1 twin, 1 triple, 1 family suite **Open:** All year

Site: P **Payment:** **Property:** **Children:** **Catering:** **Room:**

WARWICK, Warwickshire *Map ref 2B1* SatNav CV34 5QR B

enjoyEngland.com ★★★ GUEST HOUSE

B&B PER ROOM PER NIGHT
S: £35.00 - £45.00
D: £55.00 - £65.00

Jersey Villa Guest House, Warwick

69 Emscote Road, Warwick CV34 5QR **T:** (01926) 730336 / 07929 338321
E: info@jerseyvillaguesthouse.co.uk
W: www.jerseyvillaguesthouse.co.uk

Jersey Villa Guest House is located on the borders of Warwick and Royal Leamington Spa. The guest house offers quality bed and breakfast accommodation. Both towns are within walking distance, Warwick Castle is a mere 15 minute walk. **Directions:** Warwick Railway Station, come out onto Broad Street, turn left into Emscote Road, continue for 5 minutes, turn left into Jersey Villa Guest House. **Bedrooms:** Family room sleeps up to 5. Doubles, singles and twins. All rooms large, with en suite, welcome tray etc. **Open:** All year

Site: P **Property:** **Children:** 5 **Catering:** **Room:**

BIRMINGHAM, West Midlands *Map ref 4B3* SatNav B26 1DD B

enjoyEngland.com ★★★ GUEST HOUSE

Central Guest House

1637 Coventry Road, Yardley, Birmingham B26 1DD **T:** (0121) 706 7757
E: stay@centralguesthouse.com
W: www.centralguesthouse.com **£ BOOK ONLINE**

We are a small, family run guest house. A home from home, close to all local facilities. A full English breakfast is included in the price. Parking available. Ironing facilities and TV in all rooms. Telephone available. Children welcome. All our rooms are non-smoking. Please contact for 2015 Rates. **Directions:** Please contact. **Bedrooms:** All rooms en suite, apart for single room with private facilities. Tea & coffee making facilities. Hairdryer in all rooms. **Open:** All Year

Site: P **Payment:** **Property:** **Children:** **Room:**

WORCESTER, Worcestershire *Map ref 2B1* SatNav WR5 2JT B

enjoyEngland.com ★★★ BED & BREAKFAST

B&B PER ROOM PER NIGHT
S: £45.00
D: £55.00 - £59.00

Holland House

210 London Road, Worcester WR5 2JT **T:** (01905) 353939 **F:** 01905 353939
E: beds@holland-house.me.uk
W: www.holland-house.me.uk **£ BOOK ONLINE**

A warm welcome awaits you at this Victorian mid-terrace house, situated within walking distance of the cathedral. It retains many original features and offers fully en suite rooms throughout. **Directions:** We are situated on A44 approximately half way between M5/J7 and the cathedral. **Bedrooms:** 2 double, 1 twin **Open:** All year

Payment: **Property:** **Children:** **Catering:** **Room:**

Don't Miss...

Castle Howard

Malton, North Yorkshire YO60 7DA
(01653) 648444
www.castlehoward.co.uk
A magnificent 18th century house situated in breathtaking parkland, dotted with temples, lakes statues and fountains; plus formal gardens, woodland garden and ornamental vegetable garden. Inside the House guides share stories of the house, family and collections, while outdoor-guided tours reveal the secrets of the architecture and landscape.

National Media Museum

Bradford, West Yorkshire BD1 1NQ
0870 701 0200
www.nationalmediamuseum.org.uk
The Museum is home to over 3.5 million items of historical significance including the National Photography, National Cinematography, National Television and National New Media Collections. Admission to the National Media Museum is free (charges apply for cinemas/IMAX).

National Railway Museum

York, North Yorkshire YO26 4XJ
0844 815 3139
www.nrm.org.uk
Awesome trains, interactive fun – and the world's largest railway museum make for a great day out.

The Deep

Hull, East Riding of Yorkshire HU1 4DP
(01482) 381000
www.thedeep.co.uk
Full with over 3500 fish and more than 40 sharks, The Deep tells the amazing story of the world's oceans through stunning marine life, interactives and audio-visual presentations making it a fun-filled family day out for all ages.

Yorkshire Wildlife Park

Doncaster, South Yorkshire DN3 3NH
(01302) 535057
www.yorkshirewildlifepark.co.uk2
A fabulous fun day and animal experience. Walk through 'Lemur Woods' and meet these mischievous primates, or come face to face with the wallabies in Wallaby Walk.

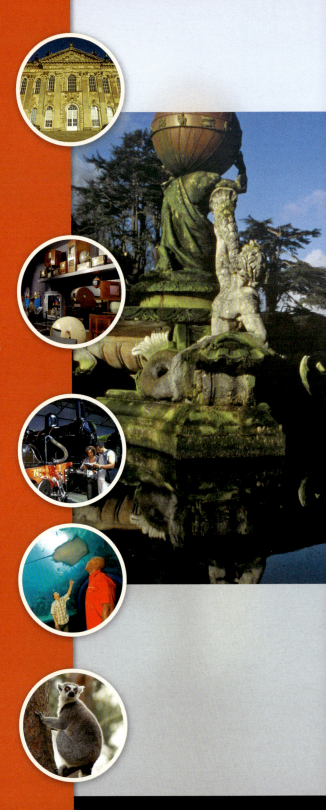

Yorkshire

Yorkshire

Yorkshire, the largest county in England, is one of the most popular and boasts award-winning culture, heritage and scenery. There's cosmopolitan Leeds, stylish Harrogate and rural market towns full of charm and character. The wild moors and deserted dales of the Yorkshire Dales and North York Moors National Parks are majestic in their beauty and the county has a spectacular coastline of rugged cliffs and sandy beaches. The region also has a wealth of historic houses, ruined castles, abbeys and fortresses for visitors to discover.

Explore – Yorkshire

North Yorkshire

Steeped in history, North Yorkshire boasts some of the country's most splendid scenery. Wherever you go in The Dales, you'll be faced with breathtaking views and constant reminders of a historic and changing past. In medieval days, solid fortresses like Richmond and Middleham were built to protect the area from marauding Scots. Ripley and Skipton also had their massive strongholds, while Bolton Castle in Wensleydale once imprisoned Mary, Queen of Scots. The pattern of history continues with the great abbeys, like Jervaulx Abbey, near Masham, where the monks first made Wensleydale cheese and the majestic ruins of Fountains Abbey in the grounds of Studley Royal. Between the Dales and the North York Moors, Herriot Country is named for one of the world's best loved writers, James Herriot, who made the area his home for more than 50 years and whose books have enthralled readers with tales of Yorkshire life.

Hotspot: Take a classic steam train from Pickering to Grosmont on the famous North Yorkshire Moors Railway for breathaking scenery. www.nymr.co.uk

Escape to the wild, deserted North York Moors National Park with its 500 square miles of hills, dales, forests and open moorland, neatly edged by a spectacular coastline. Walking, cycling and pony trekking are ideal ways to savour the scenery and there are plenty of greystone towns and villages dotted throughout the Moors that provide ideal bases from which to explore. From Helmsley, visit the ruins of Rievaulx Abbey, founded by Cistercian monks in the 12th century or discover moorland life in the Ryedale Folk Museum at Hutton-le-Hole. The Beck Isle Museum in Pickering provides an insight into the life of a country market town and just a few miles down the road you'll find Malton, once a Roman fortress, and nearby Castle Howard, the setting for Brideshead Revisited.

Hotspot: The Forbidden Corner is a unique labyrinth of tunnels, chambers, follies and surprises in the heart of the beautiful Yorkshire Dales. www.theforbiddencorner.co.uk

Leeds & West Yorkshire

For centuries cloth has been spun from the wool of the sheep grazing in the Pennine uplands and the fascinating story of this industrial heritage can be seen in the numerous craft centres and folk museums throughout West Yorkshire. To enjoy the countryside, take a trip on the steam hauled Keighley and Worth Valley Railway. Not far from Haworth is Bingley, where the Leeds & Liverpool canal makes its famous uphill journey, a route for the coal barges in days gone by, nowadays replaced by holidaymakers in gaily painted boats. Leeds itself is a vibrant city with its Victorian shopping arcades, Royal Armories Museum and lively arts scene.

Hotspot: Stop off at **Haworth,** home of the Bronte sisters, to visit The Bronte Parsonage museum and experience the rugged atmosphere of Wuthering Heights. www.bronte.org.uk

York

Wherever you turn within the city's medieval walls, you will find glimpses of the past. The splendours of the 600-year old Minster, the grim stronghold of Clifford's Tower, the National Railway Museum, the medieval timbers of the Merchant Adventurers' Hall and the fascinating Jorvik Viking Centre all offer an insight into the history of this charming city. Throughout the city, statues and monuments remind the visitor that this was where Constantine was proclaimed Holy Roman Emperor, Guy Fawkes was born and Dick Turpin met his end.

Modern York is has excellent shopping, a relaxed cafe culture, first class restaurants and bars, museums, tours and attractions. Whether you visit for a romantic weekend or a fun-filled family holiday, there really is something for everyone.

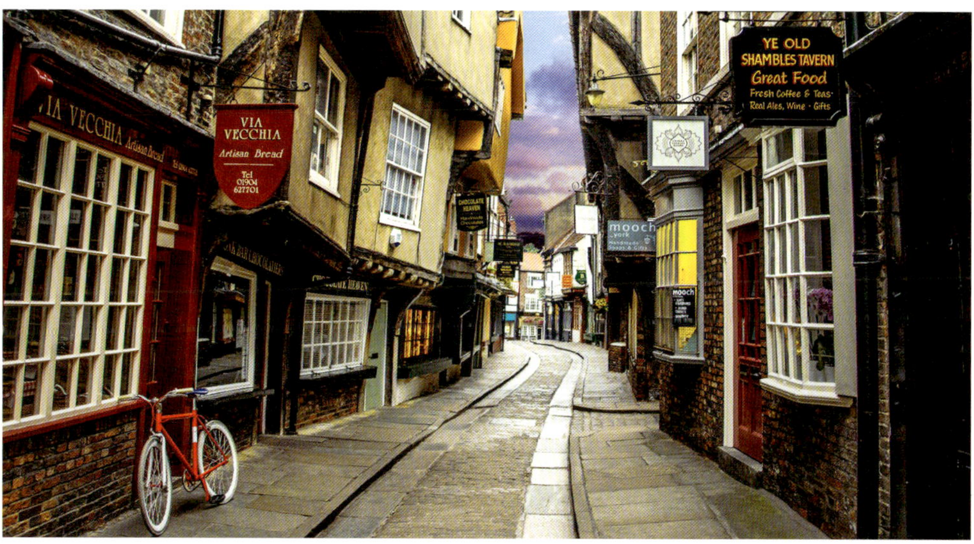

Yorkshire Coastline

The Yorkshire coastline is one of the UK's most naturally beautiful and rugged, where pretty fishing villages cling to rocky cliffs, in turn towering over spectacular beaches and family-friendly seaside destinations.

At the northern end of the coastline, Saltburn is a sand and shingle beach popular with surfers and visitors can ride the Victorian tram from the cliff to the promenade during the summer. Whitby is full of quaint streets and bestowed with a certain Gothic charm. At Scarborough, one of Britain's oldest seaside resorts, the award-winning North Bay and South Bay sand beaches are broken by the rocky headland, home to the historic Scarborough Castle. Filey, with its endless sands, has spectacular views and a 40-mile stretch of perfect sandy beach sweeps south from the dramatic 400 ft high cliffs at Flamborough Head. Along this coastline you can find the boisterous holiday destination of Bridlington, or a gentler pace at pretty Hornsea and Withernsea.

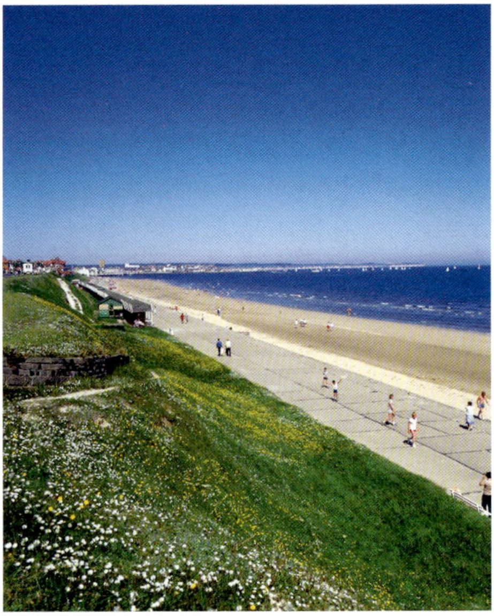

Hotspot: With its 3,000 year history, stunning location and panoramic views over the dramatic Yorkshire coastline, Scarborough Castle is one of the finest tourist attractions in Yorkshire. www.english-heritage.org.uk

East Yorkshire

From cosmopolitan Hull to the hills and valleys of the Yorkshire Wolds, East Yorkshire is wonderfully diverse. A landscape of swirling grasslands, medieval towns, manor houses and Bronze Age ruins contrasting with the vibrant energy and heritage of the Humber. The Wolds are only a stones throw from some great seaside resorts and Beverley, with its magnificent 13th century minster and lattice of medieval streets, is just one of the many jewels of architectural heritage to be found here. Hull is a modern city rebuilt since the war, linked to Lincolnshire via the impressive 1452 yd Humber Bridge.

Hotspot: The St Leger at Doncaster Racecourse is the oldest classic horse race in the world, and the town celebrates in style with a whole festival of events. www.visitdoncaster.co.uk

South Yorkshire

The historic market town of Doncaster was founded by the Romans and has a rich horseracing and railway heritage. The area around Sheffield - the steel city - was once dominated by the iron and steel industries and was the first city in England to pioneer free public transport. The Industrial Museum and City Museum display a wide range of Sheffield cutlery and oplate. Today, Meadowhall shopping centre, with 270 stores under one roof, is a must-visit for shopaholics.

Indulge – Yorkshire

Indulge in a spot of retail therapy with a trip to **Leeds**. The Grand Arcade is one of the oldest shopping arcades in Leeds City Centre and is well worth a visit for its independent retailers. The stunning architecture of the Victoria Quarter's Grade II* arcades are a spectacular setting for a shopping spree, while VQ is home to over 75 of the world's leading fashion and lifestyle brands, including Vivienne Westwood, Paul Smith, Louis Vuitton, Mulberry and Illamasqua.

Tantalise your taste buds with traditional fish & chips from **The Quayside**, the UK's Fish and Chip Shop of the year 2014. Find them at 7 Pier Road, Whitby. (01947) 825346 or visit www.whitbyfishandchips.com

The bustling **Lewis & Cooper** store in Northallerton has been a multi award-winning independent gourmet food store since 1899 and is packed with flavoursome foodie treats, fine wines, delicious gift baskets and sumptuous food hampers. Treat yourself to a mouth watering picnic spread and head out into the surrounding countryside.
www.lewisandcooper.co.uk

Enjoy an elegant afternoon tea at the famous **Bettys Cafe Tea Rooms**, Harrogate. Speciality teas, dainty sandwiches, handmade cakes and scones, and splendid surroundings make this a truly indulgent occasion and you can even buy your favourites from the bakery to take home.
(01423) 814070 or visit www.bettys.co.uk

Feel relaxed, exhilarated and cleansed after a visit to the **Turkish Baths** in Harrogate. The unique Royal Baths building first opened in 1896 and today you can enjoy a contemporary spa experience in magnificent surroundings. Treatments, refreshments and a spot of lunch are all available.
(01423) 556746 or visit www.turkishbathsharrogate.co.uk

Visit – Yorkshire

Attractions with this sign participate in the Visitor Attraction Quality Assurance Scheme.

North Yorkshire

Flamingo Land Theme Park and Zoo
Malton, North Yorkshire YO17 6UX
0871 911 8000
www.flamingoland.co.uk
One-price family funpark with over 100 attractions, 5 shows and Europe's largest privately-owned zoo.

Grassington Festival
June, Grassington, North Yorkshire
www.grassington-festival.org.uk
15 days of music and arts in the Yorkshire Dales.

Malton Food Lovers Festival
May, Malton, North Yorkshire
www.maltonyorkshire.co.uk
Fill up on glorious food and discover why Malton is considered 'Yorkshire's Food Town' with mountains of fresh produce.

Ripon International Festival
September, Ripon, North Yorkshire
www.riponinternationalfestival.com
A festival packed with music events, solo dramas, intriguing theatre, magic, fantastic puppetry, literary celebrities, historical walks - and more!

Scarborough Jazz Festival
September, Scarborough, North Yorkshire
www.jazz.scarboroughspa.co.uk
Offering a variety and range of jazz acts with a balanced programme of predominantly British musicians, with the addition of a few international stars.

Scarborough Seafest
July, Scarborough, North Yorkshire
www.discoveryorkshirecoast.com
Seafest celebrates Scarborough's maritime heritage and brings together seafood kitchen cooking demonstrations, exhibitor displays and musical performances.

Swaledale Festival
May - June, Various locations, North Yorkshire
www.swaledale-festival.org.uk
Varied programme of top-quality events, individually ticketed, realistically priced, and spread over two glorious weeks.

The Walled Garden at Scampston
Malton, North Yorkshire YO17 8NG
(01944) 759111
www.scampston.co.uk
An exciting 4 acre contemporary garden, created by Piet Oudolf, with striking perennial meadow planting as well as traditional spring/autumn borders.

York

York Early Music Festival
July, York, North Yorkshire
www.ncem.co.uk
The 2015 festival takes as its starting point the 600th anniversary of the Battle of Agincourt and features cross-currents between France and England from the Middle Ages through to the Baroque.

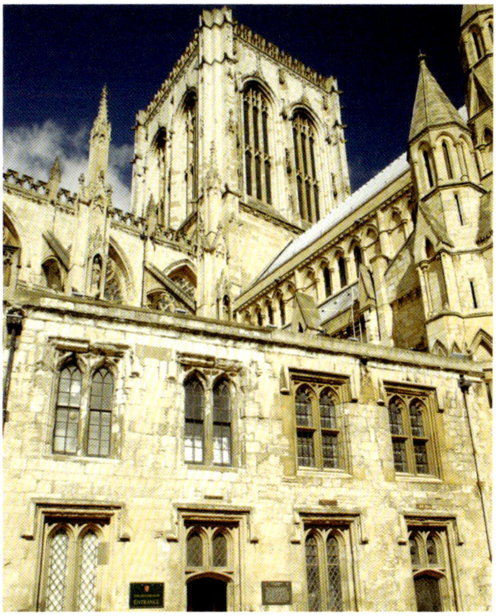

JORVIK Viking Centre
York, North Yorkshire YO1 9WT
(01904) 615505
www.jorvik-viking-centre.co.uk
Travel back 1000 years on board your time machine through the backyards and houses to the bustling streets of Jorvik.

York Boat Guided River Trips
North Yorkshire YO1 7DP
(01904) 628324
www.yorkboat.co.uk
Sit back, relax and enjoy a drink from the bar as the sights of York city and country sail by onboard a 1 hour Guided River Trip with entertaining live commentary.

York Minster
York, North Yorkshire YO1 7JN
(0)1904 557200
www.yorkminster.org
Regularly voted one of the most popular things to do in York, the Minster is not only an architecturally stunning building but is a place to discover the history of York over the centuries, its artefacts and treasures.

Yorkshire Air Museum
York, North Yorkshire YO41 4AU
(01904) 608595
www.yorkshireairmuseum.org
The Yorkshire Air Museum is based on a unique WWII Bomber Command Station with fascinating exhibits and attractive award-winning Memorial Gardens.

Leeds & West Yorkshire

Eureka! The National Children's Museum
Halifax, West Yorkshire HX1 2NE
(01422) 330069
www.eureka.org.uk
Eureka! The National Children's Museum is a magical place where children play to learn and grown-ups learn to play.

Harewood House
Leeds, West Yorkshire LS17 9LG
(0113) 218 1010
www.harewood.org
Harewood House, Bird Garden, Grounds and Adventure Playground - The Ideal day out for all the family.

Haworth 1940's Weekend
May, Haworth, West Yorkshire
www.haworth1940sweekend.co.uk
A fabulous weekend celebrating and comemorating the 1940s.

Leeds Festival
August, Wetherby, Leeds
www.leedsfestival.com
From punk and metal, through rock, alternative and indie to dance, Leeds offers music fans a chance to see hot new acts, local bands, huge stars and exclusive performances.

Lotherton Hall & Gardens
Leeds, West Yorkshire LS25 3EB
(0113) 264 5535
www.leeds.gov.uk/lothertonhall
Lotherton is an Edwardian country house set in beautiful grounds with a bird garden, red deer park and formal gardens.

National Coal Mining Museum for England
Wakefield, West Yorkshire WF4 4RH
(01924) 848806
www.ncm.org.uk
The National Coal Mining Museum offers an exciting and enjoyable insight into the working lives of miners through the ages.

Pontefract Liquorice Festival
July, Wakefield, West Yorkshire
www.yorkshire.com
The festival celebrates this unusual plant, the many wonderful products created from it and its historic association with the town.

Royal Armouries Museum
Leeds, West Yorkshire LS10 1LT
0870 034 4344
www.royalarmouries.org
Over 8,000 objects displayed in five galleries - War, Tournament, Oriental, Self Defence and Hunting. Among the treasures are Henry VIII's tournament armour and the world record breaking elephant armour. Regular jousting and horse shows.

Xscape Castleford
Castleford, West Yorkshire WF10 4TA
(01977) 5230 2324
www.xscape.co.uk
The ultimate family entertainment awaits! Dine, bowl, snow, skate, climb, movies, shop, dance on ice.

Yorkshire Sculpture Park
West Bretton,
West Yorkshire WF4 4LG
(01924) 832631
www.ysp.co.uk
YSP is an extraordinary place that sets out to challenge, inspire, inform and delight.

East Yorkshire

East Riding Rural Life Museum
Beverley, East Yorkshire HU16 5TF
(01482) 392777
www.museums.eastriding.gov.uk
Working early 19th century four-sailed Skidby Windmill, plus Museum of East Riding Rural Life.

Ferens Art Gallery
Hull, East Riding of Yorkshire HU1 3RA
(01482) 613902
www.hullcc.gov.uk/museums
Combines internationally renowned permanent collections with a thriving programme of temporary exhibitions.

RSPB Bempton Cliffs Reserve
Bridlington, East Riding of Yorkshire YO15 1JF
(01262) 851179
www.rspb.org.uk
A family favourite, and easily the best place in England to see, hear and smell seabirds! More than 200,000 birds (from April to August) make the towering chalk cliffs seem alive.

Skipsea Castle
Hornsea, East Riding of Yorkshire
0870 333 1181
www.english-heritage.org.uk/daysout/properties/skipsea-castle/
The remaining earthworks of a motte-and-bailey castle dating from the Norman era.

Treasure House and Art Gallery
Beverley, East Riding of Yorkshire HU17 8HE
(01482) 392790
www.museums.eastriding.gov.uk/treasure-house-and-beverley-art-gallery
Enthusiasts for East Riding history can access archive, library, art gallery and museum material. Exhibitions.

Wilberforce House
Hull, East Riding of Yorkshire HU11NQ
(01482) 300300
www.hullcc.gov.uk/museums
Slavery exhibits, period rooms and furniture, Hull silver, costume, Wilberforce and abolition.

South Yorkshire

RSPB Old Moor Nature Reserve
Barnsley, South Yorkshire S73 0YF
(01226) 751593
www.rspb.org.uk
Whether you're feeling energetic or just fancy some time out visit Old Moor to get closer to the wildlife.

Brodsworth Hall and Gardens
Doncaster, South Yorkshire DN5 7XJ
(01302) 722598
www.english-heritage.org.uk/daysout/properties/brodsworth-hall-and-gardens
One of England's most complete surviving Victorian houses. Inside many of the original fixtures & fittings are still in place, although faded with time. Outside the 15 acres of woodland & gardens have been restored to their 1860's heyday.

Magna Science Adventure Centre
Rotherham, South Yorkshire S60 1DX
(01709) 720002
www.visitmagna.co.uk
Magna is the UK's 1st Science Adventure Centre set in the vast Templeborough steelworks in Rotherham. Fun is unavoidable here with giant interactives.

Sheffield Botanical Gardens
South Yorkshire S10 2LN
(0114) 268 6001
www.sbg.org.uk
Extensive gardens with over 5,500 species of plants, Grade II Listed garden pavillion.

Sheffield: Millennium Gallery
South Yorkshire S1 2PP
(0114) 278 2600
www.museums-sheffield.org.uk
One of modern Sheffield's landmark public spaces. Whether you're in town or just passing through, the Gallery always has something new to offer.

Tourist Information Centres

When you arrive at your destination, visit the Tourist Information Centre for quality assured help with accommodation and information about local attractions and events, or email your request before you go.

Aysgarth Falls	Aysgarth Falls National Park Centre	01969 662910	aysgarth@yorkshiredales.org.uk
Beverley	34 Butcher Row	01482 391672	beverley.tic@eastriding.gov.uk
Bradford	Brittainia House	01274 433678	bradford.vic@bradford.gov.uk
Bridlington	25 Prince Street	01262 673474/ 01482 391634	bridlington.tic@eastriding.gov.uk
Brigg	The Buttercross	01652 657053	brigg.tic@northlincs.gov.uk
Danby	The Moors National Park Centre	01439 772737	moorscentre@northyorkmoors.org.uk
Doncaster	Blue Building	01302 734309	tourist.information@doncaster.gov.uk
Filey	The Evron Centre	01723 383637	fileytic2@scarborough.gov.uk
Grassington	National Park Centre	01756 751690	grassington@yorkshiredales.gov.uk
Halifax	The Piece Hall	01422 368725	halifax@ytbtic.co.uk
Harrogate	Royal Baths	01423 537300	tic@harrogate.gov.uk
Hawes	Dales Countryside Museum	01969 666210	hawes@yorkshiredales.org.uk
Haworth	2/4 West Lane	01535 642329	haworth.vic@bradford.gov.uk
Hebden Bridge	New Road	01422 843831	hebdenbridge@ytbtic.co.uk
Holmfirth	49-51 Huddersfield Road	01484 222444	holmfirth.tic@kirklees.gov.uk
Hornsea	Hornsea Museum	01964 536404	hornsea.tic@eastriding.gov.uk

Horton-In-Ribblesdale	Pen-y-ghent Cafe	01729 860333	mail@pen-y-ghentcafe.co.uk
Huddersfield	Huddersfield Library	01484 223200	huddersfield.information@kirklees.gov.uk
Hull	1 Paragon Street	01482 223559	tourist.information@hullcc.gov.uk
Humber Bridge	North Bank Viewing Area	01482 640852	humberbridge.tic@eastriding.gov.uk
Ilkley	Town Hall	01943 602319	ilkley.vic@bradford.gov.uk
Ingleton	The Community Centre Car Park	015242 41049	ingleton@ytbtic.co.uk
Knaresborough	9 Castle Courtyard	01423 866886	kntic@harrogate.gov.uk
Leeds	The Arcade	0113 242 5242	tourinfo@leedsandpartners.com
Leeming Bar	The Yorkshire Maid, 88 Bedale Road	01677 424262	thelodgeatleemingbar@btconnect.com
Leyburn	The Dales Haven	01969 622317	
Malham	National Park Centre	01969 652380	malham@ytbtic.co.uk
Otley	Otley Library & Tourist Information	01943 462485	otleytic@leedslearning.net
Pateley Bridge	18 High Street	0845 389 0177	pbtic@harrogate.gov.uk
Pickering	Ropery House	01751 473791	pickeringtic@btconnect.com
Reeth	Hudson House, The Green	01748 884059	reeth@ytbtic.co.uk
Richmond	Friary Gardens	01748 828742	hilda@richmondtouristinformation.co.uk
Ripon	Minster Road	01765 604625	ripontic@harrogate.gov.uk
Rotherham	40 Bridgegate	01709 835904	tic@rotherham.gov.uk
Scarborough	Brunswick Shopping Centre	01723 383636	scarborough2@scarborough.gov.uk
Scarborough (Harbourside)	Harbourside TIC	01723 383636	scarborough2@scarborough.gov.uk
Selby	Selby Library	0845 034 9540	selby@ytbtic.co.uk
Settle	Town Hall	01729 825192	settle@ytbtic.co.uk
Sheffield	Unit 1 Winter Gardens	0114 2211900	visitor@marketingsheffield.org
Skipton	Town Hall	01756 792809	skipton@ytbtic.co.uk
Sutton Bank	Sutton Bank Visitor Centre	01845 597426	suttonbank@northyorkmoors.org.uk
Todmorden	15 Burnley Road	01706 818181	todmorden@ytbtic.co.uk
Wakefield	9 The Bull Ring	0845 601 8353	tic@wakefield.gov.uk
Wetherby	Wetherby Library & Tourist Centre	01937 582151	wetherbytic@leedslearning.net
Whitby	Langborne Road	01723 383637	whitbytic@scarborough.gov.uk
Withernsea	Withernsea Lighthouse Museum	01964 615683/ 01482 486566	withernsea.tic@eastriding.gov.uk
York	1 Museum Street	01904 550099	info@visityork.org

Regional Contacts and Information

For more information on accommodation, attractions, activities, events and holidays in Yorkshire, contact one of the following regional or local tourism organisations.

Welcome to Yorkshire
www.yorkshire.com
(0113) 322 3500

Stay – Yorkshire

Entries appear alphabetically by town name in each county. A key to symbols appears on page 7

BEVERLEY, East Yorkshire Map ref 4C1 SatNav HU17 8EG B

enjoyEngland.com ★★★★★ BED & BREAKFAST

B&B PER ROOM PER NIGHT
S: £55.00 - £75.00
D: £80.00 - £120.00

Newbegin B&B

Newbegin House, 10 Newbegin, Beverley, East Yorkshire HU17 8EG **T:** (01482) 888880
E: wsweeney@wsweeney.karoo.co.uk
W: www.newbeginhousebbbeverley.co.uk

Beverley's only 5 Star B&B. Warm welcome in beautiful Georgian mansion 100 metres from Saturday Market. Three luxurious en suite guest bedrooms, including one family room, king sized beds; splendid dining room; free parking. **Directions:** 100 metres on foot from Saturday Market. By car, approach from Westwood Road and go down Newbegin (one way) to number 10 on left. **Bedrooms:** 2 double, 1 family suite **Open:** All year

Site: P **Leisure:** **Property:** **Children:** **Catering:** **Room:**

BEVERLEY, East Yorkshire Map ref 4C1 SatNav HU17 9SH H

enjoyEngland.com ★★★ HOTEL

B&B PER ROOM PER NIGHT
S: £92.50 - £155.00
D: £120.00 - £190.00
EVENING MEAL PER PERSON
£30.00 - £40.00

Tickton Grange Hotel & Restaurant

Tickton, Near Beverley, East Yorkshire HU17 9SH **T:** (01964) 543666 **F:** 01964 542556
E: info@ticktongrange.co.uk
W: www.ticktongrange.co.uk **£ BOOK ONLINE**

Set within 4 acres of grounds our beautiful country house offers bedrooms a million miles away from formulaic sameness. Dine in our award winning restaurant Hide & enjoy dishes prepared with ingredients supplied by local artisan producers. **Directions:** Two miles outside of Beverley on the A1035 **Bedrooms:** En suite, tv, tea, coffee and homemade flapjack **Open:** All year

Site: P **Payment:** **Property:** **Children:** **Catering:** **Room:**

BOLTBY, North Yorkshire Map ref 5C3 SatNav YO7 2DY B

enjoyEngland.com ★★★★ GUEST ACCOMMODATION

Willow Tree Cottage

Boltby, Thirsk, North Yorkshire YO7 2DY **T:** (01845) 537406 **E:** townsend.sce@virgin.net
W: www.willowtreecottageboltby.co.uk

The B&B room - large and luxurious, wonderful views with balcony, en suite bathroom and kitchenette, sitting area.
The Studio - a self-contained flat, separate entrance, kitchen, shower room & wood burner, own garden. Self-catering or B&B. Please see website or phone owner for 2015 prices.
Directions: From Thirsk take the A170 Scarborough Road follow signs to Felixkirk and Boltby. In Boltby follow road up hill. At bend sign take LH U turn to Willow Tree Cottage. **Bedrooms:** 2: A Luxurious B&B and 1 self-contained studio. **Open:** All year

Site: P **Leisure:** **Property:** **Children:** **Catering:** **Room:**

CLOUGHTON, North Yorkshire Map ref 5D3 SatNav YO13 0AR B

enjoyEngland.com ★★★ GUEST ACCOMMODATION

B&B PER ROOM PER NIGHT
S: £41.00 - £58.00
D: £82.00 - £116.00
EVENING MEAL PER PERSON
£17.00

Cober Hill

Newlands Road, Cloughton, Scarborough YO13 0AR **T:** (01723) 870310 **F:** 01723 870271
E: enquiries@coberhill.co.uk
W: www.coberhill.co.uk

Impressive Edwardian building, with new annexes, set in a beautiful, peaceful and tranquil location between Scarborough and Whitby, in the North York Moors National Park and overlooking the Heritage Coast. Perfect for relaxation and inspiration, 6 acres of stunning grounds and superb sea views. Groups tariffs available. **Directions:** 6 miles north of Scarborough and 15 miles south of Whitby 100 yards off the A171 Scarborough to Whitby road. **Bedrooms:** 22 single, 6 double, 25 twin, 10 family **Open:** All year

Site: P **Payment:** **Leisure:** **Property:** **Children:** **Catering:** **Room:**

EGTON BRIDGE, North Yorkshire Map ref 5D3 SatNav YO21 1XD B

★★★★ GUEST HOUSE — Gold AWARD

B&B PER ROOM PER NIGHT
S: £68.00
D: £89.00 - £145.00

Broom House at Egton Bridge

Broom House Lane, Egton Bridge, Whitby, North Yorkshire YO21 1XD **T:** (01947) 895279
E: mw@broom-house.co.uk
W: www.broom-house.co.uk **£ BOOK ONLINE**

Beautiful National Park Countryside, Moorland & the Whitby coastline, combine to offer the ultimate luxury hideaway. This delightful setting is an ideal base for relaxing, walking, bird watching etc. **Directions:** Please refer to website. **Bedrooms:** 2 double, 1 twin, 2 king size, 3 suite **Open:** All year except Christmas

Site: P **Payment:** **Leisure:** **Property:** **Catering:** **Room:**

FILEY, North Yorkshire Map ref 5D3 SatNav YO14 9JA B

★★★★ GUEST HOUSE — Silver AWARD

B&B PER ROOM PER NIGHT
S: £60.00 - £90.00
D: £74.00 - £95.00

Abbot's Leigh Guest House

7 Rutland Street, Filey YO14 9JA **T:** (01723) 513334
W: www.abbotsleighguesthouse.co.uk **£ BOOK ONLINE**

Experience quality surroundings and traditional commitment to great service at Abbots Leigh where a warm welcome and an award wining breakfast awaits. You can expect high standards of housekeeping, locally sourced produce and home baking all in a great location, we hope you will be as satisfied as many guests have been before. **Bedrooms:** Double, superking, twin and ground floor rooms **Open:** All year except Christmas

Payment: **Leisure:** **Property:** **Catering:** **Room:**

FILEY, North Yorkshire Map ref 5D3 SatNav YO14 9JA B

★★★★★ GUEST HOUSE

B&B PER ROOM PER NIGHT
S: £60.00 - £97.00
D: £80.00 - £117.00

All Seasons Guesthouse

11 Rutland Street, Filey YO14 9JA **T:** (01723) 515321 **E:** lesley@allseasonsfiley.co.uk
W: www.allseasonsfiley.co.uk **£ BOOK ONLINE**

All Seasons combines contemporary elegance and modern convenience with traditional warmth and hospitality. A five Star Michelin recommended guest house in Filey. **Directions:** From A165 follow signs for Filey at roundabout (bus station on right). Next right into West Avenue, Rutland Street is the 2nd left. **Bedrooms:** 3 double, 2 twin/2 family, 1 suite **Open:** All year

Payment: **Leisure:** **Property:** **Children:** 10 **Catering:** **Room:**

HARROGATE, North Yorkshire Map ref 4B1 SatNav HG1 2JD H

Cairn Hotel

Ripon Road, Harrogate, North Yorkshire HG1 2JD **T:** (01423) 504005 **F:** 01423 500056
E: salescairn@strathmorehotels.com
W: www.strathmorehotels.com **£ BOOK ONLINE**

enjoyEngland.com ★★★ HOTEL

B&B PER ROOM PER NIGHT
S: £50.00 - £130.00
D: £80.00 - £180.00

HB PER PERSON PER NIGHT
£60.00 - £150.00

SPECIAL PROMOTIONS
Free child places 0-4 years. Half-price 5-14 years. Christmas and New Year breaks available. Special last minute breaks. See website.

Built during Harrogate's period as a spa town, stylish and comfortable decor goes hand in hand with gracious hospitality to offer a welcome that is second to none. This charming hotel is only five minutes walk from the town centre - ideal for leisure breaks, meetings/conferences and exhibitions.

Directions: By car: 7 miles off the north/south A1 and 17 miles from the M1/M62. By rail: Harrogate station. By air: Leeds/Bradford airport (12 miles).

Bedrooms: 13 single, 48 double, 65 twin, 8 family, 1 suite
Open: All year

Site: **Payment:** **Leisure:** **Property:** **Children:** **Catering:**
Room:

HARROGATE, North Yorkshire Map ref 4B1 SatNav HG3 2LW B

Cold Cotes Guest Accommodation, Gardens & Nursery

Cold Cotes Road, Felliscliffe, Harrogate HG3 2LW **T:** (01423) 770937
E: info@coldcotes.com
W: www.coldcotes.com

enjoyEngland.com ★★★★★ GUEST ACCOMMODATION — enjoyEngland.com Gold AWARD

B&B PER ROOM PER NIGHT
S: £50.00 - £99.00
D: £50.00 - £99.00

EVENING MEAL PER PERSON
£7.50

On the edge of Nidderdale in the picturesque Yorkshire Dales. Guests say 'a special and relaxing place to stay, tranquil setting, beautiful and comfortable rooms, excellent food with an inspiring garden.' Convenient for RHS Harlow Carr. **Directions:** A59 west of Harrogate for 7 miles to Black Bull pub. Turn right after the pub onto Cold Cotes Road then third entrance on right.
Bedrooms: All rooms have king or super king beds (+ 2 twins)
Open: All year

Site: P **Payment:** **Leisure:** **Property:** **Catering:** **Room:**

HARROGATE, North Yorkshire Map ref 4B1 SatNav HG1 5JU B

enjoyEngland.com ★★★★ GUEST HOUSE

B&B PER ROOM PER NIGHT
S: £48.00 - £60.00
D: £68.00 - £80.00

Coppice Guest House

9 Studley Road, Harrogate, North Yorkshire, UK HG1 5JU **T:** (01423) 569626
E: coppice@guesthouseharrogate.com
W: www.guesthouseharrogate.com **£ BOOK ONLINE**

The Coppice Guest House B&B Harrogate. Quietly located on tree lined avenue 5 minutes walk from Harrogate town centre. Luxury en suite rooms. Free WiFi. Free parking. Full English or light breakfasts.

A warm friendly welcome awaits you. Cycling or driving through time in the Yorkshire Dales. Fantastic Views. The breathtaking Yorkshire. The Coppice into The Dales is just a 10 minute Drive.

Directions: Studley Road is off Kings Road close to The Conference Centre Kings Road is off the A59. The Coppice is close to the train and bus stations.

Bedrooms: 1 single, 2 double, 1 twin, 1 family
Open: All year

Payment: £ € **Leisure:** **Property:** **Children:** **Catering:** **Room:**

HARROGATE, North Yorkshire Map ref 4B1 SatNav HG3 1JH H

enjoyEngland.com ★★★★ HOTEL — enjoyEngland.com Gold AWARD

B&B PER ROOM PER NIGHT
S: £140.00 - £555.00
D: £165.00 - £590.00

Rudding Park

Follifoot, Harrogate, North Yorkshire HG3 1JH **T:** (01423) 871350 **F:** 01423 872286
E: reservations@ruddingpark.com
W: www.ruddingpark.co.uk

The award winning hotel offers 90 bedrooms, 2 AA Rosette Clocktower Restaurant, spa, gym, private cinema, two golf courses and extensive conference and banqueting facilities. **Directions:** Situated three miles south of Harrogate, Rudding Park lies just off the A658 linking the A61 from Leeds to the A59 York Road. **Bedrooms:** 90 Double/twin including 11 family and 8 suites **Open:** All year

Site: P **Payment:** £ € **Leisure:** **Property:** **Children:** **Catering:** **Room:**

HAWES, North Yorkshire Map ref 5B3 SatNav DL8 3PT H

enjoyEngland.com ★★ HOTEL — enjoyEngland.com Gold AWARD

B&B PER ROOM PER NIGHT
S: £73.00 - £195.00
D: £124.00 - £195.00
EVENING MEAL PER PERSON
£37.00

Stone House Hotel

Sedbusk, Hawes, Wensleydale DL8 3PT **T:** (01969) 667571 **F:** 01969 667720
E: reception@stonehousehotel.co.uk
W: www.stonehousehotel.com **£ BOOK ONLINE**

A classic Edwardian Country House Hotel with delicious food, log fires and quality bedrooms. Discover the perfect setting for a revitalising short break in the Yorkshire Dales National Park. Secure storage available for mountain and motor bikes. **Directions:** Hotel is sign posted from Hawes (half mile). **Bedrooms:** 1 single, 11 dble, 5 twin, 1 family, 6 suite **Open:** Closed January

WALKERS WELCOME — CYCLISTS WELCOME **Site:** P **Payment:** £ **Leisure:** **Property:** **Children:** **Catering:** **Room:**

KIRKBY MALZEARD, North Yorkshire Map ref 5C3 SatNav HG4 3SR B

B&B PER ROOM PER NIGHT
S: £55.00 - £70.00
D: £80.00 - £95.00

Cowscot House

Back Lane, Kirkby Malzeard, Ripon, N. Yorkshire HG4 3SR **T:** (01765) 658181
E: liz@cowscothouse.co.uk
W: www.cowscothouse.co.uk **£ BOOK ONLINE**

Cowscot House offers a high standard of accommodation in a sympathetically converted stone barn and stables on the edge of a popular village. All the en suite bedrooms are on the ground floor in a peaceful setting. **Directions:** From Ripon direction enter Kirkby Malzeard and continue down Main Street. Take right turn just after Highside Butchers turning immediately left into Back Lane. **Bedrooms:** 3 double, 1 twin **Open:** All year

Site: **P** **Payment:** **Leisure:** **Property:** **Children:** **Catering:** **Room:**

MALTON, North Yorkshire Map ref 5D3 SatNav YO17 7EG B

B&B PER ROOM PER NIGHT
S: £85.00 - £96.00
D: £120.00 - £145.00

Old Lodge Malton

Old Maltongate, Malton YO17 7EG **T:** (01653) 690570 **F:** 01653 690652
E: info@theoldlodgemalton.com
W: www.theoldlodgemalton.com **£ BOOK ONLINE**

Tudor mansion with luxurious four-poster bedrooms. Great restaurant serving freshly prepared, locally-sourced food. All-day Yorkshire Sunday lunch. All-day tea, coffee and clotted cream scones. Super gardens. **Directions:** Take the Malton exit from the A64. We are approx. 250 yards from the town centre, towards Old Malton. We're behind a big, old wall. **Bedrooms:** 20 double (onsite), 8 double (offsite) **Open:** All year

Site: **P** **Payment:** € **Leisure:** **Property:** **Children:** **Catering:** **Room:**

NORTHALLERTON, North Yorkshire Map ref 5C3 SatNav DL6 2PB B

B&B PER ROOM PER NIGHT
S: £40.00 - £50.00
D: £70.00 - £110.00
EVENING MEAL PER PERSON
£12.00 - £23.00

Lovesome Hill Farm

Lovesome Hill Farm, Lovesome Hill, Northallerton, North Yorkshire DL6 2PB
T: (01609) 772311 **E:** lovesomehillfarm@btinternet.com
W: www.lovesomehillfarm.co.uk

Relax over tea and home-made biscuits. Savour our award winning breakfast using fresh farm produce. Family occasion, break or business, ideally placed near Northallerton the heart of North Yorkshire. Lambing breaks. Romantic breaks with use of hot tub. **Directions:** Four miles North of Northallerton on the A167 towards Darlington, situated on the right hand side. **Bedrooms:** 1 single, 2 double, 1 twin, 1 family **Open:** Closed rarely

Site: **P** **Payment:** € **Leisure:** **Property:** **Children:** **Catering:** **Room:**

PICKERING, North Yorkshire Map ref 5D3 SatNav YO18 7JY B

B&B PER ROOM PER NIGHT
S: £48.00
D: £75.00

The Old Forge Bed & Breakfast

The Old Forge, Wilton, Pickering, North Yorkshire YO18 7JY **T:** (01751) 477399
E: theoldforge1@aol.com
W: www.forgecottages.co.uk

Dating from 1701. Comfortable, quality, relaxing, Bed and Breakfast. Private parking. Near Pickering Steam Railway, Dalby Forest, Yorkshire Moors, Eden Camp, fishing. Cyclists and walkers welcome. Close to Thornton-le-Dale. Excellent public transport. Please contact for special Offers. **Directions:** Follow the A170 Pickering Scarborough road. Turn left in Wilton, just after the bus stop. Park in courtyard behind The Old Forge. Sign on building.
Bedrooms: Comfortable, cosy and relaxing en suite rooms
Open: All year

Site: **P** **Leisure:** **Property:** **Children:** **Catering:** **Room:**

REETH, North Yorkshire Map ref 5B3 SatNav DL11 6QX B

Cambridge House

Arkengarthdale Road, Reeth, North Yorkshire DL11 6QX **T:** (01748) 884633
E: info@cambridgehousereeth.co.uk
W: www.cambridgehousereeth.co.uk

enjoyEngland.com ★★★★★ GUEST ACCOMMODATION

B&B PER ROOM PER NIGHT
S: £45.00
D: £88.00

SPECIAL PROMOTIONS
Winter mid- week 3 for 2 until March 20th, normal terms and conditions apply.

Cambridge House is a luxury 5* country guest house situated on the egde of Reeth in beautiful Swaledale, with stunning views, from all rooms, across the dale towards Grinton Moor. We are ideally situated for walking, cycling or just relaxing and taking in the beautiful scenery. We have 5 ensuited rooms. Relax in the guest lounge or conservatory.You will find a warm welcome at Cambridge House

Directions: We are 400m from the village green on Arkengarthdale Road, signposted from the green.

Bedrooms: All en suite rooms with a bath and shower except the single which has a shower. Tea and coffee in rooms, TV, luxury toiletries and bathrobes. WiFi
Open: All year except Christmas.

Site: P **Payment:** £ € **Leisure:** **Property:** **Children:** 14 **Catering:**
Room: TV DVD

RIPON, North Yorkshire Map ref 5C3 SatNav HG4 2BU H

The Ripon Spa Hotel

Park Street, Ripon HG4 2BU **T:** (01765) 602172 **F:** 01765 690770
E: sales@spahotelripon.co.uk
W: www.riponspa.com **£ BOOK ONLINE**

enjoyEngland.com ★★★ HOTEL

B&B PER ROOM PER NIGHT
S: £65.00 - £105.00
D: £69.00 - £129.00

EVENING MEAL PER PERSON
£12.95 - £22.95

Short walk from the centre of the ancient city of Ripon with its magnificent Cathedral, the hotel stands in award-winning landscaped gardens. You will discover traditional hospitality, croquet lawns, free on-site parking & free Wi-Fi. Fountains Abbey and Yorkshire Dales National Park nearby. **Directions:** Please see website for directions. **Bedrooms:** 4 single, 19 double, 15 twin & 2 family **Open:** All year

Site: **Payment:** £ € **Property:** **Children:**
Catering: **Room:** TV

SALTBURN-BY-THE-SEA, North Yorkshire Map ref 5C3 SatNav TS12 2QX B

The Arches Country House

Low Farm, Ings Lane, Brotton, Salturn-By-The-Sea, North Yorkshire TS12 2QX
T: (01287) 677512 **F:** 01287 677150 **E:** sales@gorallyschool.co.uk
W: www.thearcheshotel.co.uk **£ BOOK ONLINE**

B&B PER ROOM PER NIGHT
S: £45.00 - £60.00
D: £70.00 - £80.00

SPECIAL PROMOTIONS
Check website for special offers.

The Arches Country House is an independent, family owned and run accommodation located not far from Saltburn in North Yorkshire. We pride ourselves on our relaxed and informal atmosphere. We offer bed and breakfast. We also offer functions and a conference facility. Licenced to hold Civil Ceremony Weddings.

Directions: From North A1(M) Jct 60, A689 to A19 for Thirsk. From A19 to A174 toward Redcar, through Saltburn & Brotton. Stay on main road, 2nd left to St Margarets Way, past houses, past golf club, turn right.

Bedrooms: All rooms en suite. Flat screen TV, tea & coffee making facilities. Four poster room, family, single, double, twin rooms, ground floor available
Open: All Year except Christmas and New Year

Site: P **Payment:** **Leisure:** **Property:** **Children:** **Catering:**
Room:

SCARBOROUGH, North Yorkshire Map ref 5D3 SatNav YO11 1XX B

Empire Guesthouse

39 Albemarle Crescent, Scarborough YO11 1XX **T:** (01723) 373564
E: gillian@empire1939.wanadoo.co.uk
W: empireguesthouse.co.uk

B&B PER ROOM PER NIGHT
S: £24.00 - £27.00
D: £54.00

The Empire overlooks pleasant gardens located in the centre of town, ideally situated for all Scarborough's many attractions and town centre amenities. Every effort made to make your visit enjoyable. Evening meals available from Easter until the end of September. **Directions:** The Empire is 5mins from bus & rail terminals. We extend a very warm welcome to all our guests. **Bedrooms:** 2 single, 1 double, 1 twin, 1 family, 3 suite **Open:** All year except Christmas and New Year

Property: **Children:** **Catering:** **Room:**

SCARBOROUGH, North Yorkshire Map ref 5D3 SatNav YO12 7HU B

Howdale

121 Queen's Parade, Scarborough YO12 7HU **T:** (01723) 372696
E: mail@howdalehotel.co.uk
W: www.howdalehotel.co.uk/ve

B&B PER ROOM PER NIGHT
S: £24.00 - £29.00
D: £54.00 - £72.00

A cosy stay at the Howdale ensures your visit to Scarborough is perfect! Close to town. Stunning views over Scarborough North Bay & Castle. Fantastic delicious breakfast. Spotless, comfortable, friendly, efficient! Free parking. **Directions:** At traffic lights opposite railway station turn left. Next traffic lights turn right. At 1st roundabout turn left. Property is 0.5 miles on the right.
Bedrooms: 1 single, 11 double, 2 twin, 1 family
Open: March to October

Site: P **Payment:** **Property:** **Children:** **Room:**

SCARBOROUGH, North Yorkshire Map ref 5D3 SatNav YO11 3TP

B&B PER ROOM PER NIGHT
S: £45.00 - £50.00
D: £76.00 - £85.00
EVENING MEAL PER PERSON
£15.00 - £25.00

Killerby Cottage Farm

Killerby Cottage Farm, Killerby Lane, Cayton, Scarborough YO11 3TP **T:** (01723) 581236
E: val@killerbycottagefarm.co.uk
W: www.killerbycottagefarm.co.uk **£ BOOK ONLINE**

Situated between the seaside resorts of Scarborough and Filey, 1.5 miles from Cayton Bay next to the Stained Glass Centre. The farmhouse has been converted from 2 cottages and is tastefully decorated. Good food, lovely garden, warm welcome. **Directions:** Situated just off the B1261 between Cayton and Lebberston **Bedrooms:** 2 double, 1 twin/double **Open:** All year except Christmas and New Year

Site: P **Payment:** € **Property:** **Catering:** **Room:** TV DVD

SCARBOROUGH, North Yorkshire Map ref 5D3 SatNav YO13 0ER

B&B PER ROOM PER NIGHT
S: £44.00 - £55.00
D: £72.00 - £100.00

Smugglers Rock Country House

Staintondale Road, Ravenscar, Scarborough YO13 0ER **T:** (01723) 870044
E: info@smugglersrock.co.uk
W: www.smugglersrock.co.uk **£ BOOK ONLINE**

Built in approximately 1840, the house is situated in Ravenscar in the beautiful North Yorkshire Moors National Park with panoramic sea and countryside views and wonderful walks in every direction. An ideal base for exploring the area. **Directions:** Off A171 (Scarborough to Whitby Road), situated 0.5 miles before Ravenscar village. **Bedrooms:** 1 single, 4 double, 2 twin, 1 family **Open:** Easter to end of October

Site: P **Payment:** **Leisure:** **Property:** **Children:** 5 **Catering:** **Room:** TV

SCARBOROUGH, North Yorkshire Map ref 5D3 SatNav YO12 7HY

B&B PER ROOM PER NIGHT
S: £35.50 - £37.00
D: £58.00 - £70.00

SPECIAL PROMOTIONS
Oct-May inclusive (excl Bank Holidays): reduction of £1.50pppn when staying 2 nights or more.

The Whiteley

99-101 Queens Parade, Scarborough YO12 7HY **T:** (01723) 373514 **F:** 01723 373007
E: thewhiteley@gmail.com
W: www.yorkshirecoast.co.uk/whiteley

Small, family-run, non-smoking, licensed guest accommodation located in an elevated position overlooking the North Bay, close to the town centre and ideally situated for all amenities. The bedrooms are well co-ordinated and equipped with useful extras, many with sea views. Good home cooking is served in the traditional dining room.

Directions: Left at traffic lights near railway station, right at next lights, Castle Road to roundabout. Left onto North Marine Road. 2nd right onto Queens Parade.

Bedrooms: 7 double, 3 family
Open: All year except Christmas and New Year

Site: P **Payment:** **Property:** **Children:** 3 **Catering:** **Room:** TV

For **key to symbols** see page 7

SINNINGTON, North Yorkshire Map ref 5C3 SatNav YO62 6SQ B

Fox and Hounds

Main Street, Sinnington, Nr Pickering, North Yorkshire YO62 6SQ **T:** (01751) 431577
F: 01751 432791 **E:** fox.houndsinn@btconnect.com
W: www.thefoxandhoundsinn.co.uk **£ BOOK ONLINE**

B&B PER ROOM PER NIGHT
S: £59.00 - £84.00
D: £70.00 - £170.00
EVENING MEAL PER PERSON
£8.95 - £22.95

SPECIAL PROMOTIONS
2 and 3 night breaks often available throughout the year for reduced rates. Telephone or see website for last-minute offers.

The Fox and Hounds Inn is an 18th century coaching inn which is located in the quiet village of Sinnington, on the edge of the North York Moors National Park, just off the A170 Pickering to Kirbymoorside road.

Directions: Between Pickering and Kikbymoorisde on the A170.

Bedrooms: 8 double, 2 twin
Open: All year except Christmas

Site: P **Payment:** **Property:** **Children:** **Catering:** **Room:**

SKIPTON, North Yorkshire Map ref 4B1 SatNav BD23 4EA H

Coniston Hotel and Country Estate

Coniston Cold, Skipton BD23 4EA **T:** (01756) 748080 **F:** 01756 749487
E: reservations@theconistonhotel.com
W: www.theconistonhotel.com **£ BOOK ONLINE**

B&B PER ROOM PER NIGHT
S: £99.00 - £131.00
D: £116.00 - £150.00
EVENING MEAL PER PERSON
£10.00 - £32.00

Set in 1400 acre estate with stunning views, warm friendly welcome awaits, perfect location as a base to explore the Dales. Estate activities include Clay pigeon shooting, Land Rover Experience, Archery and Fishing. **Directions:** On the A65 between Skipton (7 miles) and Settle (9 miles) at Coniston Cold. Just 8 miles from Malham. **Bedrooms:** 65 double, 6 family
Open: All year

Site: P **Payment:** € **Leisure:** **Property:** **Children:** **Catering:** **Room:**

THIRSK, North Yorkshire Map ref 5C3 SatNav YO7 2AL B

Low Osgoodby Grange

Low Osgoodby Grange, Bagby, Thirsk, North Yorkshire YO7 2AL **T:** (01845) 597241
E: lowosgoodbygrange@gmail.com
W: www.lowosgoodbygrange.com

B&B PER ROOM PER NIGHT
S: £55.00
D: £70.00 - £80.00

A warm welcome awaits at Georgian farm 4 star silver family run B&B situated below the Hambleton Hills. All en suite rooms, to high standard with breakfast using local produce. Ideal location for visiting attractions and local restaurants. **Directions:** Situated 5 miles out of Thirsk off the A170 between the villages of Bagby and Kilburn. **Bedrooms:** 1 double, 1 king size, 1 family double and single **Open:** All year except christmas

Site: P **Leisure:** **Property:** **Children:** **Catering:** **Room:**

WEST WITTON, North Yorkshire Map ref 5B3 SatNav DL8 4LU

The Old Star

Main Street, West Witton, Leyburn, North Yorkshire DL8 4LU **T:** (01969) 622949
E: enquiries@theoldstar.com
W: www.theoldstar.com

B&B PER ROOM PER NIGHT
S: £32.00 - £40.00
D: £58.00 - £66.00

Former 18th century coaching inn set in the heart of Wensleydale with good views, oak beams, log fire, cottage gardens and a friendly atmosphere. Excellent centre for walking and exploring the Dales. Two nearby pubs serve good food and ale. **Directions:** West Witton is on the A684, 4 miles west of Leyburn. Northallerton is our nearest station, there is a bus from Northallerton to West Witton via Bedale. **Bedrooms:** 4 double, 1 twin, 2 flexible/family, 5 are en suite **Open:** All year except Christmas

Site: P **Payment:** € **Leisure:** **Property:** **Children:** **Catering:** **Room:**

WHITBY, North Yorkshire Map ref 5D3 SatNav YO21 1QL

Bagdale Hall, No. 4 & Lodge

1 Bagdale, Whitby YO21 1QL **T:** (01947) 602958 **F:** 01947 820714
E: bagdale@btconnect.com
W: www.bagdale.co.uk

B&B PER ROOM PER NIGHT
S: £70.00 - £130.00
D: £90.00 - £240.00

EVENING MEAL PER PERSON
£15.00 - £35.00

Whitby, Yorkshire. Bagdale Hall is an old Tudor Manor House dating back to 1516. No.4 Bagdale is a Georgian town house built around 1790. Bagdale Lodge is a large detached Georgian house circa 1770. **Directions:** Bagdale Hall is located in the centre of town a 2 minute walk to Whitby Harbour. **Bedrooms:** 21 dble, 2 twin, 4 suite **Open:** All year

Site: P **Payment:** **Leisure:** **Property:** **Children:** **Catering:** **Room:**

WHITBY, North Yorkshire Map ref 5D3 SatNav YO21 3QN

Sneaton Castle Centre

Castle Road, Whitby YO21 3QN **T:** (01947) 600051 **F:** 01947 603490
E: reception@sneatoncastle.co.uk
W: www.sneatoncastle.co.uk

B&B PER ROOM PER NIGHT
S: £44.45
D: £88.90

EVENING MEAL PER PERSON
£10.00

SPECIAL PROMOTIONS
Sunday to Thursday from 2 November - 26 March - 3 nights B&B £119 per person (based on 2 people sharing: £129 for single occupancy). Supper included on one evening. Disabled access available.

Set in the stunning grounds and gardens of Sneaton Castle, on the outskirts of Whitby and on the edge of the North York Moors and near the seashore. We offer high quality en suite accommodation and an excellent Yorkshire breakfast. Ample free and safe parking.

Directions: Please refer to website.

Bedrooms: 1 double, 8 twin and 3 family
Open: All year except Christmas and New Year

Site: P **Payment:** **Leisure:** **Property:** **Children:** **Catering:** **Room:**

YORK, North Yorkshire Map ref 4C1 SatNav YO23 1NX B

Avondale Guest House

61 Bishopthorpe Road, York, North Yorkshire YO23 1NX **T:** (01904) 633989 / 07958 021024
E: kaleda@avondaleguesthouse.co.uk
W: www.avondaleguesthouse.co.uk **£ BOOK ONLINE**

enjoyEngland.com ★★★ GUEST ACCOMMODATION

B&B PER ROOM PER NIGHT
S: £46.00 - £50.00
D: £75.00 - £95.00

Avondale, a lovely Victorian home, short walk to medieval walls, city, attractions, river walks, racecourse and station. Comfortable en suite rooms with award winning fresh breakfast menu, try our Whisky Porridge. **Directions:** Short walk from train/bus station. Drive from south A19, A1 or A64, from north A19 or A59. Find us easily from instructions on website. **Bedrooms:** 1 single, 3 double, 1 twin/king, 1 family **Open:** All year except Christmas

Site: P **Payment:** £ **Property:** **Children:** **Catering:** **Room:**

YORK, North Yorkshire Map ref 4C1 SatNav YO23 2RB B

Bracken Lodge Bed & Breakfast

10 Main Street, Bishopthorpe, York YO23 2RB **T:** (01904) 500703
E: stay@bracken-lodge.co.uk
W: www.brackenlodgeyork.co.uk **£ BOOK ONLINE**

enjoyEngland.com ★★★★ GUEST ACCOMMODATION

B&B PER ROOM PER NIGHT
S: £65.00 - £80.00
D: £80.00 - £90.00

Bracken Lodge Bed and Breakfast is situated in Bishopthorpe, 3 miles from York and has 3 rooms, 1 x king size double/twin, 1 x king size double and 1 x double all with en suite. Private car parking, quiet location, close to York racecourse. **Directions:** From A64 take exit toward York (West)/A1036 follow signs to Bishopthorpe. From Sim Balk Lane turn left on to Main St, Bracken Lodge is on right. **Bedrooms:** En suite, flat screen TV, tea & coffee in Rooms. **Open:** All Year except Christmas and New Year

Site: P **Leisure:** **Room:**

YORK, North Yorkshire Map ref 4C1 SatNav YO30 7BT B

Georgian House and Mews

35 Bootham, York YO30 7BT **T:** (01904) 622874 **F:** 01904 623823 **E:** york1e45@aol.com
W: www.georgianhouse.co.uk **£ BOOK ONLINE**

enjoyEngland.com ★★★ GUEST ACCOMMODATION

B&B PER ROOM PER NIGHT
S: £40.00 - £48.00
D: £60.00 - £90.00

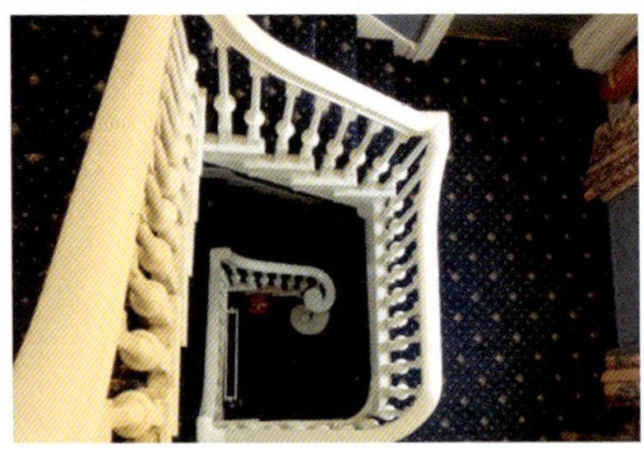

City centre guesthouse, 100 yards from City walls and 350 yards from York Minster. This is the best located guesthouse in York and we have a mixture of 3 and 4 star accommodation between Georgian House and Georgian Mews and are the cheaper option to the hotels in the area. Parking is available nearby for £4.50 per day. Please note, smoking is not allowed anywhere on the premises

Directions: By car, enter York by the A19 Thirsk roundabout and we are situated on the left after about 2.1 miles.

Bedrooms: All rooms are en suite with flat screen tv, tea making, hairdryer etc
Open: All year except Christmas

Payment: £ **Leisure:** **Property:** **Children:** **Catering:** **Room:**

YORK, North Yorkshire *Map ref 4C1* *SatNav YO30 7AH* B

enjoyEngland.com ★★★ GUEST ACCOMMODATION

B&B PER ROOM PER NIGHT
S: £35.00 - £45.00
D: £50.00 - £85.00

Grange Lodge Guest House

52 Bootham Crescent, York YO30 7AH **T:** (01904) 621137 / 07912 505390 **F:** 01904 627654
E: grange-lodge@btconnect.com
W: www.grange-lodge.com

Attractive, tastefully-furnished Victorian town house with a friendly atmosphere. Special emphasis is given to food, cleanliness and hospitality. **Directions:** A64 leading to York, take the A1237 and join A19 towards York city centre. **Bedrooms:** 4 standard doubles, 1 deluxe double, 1 triple, 1 twin, 1 single. All en suite. **Open:** All year except Christmas

Site: P **Payment:** **Leisure:** **Property:** **Children:** **Catering:** **Room:**

YORK, North Yorkshire *Map ref 4C1* *SatNav YO30 7DH* H

enjoyEngland.com ★★★ HOTEL · enjoyEngland.com Silver AWARD

B&B PER ROOM PER NIGHT
S: £70.00 - £110.00
D: £95.00 - £175.00
EVENING MEAL PER PERSON
£12.95 - £23.95

Hedley House Hotel & Apartments

3 Bootham Terrace, York YO30 7DH **T:** (01904) 637404 **F:** 01904 639774
E: greg@hedleyhouse.com
W: www.hedleyhouse.com **£ BOOK ONLINE**

Award wining 3 star city centre hotel. In a quiet location, serving fabulous homemade food from local suppliers. Beautician (massage and nails etc), lounge bar, Jacuzzi and Sauna. Free Wi-Fi and off street parking. **Directions:** From south A1 A64 A1237 York North - A19 city centre under footbridge 2nd right. From North A1 A59 A1237 York North A19 as above **Bedrooms:** 2 single, 7 double, 6 twin, 11 family **Open:** All year except Christmas

Site: P **Payment:** **Leisure:** **Property:** **Children:** **Catering:** **Room:**

YORK, North Yorkshire *Map ref 4C1* *SatNav YO30 2AY* B

enjoyEngland.com ★★★★ GUEST ACCOMMODATION · enjoyEngland.com Gold AWARD

B&B PER ROOM PER NIGHT
S: £55.00 - £65.00
D: £76.00 - £90.00
EVENING MEAL PER PERSON
£16.00 - £28.00

The Manor House

Main Street, Linton-on-Ouse, York YO30 2AY **T:** (01347) 848391
E: info@manorguesthouse.co.uk
W: www.manorguesthouse.co.uk **£ BOOK ONLINE**

Relax in beautiful listed Georgian Manor House with award winning spacious, comfortable rooms and ground-floor apartment. Lovely gardens, private parking. In lovely village with riverside walks, 3 nearby pubs with restaurants. 10 mins drive to York park & ride, ideal for Dales and Moors. **Directions:** From bypass/A1237 roundabout north A19. 2 miles turn left at Shipton. 2 miles turn left, follow to Linton. Last house on right. **Bedrooms:** 1 single, 2 double/twin, 2 family, 2 suites **Open:** All year except Christmas & New Year

Site: P **Payment:** € **Leisure:** **Property:** **Children:** **Catering:** **Room:**

YORK, North Yorkshire *Map ref 4C1* *SatNav YO1 6DH* H

enjoyEngland.com ★★ HOTEL

B&B PER ROOM PER NIGHT
S: £80.00 - £110.00
D: £90.00 - £120.00
EVENING MEAL PER PERSON
£9.95 - £27.00

The Queens Hotel

Queens Staith Road, Skeldergate, York YO1 6DH **T:** (01904) 611321 **F:** 01904 611388
E: sales@queenshotel-york.com
W: www.queenshotel-york.com

Ideally located on the banks of the river in the heart of the city of York, The Queens Hotel offers quality accommodation for leisure, families and groups. The restaurant is open daily and serves breakfast and dinner. A warm welcome awaits.
Bedrooms: 30 double, 25 twin, 23 family **Open:** All year

Payment: **Property:** **Children:** **Catering:** **Room:**

YORK, North Yorkshire Map ref 4C1 SatNav YO31 7TQ B

York House

62 Heworth Green, York YO31 7TQ **T:** (01904) 427070 **F:** 01904 427070
E: info@yorkhouseyork.co.uk
W: www.yorkhouseyork.co.uk **£ BOOK ONLINE**

enjoyEngland.com ★★★★ GUEST ACCOMMODATION

B&B PER ROOM PER NIGHT
S: £35.00 - £40.00
D: £90.00 - £110.00

SPECIAL PROMOTIONS
Early Bird Payment discount scheme of 10% on double and twin rooms on bookings made and paid 14 days prior to date of arrival.

Located a short stroll from the heart of one of Europe's most historic cities, York House is the perfect base for a visit to York or the surrounding area. A Georgian house with later additions, rooms feature all the modern conveniences you could possibly need for a relaxing, enjoyable stay.

Directions: North East of York, A1036 signed city centre. Straight over 2 roundabouts and 2 sets of traffic lights, next mini roundabout 3rd exit. York House 300 yards on left.

Bedrooms: 1 single, 6 double, 1 twin
Open: All year except Christmas and New Year

Site: P **Payment:** **Property:** **Catering:** **Room:**

DONCASTER, South Yorkshire Map ref 4C1 SatNav DN2 6AD H

Earl of Doncaster Hotel

Bennetthorpe, Doncaster DN2 6AD **T:** (01302) 361371 **F:** 01302 321858
E: reception@theearl.co.uk
W: www.theearl.co.uk

enjoyEngland.com ★★★★ HOTEL
enjoyEngland.com Silver AWARD

SPECIAL PROMOTIONS
Please contact us for prices.

The Earl of Doncaster Hotel is superbly located within 500 metres of Doncaster Racecourse and the town centre, offering free on site parking. This impressive Art Deco, 4 Star, Classic British Hotel, has beautifully designed executive bedrooms, a stylish restaurant and a magnificent Ballroom that epitomises all the character and charm of the hotel. The Earl – one of Doncaster's best kept secrets.

Directions: Follow the signs for Doncaster Racecourse, at the roundabout take the A638 (Bennetthorpe) towards the town centre, the hotel is located on the left and car park is situated at the rear of the hotel.

Bedrooms: En suite, flat screen TVs, Wi-Fi, tea & coffee Facilities, 24 hour room service, climate control, iron & ironing boards
Open: All year

Site: P **Payment:** **Leisure:** **Property:** **Children:** **Catering:** **Room:**

DONCASTER, South Yorkshire Map ref 4C1 SatNav DN10 6QU B

Home Farm and Lodge

Home Farm, High Street, Austerfield, Doncaster, South Yorkshire DN10 6QU
T: 07516 102676 **E:** homefarmandlodge@yahoo.co.uk
W: www.homefarmandlodge.co.uk **£ BOOK ONLINE**

enjoyEngland.com ★★★★ GUEST ACCOMMODATION
enjoyEngland.com Silver AWARD

B&B PER ROOM PER NIGHT
S: £45.00 - £55.00
D: £65.00 - £75.00

SPECIAL PROMOTIONS
Free wi-fi in all rooms and off road parking with cctv. Reduced rates for long term residents of 3 months or more.

Converted self contained barns set in idyllic gardens, near Bawtry perfect for long term residents or a romantic short break. All rooms have a comfy sofa, tv & dvd player, kettle, toaster, microwave & fridge. All rooms are en suite with bath & shower. All the accommodation opens up onto the garden area which residents are encouraged to use, this all makes Home Farm a home from home place to stay.

Directions: Home Farm is situated on the A614 in Austerfield, 1 mile from Bawtry and 6 miles from Doncaster.

Bedrooms: All rooms have a comfy sofa, tv & dvd player, kettle, toaster, microwave & fridge. Tea/coffee fresh orange juice, cereals, milk, jams/marmalade, bread
Open: Open all year round

Site: P **Payment:** **Leisure:** **Property:** **Children:** **Room:**

SHEFFIELD, South Yorkshire Map ref 4B2 SatNav S6 6HE B

Padley Farm B & B

Dungworth Green, Dungworth, Bradfield, Sheffield, South Yorkshire S6 6HE
T: (0114) 285 1427 **E:** lindabestall@sky.com
W: www.padleyfarm.co.uk **£ BOOK ONLINE**

enjoyEngland.com ★★★★ BED & BREAKFAST

B&B PER ROOM PER NIGHT
S: £40.00 - £65.00
D: £65.00

Set in the peaceful village of Dungworth, each room boasts wonderful panoramic views over the countryside and to Sheffield. The 17th century building has been converted to facilitate all today's comforts with en suite showers. **Directions:** A6101 through Hillsbrough. Take 3rd exit at Mailin Bridge to Loxley B6077. Left at Dam Flask then left up Briers house lane B6070. Next left.
Bedrooms: All rooms have freeview, DVD TVs & hairdryers
Open: All year except New Year

Site: P **Payment:** **Leisure:** **Property:** **Children:** **Catering:** **Room:**

HAWORTH, West Yorkshire Map ref 4B1 SatNav BD22 8EZ B

Ashmount Country House

Mytholmes Lane, Haworth BD22 8EZ **T:** (01535) 645726 **E:** info@ashmounthaworth.co.uk
W: www.ashmounthaworth.co.uk **£ BOOK ONLINE**

B&B PER ROOM PER NIGHT
S: £75.00 - £99.00
D: £95.00 - £245.00

EVENING MEAL PER PERSON
£15.00 - £45.00

SPECIAL PROMOTIONS
Please see our website for special offers.

Our Victorian house offers luxury bed & breakfast accommodation with a fantastic AA awarded restaurant. With many original features and antique furniture. The house was built by the Bronte family's Dr Ingham, it has fabulous gardens, wonderful views and private parking. We aim to provide a romantic retreat for our guests with hot tub rooms available. We also cater for Weddings and private parties.

Bedrooms: All rooms are en suite and with flat screen tvs, some with four-poster beds, feature baths and hot tubs in selected rooms
Open: All year

Site: P **Payment:** **Property:** **Catering:** **Room:**

HAWORTH, West Yorkshire Map ref 4B1 SatNav BD22 9SG B

Leeming Wells

Long Causeway, Oxenhope, Keighley, West Yorkshire BD22 9SG **T:** (01535) 646757
F: 01535 648992 **E:** info@leemingwells.co.uk
W: www.leemingwells.co.uk

B&B PER ROOM PER NIGHT
S: £55.00 - £65.00
D: £70.00 - £80.00

Leeming Wells offers 4* accommodation in an amazing setting in Oxenhope, near Haworth. With beautiful en suite bedrooms you can relax in our Swimming Pool with the backdrop of Yorkshire rolling countryside. Breakfast at Dog & Gun next door. **Directions:** By car: Haworth 9 minutes. Skipton Market Town 30 minutes. Bradford Alhambra Theatre 20 minutes. **Bedrooms:** En suite, flat screen TV, tea/coffee and biscuit tray **Open:** All year

Site: P **Payment:** **Leisure:** **Property:** **Children:** **Catering:**
Room:

KEIGHLEY, West Yorkshire Map ref 4B1 SatNav BD22 0QE B

Middle Slippery Ford Barn

Middle Slippery Ford Barn, Slippery Ford Lane, Oakworth, Keighley, West Yorkshire BD22 0QE **T:** (01535) 636972 **E:** stay@middleslipperyfordbarn.co.uk
W: www.middleslipperyfordbarn.co.uk

enjoyEngland.com ★★★★ GUEST ACCOMMODATION

enjoyEngland.com Silver AWARD

B&B PER ROOM PER NIGHT
D: £85.00 - £115.00

Built in the early 17th Century, Middle Slippery Ford Barn is a converted barn which forms part of a grade II listed farmhouse. Situated in beautiful Yorkshire moorland with little passing traffic and breath-taking views of the stunning Yorkshire hills. Sunsets can be spectacular and we're sure you will be captivated by the open farmland and our rural location.

All three guest rooms have fabulous interiors and private luxury en suite bathrooms. In addition to luxury showers, two of our rooms also have fabulous free-standing claw foot baths. Sumptuous king size beds with quality bedding, bespoke luxury designed interiors, wall-mounted digital televisions and mood lighting.

Directions: Middle Slippery Ford Barn is situated in a pretty secluded valley – 2.8 miles from the village of Oakworth, and 2.7 miles from the village of Sutton in Craven.

Open: All Year

WALKERS WELCOME CYCLISTS WELCOME

Site: P **Payment:** **Leisure:** **Property:** **Room:**

LEEDS, West Yorkshire Map ref 4B1 SatNav LS25 5LQ

Best Western Plus Milford Hotel

Great North Road, Peckfield, Leeds, West Yorkshire LS25 5LQ **T:** (01977) 681800
F: 01977 681245 **E:** reception@mlh.co.uk
W: www.milfordhotel.co.uk **£ BOOK ONLINE**

Best Western PLUS

AA ★★★ Hotel

B&B PER ROOM PER NIGHT
S: £51.00 - £121.00
D: £63.00 - £133.00
EVENING MEAL PER PERSON
£14.95 - £25.00

A modern hotel privately owned and managed, located between Leeds & York with full air conditioning to all en suite rooms. Free Wi-Fi offered to all our residents and conference delegates. Free car parking. Recommended by Tripadvisor. B+B per room per night from £51. **Directions:** Located on the outskirts of Leeds, just off the A1(M) junction 42. A63 Peckfield, visit local area page on hotel website for further directions **Bedrooms:** Offering standard double, twin and Superior Rooms **Open:** All Year

Site: P **Payment:** **Property:** **Children:** **Catering:** **Room:**

Don't Miss...

Blackpool Illuminations

Sept-Nov, Blackpool
www.blackpool-illuminations.net
This world famous display lights up Blackpool's promenade with over 1 million glittering lights that will make you oooh and aaah in wonder. Head for the big switch on or buy tickets for the Festival Weekend.

Chester Zoo

Cheshire CH2 1EU
(01244) 380280
www.chesterzoo.org
The UK's number one zoo with over 11000 animals and 400 different species, including some of the most exotic and endangered species on the planet.

Jodrell Bank Discovery Centre

Macclesfield, Cheshire SK11 9DL
(01477) 571766
www.jodrellbank.net
A great day out for all the family, explore the wonders of the universe and learn about the workings of the giant Lovell Telescope.

Muncaster Castle

Ravenglass, Cumbria CA18 1RQ
(01229) 717614
www.muncaster.co.uk
Medieval Muncaster Castle is a treasure trove of paintings, silver, embroideries and more. With acres of Grade 2 woodland gardens, famous for rhododendrons and breathtaking views of the Lake District.

Tate Liverpool

Merseyside L3 4BB
(0151) 702 7400
www.tate.org.uk/liverpool
Tate Liverpool presents displays and international exhibitions of modern and contemporary art in beautiful light filled galleries and is free to visit except for special exhibitions.

North West

Cheshire, Cumbria, Lancashire, Greater Manchester, Merseyside

The breathtaking scenery of the Lake District dominates the North West, but urban attractions such as cosmopolitan Manchester and Liverpool, with its grand architecture and cultural credentials, have much to recommend them. Further afield, you can explore the Roman and Medieval heritage of Chester, discover Lancashire's wealth of historic houses and gardens, or make a date for one of the huge variety of events that take place in this region throughout the year.

Explore – North West

Cheshire

The charms of the old walled city of Chester and the picturesque villages that dot Cheshire's countryside contrast sharply with the industrial towns of Runcorn and Warrington. Iron age forts, Roman ruins, Medieval churches, Tudor cottages and elegant Georgian and Victorian stately homes are among the many attractive sights of the county. South Cheshire, like Cumbria to the north, has long been the home of the wealthy from Manchester and Liverpool and boasts a huge selection of of excellent eateries. It also has peaceful, pretty countryside, and is within easy reach of the wilder terrain of the Peak District and North Wales.

Hotspot: Walk the city walls, step inside the magnificent gothic Cathedral, take a cruise along the River Dee or browse the picturesque medieval shopping streets of Eastgate and Watergate - Chester has over 2000 years of Roman and Medieval history to show you, as well as some seriously good shopping and eating on offer too!

Hotspot: Explore the breathtaking beauty of England's largest lake with a cruise on Lake Windermere for the most scenic views of the Lakeland fells.

Cumbria

In this lovely corner of England, there is beauty in breathtaking variety. The area is loved by many who come back time and again to its inspirational magic, brilliant blue lakes and craggy mountain tops. The central Lake District with its mountains, lakes and woods is so well known that there is a tendency to forget that the rest of Cumbria contains some of the most varied and attractive landscape in Britain. In the east of the county, the peaceful Eden Valley is sheltered by the towering hills of the Pennines, with charming little red sandstone villages and reminders of the Roman occupation everywhere. Alston, with its cobbled streets is the highest town in England, and has been used for numerous TV location sets.

Cumbria's long coastline is full of variety with rocky cliffs, sea birds, sandy estuaries, miles of sun-trap sand dunes and friendly harbours. In Autumn the deciduous woodlands and bracken coloured hillsides glow with colour. In Winter, the snow covered mountain tops dazzle magnificently against blue skies. In Spring, you can discover the delights of the magical, constantly changing light and the joy of finding carpets of wild flowers.

The Lake District is an outdoor enthusiasts paradise offering everything from walking and climbing to orienteering, potholing, cycling, riding, golf, sailing, sailboarding, canoeing, fishing and waterskiing. A great way to take in the beauty of this unique area is to plan your own personal route on foot, or cycle one of the many formal trails such as the Cumbria Cycle Way. The Cumbrian climate is ideal for gardens and the area is famous for the rhododendrons and azaleas which grow here in abundance. If you fancy a break from the great outdoors there is a wealth of historic houses, from small cottages where famous writers have lived to stately homes, that have seen centuries of gracious living and architectural importance.

Hotspot: Cholmondeley Castle Garden in Cheshire is among the most romantically beautiful gardens in the country. Visitors can enjoy the tranquil Temple Water Garden, Ruin Water Garden, memorial mosaic, Rose garden & many mixed borders. www.cholmondeleycastle.com

Lancashire

Lancashire's Forest of Bowland is an area of outstanding natural beauty with wild crags, superb walks, streams, valleys and fells. Blackpool on the coast has been the playground of the North West for many years and still draws millions of holiday makers every year, attracted to its seven miles of beach, illuminations, Pleasure Beach Amusement Park and golf. Morecambe, Southport, Lytham St Annes and Fleetwood also offer wide beaches, golf and bracing walks. Lancaster, a city since Roman times, has fine museums, a castle and an imitation of the Taj Mahal, the Ashton Memorial.

Manchester

Manchester's prosperity can be traced back to the 14th century when Flemish weavers arrived to transform a market town into a thriving boom city at the forefront of the Industrial Revolution. Now known as The Capital of the North, the city is rich in culture with plenty of galleries, museums, libraries and theatres. The City Art Gallery displays its famous pre-Raphaelite collection while the Halle Orchestra regularly fills the Bridgewater Hall. At Granada Studios you can still tour the set of Coronation Street and you can find quality shopping locations and sporting (particularly football) traditions. Cosmopolitan Manchester makes a great place to stay for a spot of retail therapy too!

Hotspot: Set in a stunning waterside location at the heart of the redeveloped Salford Quays in Greater Manchester, The Lowry is an architectural gem that brings together a wide variety of performing and visual arts, including the works of LS Lowry and contemporary exhibitions. www.thelowry.com

Merseyside

Liverpool was an important city long before The Beatles emerged from their Cavern in the Swinging Sixties. It grew from a village into a prosperous port, where emigrants sailed for the New World and immigrants arrived from Ireland. Today the ocean going liners are fewer, but the revitalised dock complex ensures that the city is as vibrant as ever. Liverpool's waterfront regeneration flagship is the Albert Dock Village, which includes the Maritime Museum and Tate Gallery Liverpool. The city has two modern cathedrals, a symphony orchestra, plenty of museums and Britain's oldest repertory theatre The Playhouse. In recent years, Liverpool has seen the opening of an extensive range of cafés, restaurants and accommodation to suit all tastes and budgets.

Hotspot: Discover objects rescued from the Titanic among the treasures at the Merseyside Maritime Museum, one of the venues that make up the National Museums Liverpool, an eclectic group of free museums and galleries. www.liverpoolmuseums.org.uk

Indulge – North West

Treat yourself to delicious sandwiches, scones, cakes, a nice chilled glass of Champagne and breathtaking views at the **White Star Grand Hall**, 30 James Street, Liverpool. Formerly the White Star Line's first-class lounge, the superb architecture recreates the splendour of a more glamorous era. www.rmstitanichotel.co.uk

One for the boys? Experience the world's greatest sport at the **National Football Museum** in Manchester. Whether you're a diehard football fan, planning a visit with your family or on a weekend break to the great city of Manchester, visit the world's biggest and best football museum. www.nationalfootballmuseum.com

Indulge in some seriously foodie fun at the 10th Anniversary of the **World's Original Marmalade Awards & Festival** at historic Dalemain Mansion & Gardens, in the Lake District. With a range of events including of course, delicious marmalade tasting. Saturday 28th Feb-Sun 1st Mar 2015. www.dalemainmarmaladeawards.co.uk

Enjoy a sophisticated feast at Simon Radley's chic, award-winning **Restaurant at the Chester Grosvenor** which has retained its Michelin star since 1990 and holds 4 AA Rosettes. (01244) 324024 www.chestergrosvenor.com

Take a trip on a steam-hauled dining train with the **East Lancashire Railway** and step into a world of vintage glamour and sophistication. Excellent food and a relaxed and friendly atmosphere in plush surroundings capture the essence of bygone days. www.eastlancsrailway.org.uk

Visit – North West

Attractions with this sign participate in the Visitor Attraction Quality Assurance Scheme.

Cheshire

Arley Hall & Gardens
Northwich, Cheshire CW9 6NA
(01565) 777353
www.arleyhallandgardens.com
Arley Hall's gardens are a wonderful example of the idea that the best gardens are living works of art.

Catalyst Science Discovery Centre
Widnes, Cheshire WA8 0DF
(0151) 420 1121
www.catalyst.org.uk
Interactive science centre whose aim is to make science exciting and accessible to people of all ages and abilities.

Chester Cathedral
Cheshire CH1 2HU
(01244) 324756
www.chestercathedral.com
A must-see for Chester, a beautiful cathedral with a fascinating history.

Go Ape! Hire Wire Forest Adventure - Delamere
Northwich, Cheshire CW8 2JD
(0845) 643 9215
www.goape.co.uk
Take to the trees and experience an exhilarating course of rope bridges, tarzan swings and zip slides, all set high above the forest floor.

Grosvenor Park Open Air Theatre
July-August, Grosvenor Park, Chester, Cheshire
www.grosvenorparkopenairtheatre.co.uk
The greatest open air theatre outside of London returns for a summer of exciting performances.

©Val Corbett

Hare Hill Gardens
Macclesfield, Cheshire SK10 4QB
(01625) 584412
www.nationaltrust.org.uk/harehill
A small but perfectly formed and tranquil woodland garden.

National Waterways Museum
Ellesmere Port, Cheshire CH65 4FW
(0151) 335 5017
www.canalrivertrust.org.uk
Unlock the wonders of our waterways.

RHS Flower Show Tatton Park
July, Tatton Park, Knutsford, Cheshire
www.rhs.org.uk
A fantastic display of flora and fauna and all things garden related in stunning Cheshire countryside.

Cumbria

Coniston Water Festival
July, Coniston Water, Lake District, Cumbria
www.conistonwaterfestival.org.uk
Features fun activities and events focused on the Coniston lake and the unique aspects of water-related culture and sport.

Grizedale Forest Visitor Centre
Hawkshead, Cumbria LA22 0QJ
(01229) 860010
www.forestry.gov.uk/northwestengland
Grizedale Forest offers a range of activities for all ages through the year, from mountain biking to relaxing walks, Go-Ape to the sculpture trails.

Holker Hall & Gardens
Grange-over-Sands, Cumbria LA11 7PL
(01539) 558328
www.holker.co.uk
Home to Lord and Lady Cavendish, Victorian wing, glorious gardens, parkland and woodlands.

Museum of Lakeland Life
Kendal, Cumbria LA9 5AL
(01539) 722464
www.lakelandmuseum.org.uk
This award winning museum takes you and your family back through time to tell the story of the Lake District and its inhabitants.

Penrith Castle
Cumbria CA11 7HX
(01912) 691200
www.english-heritage.org.uk/daysout/properties/penrith-castle/
The mainly 15th Century remains of a castle begun by Bishop Strickland of Carlisle and developed by the Nevilles and Richard III.

Ravenglass & Eskdale Railway
Cumbria CA18 1SW
(01229) 717171
www.ravenglass-railway.co.uk
Heritage steam engines haul open-top and cosy covered carriages from the Lake District coastal village of Ravenglass to the foot of England's highest mountains.

South Lakes Safari Zoo
Dalton-in-Furness, Cumbria LA15 8JR
(01229) 466086
www.southlakessafarizoo.com
The ultimate interactive animal experience. Get close to wildlife at Cumbria's top tourist attraction.

Ullswater Steamers
Cumbria CA11 0US
(01768) 482229
www.ullswater-steamers.co.uk
The 'Steamers' create the perfect opportunity to combine a cruise with some of the most famous and spectacular walks in the lake District.

Windermere Lake Cruises, Lakeside
Newby Bridge, Cumbria LA12 8AS
(01539) 443360
www.windermere-lakecruises.co.uk
Steamers and launches sail daily between Ambleside, Bowness and Lakeside.

Great North Swim
June, Windermere, Cumbria
www.greatswim.org
Europe's biggest open water swim series comes to the Lake District.

The World of Beatrix Potter
Bowness, Cumbria LA23 3BX
(01539) 488444
www.hop-skip-jump.com
A magical indoor attraction that brings to life all 23 Beatrix Potter's Peter Rabbit tales.

Lancashire

Blackpool Dance Festival
May, Blackpool, Lancashire
www.blackpooldancefestival.com
The world's first and foremost festival of dancing.

Blackpool Pleasure Beach
Blackpool, Lancashire FY4 1EZ
(0871) 222 1234
www.blackpoolpleasurebeach.com
The UK's most ride intensive theme park and home to the legendary Big One and Valhalla.

Clitheroe Food Festival
August, Clitheroe, Lancashire
www.clitheroefoodfestival.com
Celebrating the very finest Lancashire food and drink produces. Includes chef demos, tastings and cookery workshops.

Farmer Ted's Farm Park
Ormskirk, Lancashire L39 7HW
(0151) 526 0002
www.farmerteds.com
An interactive children's activity park, sited on a working farm within the beautiful Lancashire countryside.

Garstang Walking Festival
May, Garstang, Lancashire
www.visitlancashire.com
A celebration of springtime in the stunning countryside of Garstang and the surrounding area. Guided walks and activities for all the family.

Lytham Proms Festival
August, Lytham & St Annes, Lancashire
www.visitlancashire.com
Summer proms spectacular with shows from leading performers.

Sandcastle Waterpark
Blackpool, Lancashire FY4 1BB
(01253) 343602
www.sandcastle-waterpark.co.uk
The UK's Largest Indoor Waterpark and with 18 slides and attractions.

Ribchester Roman Museum
Preston, Lancashire PR3 3XS
(01254) 878261
www.ribchesterromanmuseum.org
Lancashire's only specialist Roman museum, located on the North bank of the beautiful River Ribble.

Wyre Estuary Country Park
Thornton Lancashire FY5 5LR
(01253) 857890
www.wyre.gov.uk
The award winning Wyre Estuary Country Park offers year-round activities and events for all the family including ranger-led walks, environmentally themed activities and annual events like the Family Sculpture Day.

Manchester

East Lancashire Railway

Bury, Greater Manchester BL9 0EY
(0161) 764 7790
www.eastlancsrailway.org.uk
The beautifully restored East Lancashire Railway takes you on a captivating journey to discover the region's rich transport heritage.

Greater Manchester Marathon in Trafford

April, Trafford, Manchester
www.greatermanchestermarathon.com
The UK's flattest, fastest and friendliest Marathon with a superfast course, great entertainment, outstanding crowd support and glorious finish at Manchester United Football Club.

Manchester Art Gallery

Greater Manchester M2 3JL
(0161) 235 8888
www.manchestergalleries.org
Houses one of the country's finest art collections in spectacular Victorian and Contemporary surroundings. Also changing exhibitions and a programme of events and a host of free family friendly resources.

Manchester Histories Festival

March, Various city centre locations
www.manchesterhistoriesfestival.org.uk
The ten-day MHF celebrates the heritage and history of Manchester across numerous city centre venues. The festival offers a fantastic opportunity to explore and learn this great city and is a great event for old and young alike.

Whitworth Art Gallery

Manchester M15 6ER
(0161) 275 7450
www.manchester.ac.uk/whitworth
The Whitworth Art Gallery is home to an internationally-famous collection of British watercolours, textiles and wallpapers.

Manchester Museum

Greater Manchester M13 9PL
(0161) 275 2648
www.manchester.ac.uk/museum
Found on Oxford Road, on The University of Manchester campus (in a very impressive gothic-style building). Highlights include Stan the T.rex, mummies, live animals such as frogs and snakes, object handling and a varied programme of events.

Manchester United Museum & Tour Centre

Greater Manchester M16 0RA
(0161) 868 8000
www.manutd.com
The official museum and tour offers every football fan a unique insight into Manchester United Football Club and a fantastic day out.

People's History Museum

Greater Manchester M3 3ER
(0161) 838 9190
www.phm.org.uk
National centre for the collection, conservation, interpretation and study of material relating to the history of working people in Britain.

Ramsbottom Chocolate Festival

April, Ramsbottom, Greater Manchester
www. ramsbottomchocolatefestival.com
Alongside the two-day chocolate market expect interactive workshops and activities for adults/children, alfresco dining, chocolate real ale tour, music, competitions, Giant Easter Egg display, and much more.

Saddleworth and District Whit Friday Brass Band Contest

June, Oldham, Greater Manchester
www.whitfriday.brassbands.saddleworth.org
Well over a hundred brass bands compete in contests at venues scattered around the moorland villages and towns on the western edge of the Pennines. All of the contests are open-air, many in delightful surroundings.

Merseyside

Beatles Story
Liverpool, Merseyside L3 4AD
(0151) 709 1963
www.beatlesstory.com
Located within Liverpool's historic Albert Dock, the Beatles Story is a unique visitor attraction that transports you on an enlightening and atmospheric journey into the life, times, culture and music of the Beatles.

Birkenhead Festival of Transport
September, Birkenhead, Merseyside
www.bheadtransportfest.com
Featuring classic cars, steam engines and other modes of vintage transport.

Croxteth Hall & Country Park
Liverpool, Merseyside L12 0HB
(0151) 233 6910
www.liverpoolcityhalls.co.uk/croxteth-hall/
Stately home with 500 acres estate including visitor farm, Victorian walled garden and seasonal events.

The Gallery Liverpool
Merseyside L8 5RE
(0151) 709 2442
www.thegalleryliverpool.co.uk
Set in the heart of Liverpool's Independent Cultural District, the gallery occupies the entire upper floor of the industrial premises of John O'Keeffe and Son Ltd.

Grand National
April, Aintree, Merseyside
www.aintree.co.uk
The most famous horse race over jumps takes place over the challenging Aintree fences.

Knowsley Safari Park
Merseyside L34 4AN
(0151) 430 9009
www. knowsleysafariexperience.co.uk
Enjoy a 5 mile safari through 450 acres of historic parkland.

Liverpool Football Club
Merseyside L4 0TH
(0151) 260 6677
www.liverpoolfc.com
Meet an LFC Legend; get your photograph with one of our many trophies or indulge yourself in one of our award winning Experience Days.

Liverpool Sound City
May, Bramley Moore Dock, Liverpool
www.liverpoolsoundcity.co.uk
An unrivalled 3-day festival of incredible live music and arts that includes a groundbreaking 2-day music and digital industry conference.

Speke Hall, Gardens & Estate
Liverpool, Merseyside L24 1XD
(0151) 427 7231
www.nationaltrust.org.uk/main/w-spekehall
One of the most famous half timbered houses in Britain, dating from the 15th century.

Walker Art Gallery
Liverpool, Merseyside L3 8EL
(0151) 478 4199
www.walkerartgallery.org.uk
Home to outstanding works by Rubens, Rembrandt, Poussin, Gainsborough and Hogarth, the Walker Art Gallery is one of the finest art galleries in Europe

Wirral Folk on the Coast Festival
June, Wirral, Merseyside
www.wirralfolkonthecoast.com
All-on-one-site friendly festival at Whitby Sports & Social Club, with fine music real ale and good food being served plus many more visitor attractions.

World Museum Liverpool
Merseyside L3 8EN
(0151) 478 4393
www.liverpoolmuseums.org.uk/wml
One of Britain's finest museums, with extensive collections from the Amazonian Rain Forest to the mysteries of outer space.

Tourist Information Centres

When you arrive at your destination, visit the Tourist Information Centre for quality assured help with accommodation and information about local attractions and events, or email your request before you go.

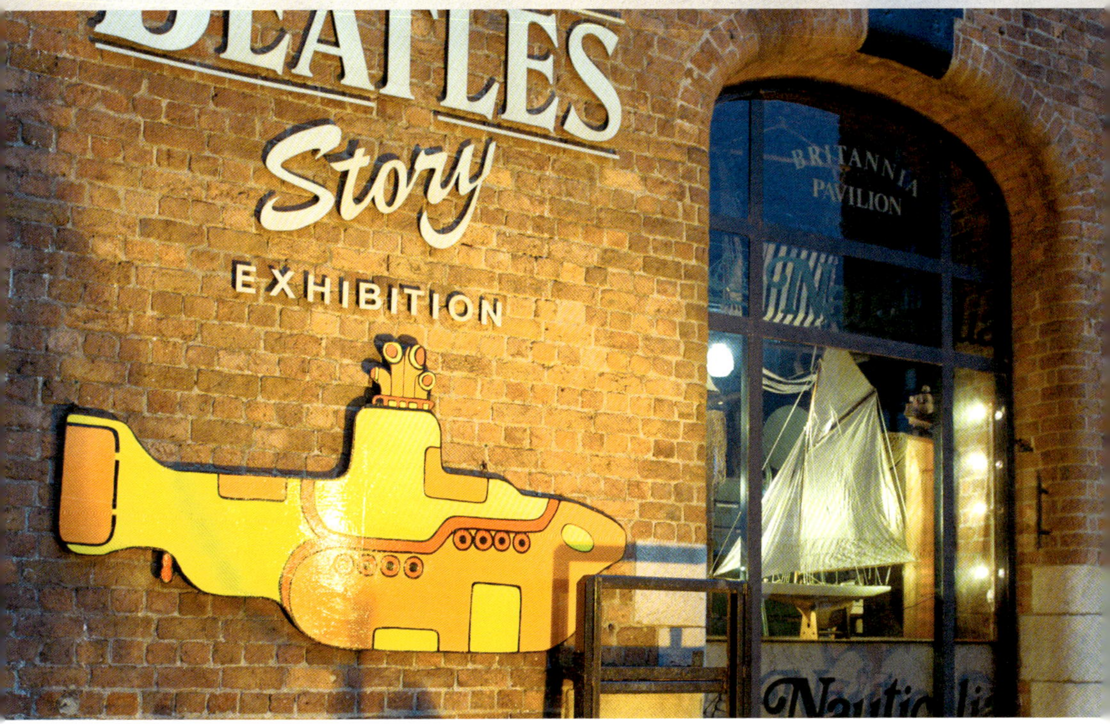

Accrington	Town Hall	01254 380293	information@leisureinhyndburn.co.uk
Alston Moor	Town Hall	01434 382244	alston.tic@eden.gov.uk
Altrincham	20 Stamford New Road	0161 912 5931	tourist.information@trafford.gov.uk
Ambleside	Central Buildings	015394 32582	tic@thehubofambleside.com
Appleby-In-Westmorland	Moot Hall	017683 51177	tic@applebytown.org.uk
Barnoldswick	Post Office Buildings	01282 666704 / 661661	tourist.info@pendle.gov.uk
Barrow-In-Furness	Forum 28	01229 876543	touristinfo@barrowbc.gov.uk
Blackburn	Blackburn Market	01254 688040	visit@blackburn.gov.uk
Blackpool	Festival House, The People's Promenade	01253 478222	tic@blackpool.gov.uk
Bolton	Central Library Foyer	01204 334321 / 334271	tourist.info@bolton.gov.uk
Bowness	Glebe Road	015394 42895	bownesstic@lakedistrict.gov.uk
Brampton	Moot Hall	016977 3433/ 01228 625600	bramptontic@gmail.co.uk
Broughton-In-Furness	Town Hall	01229 716115	broughtontic@btconnect.com
Burnley	Regeneration and Planning Policy	01282 477210	tic@burnley.gov.uk
Bury	The Fusilier Museum	0161 253 5111	touristinformation@bury.gov.uk
Carlisle	Old Town Hall	01228 625600	tourism@carlisle.gov.uk
Chester (Town Hall)	Town Hall	0845 647 7868	welcome@chestervic.co.uk
Cleethorpes	Victoria Square	01253 853378	cleveleystic@wyrebc.gov.uk
Clitheroe	Platform Gallery & VIC	01200 425566	tourism@ribblevalley.gov.uk
Cockermouth	4 Old Kings Arms Lane	01900 822634	cockermouthtouristinformationcentre@ btconnect.com

Congleton	Town Hall	01260 271095	congletontic@cheshireeast.gov.uk
Coniston	Ruskin Avenue	015394 41533	mail@conistontic.org
Discover Pendle	Boundary Mill Stores	01282 856186	discoverpendle@pendle.gov.uk
Egremont	12 Main Street	01946 820693	lowescourt@btconnect.com
Ellesmere Port	McArthur Glen Outlet Village	0151 356 5562	enquiries@cheshiredesigneroutlet.com
Garstang	1 Cherestanc Square	01995 602125	garstangtic@wyrebc.gov.uk
Glennridding Ullswater	Bekside Car Park	017684 82414	ullswatertic@lakedistrict.gov.uk
Grange-Over-Sands	Victoria Hall	015395 34026	council@grangeoversands.net
Kendal	25 Stramongate	01539 735891	info@kendaltic.co.uk
Keswick	Moot Hall	017687 72645	keswicktic@lakedistrict.gov.uk
Kirkby Stephen	Market Square	017683 71199	visit@uecp.org.uk
Lancaster	The Storey	01524 582394	lancastervic@lancaster.gov.uk
Liverpool Albert Dock	Anchor Courtyard	0151 233 2008	jackie.crawford@liverpool.gov.uk
Liverpool John Lennon Airport	Information Desk	0151 907 1058	information@liverpoolairport.com
Lytham St Annes	c/o Town Hall	01253 725610	touristinformation@fylde.gov.uk
Macclesfield	Town Hall	01625 378123 / 378062	karen.connon@cheshireeast.gov.uk
Manchester	45-50 Piccadilly Plaza	0871 222 8223	touristinformation@visitmanchester.com
Maryport	The Wave Centre	01900 811450	info@thewavemaryport.co.uk
Millom	Millom Council Centre	01946 598914	millomtic@copelandbc.gov.uk
Morecambe	Old Station Buildings	01524 582808	morecambevic@lancaster.gov.uk
Nantwich	Civic Hall	01270 537359	nantwichtic@cheshireeast.gov.uk
Northwich	Information Centre	01606 288828	infocentrenorthwich@cheshirewestandchester.gov.uk
Oldham	Oldham Library	0161 770 3064	tourist@oldham.gov.uk
Pendle Heritage Centre	Park Hill	01282 677150	pendleheritagecentre@htnw.co.uk
Penrith	Middlegate	01768 867466	pen.tic@eden.gov.uk
Preston	The Guildhall	01772 253731	tourism@preston.gov.uk
Rheged	Redhills	01768 860015	tic@rheged.com
Rochdale	Touchstones	01706 924928	tic@link4life.org
Rossendale	Rawtenstall Queens Square	01706 227911	rawtenstall.library@lancashire.gov.uk
Saddleworth	Saddleworth Museum	01457 870336	saddleworthtic@oldham.gov.uk
Salford	The Lowry, Pier 8	0161 848 8601	tic@salford.gov.uk
Sedbergh	72 Main Street	015396 20125	tic@sedbergh.org.uk
Silloth-On-Solway	Solway Coast Discovery Centre	016973 31944	sillothtic@allerdale.gov.uk
Southport	112 Lord Street	01704 533333	info@visitsouthport.com
Stockport	Staircase House	0161 474 4444	tourist.information@stockport.gov.uk
Ulverston	Coronation Hall	01229 587120 / 587140	ulverstontic@southlakeland.gov.uk
Windermere	Victoria Street	015394 46499	info@ticwindermere.co.uk

Regional Contacts and Information

For more information on accommodation, attractions, activities, events and holidays in North West England, contact one of the following regional or local tourism organisations. Their websites have a wealth of information and many produce free publications to help you get the most out of your visit.

Visit Chester
www.visitchester.com

Cumbria Tourism
T (01539) 822 222
E info@cumbriatourism.org
www.golakes.co.uk

Visit Lancashire
T (01257) 226600 (Brochure request)
E info@visitlancashire.com
www.visitlancashire.com

Visit Manchester
T 0871 222 8223
E touristinformation@visitmanchester.com
www.visitmanchester.com

Visit Liverpool
T (0151) 233 2008 (information enquiries)
T 0844 870 0123 (accommodation booking)
E info@visitliverpool.com (accommodation enquiries)
E liverpoolvisitorcentre@liverpool.gov.uk (information enquiries)
www.visitliverpool.com

Stay – North West

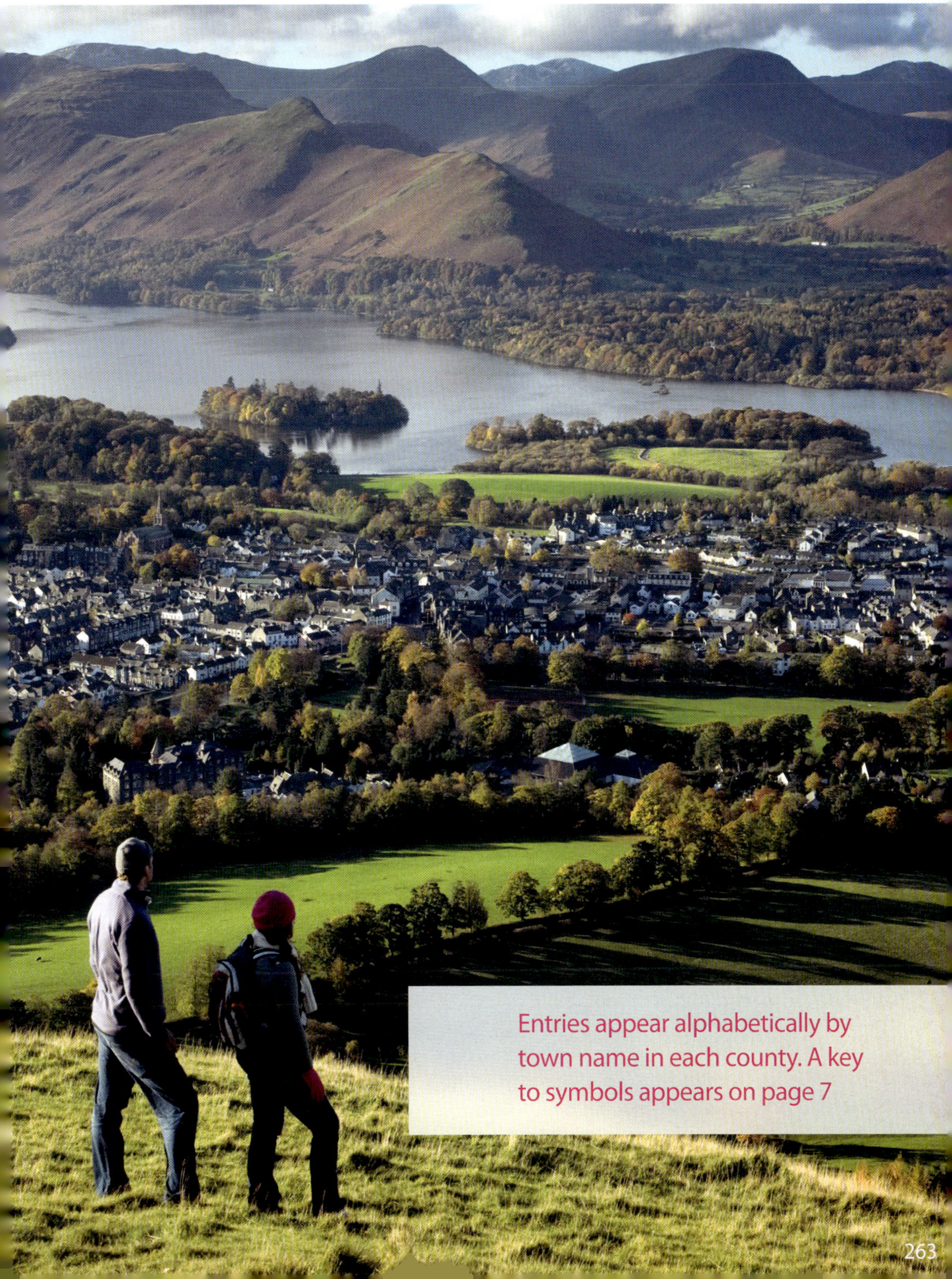

Entries appear alphabetically by town name in each county. A key to symbols appears on page 7

CHESTER, Cheshire Map ref 4A2 SatNav CH2 2AP H

Brookside Hotel

Brook Lane, Newton, Chester CH2 2AP **T:** (01244) 381943 **F:** 01244 651910
E: info@brookside-hotel.co.uk
W: www.brookside-hotel.co.uk **£ BOOK ONLINE**

enjoyEngland.com ★★★ HOTEL

B&B PER ROOM PER NIGHT
S: £50.00 - £69.00
D: £69.00 - £149.00

EVENING MEAL PER PERSON
£13.95 - £25.50

SPECIAL PROMOTIONS
Please check out our Chester Zoo packages & special breaks available by contacting the hotel directly.

Brookside Hotel is affordable luxury. Free secure parking in either of our 2 car parks (most city centre hotels charge £10 / £15 per night) Free Fibre Optic Wi-Fi in all rooms. All rooms individually styled & en suite with flat screen TV, DVD player, toiletries & serviced daily by our professional H/K team. Family run with full bar & restaurant. Quiet & cosy just 10 minute walk from the city centre.

Directions: Please visit our website or call the hotel for directions.

Bedrooms: 4 Singles, 12 doubles, 8 twins, 4 family. Most rooms have been refurbished with new decor and modern bathrooms. Each room has complimentary beverage tray
Open: All year except Christmas and New Year

WALKERS WELCOME · FAMILIES WELCOME · CYCLISTS WELCOME

Site: P **Payment:** **Leisure:** **Property:** **Children:**
Catering: **Room:**

CHESTER, Cheshire Map ref 4A2 SatNav 28CH4 8JQ B

Mitchell's of Chester Guest House

28 Hough Green, Chester CH4 8JQ **T:** (01244) 679004
E: welcome@mitchellsofchester.com
W: www.mitchellsofchester.com **£ BOOK ONLINE**

enjoyEngland.com ★★★★★ GUEST HOUSE

B&B PER ROOM PER NIGHT
S: £65.00 - £98.00
D: £82.00 - £98.00

Highly recommended by good guides. Relax in this tastefully restored Victorian residence with rooms having hospitality tray, clock/radio, TV, free Wi Fi, hairdryer and many other comforts. Easy 20 minutes walking to city. Off-road car park. **Directions:** Leave south side of Chester on A483, turn right on to A5104 (Saltney). This is Hough Green . We are 300m along on the right. **Bedrooms:** 3 doubles. Can be let as singles **Open:** All year except Christmas

Site: P **Payment:** **Leisure:** **Property:** **Catering:** **Room:**

ALSTON, Cumbria Map ref 5B2 SatNav CA9 3HX B

enjoyEngland.com ★★★ INN

B&B PER ROOM PER NIGHT
S: £40.00 - £48.00
D: £70.00 - £80.00

EVENING MEAL PER PERSON
£12.00 - £18.00

SPECIAL PROMOTIONS
£52-£62 per person dinner bed and breakfast

Cumberland Inn

Townfoot, Alston, Cumbria CA9 3HX **T:** (01434) 381875
E: stay@cumberlandinnalston.com
W: www.cumberlandinnalston.com **£ BOOK ONLINE**

Stay at the Cumberland Inn for real ales, real fires and a real family welcome. Our homemade, hearty food is perfect after a busy day out. We welcome muddy boots, dogs and bikes. Local CAMRA pub of the year 2009, 2010 and again in 2011.

Directions: On A686 from north or south. Location roadside in Alston, opposite Town Hall.

Bedrooms: 2 double, 2 twin, 1 family
Open: All year except Christmas

Site: **Payment:** **Leisure:** **Property:** **Children:** **Catering:**
Room:

AMBLESIDE, Cumbria Map ref 5A3 SatNav LA22 0EE B

enjoyEngland.com ★★★★ GUEST ACCOMMODATION

B&B PER ROOM PER NIGHT
D: £82.00 - £130.00

Rothay Garth

Rothay Road, Ambleside, Cumbria LA22 0EE **T:** (015394) 32217 **F:** 015394 34400
E: book@rothay-garth.co.uk
W: www.rothay-garth.co.uk **£ BOOK ONLINE**

"One of the best positions in the Lake District."

The Rothay Garth has a superb position combining glorious mountain views, access to Windermere Lake and Ambleside. A traditional Victorian Lakeland slate building set in its own landscaped garden, The Rothay Garth offers en suite facilities, resident's lounge, bar, conservatory and a large private car park. We pride ourselves on our friendly and personal family service. A warm welcome awaits.

Directions: From M6 jct 36, follow A590/A591 for 19 miles to Ambleside. Continue on main road through Ambleside, at bottom of Wansfell Road turn right, keep in right-hand lane, Rothay Garth car park 50yds on the right.

Bedrooms: All of our rooms are equipped with tea and coffee making facilities, colour TV, radio and hairdryer.
Open: All year except 5/12 until 27/12

WALKERS WELCOME CYCLISTS WELCOME

Site: **Payment:** **Leisure:** **Property:** **Children:** **Catering:**
Room:

AMBLESIDE, Cumbria Map ref 5A3 SatNav LA22 0EP

enjoyEngland.com ★★★★ INN

B&B PER ROOM PER NIGHT
S: £44.00 - £68.00
D: £79.00 - £179.00

EVENING MEAL PER PERSON
£11.00 - £25.00

Wateredge Inn

Waterhead Bay, Ambleside, Cumbria LA22 0EP **T:** (015394) 32332 **F:** 015394 31878
E: stay@wateredgeinn.co.uk
W: www.wateredgeinn.co.uk **£ BOOK ONLINE**

Delightfully situated 22 bedroom Inn on the shores of Windermere at Waterhead Bay. Enjoy country Inn style dining, freshly prepared bar meals, real ales and fine wines all served overlooking the lake. **Directions:** From M6 jct 36 follow A591 through to Ambleside. At Waterhead bear left at traffic lights, Wateredge is on left at end of promenade. **Bedrooms:** Lake & Fell Views, Wi-Fi, TV, tea & coffee **Open:** All year except Christmas

Site: P **Payment:** **Leisure:** **Property:** **Children:** **Catering:** **Room:** TV

BASSENTHWAITE, Cumbria Map ref 5A2 SatNav CA12 4QG

enjoyEngland.com ★★★ HOTEL

B&B PER ROOM PER NIGHT
D: £60.00 - £150.00

HB PER PERSON PER NIGHT
£114.00 - £189.00

Ravenstone Lodge Hotel

Bassenthwaite, Keswick CA12 4QG **T:** (01768) 776629
E: enquiries@ravenstonelodge.co.uk
W: www.ravenstonelodge.co.uk **£ BOOK ONLINE**

A small privately owned hotel set in 5 acres of grounds between Skiddaw & Bassenthwaite Lake with a unique atmosphere and with a restaurant with an AA rosette for culinary excellence plus a bistro serving less formal food. **Directions:** 5 miles north of Keswick on the A591. **Bedrooms:** 1 luxury super king, 5 dble, 2 twin, 1 family **Open:** All year except Christmas

Site: **Payment:** € **Leisure:** **Property:** **Children:** **Catering:** **Room:** TV

BOWNESS-ON-WINDERMERE, Cumbria Map ref 5A3 SatNav LA23 3HH

enjoyEngland.com ★★★ COUNTRY HOUSE HOTEL

B&B PER ROOM PER NIGHT
S: £80.00 - £110.00
D: £95.00 - £185.00

EVENING MEAL PER PERSON
£27.50 - £45.00

Burn How Garden House Hotel

Back Belsfield Road, Bowness-on-Windermere, Windermere, Cumbria LA23 3HH
T: (015394) 46226 **F:** 015394 47000 **E:** info@burnhow.co.uk
W: www.burnhow.co.uk **£ BOOK ONLINE**

The unique Burn How Hotel has individually designed rooms set in the privacy of our gardens. An oasis in the middle of bustling Bowness but only a 2 minute stroll to the village or lake Windermere. **Open:** All year except 15th Dec to 27th Dec

Site: P **Payment:** **Leisure:** **Property:** **Children:** **Catering:** **Room:** TV

BOWNESS-ON-WINDERMERE, Cumbria Map ref 5A3 SatNav LA23 3EW

enjoyEngland.com ★★★ BED & BREAKFAST
enjoyEngland.com Silver AWARD

B&B PER ROOM PER NIGHT
S: £45.00 - £65.00
D: £65.00 - £95.00

May Cottage B&B

Kendal Road, Bowness-on-Windermere, Cumbria, England LA23 3EW
T: (01539) 446478 / 07793 056322 **E:** bnb@maycottagebowness.co.uk
W: www.maycottagebowness.co.uk **£ BOOK ONLINE**

Super, location, close to Lake Windermere, restaurants and shops. Free parking, Wi-Fi & leisure facilities. Hearty breakfasts; comfortable, light rooms with high spec en suites. High standards of cleanliness. We care! Come, relax & enjoy! **Directions:** North: M6/J39/A6 Shap Rd. East: A65. South: M6/J36/A590/A591. Trains: Oxenholme to Windermere. Please see website for more details. **Bedrooms:** 1 single, 3 double, 2 twin, 1 family **Open:** All year through

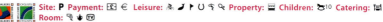

WALKERS WELCOME CYCLISTS WELCOME **Site:** P **Payment:** € **Leisure:** **Property:** **Children:** 10 **Catering:** **Room:** TV

BUTTERMERE, Cumbria Map ref 5A3 SatNav CA13 9XA

Fish Inn

Buttermere, Nr Cockermouth CA13 9XA **T:** (017687) 70253 **F:** 017687 70287
E: info@fishinnbuttermere.co.uk
W: www.fishinnbuttermere.co.uk

B&B PER ROOM PER NIGHT
S: £49.00 - £59.00
D: £97.20 - £108.00
EVENING MEAL PER PERSON
£8.00 - £15.75

Set in unbeatable surroundings a short stroll from Buttermere and Crummock waters. The Inn is comfortable and informal serving traditional food alongside local real ales, assuring you a warm welcome. **Directions:** At M6 J40 take A66 to Keswick, continue towards Cockermouth, 9 miles after Keswick roundabout turn left, follow signs B5289 Lorton and Buttermere. **Bedrooms:** 7 double (2 are superior), 2 twin, 1 family

Site: P **Payment:** **Leisure:** **Children:** **Catering:** **Room:**

CARLISLE, Cumbria Map ref 5A2 SatNav CA1 1HR

Langleigh House

6 Howard Place, Carlisle CA1 1HR **T:** (01228) 530440 **E:** langleighhouse@aol.com
W: www.langleighhouse.co.uk

B&B PER ROOM PER NIGHT
S: £30.00 - £40.00
D: £70.00 - £77.00
EVENING MEAL PER PERSON
£5.00 - £25.00

Highly recommended. Victorian house, comfortably furnished situated in a quiet conservation area with private car park, just five minutes walk from the city centre. **Directions:** Junction 43 off the M6. Drive along Warwick Road and we are the third turning on the right after St. Aidans church. **Open:** All year except Christmas and New Year

Site: P **Payment:** **Leisure:** **Property:** **Children:** **Catering:** **Room:**

CARLISLE, Cumbria Map ref 5A2 SatNav CA1 2HH

University of Cumbria - Carlisle

Fusehill Street, Carlisle, Cumbria CA1 2HH **T:** (01228) 616317 **F:** 01228 616235
E: conferences.carlisle@cumbria.ac.uk
W: www.cumbria.ac.uk/conferences

BED ONLY PER NIGHT
£20.00 - £48.00

Comfortable, modern, en suite rooms (summer only) in which to relax and unwind at the end of a busy day. Each flat has internet access and a fully equipped kitchen, plus laundry and drying facilities and a gym on site. The campus is situated just a short walk from the city centre. Within easy reach of the motorway, Hadrian's Wall and the Lake District. Ideally placed for cycling & walking routes. **Directions:** Please refer to website. **Bedrooms:** 85 single en suites (2 can be twinned) in 13 flats

Site: **Payment:** **Leisure:** **Property:** **Children:** **Catering:** **Bedroom:**

CLIFTON, Cumbria Map ref 5B2 SatNav CA10 2ER

George and Dragon

Clifton, Penrith, Cumbria CA10 2ER **T:** (01768) 865381
E: enquiries@georgeanddragonclifton.co.uk
W: www.georgeanddragonclifton.co.uk £ BOOK ONLINE

B&B PER ROOM PER NIGHT
S: £79.00 - £119.00
D: £95.00 - £155.00
EVENING MEAL PER PERSON
£12.95 - £21.95

The George and Dragon is a stylish and welcoming country inn with a lovely restaurant, cosy bar and 11 elegant yet comfortable en suite bedrooms. A great foodie destination where the menu changes seasonally and the specials daily. **Directions:** Just a few miles from Penrith and junction 40 of the M6 in Clifton village. By direct train, Penrith is just three hours from London.
Bedrooms: En suite, flat screen tv, bath or shower **Open:** All year (closed on Boxing Day)

Site: P **Payment:** **Leisure:** **Property:** **Children:** **Catering:** **Room:**

DUFTON, Cumbria Map ref 5B3 SatNav CA16 6DF B

B&B PER ROOM PER NIGHT
S: £40.00 - £42.00
D: £70.00 - £74.00

Brow Farm Bed & Breakfast

Dufton, Appleby-in-Westmorland, Cumbria CA16 6DF **T:** (01768) 352865
E: stay@browfarm.com
W: www.browfarm.com

Situated on the edge of the Pennines, with superb views from every room. Tasteful barn conversion offers rest and relaxation. Also self-catering cottages - see website for details www.browfarm.com. **Directions:** From Appleby take Dufton road for 3 miles. Farm is on right. From Penrith (A66) take Dufton road. Travel through village. Farm on left. **Bedrooms:** 2 double, 1 twin
Open: All year except Christmas

Site: P **Payment:** £ **Children:** **Room:**

GRANGE-OVER-SANDS, Cumbria Map ref 5A3 SatNav LA11 7HQ H

HB PER PERSON PER NIGHT
£91.00 - £95.00

SPECIAL PROMOTIONS
Early-season terms in April, mid-summer and autumn. Special 4-day breaks available all season.

Clare House

Park Road, Grange-over-Sands, Cumbria LA11 7HQ **T:** (01539) 533026
E: info@clarehousehotel.co.uk
W: www.clarehousehotel.co.uk

Charming hotel in its own grounds, with well-appointed bedrooms, pleasant lounges and superb bay views, offering peaceful holidays to those who wish to relax and be looked after. Delightful meals, prepared with care and pride from fresh local produce, will add greatly to the enjoyment of your stay.

Directions: From M6 jct 36 follow A590 through Grange, keep alongside sea. Clare House is on Park Road next to bandstand, between sea and road.

Bedrooms: 4 single, 2 double, 12 twin
Open: Mid March to mid December

Site: P **Payment:** £ **Property:** **Children:** **Catering:** **Room:**

GRANGE-OVER-SANDS, Cumbria Map ref 5A3 SatNav LA11 6EN H

enjoyEngland.com ★★★ HOTEL

B&B PER ROOM PER NIGHT
S: £40.00 - £100.00
D: £60.00 - £150.00

HB PER PERSON PER NIGHT
£50.00 - £120.00

SPECIAL PROMOTIONS
Free child places 0-4 years. Half-price 5-14 years. Murder Mystery and themed weekends. Christmas and New Year breaks.

Cumbria Grand Hotel

Lindale Road, Grange-over-Sands, Cumbria LA11 6EN **T:** (01539) 532331 **F:** 01539 534534
E: salescumbria@strathmorehotels.com
W: www.strathmorehotels.com **£ BOOK ONLINE**

Set in 20 acres of private gardens and woodlands, and overlooking the stunning Morecambe Bay, you will receive a warm and friendly welcome at this charming Victorian hotel. Only a short drive from Lake Windermere, there is much to see and do in the beautiful surrounding area.

Directions: By car: 15 minutes from the M6. By train: connections to Grange-over-Sands station from London, Birmingham, Leeds, Glasgow and Edinburgh.

Bedrooms: 14 single, 31 dble, 66 twin, 10 family, 3 suite
Open: All year

Site: **Payment:** **Leisure:** **Property:** **Children:** **Catering:**
Room:

HAWKSHEAD, Cumbria Map ref 5A3 SatNav LA12 8JU B

enjoyEngland.com ★★★★ FARMHOUSE

B&B PER ROOM PER NIGHT
S: £50.00
D: £76.00 - £86.00

EVENING MEAL PER PERSON
£19.00

Crosslands Farm

Rusland, Hawkshead, Cumbria LA22 8JU **T:** (01229) 860242
E: enquiries@crosslandsfarm.co.uk
W: www.crosslandsfarm.co.uk

Crosslands Farm is a early 17th century Lakeland Farmhouse set in the beautiful Rusland Valley 5 miles south of Hawkshead & near Grizedale Forest. It has delightful bedrooms, lovely bathrooms and a cosy lounge with log fire. Breakfast is served in the dining room converted from the old dairy with original slate flag floors and beams. It is an ideal base for walking and biking. Private parking.

Directions: Take the M6 at J36 follow the A590 until Newby Bridge past The Steam Railway turn right & follow the signs for Grizedale. At 4 miles turn right at y junction. Go up the little hill to the Farmhouse.

Bedrooms: 3 rooms, 1 double with en suite shower room and window seat, twin room with private bathroom & underfloor heating, 1 double room and en suite bathroom
Open: All year except Christmas. Restrictions at New Year

Site: P **Payment:** **Leisure:** **Property:** **Children:** **Catering:**
Room:

HAWKSHEAD HILL, Cumbria Map ref 5A3 SatNav LA22 0PR B

Yewfield Vegetarian Guest House

Hawkshead Hill, Hawkshead, Ambleside LA22 0PR **T:** (01539) 436765
E: derek.yewfield@btinternet.com
W: www.yewfield.co.uk

enjoyEngland.com ★★★★★ GUEST ACCOMMODATION
enjoyEngland.com Silver AWARD

B&B PER ROOM PER NIGHT
S: £60.00 - £69.00
D: £98.00 - £130.00

SPECIAL PROMOTIONS
3 night mid week break that includes 2x3 course dinners at our award winning restaurants in Ambleside: £335.00 per couple.

Yewfield is an impressive country house set in over 80 acres of private grounds, a peaceful and quiet retreat with lovely walks straight from the grounds. Following recent refurbishments, Yewfield was awarded a 5 stars VisitBritain award. We also host classical concert evenings with exceptional musicians from around the world.

Directions: One mile from Hawkshead, 4 miles from Ambleside, 2 miles past The Drunken Duck. See website for map.

Bedrooms: 8 double, 4 twin, 3 suite & 3 Apartments
Open: Closed December and January

Site: P **Payment:** **Leisure:** **Property:** **Children:** 9 **Catering:** **Room:**

HEADS NOOK, Cumbria Map ref 5B2 SatNav CA8 9EG B

String of Horses Inn

Faugh, Heads Nook, Brampton, Carlisle CA8 9EG **T:** (01228) 670297
E: info@stringofhorses.com
W: www.stringofhorses.com **£ BOOK ONLINE**

enjoyEngland.com ★★★★ GUEST ACCOMMODATION

B&B PER ROOM PER NIGHT
S: £45.00 - £55.00
D: £60.00 - £100.00

EVENING MEAL PER PERSON
£7.95 - £15.95

Dating from 1659, this traditional coaching inn is set in quiet country village only 10 minutes from Carlisle and Junction 43 of the M6 motorway. Near Hadrian's Wall and The Lake District. With great food, oak beams and panelling, real ales, log fires, free Wi-Fi and all rooms en suite.

Directions: A69 from J43 M6-Newcastle. 5 miles turn right at Lights Corby Hill/Warwick Bridge at BP Station. 1 mile through Heads Nook, turn left into Faugh.

Bedrooms: 9 double, 1 twin, 1 family
Open: All year

Site: P **Payment:** **Leisure:** **Property:** **Children:** **Catering:** **Room:**

KENDAL, Cumbria Map ref 5B3 SatNav LA9 4LD B

Beech House

40 Greenside, Kendal LA9 4LD **T:** (01539) 720385 **F:** 01539 724082 **E:** stay@beechhouse-kendal.co.uk
W: www.beechhouse-kendal.co.uk **£ BOOK ONLINE**

B&B PER ROOM PER NIGHT
S: £60.00 - £75.00
D: £80.00 - £100.00

SPECIAL PROMOTIONS
2 night minimum stay at weekends

Friendly, stylish B&B in Kendal's lovely conservation area. 5 delightful bedrooms, free parking and Wi-Fi. Kendal is a great centre with superb restaurants and walks.

8 miles from Windermere, 5 minutes walk from the town centre, The Brewery Arts Centre and Abbot Hall Art Gallery. Freshly made breakfasts with good quality locally sourced produce.

Directions: Eight miles from M6 junction 36, follow signs to Kendal, at 2nd set of traffic lights turn left, up Gillinggate, Beech House facing crossroad.

Bedrooms: 5 double
Open: All year except Christmas

Site: P **Payment:** **Leisure:** **Property:** **Catering:** **Room:**

KESWICK, Cumbria Map ref 5A3 SatNav CA12 4LJ B

Ash Tree House

Penrith Road, Keswick CA12 4LJ **T:** (01768) 772203 **E:** peterredfearn@aol.com
W: www.ashtreehouse.co.uk

B&B PER ROOM PER NIGHT
D: £64.00 - £80.00

Family run Bed and Breakfast in a former farm house built in 1841 with large garden. Comfortable en suite rooms and full English breakfast. Plenty of off road parking. **Directions:** 15 minute walk from town centre and a good base for all Lake District attractions. Detailed directions on our web site www.ashtreehouse.co.uk. **Bedrooms:** 1 double, 1 twin **Open:** All year except Christmas

Site: P **Leisure:** **Property:** **Children:** **Catering:** **Room:**

KESWICK, Cumbria Map ref 5A3 SatNav CA12 5ER B

Burleigh Mead

The Heads, Keswick CA12 5ER **T:** (01768) 775935 **E:** info@burleighmead.co.uk
W: www.burleighmead.co.uk

B&B PER ROOM PER NIGHT
D: £80.00 - £106.00

Conveniently situated between town centre and Derwentwater, our charming Victorian house offers excellent accommodation with outstanding views of surrounding fells. **Directions:** Once in Keswick follow signs for Lake and Borrowdale. The Heads is across from Central Car Park, we are 100 yards up road on right. **Bedrooms:** All en suite with fantastic views, tv, all mod cons **Open:** March to November

Site: P **Leisure:** **Property:** **Children:** 8 **Catering:** **Room:**

For **key to symbols** see page 7

KESWICK, Cumbria Map ref 5A3 SatNav CA12 4DH B

B&B PER ROOM PER NIGHT
S: £45.00
D: £35.00 - £40.00

Charnwood Guest House

6 Eskin Street, Keswick CA12 4DH **T:** (01768) 774111 **E:** sue.banister@gmail.com
W: www.charnwoodkeswick.co.uk

Elegant listed building. Close to lake and fells and in a quiet street. A warm welcome and really good food can be found at Charnwood. We cater for vegetarians. **Directions:** From A66 join the A591 to town centre and before the traffic lights turn left into Greta Street which leads to Eskin Street. **Bedrooms:** 2 double, 3 family **Open:** All year except Christmas

Payment: **Property:** **Children:** 5 **Catering:** **Room:**

KESWICK, Cumbria Map ref 5A3 SatNav CA12 4DP B

B&B PER ROOM PER NIGHT
D: £74.00 - £80.00

Greystones

Ambleside Road, Keswick, Cumbria CA12 4DP **T:** (017687) 73108 **F:** 017687 73108
E: info@greystoneskeswick.co.uk
W: www.greystoneskeswick.co.uk **£ BOOK ONLINE**

Greystones enjoys an enviable location with splendid views of the surrounding mountains yet is only a 3 minute walk to the shops, restaurants and pubs in the historic Market Square of Keswick. Private parking, secure cycle storage, drying room. **Bedrooms:** 5 x double & 2 x twin en suite rooms, flat screen TVs, tea & coffee, hairdryer, free Wi-Fi **Open:** 1st March - 31st November

Site: P **Payment:** **Property:** **Catering:** **Room:**

KESWICK, Cumbria Map ref 5A3 SatNav CA12 4DX B

B&B PER ROOM PER NIGHT
S: £36.50
D: £82.00

Lindisfarne House

21 Church Street, Keswick, Cumbria CA12 4DX **T:** (017687) 73218
E: info@lindisfarne-keswick.co.uk
W: www.lindisfarne-keswick.co.uk

Lindisfarne is a victorian house quietly situated, but within a few minutes walk to the town centre, lakes, parks and theatre by the lake. We offer clean and comfortable accommodation in our four star guest house, with a hearty breakfast. **Directions:** A66 into Keswick, take Southey Street, 3rd turning on left into Church Street. **Bedrooms:** 2 single standard, 1 single en suite (£41 prpn), 3 double en suites, 1 family (£73 prpn)/twin room **Open:** All year

Site: P **Payment:** **Leisure:** **Property:** **Children:** 5 **Catering:** **Room:**

KESWICK, Cumbria Map ref 5A3 SatNav CA124EL B

B&B PER ROOM PER NIGHT
S: £38.00 - £45.00
D: £76.00 - £90.00

Portland House

19 Leonard Street, Keswick, Cumbria CA12 4EL **T:** (017687) 74230
E: stay@portlandhouse.net
W: www.portlandhouse.net **£ BOOK ONLINE**

Portland House is situated in a quiet area just a short walk from the town centre, theatre and Derwent Water. All 6 guest bedrooms have en suite facilities including a ground floor flexible room with level access. Some parking is available. **Directions:** Keswick Penrith Rd turn left into Station St, immediately left into Southey St. 3rd left Church St. Portland House is situated on left at next corner. **Bedrooms:** All rooms have little extras to enhance your stay **Open:** Open all year except Christmas

Payment: **Leisure:** **Property:** **Catering:** **Room:**

KESWICK, Cumbria Map ref 5A3 SatNav CA12 5ES

Rooms36

36 Lake Road, Keswick CA12 5ES **T:** (01768) 772764 **F:** 01768 774416
E: andy@rooms36.co.uk / andypeters54@yahoo.com
W: www.rooms36.co.uk **£ BOOK ONLINE**

enjoyEngland.com ★★★★ GUEST HOUSE — enjoyEngland.com Silver AWARD

B&B PER ROOM PER NIGHT
S: £110.00 - £160.00
D: £120.00 - £185.00

Midway between Derwentwater & Keswick town centre. A short flat walk to the theatre by the lake with views over Hope Park towards Borrowdale - Cat Bells & Kiddaw. AA 4 Star Gold. High standards of quality, from the fresh local ingredients for breakfast, to the sheets on your bed and the Herdwick carpet from our local sheep. **Directions:** Follow sign to Borrowdale and the Lake take the Heads Road on your right Rooms36 (seymour-house) is the last property on your left. **Bedrooms:** 2 double, 4 family **Open:** All year

WALKERS WELCOME · FAMILIES WELCOME · CYCLISTS WELCOME · PETS! WELCOME

Site: P **Payment:** £ € **Leisure:** **Property:** **Children:** 1 **Catering:** **Room:** TV

KESWICK, Cumbria Map ref 5A3 SatNav CA12 4EG

Sandon Guest House

Southey Street, Keswick CA12 4EG **T:** (01768) 773648 **E:** sandonguesthouse@gmail.com
W: www.sandonguesthouse.co.uk

enjoyEngland.com ★★★★ GUEST HOUSE

B&B PER ROOM PER NIGHT
S: £40.00 - £45.00
D: £80.00 - £90.00

Charming Lakeland-stone Victorian guest house, conveniently situated for town, theatre or lake. Friendly, comfortable accommodation. Ideal base for walking or cycling holidays, storage for up to 10 bicycles. Superb English breakfast. **Directions:** 3 minutes from town centre. **Bedrooms:** 2 Super king, 2 single, 4 double, 2 twin **Open:** All year except Christmas

WALKERS WELCOME · CYCLISTS WELCOME

Site: **Payment:** £ **Leisure:** **Property:** **Children:** 4 **Catering:** **Room:** TV

KIRKBY LONSDALE, Cumbria Map ref 5B3 SatNav LA6 2AU

Copper Kettle Restaurant & Guest House

3-5 Market Street, Kirkby Lonsdale LA6 2AU **T:** (015242) 71714 **F:** 015242 71714
E: gamble_p@btconnect.com

enjoyEngland.com ★★ GUEST ACCOMMODATION

B&B PER ROOM PER NIGHT
S: £37.00
D: £50.00 - £60.00
EVENING MEAL PER PERSON
£9.00 - £12.00

Building was built in 1610-1640. Lovely restaurant on site. In town there is Ruskin's View with the river and Devil's Bridge. Lots of good walking and plenty of shops and pubs in the nearby town. Prices include breakfast. **Directions:** M6, exit 36, follow road for 5 miles. Turn into Kirkby Lonsdale on Market Street. **Bedrooms:** 2 single, 3 double, 3 twin, 2 family **Open:** All year

PETS! WELCOME

Site: P **Payment:** £ € **Leisure:** **Property:** **Children:** **Catering:** **Room:** TV

MUNCASTER, Cumbria Map ref 5A3 SatNav CA18 1RQ

Muncaster Coachmans Quarters

Muncaster Castle, Muncaster, Ravenglass CA18 1RQ **T:** (01229) 717614 **F:** 01229 717010
E: info@muncaster.co.uk
W: www.muncaster.co.uk **£ BOOK ONLINE**

enjoyEngland.com ★★★★ GUEST ACCOMMODATION

Within the magnificent Muncaster Gardens. One room has facilities for people with disabilities. Tariff includes admission to the Gardens, World Owl Centre, Meadow Vole Maze, Darkest Muncaster when operational and reduced entry to the Castle. Please contact us for 2015 rates. **Directions:** 1 mile south Ravenglass on A595. Jct 36 of M6 follow Brown Western Lake District signs. From North: from Carlisle follow A595 Cockermouth, Whitehaven, Ravenglass. **Bedrooms:** 4 double, 4 twin, 2 family. **Open:** All year

Site: P **Payment:** £ **Leisure:** **Property:** **Children:** **Room:** TV

For **key to symbols** see page 7

PORTINSCALE, Cumbria Map ref 5A3 — SatNav CA12 5RW B

★★★★ GUEST HOUSE — Gold Award

B&B PER ROOM PER NIGHT
S: £37.00 - £50.00
D: £74.00 - £84.00

Powe House

Portinscale, Keswick CA12 5RW **T:** (01768) 773611 **E:** andrewandhelen@powehouse.com
W: www.powehouse.com **£ BOOK ONLINE**

A Grade II Listed property in an ideal location for exploration of the northern and western lakes. Rooms are clean and bright, and it has a large car park. **Bedrooms:** 1 single, 4 double, 1 twin
Open: February - mid-December

Site: P **Payment:** £ **Property:** **Room:**

ROSTHWAITE, Cumbria Map ref 5A3 — SatNav CA12 5XB H

★★★ HOTEL — Gold Award

B&B PER ROOM PER NIGHT
S: £55.00 - £95.00
D: £110.00 - £190.00

EVENING MEAL PER PERSON
£16.75 - £40.00

SPECIAL PROMOTIONS
Spring, summer, autumn and winter breaks available throughout the year. Please call or check the website for details.

Scafell Hotel

Rosthwaite, Borrowdale, Keswick CA12 5XB **T:** (01768) 777208 **F:** 01768 777280
E: info@scafell.co.uk
W: www.scafell.co.uk

The Scafell Hotel is in the heart of Borrowdale Valley, considered by many to be England's finest valley. Situated almost at the foot of Great Gable and Scafell Massif, the hotel is an excellent centre for walking. Recently refurbished, the Scafell boasts great food, great service and a great atmosphere. AA Rosette, Dining Award, Gold Award and Breakfast Award. Individual and Independent for 44yrs.

Directions: From jct 40 (Penrith) of the M6 follow A46 to Keswick. From Keswick follow the B5298 for Borrowdale. Travel 6.5 miles to Rosthwaite.

Bedrooms: 3 single, 9 dble, 7 twin, 3 family, 1 suite
Open: All year

WALKERS WELCOME — CYCLISTS WELCOME

Site: **Payment:** £ € **Leisure:** **Property:** **Children:** **Catering:**
Room:

SKELWITH FOLD, Cumbria Map ref 5A3 — SatNav LA22 0HU B

★★★★ FARMHOUSE

B&B PER ROOM PER NIGHT
S: £54.00
D: £40.00 - £45.00

Holmeshead Farm

Skelwith Fold, Ambleside LA22 0HU **T:** (015394) 33048 **F:** 015394 31337
E: info@holmesheadfarm.co.uk
W: www.holmesheadfarm.co.uk

Holmeshead is a spacious 17thC farmhouse which has been updated while still retaining its character. All rooms have a peaceful atmosphere. Single room rate is offered with a supplement. **Directions:** Please contact for directions. **Bedrooms:** 1 double, 1 twin, 1 family **Open:** All year

Site: P **Leisure:** **Property:** **Children:** **Catering:** **Room:**

TROUTBECK, Cumbria *Map ref 5A2* *SatNav CA11 0SJ*

Troutbeck Inn

Troutbeck, Penrith CA11 0SJ **T:** (01768) 483635 **F:** 01768 483639
E: info@troutbeckinn.co.uk
W: www.thetroutbeckinn.co.uk **£ BOOK ONLINE**

Country hotel/inn with open fire, bar, lounge, restaurant. Quality food, wines & real ales. Dogs welcome in our bedrooms & cottages. Close to Penrith, Keswick & Ullswater. **Directions:** From J40 on M6 travel west towards Keswick. After 8 miles exit onto the A5091 to Ullswater. Troutbeck Inn is on the left. **Bedrooms:** 1 single, 4 double, 1 twin, 1 family **Open:** All year

B&B PER ROOM PER NIGHT
S: £50.00 - £55.00
D: £70.00 - £85.00
EVENING MEAL PER PERSON
£14.75 - £35.00

Site: P **Payment:** **Leisure:** **Property:** **Children:** **Catering:** **Room:**

ULVERSTON, Cumbria *Map ref 5A3* *SatNav LA12 7HD*

St Marys Mount

Belmont, Ulverston LA12 7HD **T:** (01229) 583372 **E:** gerry.bobbett@virgin.net
W: www.stmarysmount.co.uk

Guest house overlooking Morecambe Bay in own grounds. 5 minutes walk to Ulverston town centre at the foot of the Hoad Monument. Peaceful surroundings and guests can enjoy homecooked food. **Directions:** Follow the A590 into Ulverston, pass Booths. At next major roundabout take the 3rd exit onto Fountain Street. At mini roundabout take a sharp right. **Bedrooms:** 4 double, 2 twin **Open:** All year

B&B PER ROOM PER NIGHT
S: £50.00
D: £80.00
EVENING MEAL PER PERSON
£25.00

Site: P **Payment:** **Leisure:** **Property:** **Children:** **Catering:** **Room:**

WINDERMERE, Cumbria *Map ref 5A3* *SatNav LA23 3JY*

Bowfell Cottage

Middle Entrance Drive, Storrs Park, Bowness-on-Windermere, Cumbria LA23 3JY
T: (01539) 444835 **E:** annetomlinson45@btinternet.com
W: www.bowfell-cottage.co.uk

Cottage in a delightful setting, about 1mile south of Bowness off A5074, offering traditional Lakeland hospitality with comfortable accommodation and good home-cooking. Secluded parking in own grounds surrounding the property. **Directions:** From Bowness opposite church, take A5074 Kendal Rd for 1.2 miles. Turn right into Middle Entrance Drive, entrance 100 yards down Lane on left. **Bedrooms:** 1 double, 1 twin, 1 family **Open:** All year except Christmas

B&B PER ROOM PER NIGHT
S: £32.00 - £35.00
D: £60.00 - £70.00
EVENING MEAL PER PERSON
£14.50

Site: P **Leisure:** **Property:** **Children:** **Catering:** **Room:**

For **key to symbols** see page 7

WINDERMERE, Cumbria *Map ref 5A3* SatNav LA23 3NE H

Gilpin Hotel & Lake House

(formerly Gilpin Lodge Country House Hotel), Crook Road, Nr Windermere, Lake District LA23 3NE **T:** (015394) 88818 **F:** (015394) 88058 **E:** hotel@thegilpin.co.uk
W: www.thegilpin.co.uk **£ BOOK ONLINE**

B&B PER ROOM PER NIGHT
S: £225.00 - £435.00
D: £255.00 - £445.00

EVENING MEAL PER PERSON
£58.00

SPECIAL PROMOTIONS
Year round 3 to 10 night breaks from £102.50 pppn DBB. Pony trekking, tours, fishing, golf, biking and spa treatments.

This family owned and run Lake District Relais & Chateaux hotel is dedicated to nourishment, recuperation and relaxation. Gilpin Hotel has twenty luxurious rooms and suites, most leading onto the gardens, six with private hot tubs. Gilpin Lake House is a sanctuary with exquisite service, where just 6 suites enjoy 100 acres of private grounds, lake, swimming pool & the 'Jetty' spa.

Directions: Leave M6 at jct 36. Take A590/A591 to roundabout north of Kendal, then take first exit B5284 (signposted Crook, Hawkshead via ferry) for 5 miles.

Bedrooms: 7 dble, 7 twin, 12 suite
Open: All year

Site: **Payment:** **Leisure:** **Property:** **Children:** **Catering:** **Room:**

WINDERMERE, Cumbria *Map ref 5A3* SatNav LA23 2EQ B

Glenville House

Lake Road, Windermere, Cumbria LA23 2EQ **T:** (015394) 43371 **F:** 015394 48457
E: mail@glenvillehouse.co.uk
W: www.glenvillehouse.co.uk **£ BOOK ONLINE**

B&B PER ROOM PER NIGHT
S: £68.00 - £80.00
D: £70.00 - £110.00

With a relaxed tranquil atmosphere, this Victorian residence is situated a short walk from both Windermere and Bowness at the heart of the English Lake District. We are also AA 4* Rated. **Directions:** Please see website for directions **Bedrooms:** The guest house offers seven luxurious en suite rooms with colour flat screen TV's, iPod docking stations and free Wi-Fi **Open:** All year

Site: **Payment:** **Leisure:** **Property:** **Catering:** **Room:**

WINDERMERE, Cumbria *Map ref 5A3* SatNav LA23 1HF B

The Homestead Lodge

The Homestead, Troutbeck Bridge, Windermere, Cumbria LA23 1HF **T:** (01539) 443954
E: thehomesteadlodge@gmail.com
W: www.thehomesteadlodge.com

Enjoy the luxury of staying in your own private lodge with all the benefits of bed & breakfast accommodation. Picturesque lake and mountain views. Please contact us for prices. **Directions:** M6 northbound Jct 36 & follow A591 to Windermere. **Bedrooms:** 1 double room, own bathroom, lounge area

Site: **Property:** **Catering:** **Room:**

WINDERMERE, Cumbria Map ref 5A3 SatNav LA23 2AF B

enjoyEngland.com ★★★★ GUEST HOUSE

B&B PER ROOM PER NIGHT
S: £40.00 - £42.00
D: £68.00 - £84.00

Kenilworth Guest House

Holly Road, Windermere LA23 2AF **T:** (015394) 44004
E: busby@kenilworth-lake-district.co.uk
W: www.kenilworth-lake-district.co.uk **£ BOOK ONLINE**

Grand 4-star Victorian Guest House, offering warm and welcoming accommodation, centrally located in the town of Windermere. Hearty breakfasts include locally made Cumberland sausage, with vegetarian or lighter alternatives. Non-smoking throughout. Parking.
An ideal base for exploring the Lake District.

Directions: Leave A591 and drive through one-way system. After last shop, take 2nd left then 1st left - we are next to last on the right hand side.

Bedrooms: All en suite - 1 king-size double, 2 doubles, 1 twin, 1 single, 1 family (for 3 people)
Open: All year except Christmas

Site: P **Payment:** **Leisure:** **Property:** **Children:** 4 **Catering:** **Room:**

WINDERMERE, Cumbria Map ref 5A3 SatNav LA23 1LH H

enjoyEngland.com ★★★ HOTEL
enjoyEngland.com Silver AWARD

B&B PER ROOM PER NIGHT
S: £75.00
D: £150.00
EVENING MEAL PER PERSON
£46.50

Merewood Country House Hotel

Ecclerigg, Windermere, Cumbria LA23 1LH **T:** (01539) 446484 **F:** 01539 482383
E: info@merewoodhotel.co.uk
W: www.lakedistrictcountryhotels.co.uk/merewood-hotel **£ BOOK ONLINE**

A true country house of great charm and distinction set in a position of incomparable scenic beauty, with unrivalled panoramic views over Lake Windermere. Features include an oak-panelled, stained-glass hall and Edwardian conservatory bar. Merewood is open all year including Christmas and New Year. Weddings and conferences available.

Directions: Leave the M6 at junction 36 take 1st exit. At the roundabout take the 2nd exit onto the A591 and follow for approx 12 miles.

Bedrooms: 18 double, 2 family
Open: All year

Site: P **Payment:** **Leisure:** **Property:** **Children:**
Catering: **Room:**

WINDERMERE, Cumbria Map ref 5A3 SatNav LA23 1AE B

Southview House & Indoor Pool

Cross Street, Windermere, Cumbria LA23 1AE **T:** (01539) 442951
E: admin@southview.co.uk
W: www.southviewwindermere.co.uk

enjoyEngland.com ★★★★ GUEST HOUSE

B&B PER ROOM PER NIGHT
S: £52.00 - £62.00
D: £33.00 - £60.00

A warm welcome awaits you at Southview Guest House situated in the heart of Windermere in the Lake District National Park. We offer high quality bed and breakfast accommodation with our own indoor heated swimming pool and bar, exclusively for the use of our guests. **Directions:** M6, Jct 36, take A590 which turns into A591 and follow signs for Windermere. **Bedrooms:** All en suite bedrooms, 1 single, 2 classic doubles, 1 classic twin, 6 luxurious superior rooms, 1 contemporary four poster room

Site: P **Payment:** **Leisure:** **Property:** **Catering:** **Room:**

WINDERMERE, Cumbria Map ref 5A3 SatNav LA23 1BY B

Wheatlands Lodge

Old College Lane, Windermere, Cumbria LA23 1BY **T:** (01539) 443789
E: info@wheatlandslodge-windermere.co.uk
W: www.wheatlandslodge-windermere.co.uk **£ BOOK ONLINE**

enjoyEngland.com ★★★★★ GUEST ACCOMMODATION

B&B PER ROOM PER NIGHT
S: £85.00 - £115.00
D: £115.00 - £175.00

Ample parking. A variety of rooms with double, king sized, super king sized beds and a 4-poster beds and all are decorated to a high standard. All in a peaceful setting off the main road between Windermere and Bowness. Free Wi-Fi available. **Directions:** J36 M6 follow signs for Windermere A591. Turn left on to A5074 to Bowness. Go through the traffic lights and take the 2nd right by Hackney and Leigh. **Bedrooms:** En suite, flat screen tv, Wi-Fi, tea and coffee facilities **Open:** All year except Christmas

Site: P **Payment:** **Leisure:** **Property:** **Catering:** **Room:**

MANCHESTER, Greater Manchester Map ref 4B1 SatNav M23NQ H

The Midland Hotel

Peter Street, Manchester, Greater Manchester M60 2DS **T:** (0161) 236 3333
F: 0161 932 4100 **E:** midlandreservations@qhotels.co.uk
W: www.qhotels.co.uk/hotels/the-midland-manchester.aspx **£ BOOK ONLINE**

enjoyEngland.com ★★★★ HOTEL — enjoyEngland.com Silver AWARD

B&B PER ROOM PER NIGHT
S: £125.00 - £265.00
D: £135.00 - £275.00
EVENING MEAL PER PERSON
£25.00 - £89.00

This Grade II listed Edwardian building exudes elegance and style. Luxurious air conditioned bedrooms, two award winning restaurants. Great location for Manchestre Central & theatres. **Bedrooms:** En suite, SMART TV's, Air conditioned, free Wifi
Open: All year

Payment: € **Leisure:** **Property:** **Children:** **Catering:** **Room:**

SALE, Greater Manchester Map ref 4A2 SatNav M33 2AE B

Belforte House

7-9 Broad Road, Sale, Manchester M33 2AE **T:** (0161) 973 8779 **F:** 0161 973 8779
E: belfortehousehotel@aol.co.uk
W: www.belfortehousehotel.co.uk **£ BOOK ONLINE**

enjoyEngland.com ★★★★ GUEST ACCOMMODATION

B&B PER ROOM PER NIGHT
S: £38.00 - £49.95
D: £60.00 - £65.00
EVENING MEAL PER PERSON
£6.95 - £13.95

Privately owned hotel with a personal, friendly approach. Ideally located for Manchester Airport, the Metrolink and the city centre. Situated directly opposite Sale Leisure Centre. **Directions:** 1 mile from Junction 6 M60. 200 metres from Tram Station.
Bedrooms: 14 single, 4 double, 2 twin, 3 family
Open: All year except Christmas and New Year

Site: P **Payment:** **Leisure:** **Property:** **Children:** **Catering:** **Room:**

BLACKBURN, Lancashire Map ref 4A1 SatNav BB2 7NP H

enjoyEngland.com ★★★★ COUNTRY HOUSE HOTEL

enjoyEngland.com Gold AWARD

B&B PER ROOM PER NIGHT
S: £155.00 - £205.00
D: £185.00 - £285.00
HB PER PERSON PER NIGHT
£135.00 - £150.00

Stanley House Hotel & Spa

Further Lane, Mellor, Blackburn BB2 7NP **T:** (01254) 769200 **F:** 01254 769206
E: info@stanleyhouse.co.uk
W: www.stanleyhouse.co.uk **£ BOOK ONLINE**

Stanley House is an award-winning hotel, with 30 first-class bedrooms, unrivalled wedding and conference facilities, the stylish Grill on the Hill restaurant, the hugely popular Mr Fred's and a world-class spa, truly a hotel like no other. **Directions:** Located on the A677, 4 miles from the M6/M65. Preston station 6 miles. Blackpool International Airport 25 miles. Manchester International Airport 40 miles. **Open:** All year

Site: **Payment:** **Leisure:** **Property:** **Children:**
Catering: **Room:**

BLACKPOOL, Lancashire Map ref 4A1 SatNav FY1 6BP B

enjoyEngland.com ★★★★ GUEST ACCOMMODATION

enjoyEngland.com Silver AWARD

B&B PER ROOM PER NIGHT
S: £45.00 - £65.00
D: £75.00 - £99.00
EVENING MEAL PER PERSON
£15.00 - £25.00

4 Star Phildene Blackpool

5-7 St. Chads Road, Blackpool, Lancashire FY1 6BP **T:** (01253) 346141 **F:** 01253 345243
E: info@newphildenehotel.co.uk
W: newphildenehotel.co.uk **£ BOOK ONLINE**

We are ideally located 25 metres from Blackpool seafront, opposite St Chad's Headland. Just a short walk from the centre of Blackpool and all major attractions. Perfectly suited for both business and leisure guests. Child free property 18+. **Directions:** The easiest directions to give you are to make your way on to the Promenade Blackpool. St Chads Road is halfway between CentralPier and SouthPier. **Bedrooms:** 5 Single 6 Doubles 2 Premier & 1 Superior Suites **Open:** All year Except Christmas & New Year

Site: **Payment:** € **Leisure:** **Property:** **Catering:** **Room:**

BLACKPOOL, Lancashire Map ref 4A1 SatNav FY1 4PR B

enjoyEngland.com ★★★★ GUEST HOUSE

SPECIAL PROMOTIONS
We charge per person not per room. Price starts at £25 per person and all prices are based on two adults sharing.

B&B: 4 night stay for two people £132. BB&EM: 4 night stay for two people £185. Bank holidays and Illuminations do not apply.

Please check our website or telephone for further details.

Arabella

102 Albert Road, Blackpool FY1 4PR **T:** (01253) 623189 **E:** graham.waters3@virgin.net
W: www.thearabella.co.uk

We provide clean and comfortable accommodation within a family friendly atmosphere. Home cooking, dietary needs catered for, rooms are serviced daily, 5 minutes walk from the winter gardens, 10 minutes from the Tower and sea front. We do not take stag or hen parties. Specials available Mon - Fri. Prices on application.

Directions: Contact our website for google map directions.

Bedrooms: 1 single, 2 double, 2 twin, 9 family
Open: All year

Site: **Payment:** **Property:** **Children:** **Catering:** **Room:**

For **key to symbols** see page 7

BLACKPOOL, Lancashire Map ref 4A1 SatNav FY1 4JG B

enjoyEngland.com ★★★ GUEST HOUSE

B&B PER ROOM PER NIGHT
S: £27.00 - £31.00
D: £54.00 - £75.00

Ash Lodge

131 Hornby Road, Blackpool FY1 4JG **T:** (01253) 627637
E: admin@ashlodgeguesthouse.co.uk
W: www.ashlodgeguesthouse.co.uk **£ BOOK ONLINE**

Ash Lodge central Blackpool is situated in quiet residential area. It is a late Victorian house with many original features but with modern facilities and on site car park. **Directions:** M55 jct 4. Take 3rd left onto A583. Travel approx 3 miles. At 11th set of lights turn right onto Hornby Road. Ash Lodge on the right. **Bedrooms:** All rooms are en suite, with TVs, Tea & Coffee **Open:** All year except Christmas

Site: P **Payment:** **Leisure:** **Property:** **Children:** **Catering:** **Room:**

BLACKPOOL, Lancashire Map ref 4A1 SatNav FY1 5DL B

enjoyEngland.com ★★★ BED & BREAKFAST

B&B PER ROOM PER NIGHT
S: £25.00 - £35.00
D: £50.00 - £70.00

EVENING MEAL PER PERSON
£7.00 - £10.00

Blenheim Mount Hotel

207 Promenade, Blackpool FY1 5DL **T:** (01253) 625867 **F:** 01253 297611
E: bmhotel@hotmail.com
W: www.blenheimmounthotel.com **£ BOOK ONLINE**

Central seafront location overlooking the Irish Sea, where you can sit on our front patio area with a drink from our fully stocked bar, taking in our magnificent view/sunsets. We are a friendly family owned hotel with an easy going atmosphere, perfect for your family holidays so come and join us! **Directions:** End M55 follow central car parks, pass football ground at roundabout, take 2nd exit left at T junction, left to lights & right, hotel on right. **Bedrooms:** 3 single, 14 dble, 3 twin, 10 family **Open:** Most of year

Site: P **Payment:** **Leisure:** **Property:** **Children:** **Catering:** **Room:**

BLACKPOOL, Lancashire Map ref 4A1 SatNav FY2 9TA B

enjoyEngland.com ★★★ GUEST ACCOMMODATION

SPECIAL PROMOTIONS
Minimum Stay 2 Nights.

Specials for Armed Forces Week, Illuminations in October. Monday to Friday.

November Tinsel & Turkey Friday-Monday Weekends.

Christmas & New Year.

Please contact for all specials.

Brooklands

28-30 King Edward Avenue, Blackpool FY2 9TA **T:** (01253) 351479
E: brooklandsblackpool@yahoo.co.uk
W: www.brooklands-hotel.com

Recycled teenagers only, if you do not look 65, prove you are over 50. Situated in a quiet and select location, a real retreat for the over 50's. Retro adults only BB&EM. Minimum stay 2 nights. Please call for Illumination specials.

Great food, great rooms, ideal location, Tinsel & Turkey in November. Open Christmas & New Year. Car Parking available. Stair lifts and wheelchair access. Ground floor rooms, Licenced. Sorry no children. Please contact for 2015 rates.

Directions: From M55 follow signs for Promenade, once on the Prom (with the sea on your left) head north, past piers (left) and Tower (right). At Gynn roundabout proceed along the prom. King Edward Ave is the 2nd right, at the Cliffs. We are 250 yards up on the left.

Bedrooms: Mixture of single, doube and twin rooms. No single supplement. Flatscreen Freeview TV's. All rooms en suite. Tea & coffee in rooms. Some walking aids available.
Open: Easter until New Year.
Friday-Monday during November.

Site: P **Property:** **Catering:** **Room:**

BLACKPOOL, Lancashire Map ref 4A1 SatNav FY1 4QG B

enjoyEngland.com ★★★ GUEST ACCOMMODATION

B&B PER ROOM PER NIGHT
S: £22.50 - £25.00
D: £45.00 - £50.00
EVENING MEAL PER PERSON
£7.50

Cameo

30 Hornby Road, Blackpool FY1 4QG **T:** (01253) 626144
E: enquiries@blackpool-cameo.com
W: www.blackpool-cameo.com

Centrally located close to major attractions, our ten en suite bedrooms have TV/radio/alarms, tea & coffee, hairdryers and shaving points. No stag/hen parties, but everyone else is welcome. **Directions:** From the M6, take the M55 and follow the signs for Town Centre. Turn left onto Central Drive. Hornby Rd. is 2nd accessible road on the right. **Bedrooms:** All rooms double-glazed and centrally-heated **Open:** All year, excepting own holidays

Payment: **Property:** **Children:** **Catering:** **Room:**

BLACKPOOL, Lancashire Map ref 4A1 SatNav FY2 9RP H

enjoyEngland.com ★★ HOTEL

B&B PER ROOM PER NIGHT
S: £32.00 - £55.00
D: £64.00 - £125.00
HB PER PERSON PER NIGHT
£34.00 - £60.00

Doric Hotel

48-52 Queens Promenade, Blackpool FY2 9RP **T:** (01253) 352640 **F:** 01253 596842
E: info@dorichotel.co.uk
W: www.dorichotel.co.uk

Situated on Queens Promenade with breathtaking views over the Irish Sea. The Doric has become popular offering a wide range of facilities and good-value holidays for all. **Directions:** Exit M55 signposted Fleetwood A585 onto Promenade B5265 approximately 0.5miles on the right hand side. **Bedrooms:** 10 single, 20 double, 13 twin, 47 family, 13 suite **Open:** All year

Site: **Payment:** **Leisure:** **Property:** **Children:** **Catering:** **Room:**

BLACKPOOL, Lancashire Map ref 4A1 SatNav FY2 9RW H

enjoyEngland.com ★★ HOTEL

B&B PER ROOM PER NIGHT
S: £50.00 - £66.00
D: £70.00 - £100.00
EVENING MEAL PER PERSON
£11.95 - £15.00

Elgin Hotel

36-42 Queens Promenade, Blackpool FY2 9RW **T:** (01253) 353535 **F:** 01253 353790
E: info@elginhotel.com
W: www.elginhotel.com **£ BOOK ONLINE**

The Elgin is a family run hotel situated near to the Cliffs overlooking the Blackpool sands. This 89 bedroom Hotel offers 5 room types, Lift to all floors, exciting entertainment and car parking. TripAdvisor Winner of 'Certificate of Excellence Award 2014' & 'Large Hotel of the Year 2014 - Finalist - Lancashire Tourism Awards'. **Directions:** One mile north of Blackpool Tower on the promenade facing sea. **Bedrooms:** 2 single, 24 double, 25 twin and 38 family **Open:** All year.

Site: **Payment:** **Leisure:** **Property:** **Children:** **Catering:** **Room:**

BLACKPOOL, Lancashire Map ref 4A1 SatNav FY1 6AP B

enjoyEngland.com ★★★★ GUEST HOUSE

B&B PER ROOM PER NIGHT
S: £32.00 - £42.00
D: £32.00 - £35.00
EVENING MEAL PER PERSON
£12.00

Holmside House

24 Barton Avenue, Blackpool, Lancs FY1 6AP **T:** (01253) 346045
E: blackpoolholmsidehouse@talktalk.net
W: www.blackpoolholmsidehouse.co.uk

60 yards from the prom. All the facilities. Within an hour Manchester, Liverpool, the Lakes. Relax in the bar or outside with a brew. **Directions:** M55, Yeaden Way, Travelodge traffic lodge left. Traffic lights turn right, Nelson Rd left first Right. Holmside on the right. **Bedrooms:** 6 double, 1 twin, 3 family
Open: All year except Christmas

Site: P **Leisure:** **Property:** **Children:** **Catering:** **Room:**

BLACKPOOL, Lancashire Map ref 4A1 SatNav FY1 6AN

enjoyEngland.com ★★ HOTEL

B&B PER ROOM PER NIGHT
S: £28.00 - £122.00
D: £35.00 - £128.00
HB PER PERSON PER NIGHT
£39.00 - £64.00

SPECIAL PROMOTIONS
Big Reductions Early Season

Lyndene Hotel

305-315 Promenade, Blackpool FY1 6AN **T:** (01253) 346779 **F:** 01253 346466
E: enquiries@lyndenehotel.com
W: www.lyndenehotel.com **£ BOOK ONLINE**

Situated between Tower/Pleasure Beach, the Lyndene is an ideal location from which to enjoy all the resort has to offer. 140 comfortable bedrooms makes us the right choice for your stay in Blackpool. Three lifts access all floors inc ground floor rooms. Three bars, two air conditioned sea-view Cabaret lounges (entertainment nightly). Two restaurants with choice of cuisine. Bar snacks served daily.

Directions: See web page for directions.

Bedrooms: 1 single, 52 dble, 21 twin, 66 family
Open: All year round

Site: **Payment:** **Property:** **Children:** 5 **Catering:** **Room:**

BLACKPOOL, Lancashire Map ref 4A1 SatNav FY1 2HA

enjoyEngland.com ★★★ HOTEL

B&B PER ROOM PER NIGHT
S: £32.00 - £55.00
D: £64.00 - £120.00
EVENING MEAL PER PERSON
£14.95

Park House Hotel

308 North Promenade, Blackpool FY1 2HA **T:** (01253) 620081 **F:** 01253 290181
E: enquiries@blackpoolparkhousehotel.com
W: www.blackpoolparkhousehotel.com **£ BOOK ONLINE**

Ideally situated on north promenade within walking distance of town centre and all major attractions. Fabulous cuisine. Entertainment seven nights a week in our ballroom or bar lounge. **Directions:** End of M55 along Yeadon Way onto Promenade from A584 heading north approximately 1 mile. **Bedrooms:** 12 single, 34 double, 33 twin, 20 family, 4 suites **Open:** All year

Site: **Payment:** **Property:** **Children:** **Catering:** **Room:**

BLACKPOOL, Lancashire Map ref 4A1 SatNav FY1 4QJ B

The Raffles Guest Accommodation

73-77 Hornby Road, Blackpool FY1 4QJ **T:** (01253) 294713 **F:** 01253 294240
E: enquiries@raffleshotelblackpool.fsworld.co.uk
W: www.raffleshotelblackpool.co.uk **£ BOOK ONLINE**

enjoyEngland.com ★★★★ GUEST ACCOMMODATION

enjoyEngland.com Silver AWARD

B&B PER ROOM PER NIGHT
S: £36.00 - £39.00
D: £72.00 - £78.00

EVENING MEAL PER PERSON
£9.95 - £14.95

SPECIAL PROMOTIONS
3 nights for the price of 2, Mon-Fri (excl Bank Holidays), Jan-Aug.

Excellent central location for promenade, shopping centre, Winter Gardens, theatres. All rooms en suite. Licensed bar, English tea rooms, parking and daily housekeeping. Imaginative choice of menus. Listed in the Good Hotel Guide and the Which? Guide to Good Hotels. Four new luxury apartments each sleeping up to four people.

Directions: Follow signs for central car park. Exit onto Central Drive, left then right onto Hornby Road. Through 1st set of lights, on the right.

Bedrooms: 2 single, 12 double, 3 twin, 4 suite
Open: All year

Site: P **Payment:** **Leisure:** **Property:** **Children:** **Catering:**
Room:

BLACKPOOL, Lancashire Map ref 4A1 SatNav FY1 4PW B

Roselea

67 Albert Road, Blackpool FY1 4PW **T:** (01253) 622032 **E:** info@roseleahotel.com
W: www.roseleahotel.com

enjoyEngland.com ★★★ GUEST ACCOMMODATION

The Roselea is a friendly, family-run hotel with an enviable reputation for its quality accommodation, good food and efficient cheerful service, where you can relax and enjoy your holiday. Please contact us for prices. **Directions:** M6 Motorway to M55 Blackpool straight through car park, onto one-way system. Leads to Albert Road. We are half way up on the right. **Bedrooms:** 2 single, 6 double, 7 twin, 3 family **Open:** All year

Site: **Payment:** **Leisure:** **Property:** **Children:** **Catering:** **Room:**

BLACKPOOL, Lancashire Map ref 4A1 SatNav FY1 4PW H

Ruskin Hotel

55-61 Albert Road, Blackpool FY1 4PW **T:** (01253) 624063 **F:** 01253 623571
E: reception@ruskinhotel.com
W: www.ruskinhotel.com

enjoyEngland.com ★★★ HOTEL

B&B PER ROOM PER NIGHT
S: £35.00 - £79.00
D: £60.00 - £88.00

HB PER PERSON PER NIGHT
£31.00 - £71.00

Centrally located. Conference facilities, fabulous food and nightly entertainment (in season). Four bars, three dance floors, public bar and bistro. Cabaret weekends available. **Bedrooms:** 5 single, 29 dble, 24 twin, 13 family **Open:** All year

Site: **Payment:** **Leisure:** **Property:** **Children:** **Catering:**
Room:

For **key to symbols** see page 7

BLACKPOOL, Lancashire Map ref 4A1 SatNav FY1 6BP B

enjoyEngland.com ★★★★ GUEST ACCOMMODATION

B&B PER ROOM PER NIGHT
S: £30.00 - £40.00
D: £50.00 - £60.00
EVENING MEAL PER PERSON
£15.00

The Strathdon

28 St Chads Road, Blackpool FY1 6BP **T:** (01253) 343549 **E:** stay@strathdonhotel.com
W: www.strathdonhotel.com **£ BOOK ONLINE**

Veronica and Ian are proud to welcome you to The Strathdon. We are situated adjacent to the Promenade, an ideal location for the beach, piers, Pleasure Beach, the famous Blackpool Tower and Blackpool's premier entertainment venues. **Directions:** At the end of the M55 take 2nd exit onto Yeadon Way, then Seasiders Way to Blackpool FC, left at traffic lights, left at next lights, take next right. **Bedrooms:** Rooms have en suite facilities and flat screen tv **Open:** All Year except January

Payment: **Property:** **Children:** **Catering:** **Room:** TV

BLACKPOOL, Lancashire Map ref 4A1 SatNav FY1 4PR H

enjoyEngland.com ★★ HOTEL

B&B PER ROOM PER NIGHT
S: £30.00 - £50.00
D: £60.00 - £90.00
EVENING MEAL PER PERSON
£7.00 - £10.00

Sutcliffe Hotel

70-72 Albert Road, Blackpool FY1 4PR **T:** (01253) 620781 **F:** 01253 290919
E: bookings@sutcliffehotel.co.uk
W: www.sutcliffehotel.co.uk **£ BOOK ONLINE**

Book with confidence. Proprietors with 40 years hotel experience. Central location for shopping, theatres, conferences, dance and band competitions. Restaurant producing home cooked food with plenty of variety and choice. Bar Lounge. **Directions:** 5 minutes from train station and 5 minutes from end of motorway M55, following route to central car parks. **Bedrooms:** All en suite, heated, flat screen TV & tea & coffee **Open:** All year subject to maintenance

Site: P **Payment:** **Property:** **Children:** **Catering:** **Room:** TV

BLACKPOOL, Lancashire Map ref 4A1 SatNav FY1 4TA B

enjoyEngland.com ★★★ GUEST HOUSE

B&B PER ROOM PER NIGHT
S: £25.00 - £35.00
D: £50.00 - £60.00

Trentham Guest House

21 Albert Road, Blackpool FY1 4TA **T:** (01253) 290200 **E:** trenthotel@aol.com
W: www.trenthamhotelblackpool.co.uk **£ BOOK ONLINE**

A warm friendly welcome and helpful service complement the Trentham's high standards. As a family-run guest house, we take much pride in our reputation for providing comfortable accommodation in our tastefully furnished bedrooms. **Directions:** On Albert Rd opposite the shopping centre and just around the corner from the tower. **Bedrooms:** En suite, flat screen tv, tea and coffee. **Open:** All Year apart from Christmas.

Payment: **Property:** **Children:** **Catering:** **Room:** TV DVD

CLITHEROE, Lancashire Map ref 4A1 SatNav BB7 2HE B

enjoyEngland.com ★★★★ BED & BREAKFAST

B&B PER ROOM PER NIGHT
S: £45.00
D: £70.00
EVENING MEAL PER PERSON
£10.00 - £15.00

Rowan Tree

10 Railway View Road, Clitheroe BB7 2HE **T:** (01200) 427115
E: query@the-rowan-tree.org.uk
W: www.the-rowan-tree.org.uk

Luxurious en suite double/twin/family room, in a welcoming, well-appointed Victorian home. Ideally situated for town and country pursuits. Evening meal by arrangement. **Directions:** Close to bus and rail interchange. Five minute walk from town centre. **Bedrooms:** 1 double **Open:** All year

WALKERS WELCOME CYCLISTS WELCOME **Property:** **Children:** 1 **Catering:** **Room:** TV DVD

LYTHAM ST. ANNES, Lancashire Map ref 4A1 SatNav FY8 1HN H

Clifton Park Hotel

299-301 Clifton Drive South, St Annes-on-Sea, Lytham St Annes, Lancashire FY8 1HN
T: (01253) 725801 **F:** 01253 721735 **E:** info@cliftonpark.co.uk
W: www.cliftonpark.co.uk **£ BOOK ONLINE**

enjoyEngland.com ★★★ HOTEL

B&B PER ROOM PER NIGHT
S: £30.00 - £75.00
D: £60.00 - £150.00
EVENING MEAL PER PERSON
£15.00 - £22.50

Just 10 mins from Blackpool's bustling centre the Clifton Park Hotel is situated in the popular seaside resort of Lytham St Annes. The hotel boasts excellent facilities and a warm friendly atmosphere. **Directions:** From the end of the M55, follow signs for Lytham St.Annes. We are situated 150 yards on your left after St.Annes Square **Bedrooms:** All our rooms vary in shapes, sizes & styles. **Open:** All Year Round

Site: P **Payment:** **Leisure:** **Property:** **Catering:** **Room:**

THORNTON-CLEVELEYS, Lancashire Map ref 4A1 SatNav FY5 3JG H

Briardene Hotel

56 Kelso Avenue, Cleveleys FY5 3JG **T:** (01253) 338300 **F:** 01253 338301
E: briardenehotel@yahoo.co.uk
W: www.briardenehotel.co.uk

enjoyEngland.com ★★★ HOTEL

B&B PER ROOM PER NIGHT
S: £49.00 - £70.00
D: £67.00 - £97.00

SPECIAL PROMOTIONS
Special promotions available enquire with our reception. Promotions changing on a weekly/monthly basis.

Briardene Hotel is located in the centre of the Fylde Coast giving the perfect location from which to experience the unique environment that our area has to offer. The hotel has a 3 star rating, and has also just been awarded a 5 star food quality award in Restaurant and Breakfasts. Finalist for 'Small Hotel of the Year' Blackpool and Lancashire Touism.

Directions: M55 exit Junction 3, follow A585 Cleveleys, at third roundabout take first turning past Morrisons, second set of lights turn left 200 yrds on left.

Bedrooms: 2 single, 7 double, 3 twin, 2 family, 2 suite.
Open: All year

Site: **Payment:** **Leisure:** **Property:** **Children:** **Catering:**
Room:

LIVERPOOL, Merseyside Map ref 4A2 SatNav L20 3AW B

Breeze Guest House

237 Hawthorne Road, Bootle L20 3AW **T:** (0151) 933 2576 **E:** breezegh@googlemail.co.uk
W: www.breezeguesthouse.co.uk **£ BOOK ONLINE**

enjoyEngland.com ★★★★ GUEST HOUSE

B&B PER ROOM PER NIGHT
S: £35.00 - £50.00
D: £70.00 - £80.00
EVENING MEAL PER PERSON
£5.00 - £10.00

The Breeze Guesthouse is a luxury townhouse located in Bootle Village, 3 miles away from vibrant city of Liverpool home of the Beatles, Liverpool & Everton stadia & Aintree Race Course. **Directions:** Conveniently located for all modes of transport to/from Liverpool city centre, Crosby or Southport including bus, train and motorway. **Bedrooms:** 1 single, 8 twin, 1 family **Open:** All year except Christmas

Site: P **Payment:** **Property:** **Children:** **Catering:** **Room:**

LIVERPOOL, Merseyside Map ref 4A2 SatNav L1 9DA H

enjoyEngland.com ★★★★ HOTEL

B&B PER ROOM PER NIGHT
S: £86.00 - £490.00
D: £96.00 - £500.00

EVENING MEAL PER PERSON
£22.50 - £58.50

SPECIAL PROMOTIONS
Lazy Sunday Package - from £141 for two. Stay Sunday, enjoy a two course dinner in The London Carriage Works followed by a full Liverpool breakfast and a late check out of 12 noon on the Monday.

Hope Street Hotel

40 Hope Street, Liverpool, Merseyside L1 9DA **T:** (0151) 7093000 **F:** 0151 7092454
E: sleep@hopestreethotel.co.uk
W: www.hopestreethotel.co.uk **£ BOOK ONLINE**

VisitEngland Awards for Excellence 2014 SILVER WINNER

Liverpool's original boutique hotel, built around 1860 in the style of a Venetian palazzo. Reinvented and renovated in 2003 and extended in 2009 into 89 simple, stylish, contemporary and comfortable hotel rooms with a great 2 AA Rosettes restaurant - The London Carriage Works. Privately owned and independently run.

Directions: From M62, continue to end of motorway, follow signs for cathedrals (approx 3 miles). Hope Street links the two cathedrals and Hope Street Hotel is in the middle opposite the Philharmonic Hall.

Bedrooms: Oversized beds with white Egyptian cotton, solid birch and oak floors, bespoke furniture, original beams and brickwork, REN toiletries and free Wi-Fi
Open: All Year

Payment: **Leisure:** **Property:** **Children:** **Catering:**
Room:

LIVERPOOL, Merseyside Map ref 4A2 SatNav L1 9JG B

enjoyEngland.com ★★★ HOSTEL

BED ONLY PER NIGHT
£17.00

International Inn

4 South Hunter Street, Liverpool L1 9JG **T:** (0151) 709 8135 **F:** 0151 709 8135
E: info@internationalinn.co.uk
W: www.internationalinn.co.uk **£ BOOK ONLINE**

Tourist hostel, located in the heart of the city centre, near to theatres, cathedrals and nightlife. With a variety of dormitory sizes, Free tea/coffee, toast. No curfew, bedding provided. Free Wi-Fi. **Directions:** Check out our web site for full directions. We have great connections from all transport links. **Bedrooms:** 3 double, 4 twin **Open:** All year except Christmas

Payment: **Leisure:** **Property:** **Children:** **Room:** **Bedroom:**

LIVERPOOL, Merseyside Map ref 4A2 SatNav L1 9JG B

enjoyEngland.com ★★★★ HOSTEL

BED ONLY PER NIGHT
£45.00 - £62.00

International Inn Cocoon

4 South Hunter Street, Off Hardman Street, Liverpool, Merseyside L1 9JG
T: (0151) 709 8135 **F:** 0151 709 8135 **E:** info@internationalinn.co.uk
W: www.cocoonliverpool.co.uk

Conceptual, innovative, stylish, budget boutique pod hotel rooms in the heart of Liverpool's city centre. **Directions:** Check out our website for full directions. We have great connections from all transport links. **Bedrooms:** 32 en suite boutique pods located in the basement. **Open:** All Year except 24th-26th December.

Payment: **Leisure:** **Property:** **Children:** **Bedroom:**

Don't Miss...

Alnwick Castle

Northumberland NE66 1NQ
(01665) 511100
www.alnwickcastle.com
Alnwick Castle's remarkable past is filled with drama, intrigue, tragedy and romance, as well as a host of fascinating people including gunpowder plotters, kingmakers and England's most famous medieval knight: Harry Hotspur. Today, it is a significant visitor attraction with lavish State Rooms and superb art collections, as well as engaging activities and events for all ages, and all set in beautiful landscape by Northumberland-born 'Capability' Brown. Potter fans will recognise Alnwick as Hogwarts from the Harry Potter films - don't miss Potter-inspired magic shows and broomstick training!

BALTIC Centre for Contemporary Art

Gateshead, Tyne and Wear NE8 3BA
(01914) 781810
www.balticmill.com
Housed in a landmark industrial building on the south bank of the River Tyne in Gateshead, BALTIC is a major international centre for contemporary art and is the biggest gallery of its kind in the world. It presents a dynamic, diverse and international programme of contemporary visual art, ranging from blockbuster exhibitions to innovative new work and projects created by artists working within the local community.

Beamish Museum

County Durham DH9 0RG
(01913) 704000
www.beamish.org.uk
Beamish - The Living Museum of the North, is a world-famous open air museum vividly recreating life in the North East in the early 1800's and 1900's. It tells the story of the people of North East England during the Georgian, Victorian, and Edwardian periods through a costumed cast, engaging exhibits and an exciting programme of events including The Great North Festival of Transport, a Georgian Fair, The Great North Festival of Agriculture.

Durham Cathedral

County Durham DH1 3EH
(0191) 3864266
www.durhamcathedral.co.uk
Durham Cathedral is perhaps the finest example of Norman church architecture in England or even Europe. It is a World Heritage Site and houses the tombs of St Cuthbert and The Venerable Bede.

Lindisfarne Priory

Holy Island
Northumberland TD15 2RX
(01289) 389200
www.english-heritage.org.uk/lindisfarnepriory
Lying just a few miles off the beautiful Northumberland coast, Holy Island contains a wealth of history and is home to one of the region's most revered treasures, Lindisfarne Priory. The epicentre of Christianity in Anglo Saxon times and once the home of St Oswald, it was the birthplace of the Lindisfarne Gospels, one of the world's most precious books and remains a place of pilgrimage today. Take in panoramic views of the Northumbrian coast, unpack a picnic in the priory grounds, and take a break from the hustle and bustle of life. NB: watch the tides as the causeway is only open at low tide.

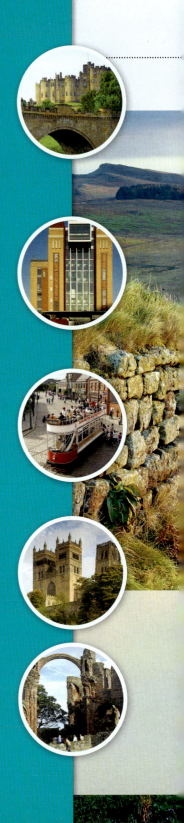

North East

County Durham, Northumberland, Tees Valley, Tyne & Wear

The North East contains two Areas of Outstanding Natural Beauty, a National Park, Hadrian's Wall, the dynamic city of Newcastle, and County Durham, with its fine cathedral and castle. This region is awash with dramatic hills, sweeping valleys, vast expanses of dune-fringed beaches and ragged cliffs with spectacular views. Littered with dramatic castles, ruins and historic houses, there are plenty of exciting family attractions and walking routes galore.

Explore – North East

County Durham & Tees Valley

Durham Cathedral, the greatest Norman building in England, was once a prison and soars grandly above the Medieval city and surrounding plain. Famed for its location as much as for its architecture, it is the burial place of both St Cuthbert, a great northern saint, and the Venerable Bede, author of the first English history.

The Vale of Durham is packed full of award-winning attractions including Locomotion: The National Railway Museum at Shildon and Beamish – The Living Museum of the North, the country's largest open air museum. Auckland Castle was the palace of Durham's unique Prince Bishops for more than 900 years. Part of the North Pennines Area of Outstanding Natural Beauty, the Durham Dales including Teesdale and Weardale, is a beautiful landscape of hills, moors, valleys and rivers, with numerous picturesque villages and market towns.

Comprising miles of stunning coastline and acres of ancient woodland, Tees Valley covers the lower, flatter area of the valley of the River Tees. This unique part of the UK, split between County Durham and Yorkshire, has nearly a hundred visitor attractions, including Preston Hall and Saltholme Nature Reserve, which can both be found in Stockton-on-Tees.

The Durham Heritage Coast, from Sunderland to Hartlepool, is one of the finest in England. The coastal path that runs along much of its length takes you on a spectacular journey of natural, historical and geological interest, with dramatic views along the shore and out over the North Sea. The historic port city of Hartlepool has award-winning attractions, a fantastic marina, beaches and countryside.

Hotspot: Durham University is home to The Oriental Museum, housing a unique collection of Chinese, Indian & Egyptian Art, and the Botanic Garden is also well worth a visit while you are there.

Hotspot: The Sage Gateshead is a concert venue and centre for musical education on the south bank of the River Tyne. It stages a varied and eclectic programme in state-of-the-art halls. www.sagegateshead.com or (0191) 443 4661 for tickets.

Newcastle & Tyne And Wear

Newcastle-upon-Tyne, once a shipbuilding centre, is a rejuvenated city of proud civic tradition with fine restaurants, theatres, and one of the liveliest arts scenes outside London. As well as the landmark Baltic, there's the Laing Art Gallery, the Great North Museum and The Sage concert venue. The Theatre Royal is the third home of the Royal Shakespeare Company and a venue for major touring companies. The Metro Centre in neighbouring Gateshead attracts shoppers from all over the country with more than 300 outlets and 11 cinema screens.

Northumberland

Northumbria, to use its ancient name, is an undiscovered holiday paradise where the scenery is wild and beautiful, the beaches golden and unspoiled, and the natives friendly. The region is edged by the North Sea, four national parks and the vast Border Forest Park. Its eastern sea boundary makes a stunning coastline, stretching 100 miles from Staithes on the Cleveland boundary, to Berwick-on-Tweed, England's most northerly town, frequently fought over and with the finest preserved example of Elizabethan town walls in the country. In between you'll find as many holiday opportunities as changes of scenery.

Step back in time 2,000 years along Hadrian's Wall, explore the hills, forests and waterfalls of the National Parks, and discover historic castles, splendid churches and quaint towns. Visitors can trace man's occupation of the region from prehistoric times through rock carvings, ancient hill forts, Saxon churches, Norman priories, medieval castles, and a wealth of industrial archaeology.

Hotspot: Take a boat trip from Seahouses to the Farne Islands - a marvellous seabird colony and breeding ground of the Atlantic Grey Seal, with more than 1,000 pups born every autumn. (01665) 721099 www.nationaltrust.org.uk/farne-islands

Housesteads Roman Fort at Haydon Bridge is the most complete example of a British Roman fort. It features magnificent ruins and stunning views of the countryside surrounding Hadrian's Wall.

The region has a rich maritime heritage too. Ruined coastal fortifications such as Dunstanburgh and fairy-tale Lindisfarne are relics of a turbulent era. Agriculture is also one of the region's most important industries. Take a trip on the Heatherslaw Light Railway, a narrow gauge line operating from Etal Village to Heatherslaw Mill, a restored waterdriven corn mill and agricultural museum near the delightful model village of Ford.

Indulge – North East

Indulge in a leisurely sightseeing trip along the **River Wear at Durham**. A one hour cruise includes sepctacular views of historic Durham City, Cathedral, Castle and bridges with full commentary including history, natural history and geography. www.princebishoprc.co.uk or call (0191) 386 9525 for sailing times and prices.

Don't miss **The Rugby World Cup 2015** which will see three matches played at **St James' Park** in Newcastle. South Africa vs Scotland, New Zealand vs Tonga and Samoa vs Scotland all take place in early October and are sure to be spectacular sporting events. www.rugbyworldcup.com

Enjoy an elegant lunch or tempting tea at the fabulous **Earl Grey Tearooms**, Howick – home of Earl Grey for whom the tea was invented. Situated in the old ballroom of the hall, it serves a variety of teas, home made and local produce, snacks and light lunches exclusively for visitors to the garden and makes a great place for a rest while exploring the arboretum and stunning gardens.
See www.howickhallgardens.org for opening times.

It's hard not to get caught up in the quirky atmosphere of **Barter Books** at the Victorian Alnwick Railway Station. This rambling, atmospheric secondhand bookshop has open fires, armchairs, a simple cafe and best of all, model trains, and is noted for its use of a barter system, whereby customers can exchange their books for credit against future purchases. It is one of the largest second-hand bookstores in Europe and an unmissable diversion if you're in this neck of the woods.
www.barterbooks.co.uk or call (01665) 604888 for opening times.

For a romantic dinner for two or a great night out with friends, dine in style at **Alnwick Garden's Treehouse Restaurant**, one of the most magical and unique restaurants to be found anywhere. Set high up in the treetops, with a roaring fire in the centre of the room and trees growing through the floor, this stunning restaurant serves local fish and seafood, meats from Northumberland's farmlands and other mouthwatering local and regional specialities.
Call (01665) 511852 for reservations.

Attractions with this sign participate in the Visitor Attraction Quality Assurance Scheme.

County Durham & Tees Valley

Adventure Valley

Durham, County Durham DH1 5SG
(01913) 868291
www.adventurevalley.co.uk
Adventure Valley, split into six Play Zones (with three under cover), you'll find the very best in family fun come rain or shine.

Billingham International Folklore Festival

August, Billingham, County Durham
www.billinghamfestival.co.uk
A festival of traditional and contemporary world dance, music and arts.

Bishop Auckland Food Festival

April, Bishop Auckland, County Durham
www.bishopaucklandfoodfestival.co.uk
Be inspired by cookery demonstrations and entertained by performers.

The Bowes Museum

Barnard Castle, County Durham DL12 8NP
(01833) 690606
www.thebowesmuseum.org.uk
The Bowes Museum houses a collection of outstanding European fine and decorative arts and offers an acclaimed exhibition programme, alongside special events and children's activities.

DLI Museum and Durham Art Gallery

Durham, County Durham DH1 5TU
(01913) 842214
www.dlidurham.org.uk
Telling the 200-year story of Durham's famous regiment. Art Gallery has changing exhibition programme.

Durham Book Festival

October/November, Durham, County Durham
www.durhambookfestival.com
With writers covering everything from politics to poetry, and fiction to feminism, there's something for everyone at the Durham Book Festival. See website for dates and full programme.

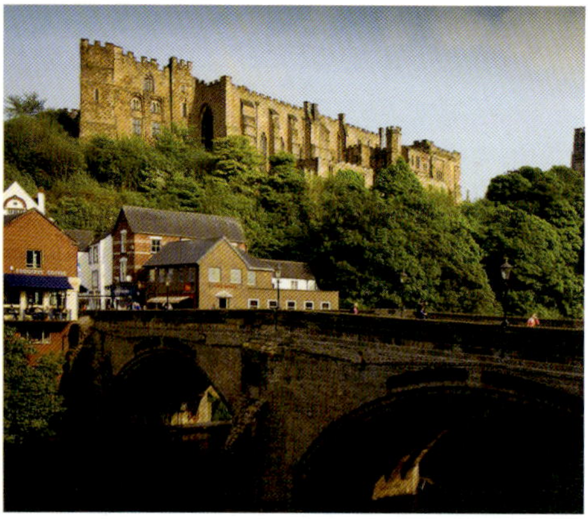

Durham Castle
County Durham DH1 3RW
(01913) 343800
www.durhamcastle.com
Durham Castle is part of the Durham City World Heritage Site and has enjoyed a long history of continuous use. Along with Durham Cathedral, it is among the greatest monuments of the Norman Conquest of Britain and is now home to students of University College, Durham. Entrance is by guided tour only, please telephone opening and tour times.

Durham Folk Party
July, Durham, County Durham
www.communigate.co.uk/ne/durhamfolkparty
It is a celebration of folk song, music and dance which began in 1990 after the demise of the excellent Durham City Folk Festival and has developed into an important part of the music year of the city.

Hall Hill Farm
Durham, County Durham DH7 0TA
(01388) 731333
www.hallhillfarm.co.uk
Award-winning farm attraction set in attractive countryside, see and touch the animals at close quarters.

Hamsterley Forest
Bishop Auckland, County Durham DL13 3NL
(01388) 488312
www.forestry.gov.uk/northeastengland
A 5,000 acre mixed woodland open to the public all year.

Hartlepool Art Gallery
Hartlepool, Tees Valley TS24 7EQ
(01429) 869706
www.hartlepool.gov.uk/info/100009/leisure_and_culture/1506/hartlepool_art_gallery/1/3
Former church building also includes the TIC and a bell tower viewing platform looking over Hartlepool.

Hartlepool's Maritime Experience
Tees Valley TS24 0XZ
(01429) 860077
www.hartlepoolsmaritimeexperience.com
An authentic reconstruction of an 18th century seaport.

Head of Steam
Tees Valley DL3 6ST
(01325) 460532
www.darlington.gov.uk/Culture/headofsteam/welcome.htm
Restored 1842 station housing a collection of exhibits relating to railways in the North East of England, including Stephenson's Locomotion, call for details of events.

High Force Waterfall
Middleton-in-Teesdale, County Durham DL12 0XH
(01833) 640209
www.rabycastle.com/high_force.htm
The most majestic of the waterfalls on the River Tees.

HMS Trincomalee
Hartlepool, Tees Valley TS24 0XZ
(01429) 223193
www.hms-trincomalee.co.uk
HMS Trincomalee, built in 1817, is one of the oldest ship afloat in Europe. Come aboard for a unique experience of Navy life two centuries ago.

Killhope, The North of England
Lead Mining Museum
Bishop Auckland, County Durham DL13 1AR
(01388) 537505
www.killhope.org.uk
Fully restored Victorian lead mine and the most complete lead mining site in Great Britain.

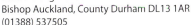

Locomotion: The National Railway Museum at Shildon
Shildon, County Durham DL4 1PQ
(01388) 777999
www.nrm.org.uk/locomotion
The first National Museum in the North East. Free admission. View over 60 vehicles, children's play area and interactive displays.

mima
Middlesbrough, Tees Valley TS1 2AZ
(01642) 726720
www.visitmima.com
mima, Middlesbrough Institute of Modern Art, is a £14.2m landmark gallery in the heart of Middlesbrough. mima showcases an international programme of fine art and applied art from the 1900s to the present day.

Preston Hall Museum and Park
Stockton-on-Tees, Tees Valley TS18 3RH
(01642) 527375
www.prestonparkmuseum.co.uk
A Georgian country house set in beautiful parkland overlooking the River Tees. A Museum of social history with a recreated Victorian street and working craftsmen.

Hotspot: *Hartlepool Museum, situated beside Hartlepool Historic Quay, includes local historical exhibits, PSS Wingfield Castle and the original lighthouse light. (01429) 860077 www.hartlepoolsmaritimeexperience.com*

Raby Castle
Staindrop, County Durham DL2 3AH
(01833) 660202
www.rabycastle.com
Home of Lord Barnard's family since 1626, includes a 200 acre deer park, gardens, carriage collection, adventure playground, shop and tearoom.

Saltburn Smugglers Heritage Centre
Saltburn-by-the-Sea, Tees Valley TS12 1HF
(01287) 625252
www.redcar-cleveland.gov.uk/museums
Step back into Saltburn's past and experience the authentic sights, sounds and smells.

Saltholme Wildlife Reserve
Middlesbrough, Tees Valley TS2 1TU
(01642) 546625
www.rspb.org.uk/reserves/guide/s/saltholme
An amazing wildlife experience in the Tees Valley.

Newcastle & Tyne And Wear

Arbeia Roman Fort and Museum
South Shields, Tyne and Wear NE33 2BB
(01914) 561369
www.twmuseums.org.uk/arbeia
Arbeia is the best reconstruction of a Roman fort in Britain and offers visitors a unique insight into the every day life of the Roman army, from the soldier in his barrack room to the commander in his luxurious house.

Centre for Life
Newcastle-upon-Tyne, Tyne and Wear NE1 4EP
(01912) 438210
www.life.org.uk
The Centre for Life is an award-winning science centre where imaginative exhibitions, interactive displays and special events promote greater understanding of science and provoke curiosity in the world around us.

Discovery Museum
Newcastle-upon-Tyne, Tyne and Wear NE1 4JA
(01912) 326789
www.twmuseums.org.uk/discovery
A wide variety of experiences for all the family to enjoy.

Evolution Festival
May, Newcastle, Tyne and Wear
www.evolutionfestival.co.uk
The North East's premier music event, taking place over a Bank Holiday.

Great North Museum: Hancock
Newcastle-upon-Tyne, Tyne and Wear NE2 4PT
(01912) 226765
www.twmuseums.org.uk/great-north-museum
See major new displays showing the wonder of the animal and plant kingdoms, spectacular objects from the Ancient Greeks and a planetarium and a life-size T-Rex.

Hatton Gallery
Newcastle-upon-Tyne, Tyne and Wear NE1 7RU
(01912) 226059
www.twmuseums.org.uk/hatton
Temporary exhibitions of contemporary and historical art. Permanent display of Kurt Schwitters' Merzbarn.

Hotspot: *Enjoy an ever-changing programme of exhibitions, live glass blowing, and banqueting and a stunning restaurant at the National Glass Museum, overlooking the River Wear.*
(01915) 155555
www.nationalglasscentre.com

Laing Art Gallery
Newcastle-upon-Tyne, Tyne and Wear NE1 8AG
(01912) 327734
www.twmuseums.org.uk/laing
The Laing Art Gallery is home to an important collection of 18th and 19th century painting, which is shown alongside temporary exhibitions of historic and contemporary art.

Newcastle Theatre Royal
Newcastle upon Tyne NE1 6BR
(0844) 811 2121
www.theatreroyal.co.uk
The Theatre Royal is a Grade I listed building situated on historic Grey Street in Newcastle-upon-Tyne. It hosts a variety of shows, including ballet, contemporary dance, drama, musicals and opera in a restored 1901 Frank Matcham Edwardian interior.

Segedunum Roman Fort, Baths & Museum
Wallsend, Tyne and Wear NE28 6HR
(01912) 369347
www.twmuseums.org.uk/segedunum
Segedunum Roman Fort is the gateway to Hadrian's Wall. Explore the excavated fort site, visit reconstructions of a Roman bath house, learn about the history of the area in the museum and enjoy the view from the 35 metre viewing tower.

Tyneside Cinema
Newcastle upon Tyne, Tyne and Wear NE1 6QG
(0845) 217 9909
www.tynesidecinema.co.uk
Showing the best films in beautiful art deco surroundings, Tyneside Cinema's programme ranges from mainstream to arthouse and world cinema. As the last surviving Newsreel theatre still operating full-time in the UK, this Grade II-listed building is a must-visit piece of lovingly restored heritage.

WWT Washington Wetland Centre
Washington, Tyne and Wear NE38 8LE
(01914) 165454
www.wwt.org.uk/visit/washington
45 hectares of wetland, woodland and wildlife reserve. Home to wildfowl, insects and flora with lake-side hides, wild bird feeding station, waterside cafe, picnic areas, sustainable garden, playground and events calendar.

Northumberland

Alnwick Beer Festival
September, Alnwick, Northumberland
www.alnwickbeerfestival.co.uk
If you enjoy real ale, or simply want to enjoy a fantastic social event, then make sure you pay this festival a visit.

The Alnwick Garden
Alnwick, Northumberland NE66 1YU
01665 511350
www.alnwickgarden.com
An exciting, contemporary design with beautiful and unique gardens, features and structures, brought to life with water and including the intriguing Poison Garden which holds dangerous plants and their stories. Fantastic eating, drinking, shopping and a range of events throughout the year.

Bailiffgate Museum
Alnwick, Northumberland NE66 1LX
(01665) 605847
www.bailiffgatemuseum.co.uk
Bailiffgate Museum brings to life the people and places of North Northumberland in exciting interactive style.

Bamburgh Castle
Northumberland NE69 7DF
(01668) 214515
www.bamburghcastle.com
A spectacular castle with fantastic coastal views. The stunning Kings Hall and Keep house collections of armour, artwork, porcelain and furniture.

Chillingham Castle
Northumberland, NE66 5NJ
01668 215359
www.chillingham-castle.com
A remarkable Medieval fortress with Tudor additions, torture chamber, shop, dungeon, tearoom, woodland walks, furnished rooms and topiary garden.

Cragside House, Gardens & Estate
Morpeth, Northumberland NE65 7PX
01669 620333
www.nationaltrust.org.uk/cragside/
Built on a rocky crag high above Debdon Burn, the house is crammed with ingenious gadgets and was the first in the world to be lit electrically. The gardens are breathtaking with 5 lakes, one of Europe's largest rock gardens, and over 7 million trees and shrubs.

Haydon Bridge Beer Festival
July, Haydon Bridge, Northumberland
www.haydonbeerfestival.co.uk
Annual celebration of the finest real ales and wines.

Hexham Abbey Festival
September-October, Hexham, Northumberland
www.hexhamabbey.org.uk
An exciting array of events to capture the imagination, bringing the very best world-class musicians and artists to Hexham.

Hexham Old Gaol
Northumberland NE46 3NH
(01434) 652349
www.hexhamoldgaol.org.uk
Tour the Old Gaol, 1330AD, by glass lift. Meet the gaoler, see a Reiver raid and try on costumes.

Kielder Castle Forest Park Centre
Northumberland NE48 1ER
(01434) 250209
www.forestry.gov.uk/northeastengland
Features include forest shop, information centre, tearoom and exhibitions. Bike hire available.

Lindisfarne Castle
(01289) 389244
www.nationaltrust.org.uk/lindisfarne-castle/
A picture perfect castle that rises from the sheer rock face at the tip of Holy Island off the Northumberland coast. It was built to defend a harbour sheltering English ships during skirmishes with Scotland and revamped by celebrated architect Edward Lutyens in 1901, today it remains relatively unchanged. Lindisfarne Castle.

RNLI Grace Darling Museum
Bamburgh, Northumberland NE69 7AE
(01668) 214910
www.rnli.org.uk/gracedarling
A museum dedicated to Grace Darling and her family, as well as all those who Save Lives at Sea.

Warkworth Castle
Warkworth, Northumberland NE65 0UJ
(01665) 711423
www.english-heritage.org.uk/warkworthcastle
Set in a quaint Northumberland town, this hill-top fortress and hermitage offers a fantastic family day out.

Tourist Information Centres

When you arrive at your destination, visit the Tourist Information Centre for quality assured help with accommodation and information about local attractions and events, or email your request before you go.

Alnwick	2 The Shambles	01670 622152/ 01670 622151	alnwick.tic@northumberland.gov.uk
Amble	Queen Street Car Park	01665 712313	amble.tic@northumberland.gov.uk
Bellingham	Station Yard	01434 220616	bellinghamtic@btconnect.com
Berwick-upon-Tweed	106 Marygate	01670 622155/ 625568	berwick.tic@northumberland.gov.uk
Bishop Auckland	Town Hall	03000 269524	bishopauckland.touristinfo@durham.gov.uk
Corbridge	Hill Street	01434 632815	corbridge.tic@northumberland.gov.uk
Craster	Craster Car Park	01665 576007	craster.tic@northumberland.gov.uk
Darlington	Central Library	01325 462034	crown.street.library@darlington.gov.uk
Durham Visitor Contact Centre	1st Floor	03000 262626	visitor@thisisdurham.com
Gateshead	Central Library	0191 433 8420	libraries@gateshead.gov.uk
Guisborough	Priory Grounds	01287 633801	guisborough_tic@redcar-cleveland.gov.uk
Haltwhistle	Westgate	01434 322002	haltwhistle.tic@northumberland.gov.uk
Hartlepool	Hartlepool Art Gallery	01429 869706	hpooltic@hartlepool.gov.uk
Hexham	Wentworth Car Park	01434 652220	hexham.tic@northumberland.gov.uk
Middlesbrough	Middlesbrough Info.	01642 729900	tic@middlesbrough.gov.uk
Middleton-in-Teesdale	10 Market Place	01833 641001	tic@middletonplus.myzen.co.uk
Morpeth	The Chantry	01670 623455	morpeth.tic@northumberland.gov.uk
Newcastle-upon-Tyne	Newcastle Gateshead	0191 277 8000	visitorinfo@ngi.org.uk
North Shields	Unit 18	0191 2005895	ticns@northtyneside.gov.uk
Once Brewed	National Park Centre	01434 344396	tic.oncebrewed@nnpa.org.uk
Otterburn	Otterburn Mill	01830 521002	tic@otterburnmill.co.uk
Saltburn by Sea	Saltburn Library	01287 622422/ 623584	saltburn_library@redcar-cleveland.gov.uk
Seahouses	Seafield Car Park	01665 720884/ 01670 625593	seahouses.tic@northumberland.gov.uk
South shields	Haven Point	0191 424 7788	tourism@southtyneside.gov.uk
Stockton-on-Tees	High Street	01642 528130	visitorinformation@stockton.gov.uk
Whitley Bay	York Road	0191 6435395	susan.clark@northtyneside.gov.uk
Wooler	The Cheviot Centre	01668 282123	wooler.tic@northumberland.gov.uk

Regional Contacts and Information

For more information on accommodation, attractions, activities, events and holidays in North East England, contact one of the regional or local tourism organisations. Their websites have a wealth of information and many produce free publications to help you get the most out of your visit.

www.visitnortheastengland.com

www.thisisdurham.com
www.newcastlegateshead.com
www.visitnorthumberland.com
www.visithadrianswall.co.uk
www.visitnorthtyneside.com
www.visitsouthtyneside.co.uk
www.seeitdoitsunderland.co.uk

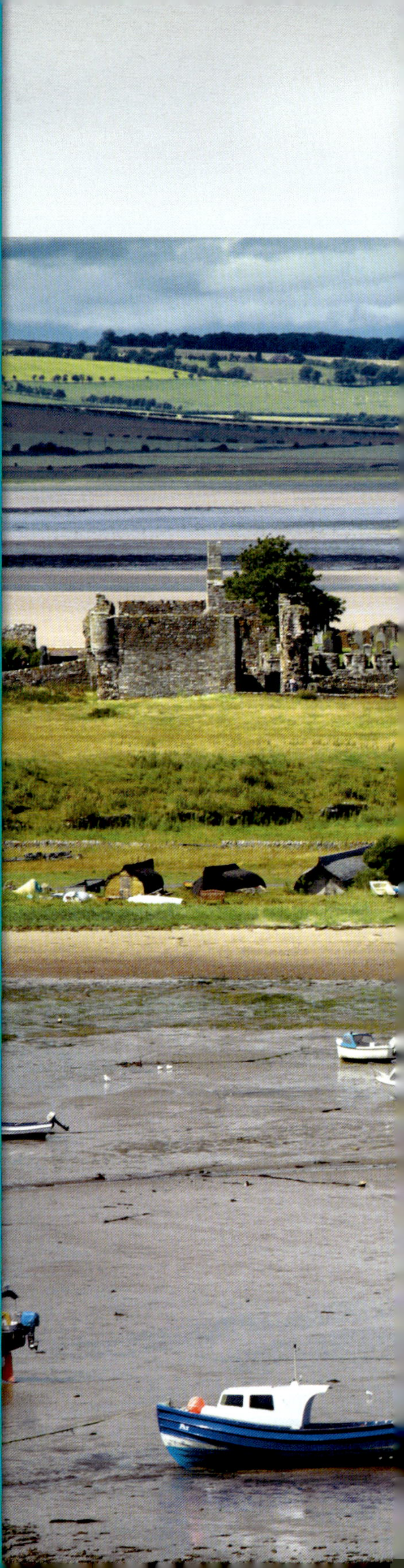

Stay – North East

Entries appear alphabetically by town name in each county. A key to symbols appears on page 7

BEAMISH, Co Durham Map ref 5C2 SatNav DH9 9UA B

B&B PER ROOM PER NIGHT
S: £45.00
D: £59.00

Bushblades Farm

Harperley DH9 9UA **T:** (01207) 232722 **E:** bushbladesfarm@hotmail.com

Welcome to our comfortable Georgian Farmhouse which we have been running for 23 years, with guests returning year after year. Relax in our conservatory or large garden. Breakfast is a cooked English breakfast or Continental breakfast if preferred (both with good choice), served in our traditional dining-room. **Directions:** Leave A1(M) jct 63 for Stanley (A693). At Stanley roundabout bear left towards Consett. 0.5 miles after traffic lights turn right to Harperley. Follow second right, go straight over crossroads up hill and farm 0.5 miles on right. **Bedrooms:** twin en suite and double en suite room. Hospitality tray, colour Freeview TV, DVD player and comfortable chairs. **Open:** All Year

Site: P **Property:** **Children:** 12 **Catering:** **Room:** TV

DURHAM, Co Durham Map ref 5C2 SatNav DH1 4PS B

B&B PER ROOM PER NIGHT
D: £100.00 - £130.00

Castle View Guest House

4 Crossgate, Durham DH1 4PS **T:** (0191) 3868852 **E:** castle_view@hotmail.com
W: www.castle-view.co.uk

Two hundred and fifty year old listed building in the heart of the old city, with woodland and riverside walks and magnificent views of the cathedral and castle. Complimentary parking. **Directions:** From A1(M) take junction 62, follow signs A690 Crook until river crossing. At traffic lights turn left into Crossgate, next to St Margarets Church. **Bedrooms:** 3 double, 2 twin **Open:** All year except Christmas and New Year

Site: **Payment:** **Property:** **Children:** 2 **Catering:** **Room:** TV

DURHAM, Co Durham Map ref 5C2 SatNav DH1 3RH B

enjoyEngland.com ★★★ GUEST ACCOMMODATION

B&B PER ROOM PER NIGHT
S: £35.00 - £40.00
D: £60.00 - £75.00

EVENING MEAL PER PERSON
£15.00 - £35.00

St Chad's College

18 North Bailey, Durham DH1 3RH **T:** (0191) 334 3358 **F:** 0191 334 3371
E: chads@durham.ac.uk
W: www.dur.ac.uk/chads/

In the heart of historic Durham, adjacent to the World Heritage Site and next to the Cathedral, St Chad's provides comfortable modern accommodation, supported by friendly service, in its range of listed buildings - a spectacular location. Group bookings welcome. **Directions:** Follow the A1(M) until the A690, direct to Durham, towards Cathedral. The college lies opposite of Durham Cathedral. **Bedrooms:** Over 150 en suite and standard bedrooms. Evening meals pre book only **Open:** Easter/Summer student vacations

Site: **Payment:** **Leisure:** **Property:** **Children:** **Catering:** **Room:**

DURHAM, Co Durham Map ref 5C2 SatNav DH1 3RJ B

enjoyEngland.com ★★★ GUEST ACCOMMODATION

B&B PER ROOM PER NIGHT
S: £34.00
D: £60.00

St John's College

3 South Bailey, Durham DH1 3RJ **T:** (0191) 3343877 **E:** s.l.hobson@durham.ac.uk
W: www.durham.ac.uk/st-johns.college

Located in the heart of Durham City alongside the cathedral, St John's offers accommodation in distinctive, historic buildings with riverside gardens. **Directions:** Take A1(M) motorway junction 62, dual carriageway A690 Gilesgate roundabout. Take third exit, second left exit, then left to Market Square, 200 yards to College. **Bedrooms:** 66 single, 15 double, 2 twin **Open:** Summer vacations only

Site: **Payment:** **Property:** **Children:** **Catering:** **Room:**

ALNWICK, Northumberland Map ref 5C1 SatNav NE66 2HJ B

enjoyEngland.com ★★★ GUEST ACCOMMODATION

B&B PER ROOM PER NIGHT
S: £44.00 - £55.00
D: £59.00 - £120.00

EVENING MEAL PER PERSON
£15.00 - £30.00

SPECIAL PROMOTIONS
Stay Mon-Thu get Thursday Half Price. Stay Fri & Sat get Sunday Half Price, Ex Bk Hols. Adaptable family rooms.

Alnwick Lodge

West Cawledge Park, Alnwick NE66 2HJ
T: (01665) 604363 / (01665) 603377 / 07881 696769 **E:** bookings@alnwicklodge.com
W: www.alnwicklodge.com £ BOOK ONLINE

Lonely Planet recommended and Trip Advisor 4* rated accommodation in beautiful Northumberland. A unique creation AD1650-2012. Alnwick Lodge, West Cawledge Park is a combination of history and rural charm with an air of sophistication, whilst linked to technology. Fascinating, uncomparable accommodation for business, pleasure, conferences, film crews and parties. Antique galleries and log fires.

Directions: 1 mile south of Alnwick. Direct access from A1 (trunk road) highway signposted to West Cawledge Park (chair on the roof).

Bedrooms: 4 single, 4 double, 3 twin and 4 family. Glamping - Foresters Wagon, Shepherds Hut, Gypsy Caravans. **Open:** All year

Site: P **Payment:** **Leisure:** **Property:** **Children:** **Catering:**
Room:

ALNWICK, Northumberland *Map ref 5C1* — *SatNav NE66 1PN*

The Bondgate Boutique

22 Bondgate Without, Alnwick, Northumberland NE66 1PN **T:** 07725 461181
E: info@thebondgate.co.uk
W: www.thebondgate.co.uk

B&B PER ROOM PER NIGHT
S: £45.00 - £65.00
D: £60.00 - £90.00

The Bondgate Boutique, accommodation in Alnwick Northumberland, offers a very private and discreet experience, with a total of 7 beautifully appointed en suite bedrooms with Twin beds, King size and Super King size beds. We are sure there is a room that is suitable for you.

This Grade II listed building is of one the oldest residential properties in Alnwick dating back to the early 18th century. Built for a Catholic family with its characterful quirky layout, exposed beams and it also has a Priest Hole within one corner of a bedroom. It all makes for a cosy stay.

Directions: Please see website.

Open: All Year except Christmas and New Year

Site: P **Payment:** **Leisure:** **Property:** **Children:** 8 **Catering:**
Room:

ALNWICK, Northumberland *Map ref 5C1* — *SatNav NE661TW*

Bow House

49 St Michaels Lane, Alnwick NE66 1TW **T:** 07809 467126
E: info@alnwickguesthouses.co.uk
W: www.alnwickguesthouses.co.uk **£ BOOK ONLINE**

B&B PER ROOM PER NIGHT
D: £80.00 - £100.00

Set in a conservation area overlooking St. Paul's Church and within two minutes walk from the local shops and restaurants. Property takes its name from the Archery practice that took place outside the town wall where the property stands. **Directions:** South, take first exit from A1 to town centre. Left before Hotspur Tower. Opposite St Pauls church. North turn right after Tower. **Bedrooms:** En suite. **Open:** All year - Excluding Christmas/Boxing & New Year's Day.

Site: **Payment:** **Leisure:** **Property:** **Children:** 10 **Room:**

AMBLE, Northumberland Map ref 5C1 SatNav NE65 0AL B

Amble Guesthouse

16 Leazes Street, Amble NE65 0AL **T:** (01665) 714661 **E:** stephmclaughlin@aol.com
W: www.ambleguesthouse.co.uk

A family run 4 bedroom guest house. All rooms en suite. In picturesque fishing port of Amble. Ten+ golf courses within twelve mile radius. Please contact us for prices. **Directions:** From main A1 follow signposts to Amble. Will supply more concise details on request by e-mail or phone. **Bedrooms:** 1 single, 1 double, 1 twin, 1 family **Open:** All year except Christmas and New Year

Payment: **Leisure:** **Property:** **Children:** 12 **Room:**

BAMBURGH, Northumberland Map ref 5C1 SatNav NE70 7EE H

Waren House Hotel

Waren Mill, Belford NE70 7EE **T:** (01668) 214581 **F:** 01668 214484
E: enquiries@warenhousehotel.co.uk
W: www.warenhousehotel.co.uk £ BOOK ONLINE

B&B PER ROOM PER NIGHT
S: £105.00 - £125.00
D: £130.00 - £190.00
HB PER PERSON PER NIGHT
£85.00 - £120.00

Traditional, award-winning country-house hotel set in landscaped grounds, this attractive Georgian house, once owned by the third Lord Derwentwater, has been extended to provide a variety of accommodation, excellent food and a wide selection of wines. There are two ground floors rooms with disabled access located in the courtyard. Children over the age of 14 are welcome. **Directions:** Please contact for directions. **Bedrooms:** 6 doubles, 4 twins and 3 suites **Open:** All year

Site: P **Payment:** € **Leisure:** **Property:** **Children:** 14 **Catering:** **Room:**

BEAL, Northumberland Map ref 5B1 SatNav TD15 2PB B

Brock Mill Farmhouse

Brock Mill, Beal, Berwick-upon-Tweed TD15 2PB **T:** (01289) 381283 **F:** 01289 381283
E: brockmillfarmhouse@btinternet.com
W: www.holyislandaccommodation.com £ BOOK ONLINE

B&B PER ROOM PER NIGHT
S: £35.00 - £50.00
D: £65.00 - £80.00

Working farm. Peaceful surroundings. Ideal for touring North Northumberland and Scottish Borders. Quality accommodation with en suite/suite and private bathrooms new for 2010. Superb English breakfasts or tasty vegetarian alternatives. **Directions:** About 1.5 miles from A1 at Beal on the Holy Island road. **Bedrooms:** Combination of double/twin/family and single **Open:** All year except Christmas

Site: P **Payment:** € **Leisure:** **Property:** **Children:** **Catering:** **Room:**

BERWICK-UPON-TWEED, Northumberland Map ref 5B1 SatNav TD15 1DU B

Alannah House

84 Church Street, Berwick upon Tweed, Northumberland TD15 1DU **T:** (01289) 307252
E: info@alannahhouse.com
W: www.alannahhouse.com

B&B PER ROOM PER NIGHT
S: £50.00 - £65.00
D: £75.00 - £80.00

Georgian town house, situated in town centre within the famous Elizabethan town walls. We have a well maintained walled garden and patio area for guests' use. Parking permits available. All rooms en suite and have digital TV. **Directions:** Enter Berwick town centre, head for town hall turn immediately left behind the hall, 400yds on the right past the police station. **Bedrooms:** 1 double, 1 triple, 1 family. All en suite **Open:** All year

Site: **Leisure:** **Property:** **Children:** **Catering:** **Room:**

For **key to symbols** see page 7

BERWICK-UPON-TWEED, Northumberland Map ref 5B1 SatNav TD15 1NF B

Castle Vale House

Railway Street, Berwick-upon-Tweed, Northumberland TD15 1NF **T:** (01289) 303699
F: 01289 466007 **E:** info@castlevalebandb.co.uk
W: www.castlevalehouse.co.uk **£ BOOK ONLINE**

enjoyEngland.com ★★★ BED & BREAKFAST

B&B PER ROOM PER NIGHT
S: £45.00 - £72.00
D: £69.00 - £85.00

SPECIAL PROMOTIONS
Please contact us by phone or email to ask about discounts on out-of-season short or long stays. Specials in Feb/Mar/Apr/Oct/Nov. 2-bed self-catering annexe also available April - October.

We welcome you to our large secluded Victorian family home standing in its own private grounds with stunning views of the river Tweed and Royal Border Bridge. It has private parking and is close to the railway station (Edinburgh or Newcastle less than an hour) . The town centre is ten minutes walk away, offering a variety of cafes and shops, and the golf course and sea are within half a mile.

Directions: Leaving the A1 from north or south, head for station (Railway St) at the north of the town. Castle Vale House is down a long drive left off Railway Street, which runs parallel to the station entrance.

Bedrooms: All rooms on first floor, en suite, tv/dvd, two chairs, tea & coffee, shower (one with bath)
Open: All year except Christmas until mid January

Site: P **Payment:** £ **Property:** **Room:** TV DVD

BERWICK-UPON-TWEED, Northumberland Map ref 5B1 SatNav TD15 2PL B

Fenham Farm Coastal Bed & Breakfast

Beal, Berwick-upon-Tweed TD15 2PL **T:** (01289) 381245 **E:** stay@fenhamfarm.co.uk
W: www.fenhamfarm.co.uk **£ BOOK ONLINE**

enjoyEngland.com ★★★★ GUEST ACCOMMODATION · enjoyEngland.com Gold AWARD

B&B PER ROOM PER NIGHT
S: £65.00 - £75.00
D: £85.00 - £95.00

Quality Bed & Breakfast accommodation in converted farm outbuildings on a beautiful coastal spot overlooking the Holy Island of Lindisfarne. 5 warm & comfortable en suite bedrooms. Delicious breakfasts served in the farmhouse. **Directions:** Fenham Farm is on the coast approximately 1.5 miles off the A1, 10 miles south of Berwick upon Tweed and 6 miles north of Belford. **Bedrooms:** 4 double/ twin, 1 family **Open:** March until November

WALKERS WELCOME · CYCLISTS WELCOME **Site:** P **Payment:** £ **Leisure:** **Property:** **Children:** **Catering:** **Room:** TV

CORBRIDGE, Northumberland Map ref 5B2 SatNav NE45 5LW B

2 The Crofts

Newcastle Road, Corbridge NE45 5LW **T:** (01434) 633046 **E:** welcome@2thecrofts.co.uk
W: www.2thecrofts.co.uk **£ BOOK ONLINE**

enjoyEngland.com ★★★★ BED & BREAKFAST · enjoyEngland.com Silver AWARD

B&B PER ROOM PER NIGHT
S: £45.00 - £55.00
D: £70.00 - £80.00

Traditional large Victorian terrace on edge of Corbridge in quiet location with friendly attention and award-winning Aga-cooked breakfast. 3 lovely guest rooms: 2 double, 1 twin, all en suite. Near Hadrian's Wall and on Hadrian cycle way. **Directions:** Full directions on website. We are on B6530 road, X85 and 685 bus routes, 25 minutes walk from railway station, 20 minute drive from airport. **Bedrooms:** 2 king-sized doubles, 1 twin bedroom, all en suite **Open:** All year

WALKERS WELCOME · CYCLISTS WELCOME **Site:** P **Payment:** £ **Leisure:** **Property:** **Children:** **Catering:** **Room:** TV

CORBRIDGE, Northumberland Map ref 5B2 SatNav NE45 5LP

The Hayes (Bed & Breakfast)

Newcastle Road, Corbridge NE45 5LP **T:** (01434) 632010 **E:** ctmm18@gmail.com
W: www.hayes-corbridge.co.uk

★★★ GUEST ACCOMMODATION

B&B PER ROOM PER NIGHT
S: £37.00 - £49.50
D: £76.00 - £79.00

Fine country house in lovely setting in historic Corbridge providing family-run well-appointed accommodation. Easy access to Hadrian's Wall, A68 and A69 and Northumbria countryside. **Directions:** From East: leave A69 at Styford roundabout follow road into Corbridge for 2 mls. From West: pass petrol station, then up hill 0.25mls. **Bedrooms:** 1 single, 3 family **Open:** All year except Christmas and New Year

Site: **Payment:** **Leisure:** **Property:** **Children:** **Catering:** **Room:**

CORNHILL-ON-TWEED, Northumberland Map ref 5B1 SatNav TD12 4UH

Collingwood Arms Hotel

Main Street, Cornhill-on-Tweed TD12 4UH **T:** (01890) 882424 **F:** 01890 883098
E: enquiries@collingwoodarms.com
W: www.collingwoodarms.com £ BOOK ONLINE

★★★ HOTEL — Gold AWARD

B&B PER ROOM PER NIGHT
D: £130.00 - £200.00

The Collingwood Arms has an enviable reputation for its Food, Service and Accommodation. Refurbished and maintained to a very high standard, a warm welcome awaits you. **Directions:** The Hotel is located on the A697 in the village of Cornhill On Tweed, about a mile South of the Scottish border. **Bedrooms:** 15 luxurious en suite rooms including 2 suites **Open:** All year

WALKERS WELCOME · FAMILIES WELCOME · CYCLISTS WELCOME · PETS! WELCOME

Site: **Payment:** **Leisure:** **Property:** **Children:** **Catering:** **Room:**

HEXHAM, Northumberland Map ref 5B2 SatNav NE47 5LU

Langley Castle Hotel

Langley-on-Tyne, Hexham NE47 5LU **T:** (01434) 688888 **F:** 01434 684019
E: manager@langleycastle.com
W: www.langleycastle.com £ BOOK ONLINE

★★★★ HOTEL — Gold AWARD

B&B PER ROOM PER NIGHT
S: £119.50 - £209.50
D: £155.00 - £279.00

HB PER PERSON PER NIGHT
£159.00 - £299.00

SPECIAL PROMOTIONS
Reserve a castle-view room and we will upgrade to a 'castle' room (if available at check-in), at no extra charge.

A genuine 14th Century Castle set in woodland estate. All rooms with facilities, some with window seats set into seven foot thick walls. Sauna, four poster beds. The magnificent drawing room, with blazing log fire, complements intimate Josephine Restaurant. Perfect to explore Hadrian's Wall, Northumberland, Bamburgh Castle, Holy Island and Borders.

Directions: Half an hour drive from Newcastle airport. From A69 take A686 for 2 miles.

Bedrooms: 27 rooms in total
Open: All year

WALKERS WELCOME · CYCLISTS WELCOME

Site: **Payment:** **Leisure:** **Property:** **Children:** **Catering:** **Room:**

For **key to symbols** see page 7

HEXHAM, Northumberland Map ref 5B2 SatNav NE46 1RS B

enjoyEngland.com ★★★★ GUEST ACCOMMODATION

B&B PER ROOM PER NIGHT
S: £50.00 - £60.00
D: £110.00 - £120.00
HB PER PERSON PER NIGHT
£80.00 - £100.00

Loughbrow House

Dipton Mill Road NE46 1RS **T:** (01434) 603351 **E:** patriciaclark351@btinternet.com
W: www.loughbrow.fsnet.co.uk

A mansion house built in 1780 set in 9 acres of garden, surrounded by own farm land looking up the North Tyne valley. Situated 1 mile from Hexham. Ample parking. **Directions:** From Hexham take B6306. After 0.25 miles take right-hand fork, Dipton Mill Road, for further 0.25 miles. Turn into drive gates, house is 0.5 miles. **Bedrooms:** 2 single, 1 double, 2 twin. **Open:** All year except Christmas and New Year

Site: P **Leisure:** **Property:** **Children:** 5 **Catering:** **Room:**

HEXHAM, Northumberland Map ref 5B2 SatNav NE48 2JT H

enjoyEngland.com ★★★ COUNTRY HOUSE HOTEL

B&B PER ROOM PER NIGHT
S: £55.00 - £74.00
D: £98.00 - £128.00
EVENING MEAL PER PERSON
£9.90 - £21.40

Riverdale Hall Hotel

Bellingham, Hexham, Northumberland NE48 2JT **T:** (01434) 220254 **F:** 01434 700002
E: reservations@riverdalehallhotel.co.uk
W: www.riverdalehallhotel.co.uk £ BOOK ONLINE

Country House Hotel with swimming pool, cricket field and salmon river. 28 rooms all with en suite facilities. Award winning restaurant (Les routiers Gold plate award), bar with open log fire, cask ales and good wines, swimming pool and sauna. Four self-catering apartments. Perfect situation for walkers on Hadrian's Wall and Pennine Way. Bellingham's 18 hole golf course opposite. Nearest hotel to Northumberland International Dark Sky Park, Kielder Water and Forest. Private salmon fishing.

Directions: Please see our website for a map and route planner.

Bedrooms: Spacious, all en suite some with balconies or patios looking south over the North Tyne River. Free wi-fi
Open: All year

Site: P **Leisure:** **Property:** **Children:** **Catering:** **Room:**

SEAHOUSES, Northumberland Map ref 5C1 SatNav NE68 7YB B

enjoyEngland.com ★★★★ BED & BREAKFAST

B&B PER ROOM PER NIGHT
S: £50.00
D: £70.00 - £75.00

Holly Trees

4 James Street, Seahouses NE68 7YB **T:** (01665) 721942
E: margaret.tucker4@btinternet.com
W: www.holly-trees.com

Margaret has been providing a warm welcome to her guests for the past eight years and she serves delicious breakfasts with her freshly baked homemade bread. **Directions:** See website for directions **Bedrooms:** 3 doubles and 1 single, all en suite. Can offer 2 twins **Open:** April - October

Site: **Leisure:** **Property:** **Children:** 12 **Catering:** **Room:**

SEAHOUSES, Northumberland Map ref 5C1 SatNav NE68 7UB B

St Cuthbert's House

192 Main Street, Seahouses, Northumberland NE68 7UB **T:** (01665) 720456
E: stay@stcuthbertshouse.com
W: www.stcuthbertshouse.com **£ BOOK ONLINE**

B&B PER ROOM PER NIGHT
S: £80.00 - £120.00
D: £100.00 - £120.00

SPECIAL PROMOTIONS
Quote 'VE Guide' when booking (online or in person) to receive a complimentary bottle of our very good House wine!

Welcome to VisitEngland's 'Best B&B in England 2014'! This time away is precious for you, and you want to feel a genuine, warm welcome, with a lovely experience you can share with your closest friends and family. These are the feelings you'll enjoy when you stay at St Cuthbert's House - a very special place.

Jeff & Jill welcome you to this historic and beautifully restored B&B on the stunning Northumberland coast. Walk to Bamburgh Castle, or take a short drive to Holy Island, or Alnwick Castle. Wide open spaces, beautiful beaches, and castles galore - all await you! Come and see...

Directions: Detailed, accurate travel information and directions are available on the 'Info' menu of our website. Call if you need help!

Bedrooms: 5-star Gold Award facilities in all rooms
Open: All year, some closed periods in winter

Site: P **Payment:** **Leisure:** **Property:** **Catering:** **Room:**

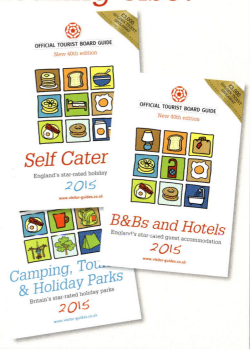

SOUTH SHIELDS, Tyne and Wear Map ref 5C2 SatNav NE33 1LH

★★★ HOTEL

B&B PER ROOM PER NIGHT
S: £74.50 - £205.00
D: £74.50 - £205.00

HB PER PERSON PER NIGHT
£54.00 - £125.00

SPECIAL PROMOTIONS
Please visit our website for special offers and forthcoming events.

Little Haven Hotel

River Drive, South Shields NE33 1LH **T:** (01914) 554455 **F:** 01914 554466
E: info@littlehavenhotel.com
W: www.littlehavenhotel.com

Uniquely situated at the gateway of the River Tyne, Little Haven Hotel boasts extensive views of the river and Little Haven Beach. Within 15 minutes of both Newcastle and Sunderland. Enjoy a varied and exciting wining and dining experience in the Boardwalk restaurant, fashionably set in the conservatory overlooking the historical River Tyne with a view to Little Haven Beach and the lively waterfront.

Directions: Please contact us for directions.

Bedrooms: 33 double, 14 twin, 4 family, 8 executive & 3 penthouse suites
Open: All year

Site: **Payment:** **Leisure:** **Property:** **Children:** **Catering:**
Room:

WASHINGTON, Tyne and Wear Map ref 5C2 SatNav NE38 7AB

★★★★ GUEST ACCOMMODATION
Silver AWARD

B&B PER ROOM PER NIGHT
D: £27.50 - £40.00

Ye Olde Cop Shop

6 The Green, Washington Village, Tyne and Wear NE38 7AB **T:** (01914) 165333
E: yeoldecopshop@btopenworld.com

Former police station built in 1866 is situated in the heart of a village steeped in history and close to the ancestral home of George Washington. Cleanliness, comfort and hospitality is of an excellent standard, with all rooms en suite and well equipped. Secure car parking with surveillance cameras to the rear.
Directions: A1M turn off junction 64, proceed to roudabout A182 join via left sliproad to sliproad A1231 third exit at roundabout. Follow signs Washington Village/Washington Old Hall to crossroads. Over crossroads 20 yards turn left, between Cross Keys and Washington Arms. **Open:** All year except christmas.

Site: P **Payment:** **Property:** **Catering:** **Room:**

A

B

1

Location Maps

Every place name featured in the regional accommodation sections of this guide has a map reference to help you locate it on the maps which follow. For example, to find Colchester, Essex, which has 'Map ref 3B2', turn to Map 3 and refer to grid square B2.

All place names appearing in the regional sections are shown with orange circles on the maps. This enables you to find other places in your chosen area which may have suitable accommodation – the place index (at the back of this guide) gives page numbers.

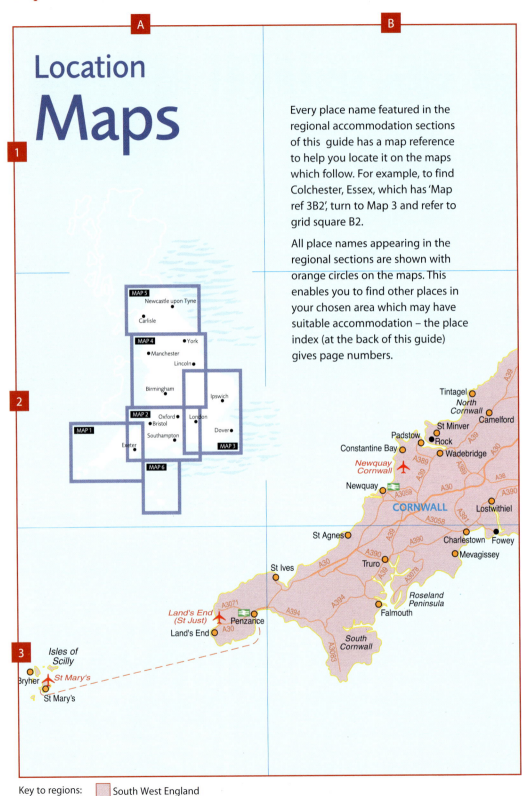

2

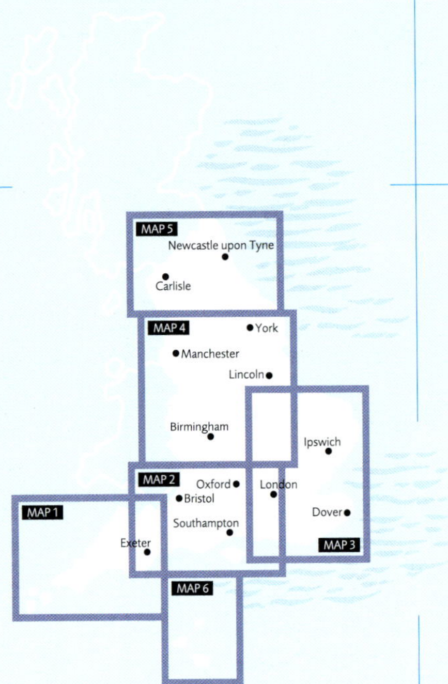

3

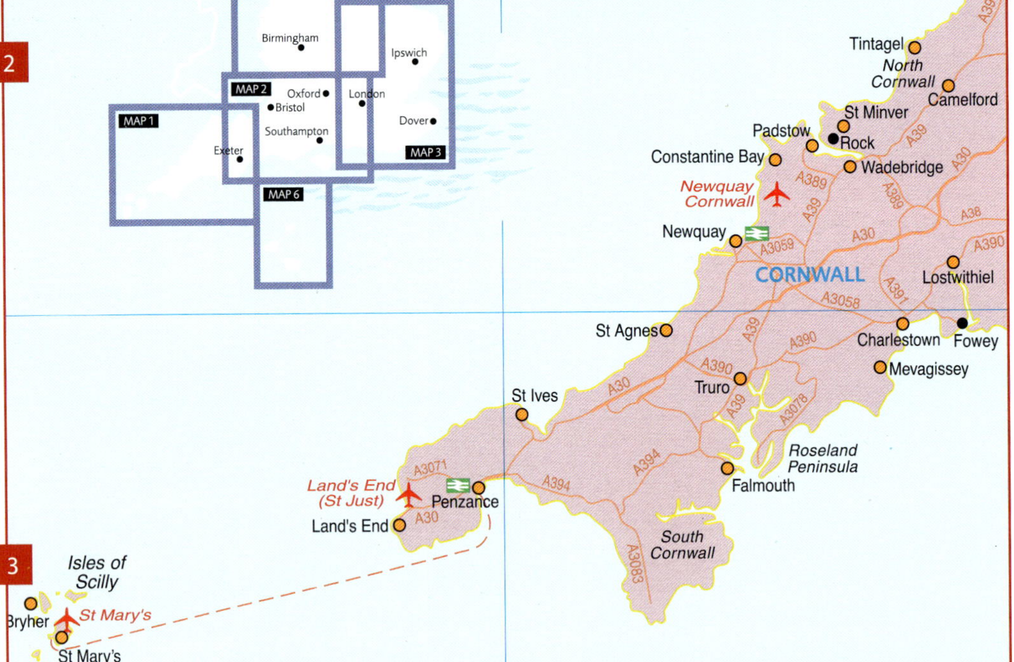

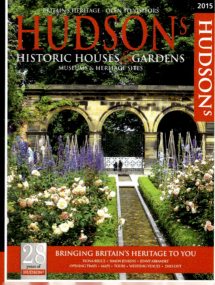

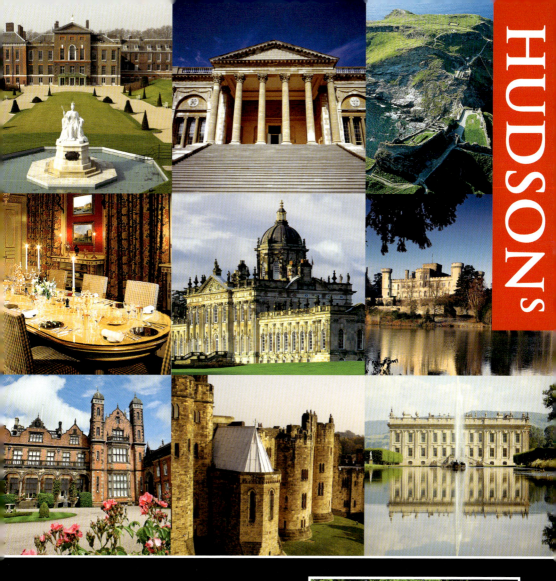

Key to regions: South West England

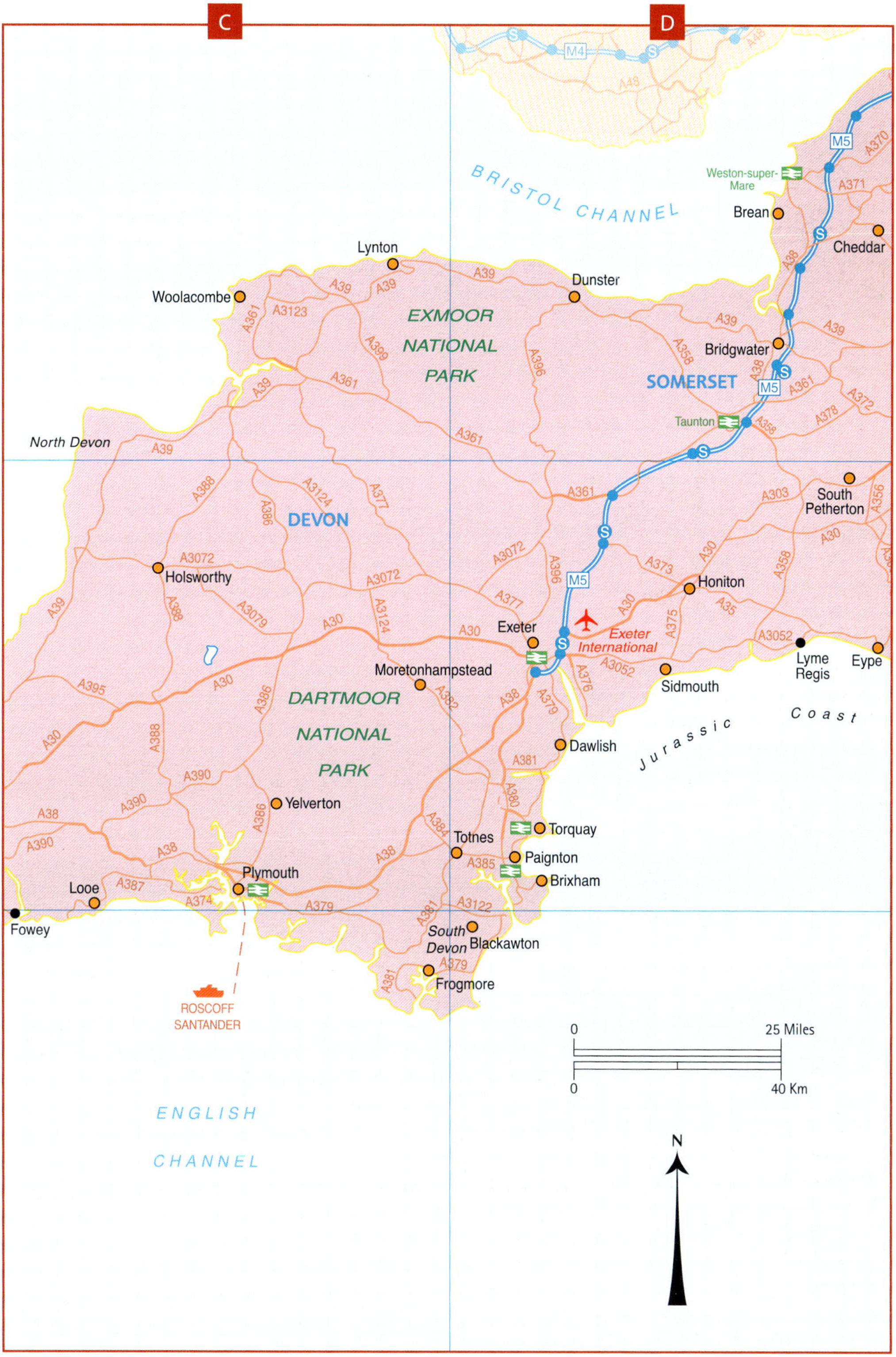

Orange circles indicate accommodation within the regional sections of this guide

Map 2

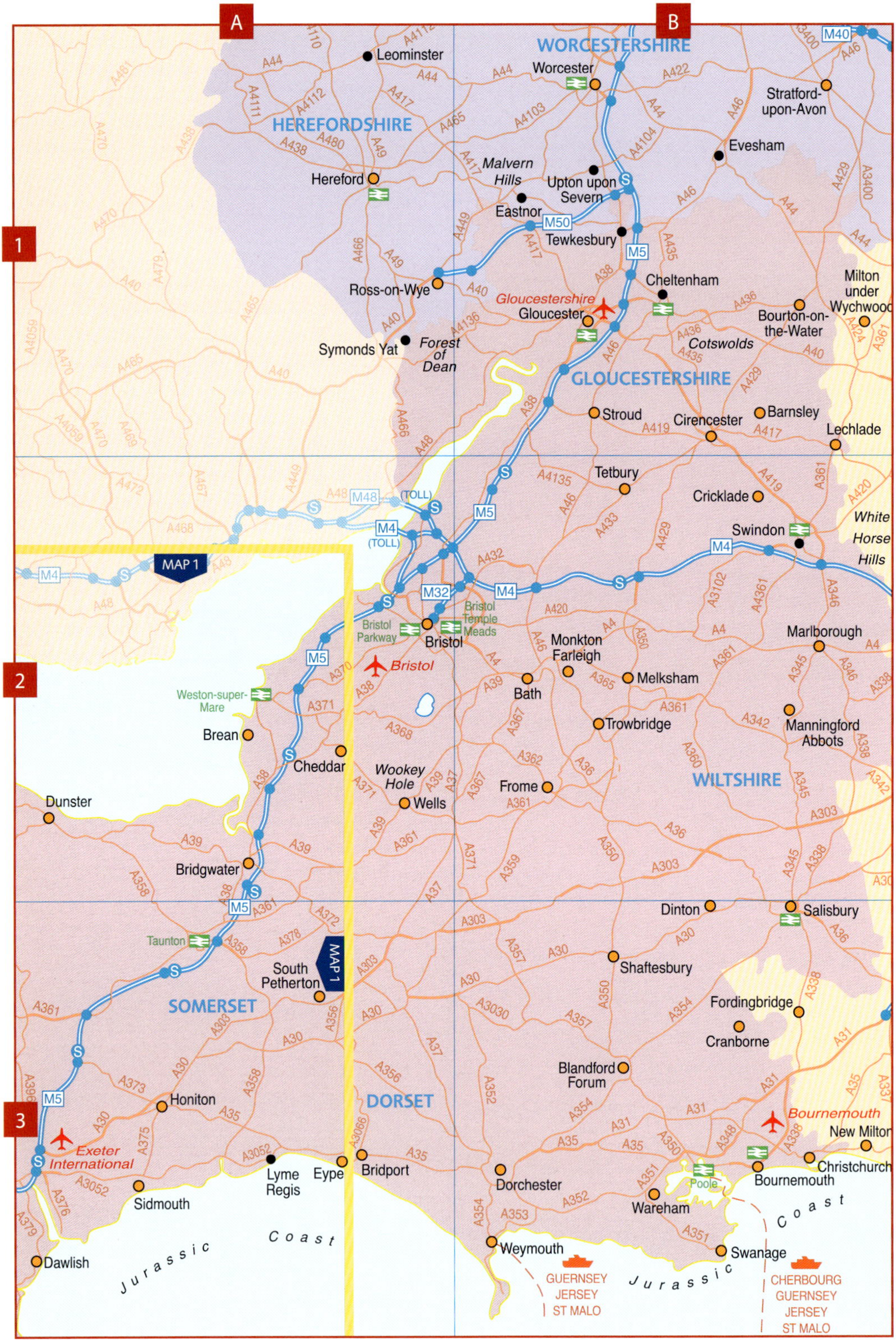

Key to regions: South West England South East England London

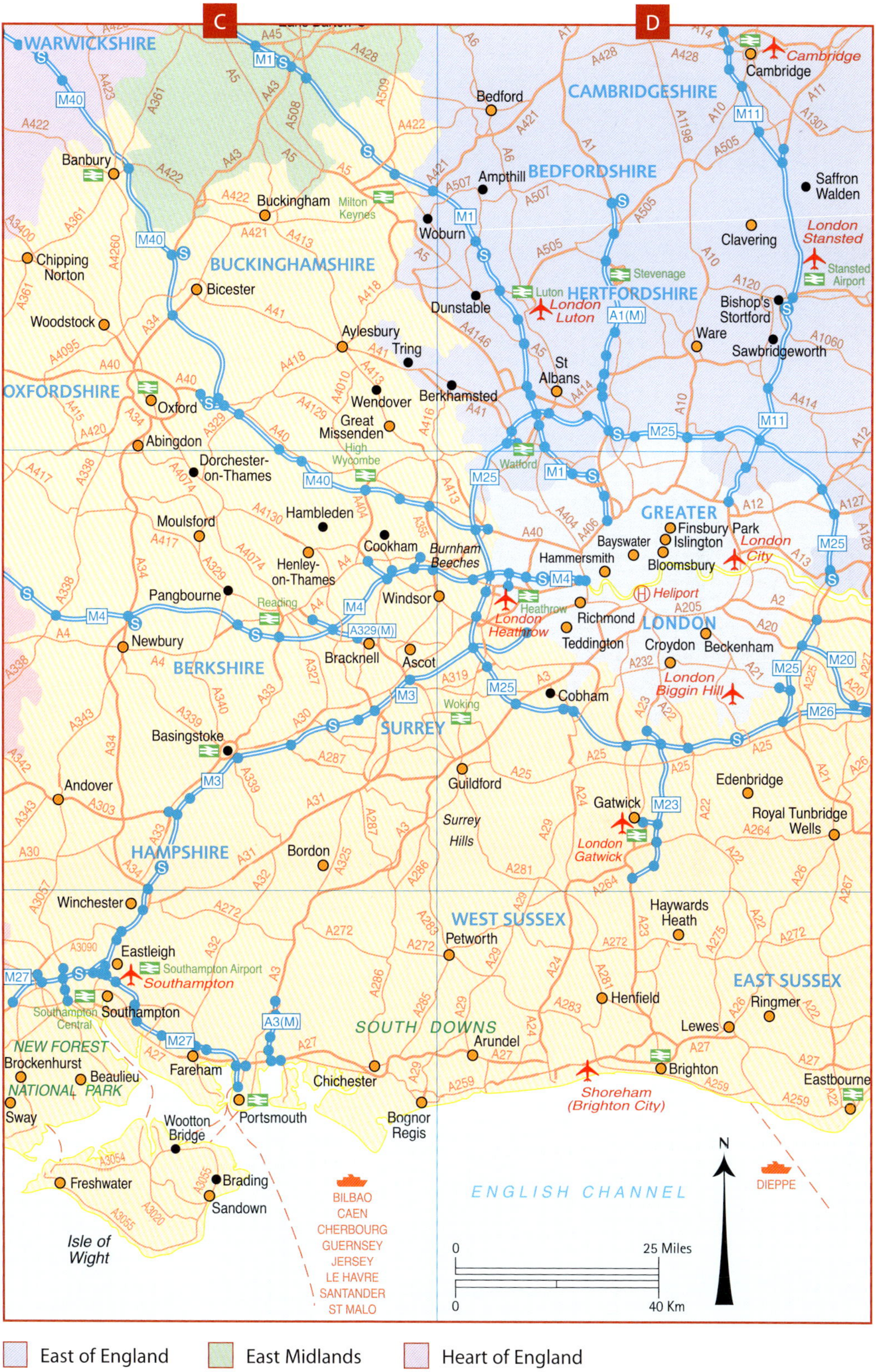

Orange circles indicate accommodation within the regional sections of this guide

Map 3

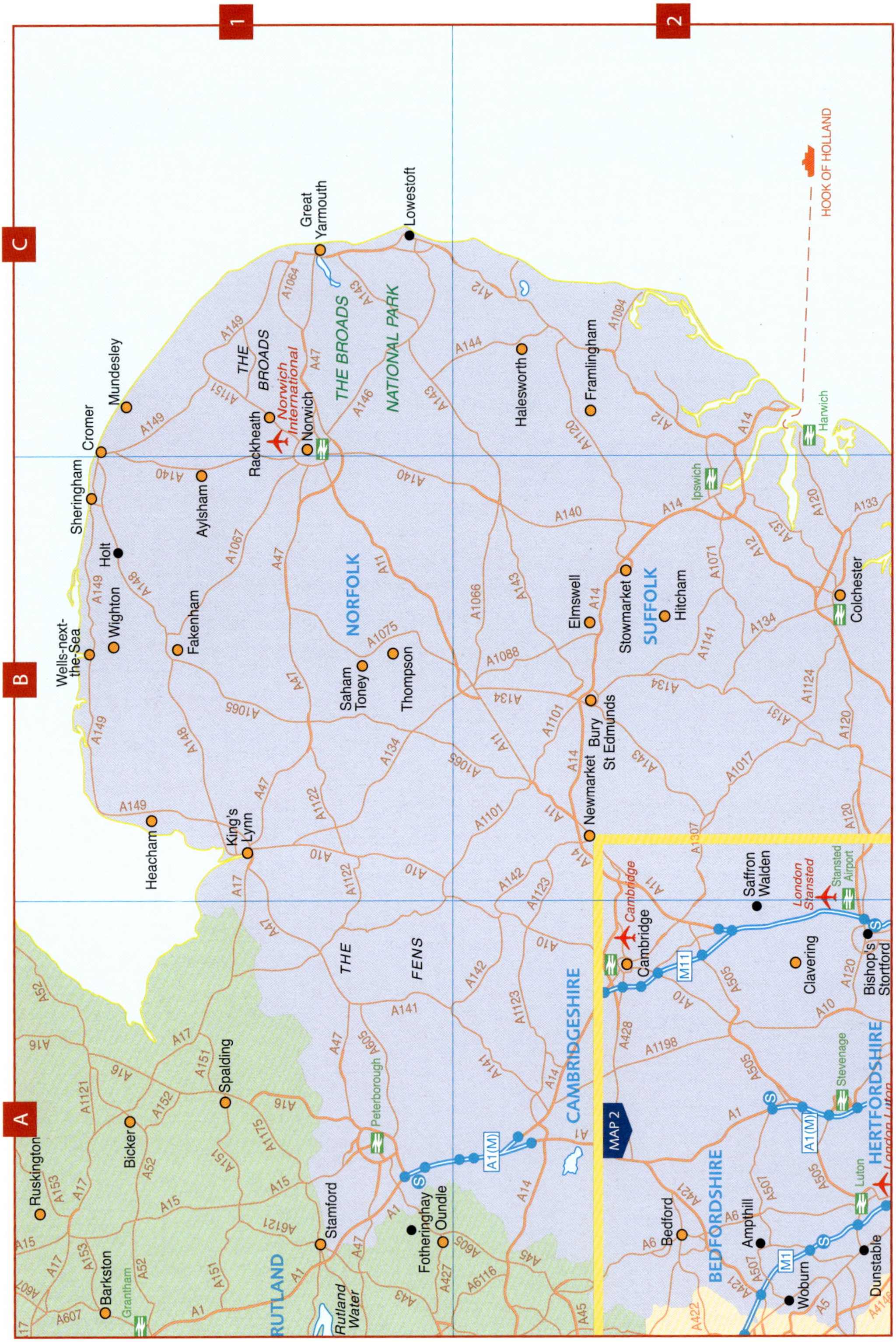

Key to regions: South East England London East of England

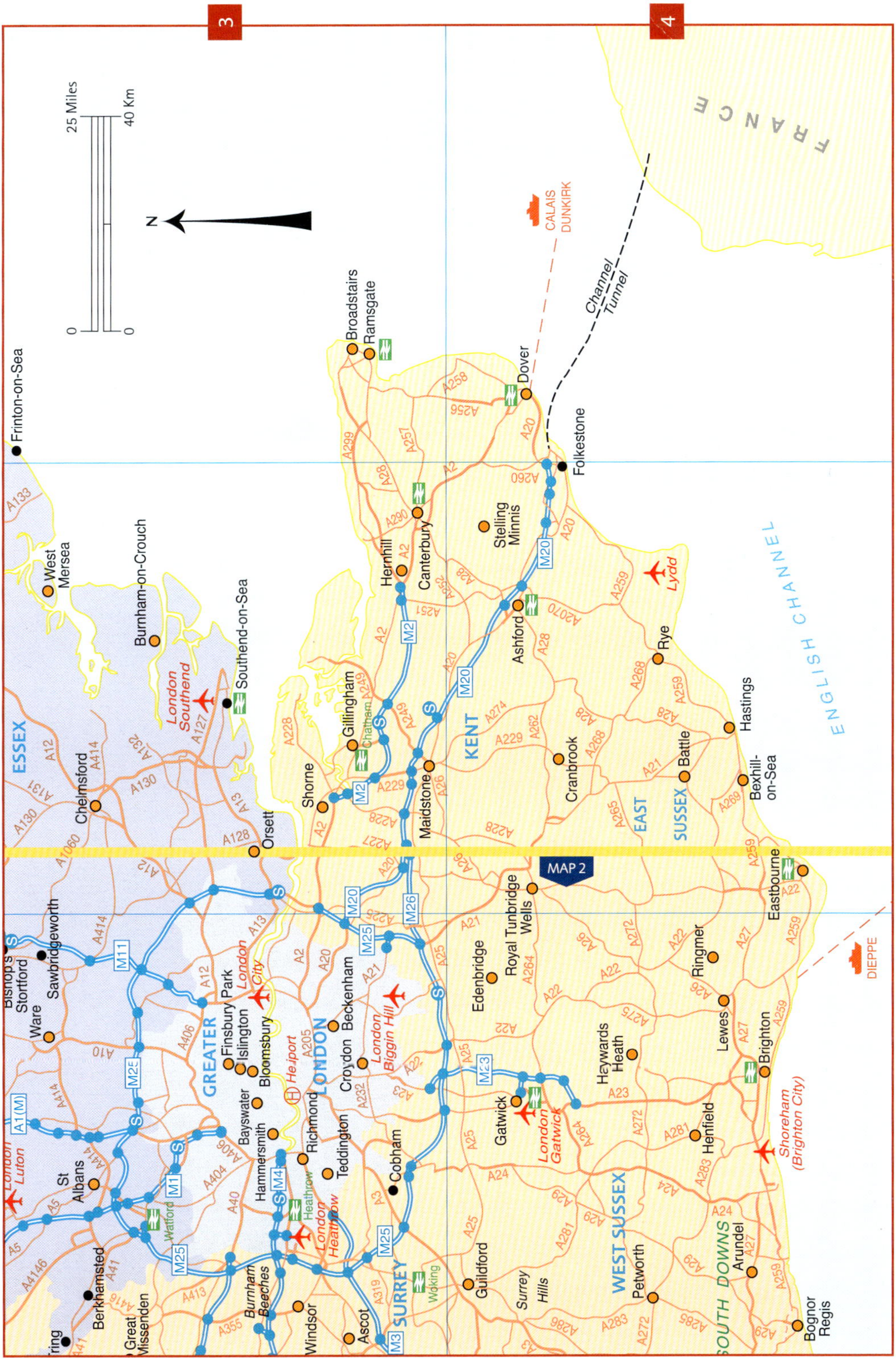

East Midlands

Orange circles indicate accommodation within the regional sections of this guide

Map 4

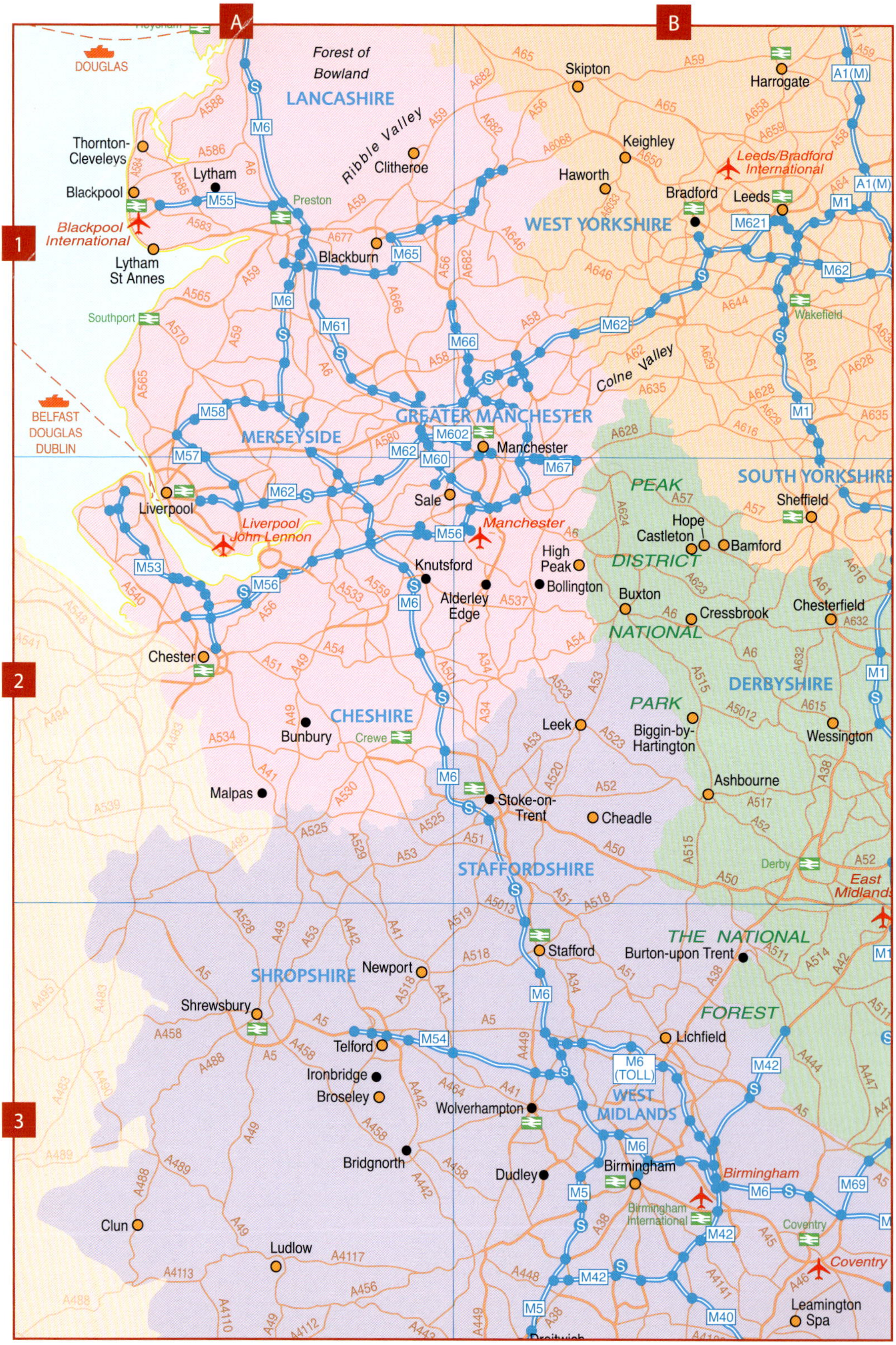

Key to regions: East of England | East Midlands | Heart of England

Yorkshire | North West England | North East England

Orange circles indicate accommodation within the regional sections of this guide

Map 5

Key to regions: Yorkshire North West England North East England

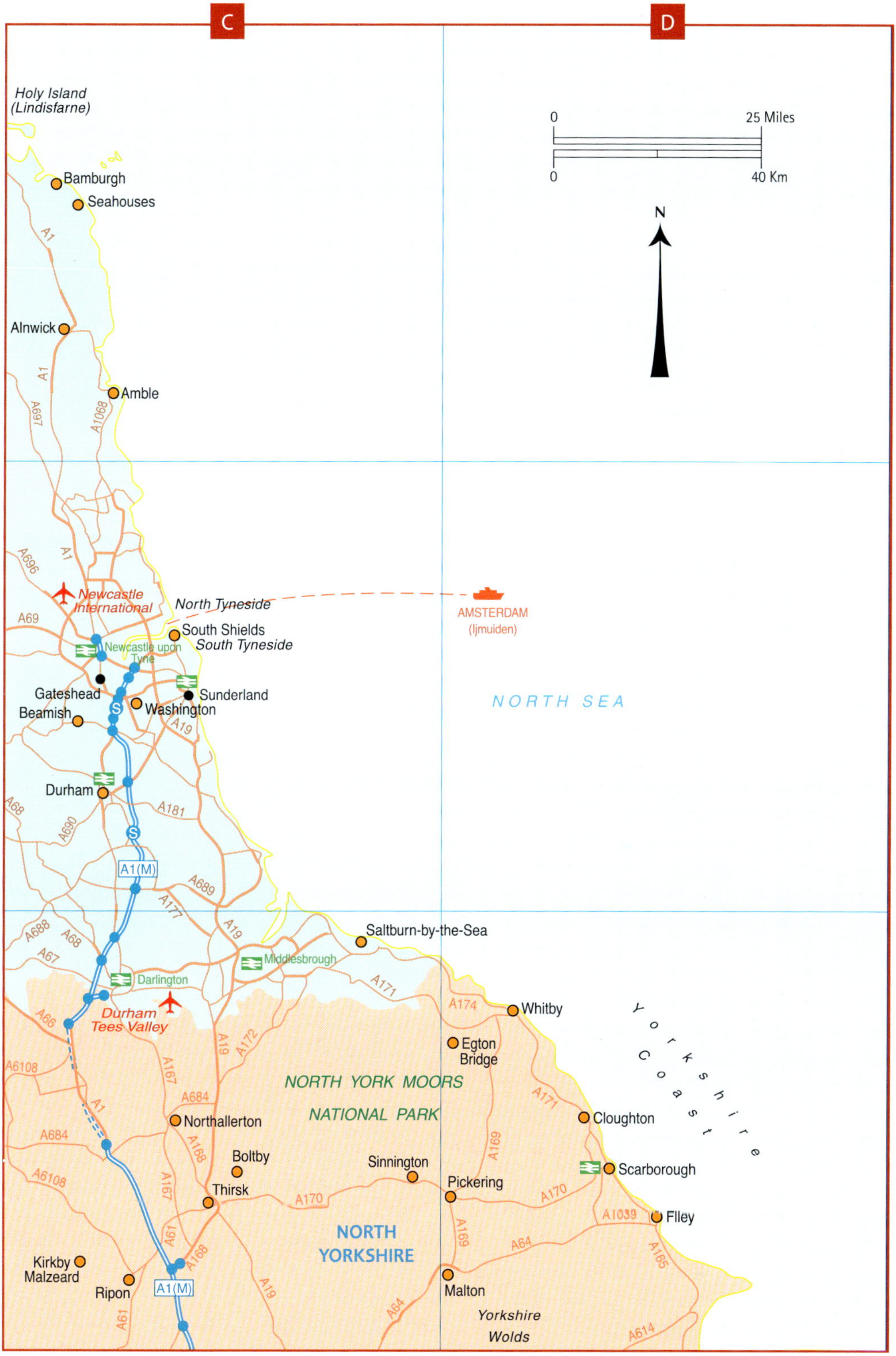

Orange circles indicate accommodation within the regional sections of this guide

Map 6

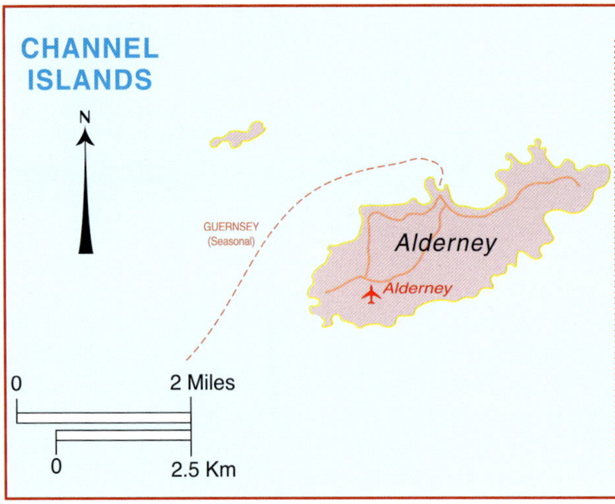

Getting to the Channel Islands

Getting to Jersey and Guernsey is simple, with regular flights from Gatwick and nine other airports. There are also fast ferry crossings from Poole and Weymouth. A traditional ferry sails from Portsmouth. You can travel easily between the islands, flights operate between Jersey, Guernsey and Alderney. Herm and Sark are reached by regular passenger ferries.

Air:

Air Southwest www.airsouthwest.com
Aurigny Air Services www.aurigny.com
Blue Islands www.blueislands.com
Flybe www.flybe.com

Sea:

Condor Ferries www.condorferries.com
Manche Iles Express www.manche-iles-express.com
Sark Shipping Company www.sarkshipping.info
Travel Trident, Herm +44 (0) 1481 721379

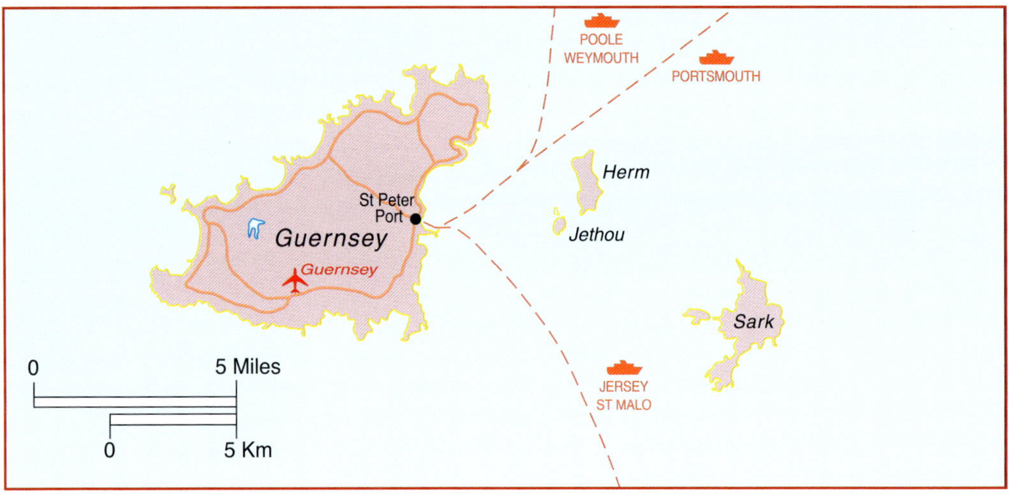

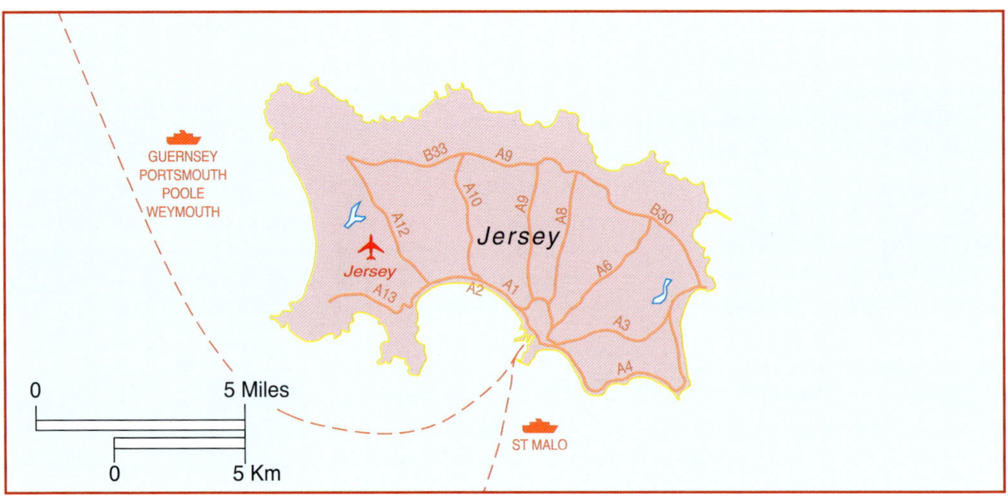

Key to regions: Channel Islands

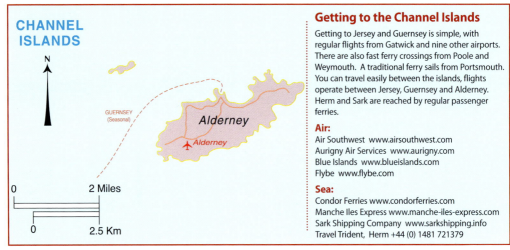

Orange circles indicate accommodation within the regional sections of this guide

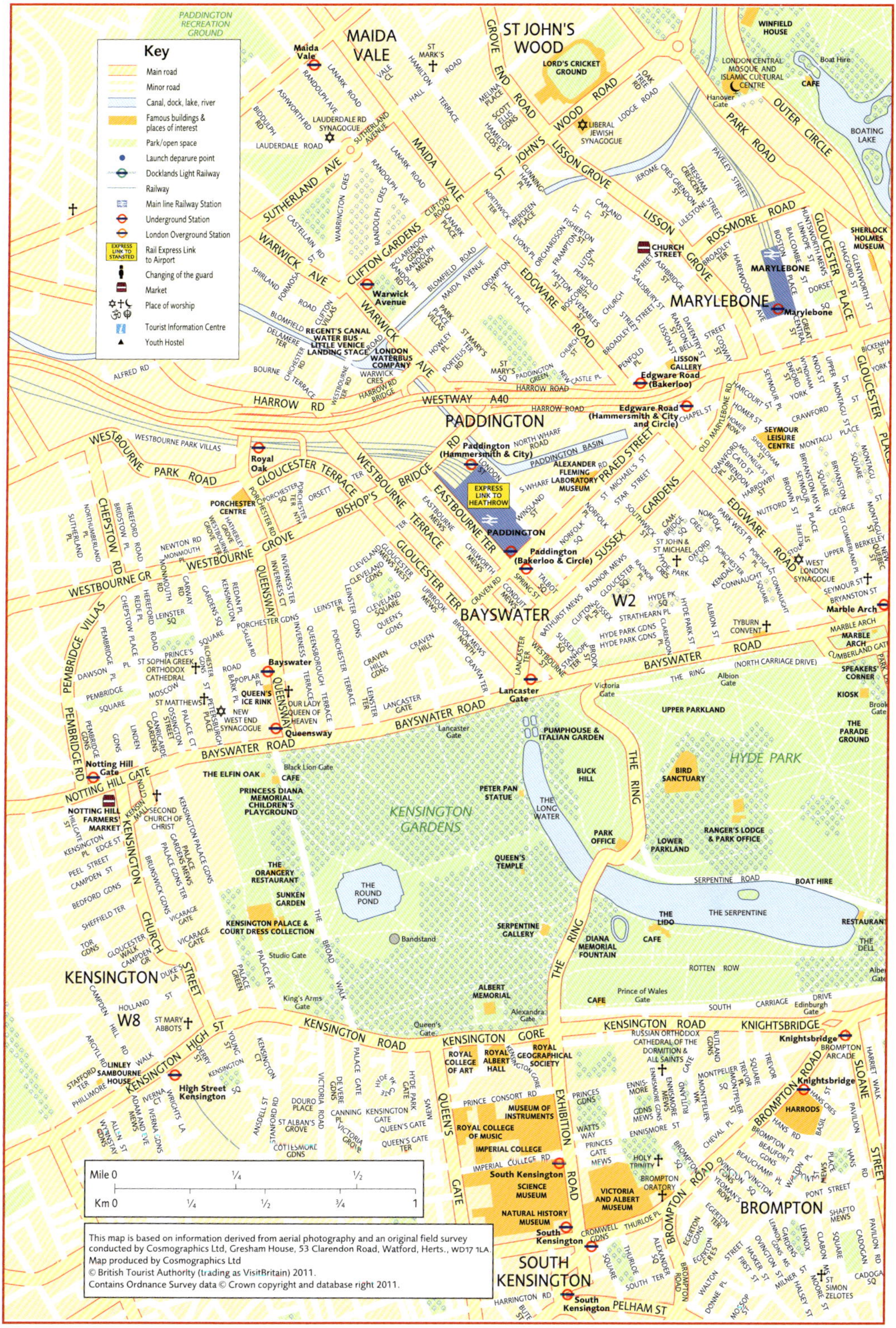
Key
Main road
Minor road
Canal, dock, lake, river
Famous buildings & places of interest
Park/open space
Launch deparure point
Docklands Light Railway
Railway
Main line Railway Station
Underground Station
London Overground Station
EXPRESS LINK TO STANSTED
Rail Express Link to Airport
Changing of the guard
Market
Place of worship
Tourist Information Centre
Youth Hostel
MAIDA VALE
ST JOHN'S WOOD
LORD'S CRICKET GROUND
PADDINGTON RECREATION GROUND
MARYLEBONE
PADDINGTON
BAYSWATER
W2
KENSINGTON
W8
KENSINGTON GARDENS
HYDE PARK
THE SERPENTINE
THE LONG WATER
THE ROUND POND
BROMPTON
SOUTH KENSINGTON
KNIGHTSBRIDGE
HARRODS
ROYAL ALBERT HALL
SCIENCE MUSEUM
NATURAL HISTORY MUSEUM
VICTORIA AND ALBERT MUSEUM
KENSINGTON PALACE & COURT DRESS COLLECTION
SHERLOCK HOLMES MUSEUM
BOATING LAKE
Marble Arch
Mile 0 ¼ ½
Km 0 ¼ ½ ¾ 1
This map is based on information derived from aerial photography and an original field survey conducted by Cosmographics Ltd, Gresham House, 53 Clarendon Road, Watford, Herts., WD17 1LA.
Map produced by Cosmographics Ltd
© British Tourist Authority (trading as VisitBritain) 2011.
Contains Ordnance Survey data © Crown copyright and database right 2011.

Map 8

London

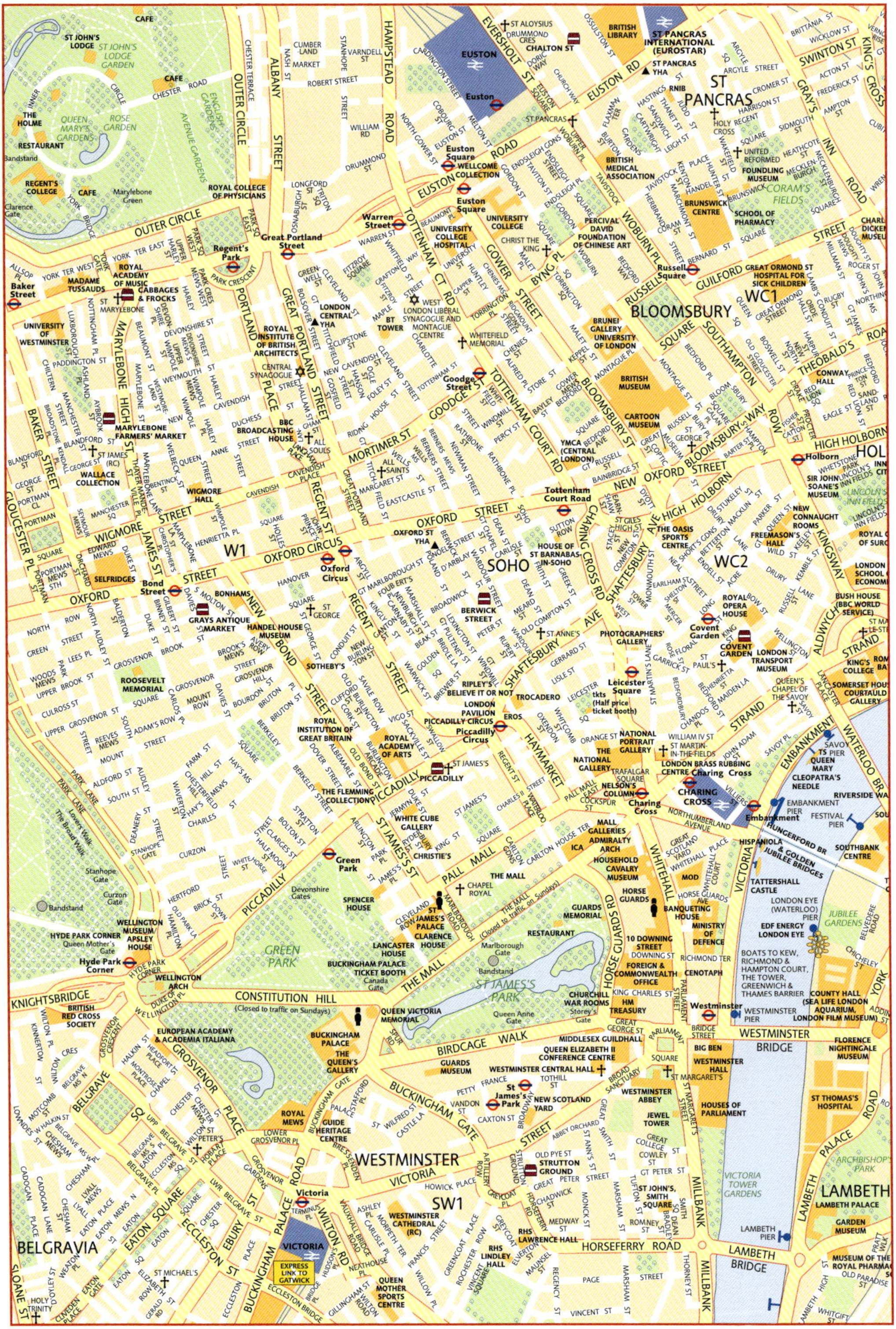

ST JOHN'S LODGE
QUEEN MARY'S GARDENS
REGENT'S COLLEGE
OUTER CIRCLE
ROYAL COLLEGE OF PHYSICIANS
Regent's Park
Great Portland Street
Baker Street
MADAME TUSSAUDS
ROYAL ACADEMY OF MUSIC
UNIVERSITY OF WESTMINSTER
EUSTON
Euston
Euston Square
Warren Street
UNIVERSITY COLLEGE HOSPITAL
UNIVERSITY COLLEGE
BRITISH LIBRARY
ST PANCRAS INTERNATIONAL (EUROSTAR)
ST PANCRAS
BRITISH MEDICAL ASSOCIATION
PERCIVAL DAVID FOUNDATION OF CHINESE ART
BRUNSWICK CENTRE
FOUNDLING MUSEUM
CORAM'S FIELDS
Russell Square
BLOOMSBURY
WC1
GREAT ORMOND ST HOSPITAL FOR SICK CHILDREN
BRUNEI GALLERY UNIVERSITY OF LONDON
BRITISH MUSEUM
CARTOON MUSEUM
Goodge Street
BT TOWER
ROYAL INSTITUTE OF BRITISH ARCHITECTS
BBC BROADCASTING HOUSE
MARYLEBONE FARMERS' MARKET
WALLACE COLLECTION
WIGMORE HALL
W1
Oxford Circus
OXFORD CIRCUS
Tottenham Court Road
Holborn
SIR JOHN SOANE'S MUSEUM
SOHO
WC2
Bond Street
SELFRIDGES
GRAYS ANTIQUE MARKET
HANDEL HOUSE MUSEUM
SOTHEBY'S
BERWICK STREET
ROYAL OPERA HOUSE
Covent Garden
COVENT GARDEN
LONDON TRANSPORT MUSEUM
ROOSEVELT MEMORIAL
ROYAL INSTITUTION OF GREAT BRITAIN
ROYAL ACADEMY OF ARTS
Piccadilly Circus
PICCADILLY CIRCUS
RIPLEY'S BELIEVE IT OR NOT
LONDON PAVILION
TROCADERO
Leicester Square
NATIONAL PORTRAIT GALLERY
THE NATIONAL GALLERY
TRAFALGAR SQUARE
NELSON'S COLUMN
Charing Cross
CHARING CROSS
Embankment
CLEOPATRA'S NEEDLE
SOMERSET HOUSE COURTAULD GALLERY
Green Park
GREEN PARK
HYDE PARK CORNER
Hyde Park Corner
WELLINGTON MUSEUM APSLEY HOUSE
WELLINGTON ARCH
SPENCER HOUSE
ST JAMES'S PALACE
CLARENCE HOUSE
LANCASTER HOUSE
ADMIRALTY ARCH
HORSE GUARDS
BANQUETING HOUSE
10 DOWNING STREET
ST JAMES'S PARK
CONSTITUTION HILL
BUCKINGHAM PALACE
THE QUEEN'S GALLERY
QUEEN VICTORIA MEMORIAL
CHURCHILL WAR ROOMS
HM TREASURY
Westminster
WESTMINSTER BRIDGE
BIG BEN
WESTMINSTER HALL
HOUSES OF PARLIAMENT
WESTMINSTER ABBEY
JEWEL TOWER
LONDON EYE (WATERLOO) PIER
EDF ENERGY LONDON EYE
COUNTY HALL (SEA LIFE LONDON AQUARIUM, LONDON FILM MUSEUM)
FLORENCE NIGHTINGALE MUSEUM
ST THOMAS'S HOSPITAL
St James's Park
NEW SCOTLAND YARD
ROYAL MEWS
WESTMINSTER
Victoria
VICTORIA
EXPRESS LINK TO GATWICK
WESTMINSTER CATHEDRAL (RC)
SW1
VICTORIA TOWER GARDENS
LAMBETH
LAMBETH PALACE
GARDEN MUSEUM
LAMBETH BRIDGE
HORSEFERRY ROAD
MILLBANK
BELGRAVIA
EATON SQUARE
KNIGHTSBRIDGE

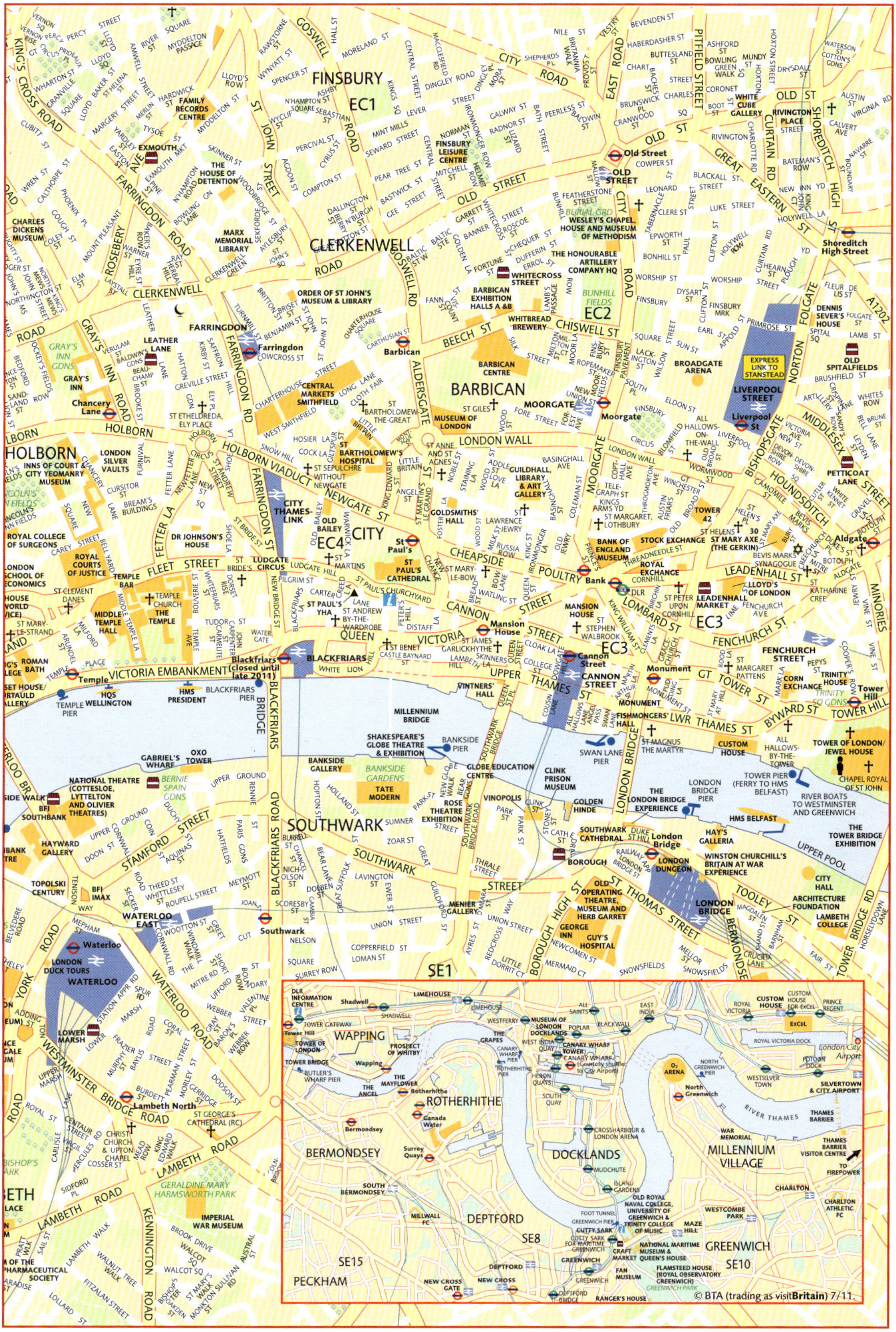
FINSBURY
EC1
CLERKENWELL
BARBICAN
EC2
CITY
EC4
EC3
HOLBORN
SOUTHWARK
SE1
WAPPING
ROTHERHITHE
BERMONDSEY
DOCKLANDS
MILLENNIUM VILLAGE
DEPTFORD
SE8
GREENWICH
SE10
SE15
PECKHAM
Farringdon
Barbican
Moorgate
Liverpool St
Old Street
Shoreditch High Street
Aldgate
Tower Hill
Monument
Bank
Mansion House
Cannon Street
Blackfriars (closed until late 2011)
Temple
St Paul's
Chancery Lane
London Bridge
Borough
Southwark
Waterloo
Lambeth North
ST PAUL'S CATHEDRAL
MUSEUM OF LONDON
BARBICAN CENTRE
TOWER OF LONDON/ JEWEL HOUSE
TATE MODERN
SHAKESPEARE'S GLOBE THEATRE & EXHIBITION
MILLENNIUM BRIDGE
HMS BELFAST
THE TOWER BRIDGE EXHIBITION
CITY HALL
NATIONAL THEATRE (COTTESLOE, LYTTELTON AND OLIVIER THEATRES)
IMPERIAL WAR MUSEUM
SOUTHWARK CATHEDRAL
LONDON DUNGEON
TOWER 42
30 ST MARY AXE (THE GHERKIN)
BANK OF ENGLAND MUSEUM
STOCK EXCHANGE
ROYAL COURTS OF JUSTICE
DR JOHNSON'S HOUSE
CHARLES DICKENS MUSEUM
EXPRESS LINK TO STANSTEAD
RIVER THAMES
O2 ARENA
© BTA (trading as visitBritain) 7/11.

Motorway Service Area Assessment Scheme

Something we all use and take for granted but how good are they?

The star ratings cover over 250 different aspects of each operation, including cleanliness, the quality and range of catering and also the quality of the physical aspects, as well as the service. It does not cover prices or value for money.

OPERATOR: EXTRA

Baldock	★★★★
Beaconsfield	★★★★
Blackburn	★★★★
Cambridge	★★★
Cullompton	★★★
Peterborough	★★★★

OPERATOR: MOTO

Birch E	★★★
Birch W	★★★
Bridgwater	★★★
Burton in Kendal	★★★
Cherwell Valley	★★★★★
Chieveley	★★★
Doncaster N	★★★★
Donington Park	★★★★
Exeter	★★★
Ferrybridge	★★★
Frankley N	★★★
Frankley S	★★★
Heston E	★★★
Heston W	★★★
Hilton Park N	★★★
Hilton Park S	★★★
Knutsford N	★★★
Knutsford S	★★★
Lancaster N	★★★
Lancaster S	★★
Leigh Delamere E	★★★★
Leigh Delamere W	★★★★
Medway	★★★
Pease Pottage	★★★
Reading E	★★★★
Reading W	★★★
Severn View	★★
Southwaite N	★★★
Southwaite S	★★★
Stafford N	★★★★
Tamworth	★★★
Thurrock	★★★★
Toddington N	★★★★
Toddington S	★★★
Trowell N	★★★
Trowell S	★★★
Washington N	★★★
Washington S	★★★★
Wetherby	★★★★
Winchester N	★★★★
Winchester S	★★★
Woolley Edge N	★★★★
Woolley Edge S	★★★★

OPERATOR: ROADCHEF

Chester	★★
Clacket Lane E	★★★
Clacket Lane W	★★
Durham	★★★
Killington Lake	★★★
Maidstone	★★★
Northampton N	★★★
Northampton S	★★★
Norton Canes	★★★★
Rownhams N	★★
Rownhams S	★★★
Sandbach N	★★
Sandbach S	★★★
Sedgemoor S	★★
Stafford S	★★★
Strensham N	★★★★
Strensham S	★★★
Taunton Deane N	★★
Taunton Deane S	★★★
Tibshelf N	★★★
Tibshelf S	★★★
Watford Gap N	★★★
Watford Gap S	★★

OPERATOR: WELCOME BREAK

Birchanger Green	★★★★
Burtonwood	★★★
Charnock Richard W	★★★
Charnock Richard E	★★★
Corley E	★★★
Corley W	★★★
Fleet N	★★★★
Fleet S	★★★
Gordano	★★★★
Hartshead Moor E	★★★
Hartshead Moor W	★★★
Hopwood Park	★★★★
Keele N	★★★
Keele S	★★★
Leicester Forest East N	★★★
Leicester Forest East S	★★★
London Gateway	★★★★
Membury E	★★★
Membury W	★★★★
Michaelwood N	★★★
Michaelwood S	★★★
Newport Pagnell S	★★★
Newport Pagnell N	★★★
Oxford	★★★★
Sedgemoor N	★★★
South Mimms	★★★★
Telford	★★★
Warwick N	★★★
Warwick S	★★★★
Woodall N	★★
Woodall S	★★★

WESTMORLAND

Tebay N	★★★★
Tebay S	★★★★★

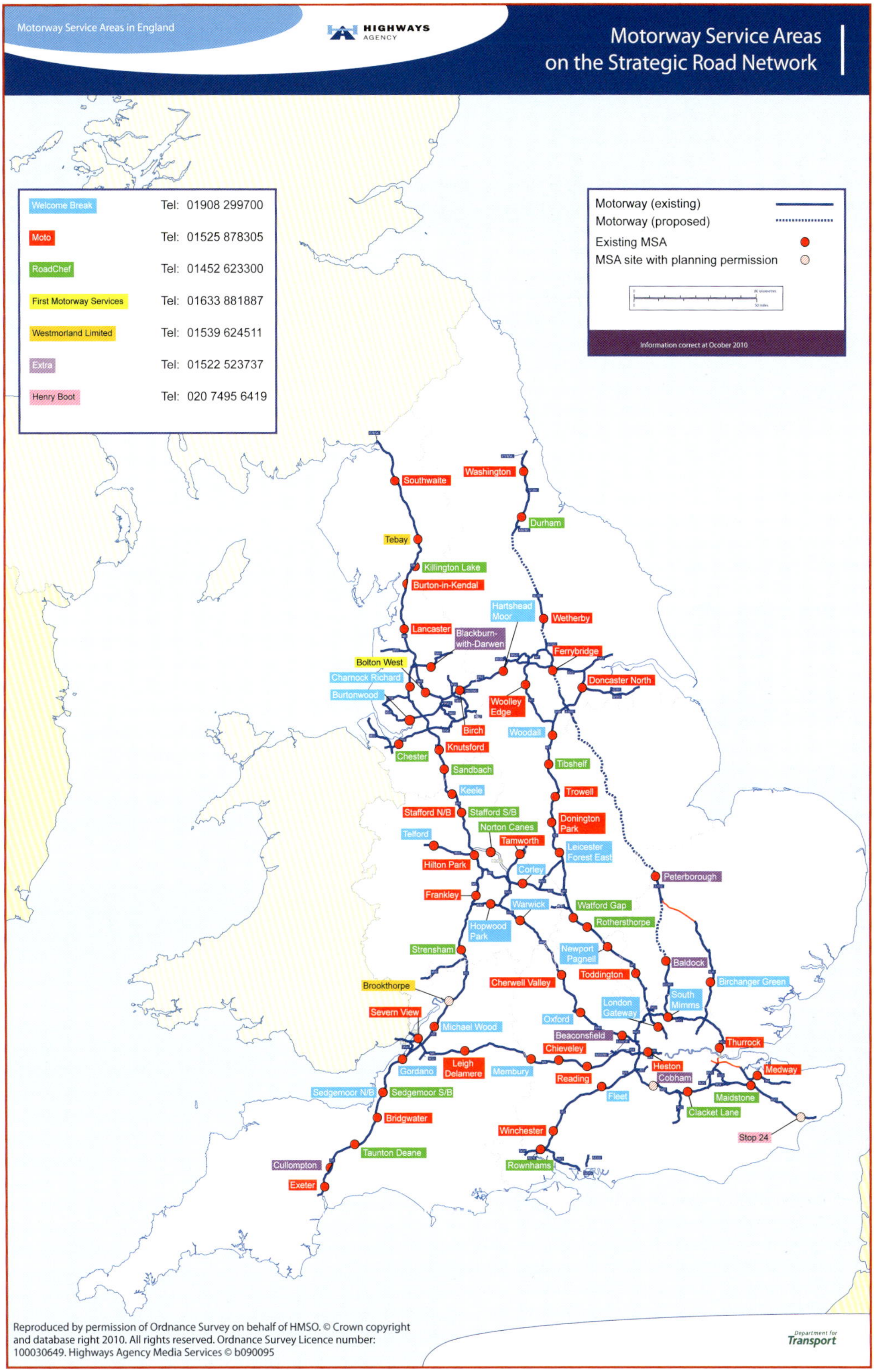
Motorway Service Areas in England
HIGHWAYS AGENCY
Motorway Service Areas on the Strategic Road Network
Welcome Break Tel: 01908 299700
Moto Tel: 01525 878305
RoadChef Tel: 01452 623300
First Motorway Services Tel: 01633 881887
Westmorland Limited Tel: 01539 624511
Extra Tel: 01522 523737
Henry Boot Tel: 020 7495 6419
Motorway (existing)
Motorway (proposed)
Existing MSA
MSA site with planning permission
Information correct at Ocober 2010
Southwaite
Washington
Durham
Tebay
Killington Lake
Burton-in-Kendal
Hartshead Moor
Wetherby
Lancaster
Blackburn-with-Darwen
Ferrybridge
Bolton West
Charnock Richard
Doncaster North
Burtonwood
Woolley Edge
Birch
Woodall
Chester
Knutsford
Tibshelf
Sandbach
Keele
Trowell
Stafford N/B
Stafford S/B
Donington Park
Norton Canes
Telford
Tamworth
Leicester Forest East
Hilton Park
Corley
Peterborough
Frankley
Warwick
Watford Gap
Hopwood Park
Rothersthorpe
Strensham
Newport Pagnell
Baldock
Brookthorpe
Cherwell Valley
Toddington
Birchanger Green
South Mimms
London Gateway
Severn View
Oxford
Michael Wood
Beaconsfield
Thurrock
Chieveley
Leigh Delamere
Heston
Medway
Gordano
Membury
Reading
Cobham
Sedgemoor N/B
Sedgemoor S/B
Fleet
Maidstone
Clacket Lane
Bridgwater
Winchester
Stop 24
Taunton Deane
Rownhams
Cullompton
Exeter
Reproduced by permission of Ordnance Survey on behalf of HMSO. © Crown copyright and database right 2010. All rights reserved. Ordnance Survey Licence number: 100030649. Highways Agency Media Services © b090095
Department for Transport

There are hundreds of "Green" places to stay and visit in England from small bed and breakfasts to large visitor attractions and activity holiday providers. Businesses displaying this logo have undergone a rigorous verification process to ensure that they are sustainable (green) and that a qualified assessor has visited the premises.

We have indicated the accommodation which has achieved a Green award... look out for the symbol in the entry.

Further Information

Advice and information

Making a booking

When enquiring about accommodation, make sure you check prices, the quality rating and other important details. You will also need to state your requirements clearly and precisely, for example:

- Arrival and departure dates, with acceptable alternatives if appropriate
- The type of accommodation you need – for example, a room with twin beds or an en suite bathroom
- The terms you want – for example, bed and breakfast only; dinner and breakfast (where provided)
- The age of any children with you, whether you want them to share your room or be next door, and any other special requirements, such as a cot
- Any particular requirements you may have, such as a special diet or a ground-floor room.

Confirmation

Misunderstandings can easily happen over the telephone, so do request a written confirmation, together with details of any terms and conditions that apply to your booking.

Deposits

If you make your reservation weeks or months in advance, you will probably be asked for a deposit, which will then be deducted from the final bill when you leave. The amount will vary from establishment to establishment and could be payment in full at peak times.

Payment on arrival

Some establishments ask you to pay for your room on arrival if you have not booked it in advance. This is especially likely to happen if you arrive late and have little or no luggage. If you are asked to pay on arrival, it is a good idea to see your room first, to make sure it meets your requirements.

Cancellations

Legal contract

When you accept accommodation that is offered to you, by telephone or in writing, you enter into a legally binding contract with the proprietor. This means that if you cancel your booking, fail to take up the accommodation or leave early, you will probably forfeit your deposit and may expect to be charged the balance at the end of the period booked if the place cannot be re-let. You should be advised at the time of the booking of what charges would be made in the event of cancelling the accommodation or leaving early, which is usually written into the property's terms and conditions. If this is not mentioned, you should ask the proprietor for any cancellation terms that apply before booking your accommodation to ensure any disputes are avoided. Where you have already paid the full amount before cancelling, the proprietor is likely to retain the money. However if the accommodation is re-let, the proprietor will make a refund to you which normally excludes the amount of the deposit.

Remember, if you book by telephone and are asked for your credit card number, you should check whether the proprietor intends to charge your credit card account, should you later cancel your reservation. A proprietor should not be able to charge your credit card account with a cancellation fee without your consent unless you agreed to this at the time of your booking. However, to avoid later disputes, we suggest you check whether this is the intention before providing your details.

Insurance

There are so many reasons why you might have to cancel your holiday, which is why we strongly advise people to take out a cancellation insurance policy.

Arrival time

If you know you will be arriving late in the evening, it is a good idea to say so when you book. If you are delayed on your way, a telephone call to say that you will be late is often appreciated.

It is particularly important to liaise with the proprietor about key collection as he or she may not be on site.

Service charges and tipping

These days many places levy service charges automatically. If they do, they must clearly say so in their offer of accommodation, at the time of booking. The service charge then becomes part of the legal contract when you accept the offer of accommodation.

If a service charge is levied automatically, there is no need to tip the staff, unless they provide some exceptional service. The usual tip for meals is 10% of the total bill.

Telephone charges

Establishments can set their own charges for telephone calls made through their switchboard or from direct-dial telephones in bedrooms. These charges are often much higher than telephone companies' standard charges (to defray the cost of providing the service).

Comparing costs

It is a condition of the quality assessment schemes that an establishment's unit charges are on display by the telephones or with the room information. It is not always easy to compare these charges with standard rates, so before using a telephone for long-distance calls, you may decide to ask how the charges compare.

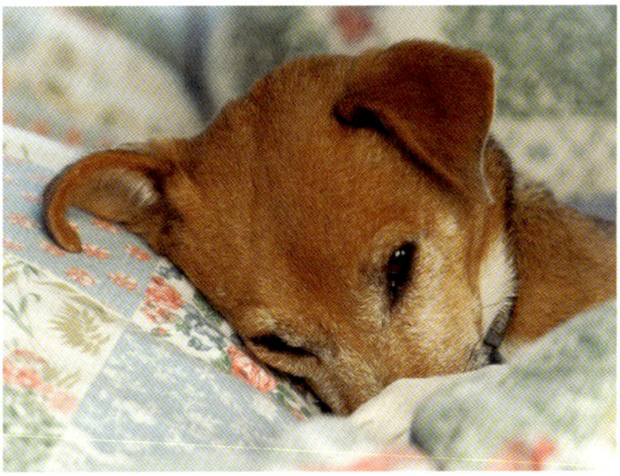

Security of valuables

You can deposit your valuables with the proprietor or manager during your stay, and we recommend you do this as a sensible precaution. Make sure you obtain a receipt for them. Some places do not accept articles for safe custody, and in that case it is wisest to keep your valuables with you.

Disclaimer

Some proprietors put up a notice that disclaims liability for property brought on to their premises by a guest. In fact, they can only restrict their liability. By law, a proprietor is liable for the value of the loss or damage to any property (except a car or its contents) of a guest who has engaged overnight accommodation, but if the proprietor has the notice on display, liability is limited to £50 for one article and a total of £100 for any one guest. The notice must be prominently displayed in the reception area or main entrance. These limits do not apply to valuables you have deposited with the proprietor for safekeeping, or to property lost through the default, neglect or wilful act of the proprietor or his staff.

Travelling with pets

Dogs, cats, ferrets and some other pets can be brought into the UK from certain countries without having to undertake six months' quarantine on arrival, provided they meet the requirements of the Pet Travel Scheme (PETS).

For full details, visit the PETS website at
w www.gov.uk/take-pet-abroad
or contact the PETS Helpline
t +44 (0)370 241 1710
e pettravel@ahvla.gsi.gov.uk
Ask for fact sheets which cover dogs and cats, ferrets or domestic rabbits and rodents.

There are no requirements for pets travelling directly between the UK and the Channel Islands. Pets entering Jersey or Guernsey from other countries need to be Pet Travel Scheme compliant and have a valid EU Pet Passport. For more information see www.jersey.com or www.visitguernsey.com.

What to expect

The proprietor/management is required to undertake the following:

Prior to booking

- To describe accurately in any advertisement, brochure, or other printed or electronic media, the facilities and services provided;
- To make clear to guests in print, electronic media and on the telephone exactly what is included in all prices quoted for accommodation, including taxes and any other surcharges. Details of charges for additional services/facilities should also be made clear, for example breakfast, leisure etc;
- To provide information on the suitability of the premises for guests of various ages, particularly for the elderly and the very young;
- To allow guests to view the accommodation prior to booking if requested.

At the time of booking

- To clearly describe the cancellation policy to guests i.e. by telephone, fax, internet/email as well as in any printed information given to guests;
- To adhere to and not to exceed prices quoted at the time of booking for accommodation and other services;
- To make clear to guests if the accommodation offered is in an unconnected annexe or similar, and to indicate the location of suchb accommodation and any difference in comfort and/ or amenities from accommodation at the property.

On arrival

- To welcome all guests courteously and without discrimination in relation to gender, sexual orientation, disability, race, religion or belief.

During the stay

- To maintain standards of guest care, cleanliness, and service appropriate to the type of establishment;
- To deal promptly and courteously with all enquiries, requests, bookings and correspondence from guests;
- To ensure complaints received are investigated promptly and courteously to an outcome that is communicated to the guest.

On departure

- To give each guest, on request, details of payments due and a receipt, if required/requested.

General

- To give due consideration to the requirements of guests with special needs, and make suitable provision where applicable;
- To ensure the accommodation, when advertised as open, is prepared for the arrival of guests at all times;
- To advise guests, at any time prior to their stay, of any changes made to their booking;
- To have a complaints handling procedure in place to deal promptly and fairly with all guest complaints;
- To hold current public liability insurance and to comply with all relevant statuory obligations including legislation applicable to fire, health and safety, planning and food safety;
- To allow, on request, VisitEngland representatives reasonable access to the establishment, to confirm that the Code of Conduct is being observed or in order to investigate any complaint of a serious nature;

Comments and complaints

Information

Other than rating information, the proprietors themselves supply descriptions of their properties and other information for the entries in this book. They have all signed a declaration to confirm that their information accurately describes their accommodation business. The publishers cannot guarantee the accuracy of information in this guide, and accept no responsibility for any error or misrepresentation. All liability for loss, disappointment, negligence or other damage caused by reliance on the information contained in this guide, or in the event of bankruptcy or liquidation or cessation of trade of any company, individual or firm mentioned, is hereby excluded. We strongly recommend that you carefully check prices and other details before you book your accommodation.

Quality signage

All establishments displaying a quality sign have to hold current membership of VisitEngland's Quality Assessment Scheme.

When an establishment is sold, the new owner has to re-apply and be re-assessed. In certain circumstances the rating may be carried forward before the property is re-assessed.

Problems

Of course, we hope you will not have cause for complaint, but problems do occur from time to time. If you are dissatisfied with anything, make your complaint to the management immediately. Then the management can take action by investigating the matter in attempts to put things right. The longer you leave a complaint, the harder it is to deal with it effectively.

In certain circumstances, the national tourist board may look into your complaint. However, they have no statutory control over establishments or their methods of operating and cannot become involved in legal or contractual matters such as financial compensation.

If you do have problems that have not been resolved by the proprietor and which you would like to bring to their attention, please write to:
Quality in Tourism, 1320 Montpellier Court, Pioneer Way, Gloucester Business Park, Gloucester, Gloucestershire GL3 4AH

About the accommodation entries

Entries

All accommodation featured in this guide has been assessed or has applied for assessment under a quality assessment scheme.

Start your search for a place to stay by looking in the 'Stay' sections of this guide, where proprietors have paid to have their establishment featured in either a standard entry (includes photograph, description, facilities and prices) or an enhanced entry (photograph(s) and extended details).

Locations

Places to stay are listed by town, city or village. If a property is located in a small village, you may find it listed under a nearby town (providing it is within a seven-mile radius).

Within each region, counties run in alphabetical order. Place names are listed alphabetically within each county, and include interesting county information and a map reference.

Map references

These refer to the colour location maps at the back of the guide. The first figure shown is the map number, the following letter and figure indicate the grid reference on the map. Only place names that have a standard or enhanced entry feature appear on the maps. Some standard or enhanced entries were included in the scheme after the guide went to press, therefore they do not appear on the maps.

Telephone numbers

Booking telephone numbers are listed below the contact address for each entry. Area codes are shown in brackets.

Prices

The prices printed are to be used as a guide only; they were supplied to us by proprietors in summer 2014.

Remember, changes may occur after the guide goes to press, therefore we strongly advise you to check prices before booking your accommodation. Prices are shown in pounds sterling, including VAT where applicable. There are many different ways of quoting prices for accommodation. We use a standardised method in the guide to allow you to compare prices. For example, when we show:

Bed and breakfast: the prices shown are per room for overnight accommodation with breakfast. The double room price is for two people. (If a double room is occupied by one person, there is sometimes a reduction in price.) Some places only provide a continental breakfast in the set price, and you may have to pay extra if you want a full English breakfast.

Evening meal: the prices shown are per person per night.

Half board: the prices shown are per person per night for room, evening meal and breakfast. These prices are usually based on two people sharing a room.

Checking prices

According to UK law, establishments with at least four bedrooms or eight beds must display their charges in the reception area or entrance. There is no legal requirement for establishments in the Channel Islands to display their prices but they should make them clear at the time of booking.

In your own interests, do make sure you check prices and what they include.

Children's rates

You will find that many places charge a reduced rate for children, especially if they share a room with their parents. Some places charge the full rate, however, when a child occupies a room which might otherwise have been let to an adult. The upper age limit for reductions for children varies from one accommodation to another, so check this when you book.

Seasonal packages and special promotions

Prices often vary through the year and may be significantly lower outside peak holiday weeks. Many places offer special package rates – fully inclusive weekend breaks, for example – in the autumn, winter and spring. A number of establishments taking an enhanced entry have included any special offers, themed breaks, etc. that are available.

You can get details of other bargain packages that may be available from the establishments themselves, regional tourism organisations or your local Tourist Information Centre (TIC). Your local travel agent may also have information and can help you make reservations.

Bathrooms

En suite bathroom means the bath or shower and wc are contained behind the main door of the bedroom. Private bathroom means a bath or shower and wc solely for the occupants of one bedroom, on the same floor, reasonably close and with a key provided. If the availability of a bath, rather than a shower, is important to you, remember to check when you book.

Meals

It is advisable to check the availability of meals and set times when making your reservation. Some smaller places may ask you at breakfast whether you want an evening meal. The prices shown in each entry are for bed and breakfast or half board, but many places also offer lunch.

Open period

If an entry does not indicate an opening period, please check directly with the establishment.

Symbols

The at-a-glance symbols included at the end of each entry show many of the services and facilities available at each establishment. You will find the key to these symbols on page 7.

Smoking

In the UK and the Channel Islands, it is illegal to smoke in enclosed public spaces and places of work. Some establishments may choose to provide designated smoking bedrooms, and may allow smoking in private areas that are not used by any staff. If you wish to smoke, it is advisable to check whether it is allowed when you book.

Alcoholic drinks

Many places listed in the guide are licensed to serve alcohol. The licence may be restricted – to diners only, for example – so you may want to check this when you book. If they have a bar this is shown by the symbol

Pets

Many places accept guests with dogs, but we advise that you check this with the proprietor before booking, remembering to ask if there are any extra charges or rules about exactly where your pet is allowed. The acceptance of dogs is not always extended to cats and it is strongly advised that cat owners contact the property well in advance of their stay.

Some establishments do not accept pets at all. Pets are welcome by arrangement where you see this symbol 8. The quarantine laws have changed and now dogs, cats and ferrets are able to come into Britain and the Channel Islands from over 50 countries. For details of the Pet Travel Scheme (PETS) please turn to page 331.

Payment accepted

The types of payment accepted by an establishment are listed in the payment accepted section. If you plan to pay by card, check that the establishment will accept the particular type of card you own before booking. Some proprietors will charge you a higher rate if you pay by credit card rather than cash or cheque. The difference is to cover the charges paid by the proprietor to the credit card company. When you book by telephone, you may be asked for your credit card number as confirmation. Remember, the proprietor may then charge your credit card account if you cancel your booking. See details of this under Cancellations on page 330.

Conferences and groups

Places which cater for conferences and meetings are marked with the symbol . Rates are often negotiable, depending on the time of year, number of people involved and any special requirements you may have.

Awaiting confirmation of rating

At the time of going to press some properties featured in this guide had not yet been assessed therefore their rating for this year could not be included. The term 'Rating Applied For' indicates this throughout your guide.

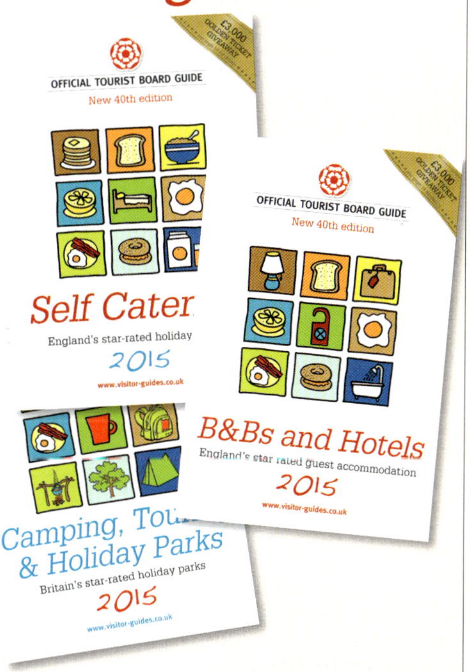

Getting around

Travelling in London

London transport

Each London Underground line has its own unique colour, so you can easily follow them on the Underground map. Most lines run through central London, and many serve parts of Greater London. Buses are a quick, convenient way to travel around London, providing plenty of sightseeing opportunities along the way. There are over 6,500 buses in London operating 700 routes every day. You will need to buy a ticket or Travel Pass before you board the bus.

London's National Rail system stretches all over London. Many lines start at the main London railway stations (Paddington, Victoria, Waterloo, Kings Cross) with links to the tube. Trains mainly serve areas outside central London, and travel overground.

Children usually travel free, or at reduced fare, on all public transport in London.

Oyster cards

Oyster cards can be used to pay fares on all London Underground, buses, Docklands Light Railway and trams, however are generally not valid for National Rail services in London.

Oyster cards are very easy to use, you just touch the card on sensors at stations or on buses and you are charged the lowest fare available for your journey. You buy credit for your journey and when it runs out you simply top up with more.

Oyster cards are available to adults only. Children below the age of 11 can accompany adults free of charge. Children between the ages of 11 and 15 can travel free on buses and trams and at child rate on Tube, DLR and London Overground services, provided they have an 11-15 Zip Oyster photocard. You can purchase an Oyster card for a fee of £5, which is refundable on its return, at any underground station, one of 3,000 Oyster points around London displaying the London Underground sign (usually shops), or from www.visitbritainshop.com, or www.oyster.tfl.gov.uk/oyster

London congestion charge

The congestion charge is £11.50 daily charge to drive in central London at certain times. Check if the congestion charge is included in the cost of your car before booking. If your car's pick up point is in the congestion-charging zone, the company may pay the charge for the first day of your hire.

Low Emission Zone

The Low Emission Zone is an area covering most of Greater London, within which the most polluting diesel-engine vehicles are required to meet specific emissions standards. If your vehicle does not, you will be required to pay a daily charge.

Vehicles affected by the Low Emission Zone are older diesel-engine lorries, buses, coaches, large vans, minibuses and other heavy vehicles such as motor caravans and motorised horse boxes. This also includes vehicles registered outside of Great Britain. Cars and motorcycles are not affected by this scheme. For more information visit www.tfl.gov.uk

Rail and train travel

Britain's rail network covers all main cities and smaller regional towns. Trains on the network are operated by a few large companies running routes from London to stations all over Britain. Therefore smaller companies that run routes in regional areas. You can find up-to-the-minute information about routes, fares and train times on the National Rail Enquiries website (www.nationalrail.co.uk). For detailed information about routes and services, refer to the train operators' websites (see page 345).

Railway passes

BritRail offer a wide selection of passes and tickets giving you the freedom to travel on all National Rail services. Passes can also include sleeper services, city and attraction passes and boat tours. Passes can usually be purchased from travel agents outside Britain or by visiting the BritRail website www.britrail.net.

Bus and coach travel

Public buses

Every city and town in Britain has a local bus service. These services are privatised and managed by separate companies. The largest bus companies in Britain are First (www.firstgroup.com/ukbus), Stagecoach (www.stagecoachbus.com) and Arriva (www.arrivabus.co.uk), and run buses in most UK towns. Outside London, buses usually travel to and from the town centre or to the busiest part of town. Most towns have a bus station, where you'll be able to find maps and information about routes. Bus route information may also be posted at bus stops.

Tickets and fares

The cost of a bus ticket normally depends on how far you're travelling. Return fares may be available on some buses, but you would usually need to buy a 'single' ticket for each individual journey.

You can also buy your ticket when boarding a bus by telling the driver where you are going. One-day and weekly travel cards are available in some towns, and these can be purchased from either the driver or from an information centre at the bus station. Tickets are valid for each separate journey rather than for a period of time, so if you get off the bus you'll need to buy a new ticket when getting on another.

Domestic flights

Flying is a time-saving alternative to road or rail when it comes to travelling around Britain. Domestic flights are fast and frequent and there are 33 airports across Britain that operate domestic routes. You will find airports marked on the maps at the front of this guide.

Domestic flight advice

Photo ID is required to travel on domestic flights. However it is advisable to bring your passport as not all airlines will accept other forms of photo identification. Please be aware of the high security measures at all airports in Britain which include include restrictions on items that may be carried in hand luggage. It is important that you check the restrictions in place with your airline prior to travel, as these can vary over time and don't forget to allow adequate time for check-in and boarding on arrival.

Cycling

Cycling is a great way to see some of England's iconic scenery and there are many networks of cycling routes available across England. The National Cycle Network offers over 10,000 miles of walking and cycling routes details for connecting towns and villages, countryside and coast across England. For more information and view these routes see page 341 or visit Sustrans at www.sustrans.co.uk.

Think green

If you'd rather leave your car behind and travel by 'green transport' to some of the attractions highlighted in this guide you'll be helping to reduce congestion and pollution as well as supporting conservation charities in their commitment to green travel.

The National Trust encourages visits made by non-car travellers and it offers admission discounts or a voucher for the tea room at a selection of its properties if you arrive on foot, cycle or public transport (you may need to produce a valid bus or train ticket if travelling by public transport.).

More information about The National Trust's work to encourage car-free days out can be found at www.nationaltrust.org.uk. (Refer to the section entitled 'Information for Visitors').

sustrans
JOIN THE MOVEMENT

Here are just some of the most popular long distance routes on the 12,000 mile Sustrans National Cycle Network. To see the Network in it's entirety and to find routes near you, visit **www.sustrans.org.uk**

Sustrans is the UK's leading sustainable transport charity working on practical projects to enable people to choose to travel in ways which benefit their health and the environment.

By car and by train

Distance chart

The distances between towns on the chart below are given to the nearest mile, and are measured along routes based on the quickest travelling time, making maximum use of motorways or dual-carriageway roads. The chart is based upon information supplied by the Automobile Association.

To calculate the distance in kilometres multiply the mileage by 1.6
For example: Brighton to Dover
82 miles x 1.6 =131.2 kilometres

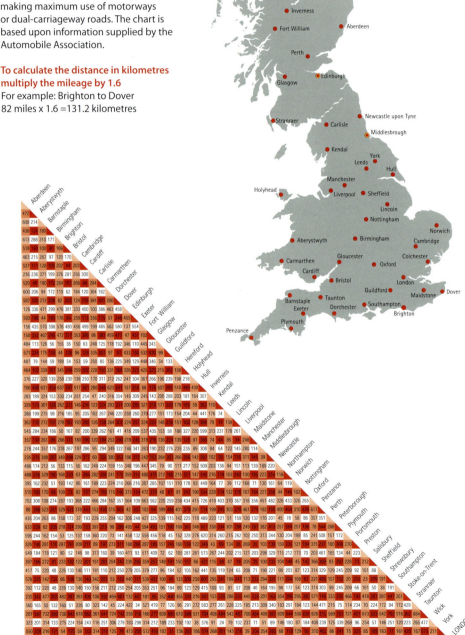

	Aberdeen	Aberystwyth	Barnstaple	Birmingham	Brighton	Bristol	Cambridge	Cardiff	Carlisle	Carmarthen	Dorchester	Dover	Edinburgh	Exeter	Fort William	Glasgow	Gloucester	Guildford	Hereford	Holyhead	Hull	Inverness	Kendal	Leeds	Lincoln	Liverpool	Maidstone	Manchester	Middlesbrough	Newcastle	Northampton	Norwich	Nottingham	Oxford	Penzance	Perth	Peterborough	Plymouth	Portsmouth	Preston	Salisbury	Sheffield	Shrewsbury	Southampton	Stoke-on-Trent	Stranraer	Taunton	Wick	York
Aberystwyth	472
Barnstaple	608	214
Birmingham	436	124	180
Brighton	613	288	210	171
Bristol	518	130	100	90	169
Cambridge	463	215	267	97	120	170
Cardiff	537	111	128	109	202	44	203
Carlisle	236	236	371	199	376	281	256	300
Carmarthen	520	48	190	172	264	107	266	68	284
Dorchester	600	206	94	172	119	62	184	120	364	182
Dover	587	326	272	208	82	205	124	239	381	301	200
Edinburgh	126	336	471	299	476	381	333	400	100	386	463	458
Exeter	593	198	44	165	178	84	259	113	356	175	57	248	455
Fort William	156	435	570	398	576	480	456	499	199	485	562	580	137	554
Glasgow	150	332	467	295	472	377	353	396	96	382	459	477	47	451	102
Gloucester	484	113	126	56	155	36	150	63	248	125	118	192	346	110	445	343
Guildford	571	224	175	128	44	106	96	139	335	201	97	97	433	150	532	430	99
Hereford	487	79	144	59	189	54	153	59	250	85	136	225	349	129	448	346	34	133
Holyhead	464	102	339	167	345	249	259	202	228	150	331	369	326	323	425	323	215	302	156
Hull	376	227	320	139	258	230	138	250	170	311	312	262	247	304	367	266	196	239	198	218
Inverness	106	496	631	459	637	541	517	561	260	546	623	641	157	616	66	176	507	595	510	488	430
Kendal	283	189	324	153	330	234	251	254	47	240	316	354	145	309	245	143	200	288	203	181	164	307
Leeds	329	173	301	120	262	211	146	230	123	224	293	271	200	285	321	219	177	220	179	165	59	383	110
Lincoln	388	199	275	98	216	185	95	205	182	267	246	220	258	260	379	277	151	173	154	204	44	441	176	74
Liverpool	362	110	272	101	278	182	193	202	126	158	264	302	224	257	324	222	148	236	151	102	128	386	79	74	139
Maidstone	545	284	234	166	50	167	82	200	339	262	161	41	416	209	537	435	153	58	186	327	220	599	313	231	178	261
Manchester	357	134	261	89	266	171	160	190	120	184	253	290	219	245	318	216	136	224	139	125	97	380	74	44	85	34	248
Middlesbrough	276	244	357	176	318	267	197	286	95	294	349	322	146	341	283	190	232	276	235	235	89	308	84	64	122	145	280	114
Newcastle	235	275	388	207	349	298	229	317	60	325	380	353	106	372	242	153	264	307	266	266	142	267	102	95	154	176	311	145	39
Northampton	486	174	212	56	133	115	56	162	249	224	159	155	348	196	447	345	79	90	111	217	152	509	203	136	94	151	113	139	189	220
Norwich	488	278	329	160	168	233	63	266	282	328	241	172	359	313	480	378	212	160	215	321	147	542	276	174	103	240	130	185	223	254	118
Nottingham	395	162	232	51	193	142	86	161	189	223	224	210	266	216	387	285	107	151	110	178	93	449	164	77	39	112	168	71	130	161	64	119
Oxford	510	160	170	68	109	73	82	107	274	169	115	146	373	154	472	370	48	67	81	242	190	534	228	174	132	176	107	164	227	258	44	146	102
Penzance	702	308	108	274	287	193	368	222	466	284	167	357	564	109	663	562	220	259	238	434	415	726	419	403	370	367	318	356	451	482	326	433	326	265
Perth	86	388	523	351	529	433	378	453	152	438	515	503	42	507	102	64	399	486	401	379	291	114	199	245	303	278	461	275	192	150	400	404	310	426	617
Peterborough	435	204	263	86	158	173	37	193	229	255	204	162	306	248	427	325	139	115	142	225	110	489	223	121	51	159	120	132	170	201	45	78	58	86	357	351
Plymouth	633	239	62	205	218	124	299	153	397	215	98	288	495	44	594	493	151	190	169	365	346	657	350	334	301	298	249	287	382	413	257	364	257	196	78	544	288
Portsmouth	596	244	162	154	53	125	137	158	360	220	73	141	458	132	558	456	118	45	152	328	276	620	314	260	215	262	102	250	313	344	130	204	188	85	241	508	157	172
Preston	326	146	281	110	287	191	209	211	89	197	273	311	188	266	287	185	157	245	160	138	122	349	43	69	134	36	269	35	103	139	159	235	121	184	375	237	180	306	270
Salisbury	549	184	118	121	90	52	145	98	313	160	39	160	411	93	511	409	72	62	105	281	261	573	267	244	202	215	121	203	298	329	115	212	173	70	203	461	165	134	44	223
Sheffield	397	166	272	91	233	182	122	201	161	263	264	247	236	256	359	257	148	191	150	157	66	421	115	38	47	79	205	39	100	131	104	148	45	142	366	309	93	297	228	73	212
Shrewsbury	417	75	220	48	226	130	140	111	181	110	212	250	279	205	379	277	96	184	52	105	162	441	135	119	124	65	208	71	190	221	98	203	87	123	314	329	129	245	209	92	161	88
Southampton	578	225	142	135	66	106	136	140	342	201	53	152	440	111	539	437	100	49	133	309	258	601	295	241	199	243	113	232	294	325	111	204	169	67	221	489	157	152	20	252	23	209	191
Stoke-on-Trent	392	112	220	48	226	130	140	150	156	211	212	250	254	205	353	251	96	184	99	123	129	415	109	93	91	57	208	46	164	195	98	172	54	123	314	303	99	245	209	66	161	50	38	191
Stranraer	235	342	477	305	482	387	363	406	106	392	469	487	132	461	181	86	352	440	355	333	276	261	153	229	288	232	445	229	201	163	354	388	295	380	571	149	333	502	466	195	418	267	287	447	261
Taunton	560	165	50	132	160	51	226	80	323	142	45	224	422	34	521	419	77	126	96	291	272	583	277	261	228	225	185	213	309	340	183	291	184	123	144	471	215	75	114	234	70	224	172	94	172	429
Wick	207	597	732	560	738	642	618	662	361	647	724	742	258	716	166	277	608	695	610	588	531	104	408	484	543	487	700	484	409	367	609	644	550	635	826	215	589	757	721	451	673	523	542	702	516	362	684
York	323	201	314	133	275	224	154	243	116	251	306	279	193	298	314	212	189	233	192	192	38	376	91	24	79	102	237	71	51	89	146	180	87	184	408	239	125	339	269	96	254	57	146	251	120	223	265	477
LONDON	550	239	216	121	54	120	59	153	314	215	125	78	413	200	512	410	102	31	136	282	186	574	268	201	143	216	39	204	254	285	68	118	129	56	310	462	86	241	75	225	85	169	163	77	161	420	167	675	211

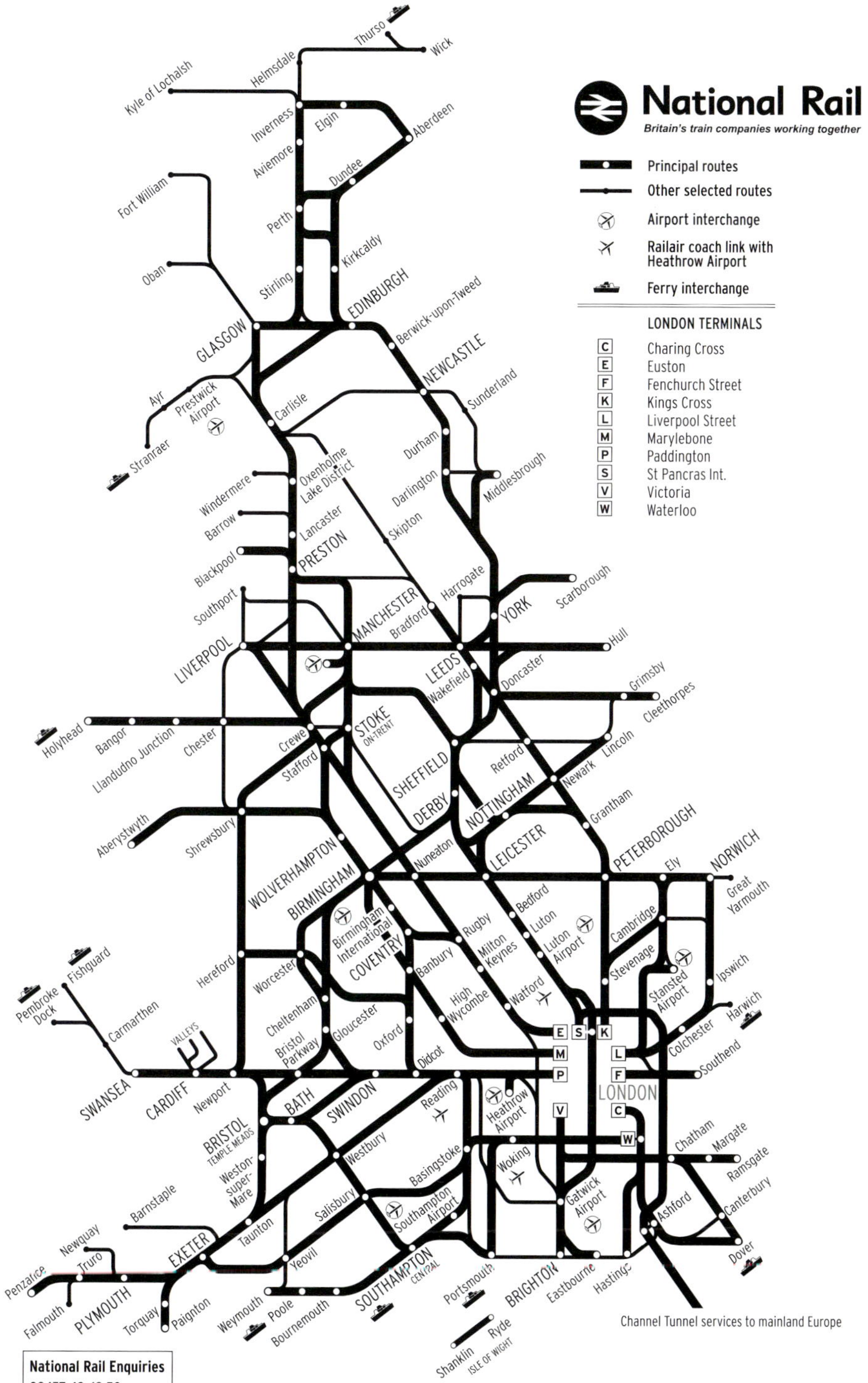

National Rail Enquiries
08457 48 49 50
www.nationalrail.co.uk

Travel information

General travel information

Streetmap	www.streetmap.co.uk	
Transport for London	www.tfl.gov.uk	0843 222 1234
Travel Services	www.departures-arrivals.com	
Traveline	www.traveline.info	0871 200 2233

Bus & coach

Megabus	www.megabus.com	0900 160 0900
National Express	www.nationalexpress.com	08717 818 178
WA Shearings	www.shearings.com	0844 824 6351

Car & car hire

AA	www.theaa.com	0800 085 2721
Green Flag	www.greenflag.com	0845 246 1557
RAC	www.rac.co.uk	0844 308 9177
Alamo	www.alamo.co.uk	0871 384 1086*
Avis	www.avis.co.uk	0844 581 0147*
Budget	www.budget.co.uk	0844 544 3407*
Easycar	www.easycar.com	
Enterprise	www.enterprise.com	0800 800 227*
Hertz	www.hertz.co.uk	0870 844 8844*
Holiday Autos	www.holidayautos.co.uk	0871 472 5229
National	www.nationalcar.co.uk	0871 384 1140
Thrifty	www.thrifty.co.uk	01494 751500

Air

Air Southwest	www.airsouthwest.com	0870 043 4553
Blue Islands (Channel Islands)	www.blueislands.com	08456 20 2122
BMI	www.flybmi.com	0844 848 4888
BMI Baby	www.bmibaby.com	0905 828 2828*
British Airways	www.ba.com	0844 493 0787
British International (Isles of Scilly to Penzance)	www.islesofscillyhelicopter.com	01736 363871*
CityJet	www.cityjet.com	0871 663 3777
Eastern Airways	www.easternairways.com	08703 669100
Easyjet	www.easyjet.com	0843 104 5000
Flybe	www.flybe.com	0871 700 2000*
Jet2.com	www.jet2.com	0871 226 1737*
Manx2	www.manx2.com	0871 200 0440*
Ryanair	www.ryanair.com	0871 246 0000
Skybus (Isles of Scilly)	www.islesofscilly-travel.co.uk	0845 710 5555
Thomsonfly	www.thomsonfly.com	0871 231 4787

Train		
National Rail Enquiries	www.nationalrail.co.uk	0845 748 4950
The Trainline	www.trainline.co.uk	0871 244 1545
UK train operating companies	www.rail.co.uk	
Arriva Trains	www.arriva.co.uk	0191 520 4000
c2c	www.c2c-online.co.uk	0845 601 4873
Chiltern Railways	www.chilternrailways.co.uk	0845 600 5165
CrossCountry	www.crosscountrytrains.co.uk	0844 811 0124
East Midlands Trains	www.eastmidlandstrains.co.uk	0845 712 5678
Eurostar	www.eurostar.com	08432 186 186*
First Capital Connect	www.firstcapitalconnect.co.uk	0845 026 4700
First Great Western	www.firstgreatwestern.co.uk	0845 700 0125
Gatwick Express	www.gatwickexpress.com	0845 850 1530
Heathrow Connect	www.heathrowconnect.com	0845 678 6975
Heathrow Express	www.heathrowexpress.com	0845 600 1515
Hull Trains	www.hulltrains.co.uk	0845 071 0222
Island Line	www.islandlinetrains.co.uk	0845 600 0650
London Midlands	www.londonmidland.com	0121 634 2040
Merseyrail	www.merseyrail.org	0151 702 2071
National Express East Anglia	www.nationalexpresseastanglia.com	0845 600 7245
National Express East Coast	www.nationalexpresseastcoast.com	0845 722 5333
Northern Rail	www.northernrail.org	0845 000 0125
ScotRail	www.scotrail.co.uk	0845 601 5929
South Eastern Trains	www.southeasternrailway.co.uk	0845 000 2222
South West Trains	www.southwesttrains.co.uk	0845 600 0650
Southern	www.southernrailway.com	0845 127 2920
Stansted Express	www.stanstedexpress.com	0845 600 7245
Translink	www.translink.co.uk	(028) 9066 6630
Transpennine Express	www.tpexpress.co.uk	0845 600 1671
Virgin Trains	www.virgintrains.co.uk	08450 008 000*

Ferry		
Ferry Information	www.discoverferries.com	0207 436 2449
Condor Ferries	www.condorferries.co.uk	0845 609 1024*
Steam Packet Company	www.steam-packet.com	08722 992 992*
Isles of Scilly Travel	www.islesofscilly-travel.co.uk	0845 710 5555
Red Funnel	www.redfunnel.co.uk	0844 844 9988
Wight Link	www.wightlink.co.uk	0871 376 1000

Phone numbers listed are for general enquiries unless otherwise stated.
* Booking line only

If you have access needs...

Guests with hearing, visual or mobility needs can feel confident about booking accommodation that participates in the National Accessible Scheme (NAS).

Look out for the NAS symbols which are included throughout the accommodation directory. Using the NAS could help make the difference between a good holiday and a perfect one!

For more information on the NAS and tips & ideas on holiday travel in England, go to: www.visitengland.com/accessforall

National Accessible Scheme index

Establishments with a detailed entry in this guide who participate in the National Accessible Scheme are listed below. At the front of the guide you can find information about the scheme. Establishments are listed alphabetically by place name.

Mobility level 1

Mobility level 2

Hearing impairment level 1

Visual impairment level 1

Gold and Silver Award winners

Establishments with a detailed entry in this guide that have achieved recognition of exceptional quality are listed below. Establishments are listed alphabetically by place name.

South West

GOLD AWARD

Barnsley, **Barnsley House** ★★★★	67
Bath, **Marlborough House Guest House** ★★★★	72
Bath (6 miles), **Lucknam Park Hotel and Spa** ★★★★★	72
Camelford, **Pendragon Country House** ★★★★★	42
Christchurch, **Druid House** ★★★★★	64
Honiton, **Combe House Devon** ★★★★	52
Lostwithiel, **Hazelmere House** ★★★★	44
Lynton, **Highcliffe House** ★★★★★	52
Sidmouth, **The Barn & Pinn Cottage Guest House** ★★★★	56
Sidmouth, **Hotel Riviera** ★★★★	56
St. Ives, **No1** ★★★★★	47
Stroud, **1 Woodchester Lodge** ★★★★	69
Stroud, **The Old Coach House** ★★★★	70
Tetbury, **Calcot Manor Hotel & Spa** ★★★★	71
Tintagel, **The Avalon** ★★★★★	47
Wareham, **Bradle Farmhouse** ★★★★	66
Wells, **Beryl** ★★★★	77

SILVER AWARD

Bath, **The Royal Hotel** ★★★	73
Bath, **The White Guest House** ★★★	74
Bridgwater, **Gurney Manor Mill** ★★★★	74
Bridport, **Chesil Beach Lodge** ★★★★	63
Bryher, **Hell Bay Hotel** ★★★★	49
Constantine Bay, **Treglos Hotel** ★★★★	42
Falmouth, **Budock Vean Hotel** ★★★★	43
Holsworthy, **Leworthy Farmhouse B&B** ★★★★	52
Lands End, **Bosavern House** ★★★★	43
Monkton Farleigh, **Muddy Duck** ★★★★	79
Salisbury, **Lodge Farmhouse Bed & Breakfast** ★★★★	80
Shaftesbury, **The Retreat** ★★★★	65
St. Minver, **Tredower Barton** ★★★	47
Stroud, **The Close B&B** ★★★★	70
Stroud, **Pretoria Villa** ★★★★	70
Torquay, **Babbacombe Guest House** ★★★★	57
Torquay, **The Downs, Babbacombe** ★★★★	59
Trowbridge, **Newhouse Farm** ★★★★	80
Truro, **Townhouse Rooms** ★★★★	48
Wadebridge, **St Enodoc Hotel Rock** ★★★★	48

South East

GOLD AWARD

SILVER AWARD

London

SILVER AWARD

East of England

GOLD AWARD

SILVER AWARD

East Midlands

GOLD AWARD

SILVER AWARD

Heart of England

SILVER AWARD

Yorkshire

GOLD AWARD

SILVER AWARD

North West

GOLD AWARD

SILVER AWARD

North East

GOLD AWARD

SILVER AWARD

Walkers Welcome & Cyclists Welcome

Establishments participating in the Walkers Welcome and Cyclists Welcome schemes provide special facilities and actively encourage these recreations. Accommodation with a detailed entry in this guide is listed below. Place names are listed alphabetically.

Walkers Welcome & Cyclists Welcome		
Abingdon-on-Thames, South East	**Abbey Guest House ★★★★GOLD**	114
Alnwick, North East	**Bow House ★★★★GOLD**	304
Ambleside, North West	**Rothay Garth ★★★★**	265
Bamford, East Midlands	**Yorkshire Bridge Inn ★★★★SILVER**	186
Battle (4.7 miles), South East	**Woodside Luxury B&B, Spa and Glamping ★★★★★GOLD**	120
Beal, North East	**Brock Mill Farmhouse ★★★★**	305
Berwick-upon-Tweed, North East	**Alannah House ★★★★SILVER**	305
Berwick-upon-Tweed, North East	**Fenham Farm Coastal Bed & Breakfast ★★★★GOLD**	306
Bicker, East Midlands	**Supreme Inns ★★★**	192
Bognor Regis, South East	**White Horses Bed & Breakfast ★★★★**	121
Bowness-on-Windermere, North West	**May Cottage B&B ★★★SILVER**	266
Bury St. Edmunds, East of England	**St Edmunds Guesthouse ★★★★SILVER**	169
Camelford, South West	**Pendragon Country House ★★★★★GOLD**	42
Canterbury, South East	**Kipps Independent Hostel ★★★**	107

Carlisle, North West	**University of Cumbria - Carlisle ★★★★**	267
Castleton, East Midlands	**Causeway House B&B ★★★**	189
Chester, North West	**Brookside Hotel ★★★**	264
Cirencester, South West	**Riverside House ★★★★**	68
Clifton, North West	**George and Dragon ★★★★**	267
Clitheroe, North West	**Rowan Tree ★★★★**	284
Clun, Heart of England	**The White Horse Inn ★★★**	213
Corbridge, North East	**2 The Crofts ★★★★ SILVER**	306
Cornhill-on-Tweed, North East	**Collingwood Arms Hotel ★★★ GOLD**	307
Cranborne, South West	**La Fosse at Cranborne ★★★★**	64
Cromer, East of England	**Northrepps Cottage Country Hotel ★★★ GOLD**	163
Dinton, South West	**Marshwood Farm B&B ★★★★**	78
Dover, South East	**Hubert House Guesthouse ★★★★ GOLD**	108
Dunster, South West	**Yarn Market Hotel ★★★**	76
Egton Bridge, Yorkshire	**Broom House at Egton Bridge ★★★★ GOLD**	235
Hawes, Yorkshire	**Stone House Hotel ★★ GOLD**	237
Heacham, East of England	**St Anne's Guest House ★★★★ SILVER**	164
Hexham, North East	**Langley Castle Hotel ★★★★ GOLD**	307
Hitcham, East of England	**Stanstead Hall ★★★★**	170
Honiton, South West	**Combe House Devon ★★★★ GOLD**	52
Hope, East Midlands	**Underleigh House ★★★★★ GOLD**	190
Keighley, Yorkshire	**Middle Slippery Ford Barn ★★★★ SILVER**	249
Keswick, North West	**Rooms36 ★★★★ SILVER**	273
Keswick, North West	**Sandon Guest House ★★★★**	273
Lincoln, East Midlands	**Welbeck Cottage Bed and Breakfast ★★★★**	193
Loughborough, East Midlands	**Bybrook Barn ★★★★**	191
Ludlow, Heart of England	**Elm Lodge B&B ★★★★**	213
Maidstone, South East	**Ash Cottage ★★★★★**	110
Mundesley, East of England	**Overcliff Lodge ★★★★ SILVER**	165
Norwich, East of England	**Marsham Arms Coaching Inn ★★★★ SILVER**	165
Norwich, East of England	**Old Rectory Hotel ★★★**	166
Plymouth, South West	**Caraneal ★★★★**	55
Rackheath, East of England	**Barn Court ★★★★**	166
Ramsgate, South East	**Glendevon Guest House ★★★★ SILVER**	111
Reeth, Yorkshire	**Cambridge House ★★★★★**	239
Ripon, Yorkshire	**The Ripon Spa Hotel ★★★**	239
Rosthwaite, North West	**Scafell Hotel ★★★ GOLD**	274
Saltburn-by-the-Sea, Yorkshire	**The Arches Country House ★★★★**	240
Shrewsbury, Heart of England	**Brompton Farmhouse ★★★★ SILVER**	214
Stroud, South West	**The Close B&B ★★★★ SILVER**	70
Sway, South East	**The Mill At Gordleton ★★★★★ SILVER**	105
Tintagel, South West	**The Avalon ★★★★★ GOLD**	47
Yelverton, South West	**Overcombe House ★★★★**	61

Walkers Welcome

Ashbourne, East Midlands	**Peak District Spa ★★★★ SILVER**	185
Barkston, East Midlands	**Kelling House ★★★★**	191
Buttermere, North West	**Fish Inn ★★★★**	267
Buxton, East Midlands	**Old Hall Hotel ★★★**	188
Eype, South West	**Eype's Mouth Country Hotel ★★★**	65
Haworth, Yorkshire	**Leeming Wells ★★★★**	248
Keswick, North West	**Portland House ★★★★ SILVER**	272
Penzance, South West	**Hotel Penzance ★★★★**	45
St. Ives, South West	**No1 ★★★★★ GOLD**	47
St. Mary's, South West	**Isles of Scilly Country Guest House ★★★**	49

Cyclists Welcome

Stroud, South West	**1 Woodchester Lodge ★★★★ GOLD**	69

Welcome Pets!

Want to travel with your faithful companion? Look out for accommodation displaying the **Welcome Pets!** sign. Participants in this scheme go out of their way to meet the needs of guests bringing dogs, cats and/or small birds. In addition to providing water and food bowls, torches or nightlights, spare leads and pet washing facilities, they'll buy in food on request, and offer toys, treats and bedding. They'll also have information on pet-friendly attractions, pubs, restaurants and recreation. Of course, not everyone is able to offer suitable facilities for every pet, so do check if there are any restrictions on type, size and number of animals when you book.

Look out for the following (WELCOME PETS! symbol) symbol in the entry.

Families and Pets Welcome

Establishments participating in the Families Welcome or Welcome Pets! schemes provide special facilities and actively encourage families or guests with pets. Accommodation with a detailed entry in this guide is listed below. Place names are listed alphabetically.

Families and Pets Welcome

Clifton, North West	**George and Dragon ★★★★**	267
Cornhill-on-Tweed, North East	**Collingwood Arms Hotel ★★★GOLD**	307
Keswick, North West	**Rooms36 ★★★★SILVER**	273
Rackheath, East of England	**Barn Court ★★★★**	166
Ripon, Yorkshire	**The Ripon Spa Hotel ★★★**	239
Torquay, South West	**Best Western Livermead Cliff Hotel ★★★**	57

Families Welcome

Abingdon-on-Thames, South East	**Abbey Guest House ★★★★GOLD**	114
Battle (4.7 miles), South East	**Woodside Luxury B&B, Spa and Glamping ★★★★★GOLD**	120
Bicker, East Midlands	**Supreme Inns ★★★**	192
Bury St. Edmunds, East of England	**St Edmunds Guesthouse ★★★★SILVER**	169
Buttermere, North West	**Fish Inn ★★★★**	267
Chester, North West	**Brookside Hotel ★★★**	264
Norwich, East of England	**Marsham Arms Coaching Inn ★★★★SILVER**	165
Norwich, East of England	**Old Rectory Hotel ★★★**	166
St. Ives, South West	**No1 ★★★★★GOLD**	47
Sway, South East	**The Mill At Gordleton ★★★★★SILVER**	105
Totnes, South West	**Lower Horner ★★★★★**	60

Pets Welcome

Dunster, South West	**Yarn Market Hotel ★★★**	76
Eastbourne, South East	**Best Western Lansdowne Hotel ★★★**	124
Kirkby Lonsdale, North West	**Copper Kettle Restaurant & Guest House ★★**	273
Oakham, East Midlands	**Barnsdale Lodge Hotel ★★★SILVER**	197
Sinnington, Yorkshire	**Fox and Hounds ★★★★SILVER**	242
St. Agnes, South West	**Little Trevellas Farm ★★★**	46
St. Mary's, South West	**Isles of Scilly Country Guest House ★★★**	49
Troutbeck, North West	**Troutbeck Inn ★★★★**	275

Swimming Pools index

If you're looking for accommodation with swimming facilities use this index to see at a glance detailed accommodation entries that match your requirement. Establishments are listed alphabetically by place name.

Outdoor pool

Budget accommodation

If you are travelling on a budget, the following establishments offer accommodation at £25 per single room per night or less, or £50 per double room per night or less. These prices are only an indication - please check carefully before confirming a reservation. Establishments are listed alphabetically by place name.

South West

Bath, **Bath YMCA** ★★★	71
Newquay, **Harrington Guest House** ★★★	45
Paignton, **Redcliffe Lodge Hotel** ★★	54
Paignton, **Rowcroft Lodge** ★★★	54
Plymouth, **Gabber Farm** ★★★	55
Salisbury, **Evening Hill**	79
St. Agnes, **Little Trevellas Farm** ★★★	46
St. Agnes, **Penkerris** ★★	46
Torquay, **Whitburn Guest House** ★★★	60

South East

Canterbury, **Kipps Independent Hostel** ★★★	107
Great Missenden, **Forge House** ★★★	100
Ramsgate, **Comfort Inn Ramsgate** ★★★	111
Royal Tunbridge Wells, **Badgers End Bed & Breakfast** ★★	112
Woodstock, **Shepherds Hall** ★★★	119

East of England

Cromer, **Cliff Cottage** ★★★★	162
Orsett, **Jays Lodge** ★★★★	161

East Midlands

Skegness, **Stepping Stones** ★★★	195

Heart of England

Leek, **Three Horseshoes Country Hotel & Spa** ★★★ **SILVER**	215

Yorkshire

Harrogate, **Cold Cotes Guest Accommodation, Gardens & Nursery** ★★★★★ **GOLD**	236
Scarborough, **Empire Guesthouse** ★★★	240
Scarborough, **Howdale** ★★★★	240
York, **Grange Lodge Guest House** ★★★	245

North West

Blackpool, **Blenheim Mount Hotel** ★★★	280
Blackpool, **Cameo** ★★★	281
Blackpool, **Holmside House** ★★★★	281
Blackpool, **Lyndene Hotel** ★★	282
Blackpool, **The Strathdon** ★★★★	284
Blackpool, **Trentham Guest House** ★★★	284
Keswick, **Charnwood Guest House** ★★★★	272
Kirkby Lonsdale, **Copper Kettle Restaurant & Guest House** ★★	273
Skelwith Fold, **Holmeshead Farm** ★★★★	274
Windermere, **Southview House & Indoor Pool** ★★★★	278

North East

Washington, **Ye Olde Cop Shop** ★★★★ **SILVER**	310

Hostel and campus accommodation

The following establishments all have a detailed entry in this guide.

Hostels		
Bath, South West	**Bath YMCA ★★★HOSTEL**	71
Brighton, South East	**Kipps Brighton ★★★HOSTEL**	122
Canterbury, South East	**Kipps Independent Hostel ★★★BACKPACKERS**	107
Guildford, South East	**Guildford YMCA ★★★★HOSTEL**	119
Liverpool, North West	**International Inn ★★★HOSTEL**	286
Liverpool, North West	**International Inn Cocoon ★★★★HOSTEL**	286

Campus accommodation		
Carlisle, North West	**University of Cumbria - Carlisle ★★★★CAMPUS**	267
Newport, Heart of England	**Lilleshall National Sports and Conferencing Centre ★★★★CAMPUS**	213
Oxford, South East	**Keble College ★★★ - ★★★★CAMPUS**	117

Index by property name

Accommodation with a detailed entry in this guide is listed below.

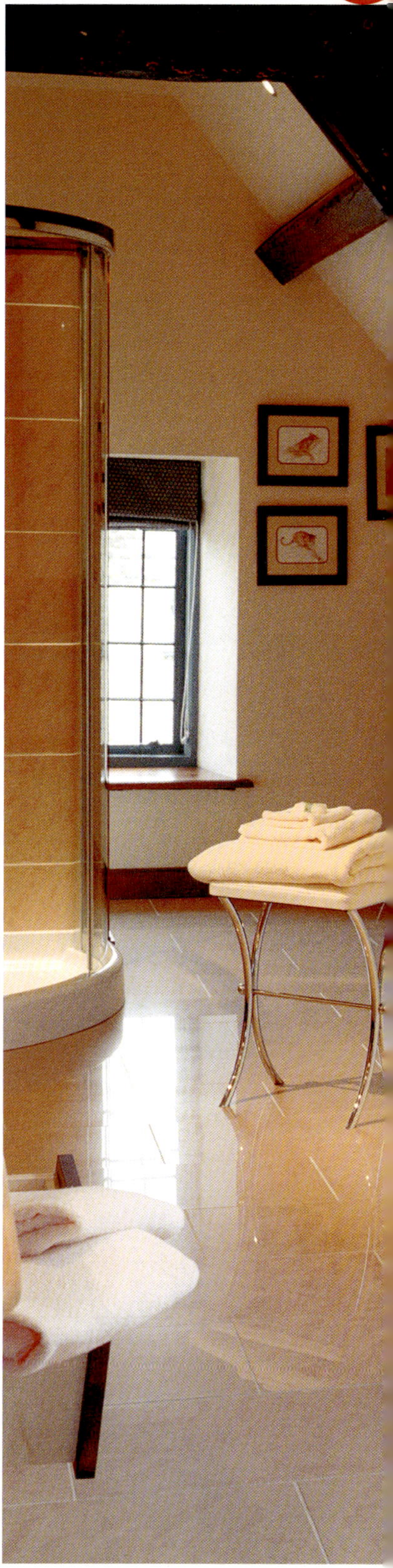

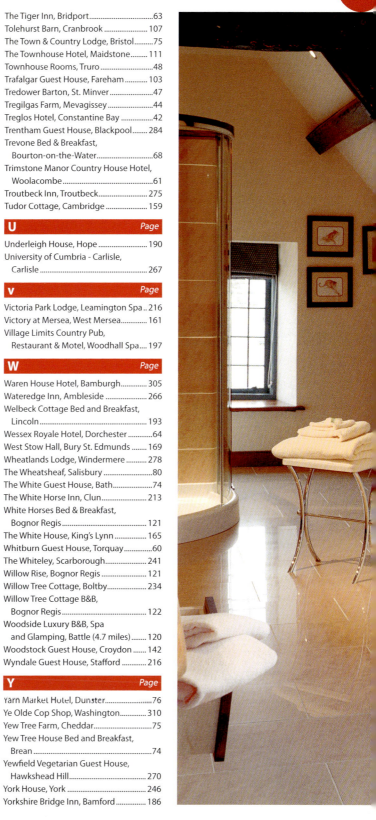

Index by place name

The following places all have detailed accommodation entries in this guide. If the place where you wish to stay is not shown the location maps (starting on page 312) will help you to find somewhere to stay in the area.

Index to display advertisers

HUDSONS MEDIA LIMITED

Published by: Hudson's Media Ltd
35 Thorpe Road, Peterborough, PE3 6AG
Tel: 01733 296910 Fax: 01733 209292

On behalf of: VisitBritain, Sanctuary Buildings, 20 Great Smith Street, London SW1P 3BT

Editor: Deborah Coulter
Editorial Contributor: Neil Pope
Production team: Deborah Coulter, Rhiannon McCluskey, Rebecca Owen-Fisher

Creative: Jamieson Eley
Advertising team: Ben Piper, Matthew Pinfold, Seanan McGrory, James O'Rawe
Email: VEguides@hudsons-media.co.uk Tel: 01733 296913
Production System: NVG – leaders in Tourism Technology. www.nvg.net
Printer: Stephens & George, Merthyr Tydfil
Retail Sales: Compass – Tel: 020 8996 5764

Photography credits: © Abbotsbury Subtropical Gardens, Alders Caravan Park, Alnwick Castle, Althorp, Andy Stammers, Arley Hall/Val Corbett, Athelhampton House, Beamish Museum, Bellingham Camping & Caravanning Club, Biddenyard Vineyard, Blair Castle, Blenheim Palace, Britain on View, Burghley, Chatsworth, Commons.Wikimedia.org, Deborah Coulter, Doddington Hall, English Heritage, Exbury Gardens/Dave Zubraski, Crafty Camping/Guy Mallinson, Getty Images: mightyisland, Harewood House, Hartland Abbey, Highclere Castle, Holker Hall, Kenilworth Castle, Knebworth House, Ladram Bay Holiday Park, Longleat Safari Park, New Lanark Mills, Pashley Manor Gardens/Helen Sinclair, Renishaw Hall/Chris Dawes, Scampston, Seafield Caravan Park, Sudeley Castle, The Alnwick Garden, The Forbidden Corner, VisitEngland, Welcome to Yorkshire, Wilton House, Woburn Safari Park.

© VisitBritain Images: Adam Burton, Andrew Orchard, Andrew Pickett, Andy Ward, Ben Selway, Chris Renton, County Durham Tourism Partnership, Craig Easton, Craig Easton, Daniel Bosworth, David Clapp, David Sellman, Eric Nathan, Grant Pritchard, Ian Shaw, Ingrid Rasmussen, James McCormick, Jason Hawkes, Joanna Henderson, Joe Cornish, John Millar, John Spaull, Kiyoshi Sakasai, Lancashire & Blackpool Tourist Board, Lee Beel, Liz Gander, Mark Thomasson, Martin Brent, Matt Cant, Melody Thornton, Nadir Khan, Olivier Roques-Rogery, Paul Underhill, Pawel Libera, PTomkins/VisitScotland, Richard Surman, Rod Edwards, Simon Kreitem, Simon Winnall, Thanet District Council, Tony Pleavin, Visit Guernsey.

Please note that all references to places to visit, products, services or experiences referred to in the editorial content are suggestions only and are not intended as endorsements of any destination, product, service or experience.

Important note: The information contained in this guide has been published in good faith on the basis of information submitted to VisitBritain by the proprietors of the premises listed, who have paid for their entries to appear. VisitBritian cannot guarantee the accuracy of the information in this guide and accepts no responsibility for any error or misrepresentations. All liability for loss, disappointment, negligence or other damage caused by reliance on the information contained in this guide, or in the event of bankruptcy, or liquidation, or cessation of trading of any company, individual, or firm mentioned is hereby excluded to the fullest extent permitted by law. Please check carefully all prices, ratings and other details before confirming a reservation.

ISBN 978-0-85101-549-1
A VisitBritain guide